Theology for the Layman

Theology for the Layman
Based on the *Summa Theologiae*
for the Holy Name Society

VOLUME I:
GOD, THE ANGELS, AND CREATION

By Dominican Priests

Introduction by Fr. Cajetan Cuddy, O.P.

AROUCA
PRESS

Each chapter in this volume was originally published as an individual pamphlet by the National Headquarters of the Holy Name Society (NYC) with ecclesiastical approval given between 1941 and 1946. They have been slightly edited for this volume.

Grateful acknowledgement extended to Fr. Cajetan Cuddy, O.P., for his introduction, helpful comments, and overall enthusiasm for this project and David Francis Sherwood who kindly obtained some difficult to find pamphlets and helped with their transcription.

Cover and layout by Allison Merrick
Photo credit: Fr. Lawrence Lew, O.P.

ISBN: 978-1-998492-10-7 (pbk)
ISBN: 978-1-998492-11-4 (hc)

Arouca Press
PO Box 55003
Bridgeport PO
Waterloo, ON N2J 3G0
Canada
www.aroucapress.com
Send inquiries to info@aroucapress.com

CONTENTS

Introduction

Theology for the Layman in the Twenty-First Century

Cajetan Cuddy, O.P.

W e generally find things that are new and innovative to be the most interesting. Considered under these aspects, *Theology for the Layman* may not immediately seem to have relevance or currency in 2024. The first chapters of *Theology for the Layman* first appeared in 1941. (These chapters were originally published as a series of pamphlets.) The last chapter was published in 1954. Thus, this project finds its origin in the mid-twentieth century—roughly seventy years ago.

A lot has happened during the past seventy years. Changes in societal structure, cultural conviction, economic means, political emphasis, and technological influence render the twenty-first century very different from the mid-twentieth century. Moreover, historians will also rightly point to the fact that a lot has changed even in the life of the Catholic Church. The Second Vatican Council, which took place not long after these pamphlets were originally published, ushered in numerous developments in Catholic life.

So, we can rightly ask: Why—in the year 2024—republish this series of popular theological writings by American Dominican priests? Does this work still possess relevance and utility today?

Things New and Things Old:
The Twenty-First Century

Regardless of one's political allegiance or temperament, all can agree that the first two decades of the twenty-first century have been anything but tranquil and uneventful. Questions, concerns, and debates have captured the attention of all people—not just intellectuals. Discussion and dispute characterize contemporary life.

The predominance of impassioned disputation has risen, largely, in conjunction with the rise of technology. The centrality of the internet has shaped how human communication takes place. In the 1940s, of course, the radio was one of the chief instruments of news and entertainment. The television would also begin to occupy a prominent place in American life during the 1950s. In the twenty-first century, however, the radio has lost its centrality. The television, although it still exists and is still utilized, has become inextricably linked to the internet. Indeed, most people employ a device that fits within their pockets (the smartphone) for all of the information needs that people in previous generations would have used newspapers or the radio to satisfy. Communication can now occur with unprecedented rapidity. Traditional forms of media and communication have begun to cede to things like online journalism, Instagram, Facebook, and Twitter or "X." Never before in human history has it been possible for everyone to learn—instantaneously—what is happening around the world. Thus, the planet has become, effectively, a smaller place. All people—everyone, no matter where they reside—can be in communication to a degree and to an extent never before experienced in all of human history.

And because technology and communication have thus advanced, all persons are exposed to the concerns that preoccupy the modern mind. Questions and controversies are prominent parts of 21st century life. In previous times, the elite intellectuals of a given period would, of course, receive attention through traditional media. Nonetheless, their influence was still rather limited—at least in comparison to that of today's societal "influencers." Engaged persons can now present ideas, raise questions, and issue critiques of alternative philosophies in a universally accessible manner. Thus, even if one lives in a remote village, far away from a metropolitan or university center, he or she can participate in an ongoing global discussion about critical elements of human life.

The universality and swiftness of modern communication continues to impact our contemporary world. Members of the twenty-first century are inescapably participants in a high level, emotionally charged, and intellectually demanding conversation about the foundations of all of human experience. Universal attention is presently devoted to issues surrounding human identity, happiness, and fulfillment. In one sense, the present interest in these issues should not surprise us. They are the most important issues in every generation. The emphasis of today's questions has, admittedly, assumed a different emphasis in the present moment. Nonetheless, the most important contemporary questions are about the same subjects that all generations discuss: human nature and the meaning of human life. Because human nature is of essential relevance to our ineradicable search for human happiness, questions about the essence of the human person will never "go out of style."

Consequently, intellectual preparation, formation, and instruction are required by all those who wish to participate, profitably and effectively, in the discourse of our time. Society does not permit modern people to be without an opinion about the hotly debated questions. Today, everyone is compelled to be, in some way, an "intellectual"—someone with ideas and convictions about what it means to be a fulfilled human person. In our present time, ideas about fundamental things are at the center of human attention. People are praised for their ideas. People are also cancelled for their ideas.

Theology for the Layman provides clear, profound, and even sublime reflection on the things that matter the most. In a word, the chapters contained in *Theology for the Layman*, accessible though they are, can teach readers how to think critically and carefully about the most important elements of human life. The following pages may be literarily simple, but their message is far from simplistic.

Facile engagement with ideas and doctrines is absent these volumes. *Theology for the Layman* can teach readers how to think critically about the most important principles of reality. This renders these volumes profoundly relevant to even secular readers today.

Of course, however, *Theology for the Layman*—as its title states—was originally written for Catholic laymen who found themselves interested in the content of the Christian faith. The Dominican priests who contributed to *Theology for the Layman* chiefly desired to present a holistic and systematic presentation of the truth about reality. The motto of their Dominican Order was (and remains) *veritas*. The truth. Thus, *Theology for the Layman* sought to inspire greater devotion in the Catholic piety of its readers through a clear presentation of the truth that is Catholic doctrine.

In terms of Catholic devotion, things in 2024 are very different from what they were in 1941. Perhaps the most prominent difference is the fact that fewer and fewer persons practice the Catholic religion. Of course, not everyone was Catholic in 1941. But, those who were Catholic, customarily recognized what the practice of the faith entailed. Moreover, they practiced the faith because they *understood* the faith. Catechesis and instruction were significant parts of parochial life. And this catechetical emphasis helps to account for the robust parochial life that characterized this prior period.

Although Mass attendance continues to decline in the twenty-first century, there is still a remnant of devout and faithful believers. There will always be a remnant. The Church of Jesus Christ can never be stamped out, as our Lord Himself promised (see Mt 16:18). The Church will always perdure. Why? *Because of God.* Jesus promised that the Church would always be. And no political miscalculation, no error, and no sin, can prevent the Church from being who she is and from doing what she has done since Christ instituted her.

Thus, today, the Church continues to exist and to work for the sanctification of souls. People continue to attend Mass. Still, it is undeniable that many of today's Catholics suffer numerous misconceptions about the faith—noticeably more misconceptions than the Catholic laity of the early twentieth century. Confusion, misinformation, and nescience about Christian doctrine is one of the most prominent features of parochial life in the twenty-first century.

We recognize that there are significant groups and devout people who, as lay persons, take the Catholic faith very seriously. They read many books. They study the Scriptures. They watch many videos, listen to many podcasts, and go on many retreats. They are eager to learn, to understand, to articulate, and even to defend the Catholic faith in the twenty-first century. Our contemporary period enjoys the efforts of a number of effective Catholic evangelists, apologists, and writers who have produced works that remain of lasting value for the informed Catholic reader.

Hence, it is not the case that Catholics today don't want to understand what the Church teaches. Christian believers are always inclined to the intelligibility of the faith. But, today, Catholics are often puzzled about how best to learn the Catholic faith. Numerous books on Christian doctrine, Catholic theology, and catechesis have appeared since 1941. Yet no book—not even those of great influence and popularity—has succeeded in communicating the cohesive fullness of the faith in a way proportionate to the level of catechesis enjoyed by Catholics in the early twentieth century.

What we lack today, thus, are accessible yet systematic and comprehensive presentations of the Catholic religion—*as a whole*. Readers of contemporary authors frequently encounter many interesting and insightful observations about aspects of Christian doctrine. What the Catholic laity find elusive—and indeed so elusive that they may not even recognize its absence—is a cohesive and reliable presentation of the Catholic faith. Such a presentation must provide definitions, must identify doctrines, and must explain dogmas. Not every Catholic author is called to produce such a cohesive work, of course. And yet, if there is a single thing that the Catholic layperson (and even the Catholic cleric) requires in the twenty-first century, it is this universal presentation of the Catholic faith.

Why, we might ask, do we need such a universal, comprehensive presentation of the faith? Is it not sufficient to understand a few key Catholic teachings and then permit a certain creative contemplation to take over our reflections on the Christian life?

The reason why a systematic and comprehensive presentation of the Catholic faith is absolutely necessary is because the Catholic faith is, itself, integrally one. Serious students of the Catholic faith cannot approach the teaching of the Church in a piecemeal fashion. The subject matter of their research does not admit to fragmented study. Because the Catholic faith is a unified whole, mature students of the Catholic religion must enter into the unified wholeness of the Church's doctrine and of Christian belief. Such a unity alone will ensure that harmful errors—mistakes in doctrinal conviction and in the spiritual life—do not derail or frustrate one's spiritual life. St. Paul enjoins us to "no longer be infants, tossed by waves and swept along by every wind of teaching arising from human trickery, from their cunning in the interests of deceitful scheming" (Eph 4:14). Those who have an incomplete grasp of the Catholic faith, unfortunately, are quite vulnerable to such tossing. And this is a theme overtly present in *Theology for the Layman*.

In lieu of an adequate, systematic understanding of the Christian religion, devout persons will necessarily turn to their own intuitions about religious experience for guidance and clarity about the Christian faith. Of course, Catholic doctrine has much to say about everyday Christian experience. (This is why the example of the saints is so important for the Christian life.) But wise teachers throughout the ages have pointed out that our own (often imprecise) sentiments about human experience frequently taint and potentially distort the truth of God. In a word, we can't understand what it means to be Catholic if we rely exclusively upon private, personal intuitions. We require something much more reliable, secure, and permanent. And, thankfully, God has provided such a reliable teaching: God's revelation of himself and what God has told us that he does in our lives—these must supremely shape our reflections on human experience. Moreover, we can only be certain about what God's revelation actually reveals through the guidance of the Church. Christ imparted to the Church, alone, the charism of determining what is authentic Christian doctrine and what is not.

In their original published form, the *Theology for the Layman* pamphlets included this summary on their back covers: "these pamphlets are numbers in a series which eventually will embrace all theology"—written "for any study group that wishes a systematic survey of Catholic Theology." Even in its original conception, then, the *Theology for the Layman* supplies a robust Catholic formation. There have been many publications in the last fifty years that manifest a great fidelity to, and love for, the Church and for the faith. Yet not all books have aspired to provide a resource that all Catholics need: a complete and systematic presentation of the Catholic faith. In this regard, *Theology for the Layman* remains an exceptional work.

Although *Theology for the Layman* is written in a simple and accessible style, these short chapters provide a systematic presentation of the Catholic faith. Of course, *Theology for the Layman's* chapters were published before the Church blessed her members with the *Catechism of the Catholic Church*. Nonetheless, the essential truths of the Christian faith have not changed. And the *Catechism* did not abrogate any of the doctrinal convictions that the Church maintained in the mid-twentieth century (and that we find exposited in the chapters that follow). The chapters contained in these volumes are still—even seventy years after their original composition—a reliable and compelling presentation of the Church's teaching as a whole. Indeed, *Theology for the Layman* can be read as a profitable complement to the Church's own, official summary of her doctrine in the *Catechism of the Catholic Church*.

If we are deprived of a comprehensive presentation of the faith, alternative accounts of the things that matter the most can beguile our thoughts and affections—accounts less wise and contrary to human flourishing. Given the dynamics of twenty-first century discourse and debate, Christian believers cannot afford to be so uninformed. Today's believers need wisdom above all. That is why this work continues to matter even today. In a very real sense, *Theology for the Layman* offers wise answers for readers living in a world consumed by impassioned questions.

Why St. Thomas Aquinas in the Twenty-First Century?

Given our above emphasis upon the value of a holistic presentation of the Christian religion in a tumultuous time, we take consolation in the fact that the authors of *Theology for the Layman* follow the lead and rely upon the writings of St. Thomas Aquinas. Of course, Thomas Aquinas is not the only theologian of importance and significance in Christian history.[1] Nonetheless, the Church has consistently and explicitly recognized in Aquinas's writings a uniquely comprehensive and faithful summary of the doctrine that she received from her founder, Jesus Christ.[2]

All of the Fathers and Doctors of the Church reward careful reading. St. Thomas is not a replacement for the whole of the Church's spiritual and intellectual patrimony. And yet, no other Doctor wrote a single work like the *Summa Theologiae*—a work that accurately presents virtually all of the essential parts of the Christian religion.

The *Summa Theologiae* was exclusively concerned with the essential truths of the Christian religion. St. Thomas highlights this myopic focus, explicitly, in the *Summa*'s general prologue. Moreover, he recognized that the truth must be articulated in a way that readers and students could understand. Thus, the supreme formality of the

---

[1] For more about Aquinas's life and legacy, see Romanus Cessario, O.P., and Cajetan Cuddy, O.P., *Thomas and the Thomists: The Achievement of St. Thomas Aquinas and His Interpreters* (Minneapolis, MN: Fortress Press, 2017); and Jean-Pierre Torrell, O.P., *Saint Thomas Aquinas— Volume I: The Person and His Work*, 3rd ed., trans. Matthew K. Minerd and Robert Royal (Washington, DC: Catholic University of America Press, 2023).

[2] For a helpful summary of the Catholic Church's endorsement of St. Thomas Aquinas, see Santiago Ramírez, O.P., "The Authority of St. Thomas Aquinas," *The Thomist* 15, no. 1 (1952): 1–109.

Summa Theologiae is pedagogical accessibility. This is supremely expressed in the very structure of the *Summa Theologiae*. Without much exaggeration, one could say that the *Summa*'s table of contents—and the order of presentation that one finds therein—is almost as important as the specific things that Aquinas says in each of the *Summa*'s discrete parts. *Theology for the Layman* reflects the great advantage of authors who intentionally follow the outline of Aquinas's wise and orderly presentation of Christian doctrine.

To summarize: Although the *Summa Theologiae* is not an easy book, it is an accessible book—to readers who make an effort to follow the sublime analysis that they encounter therein. No other single author has presented the entirety of the Catholic faith with such clarity, consistency, and universal accessibility. Consequently, the authors of *Theology for the Layman* recognize in Aquinas a useful resource for their own efforts to present the Catholic faith to the twentieth century. They deliberately follow the order of discussion and teaching that St. Thomas so carefully employed in the *Summa Theologiae*. Thus, their efforts enjoy a great utility even for those who search for wisdom in the twenty-first century.

Theology for the Layman, thus, captures the intellectual and spiritual heart of the *Summa Theologiae* without losing any of its vitality. In a word, the following pages extends the ultimate design and purpose of the *Summa Theologiae* itself: to make the essential truths of the Christian faith intelligible to those grappling with the most important questions.

Conclusion

The questions that are disputed today are questions that require intellectual engagement. One must be able, to some degree, to understand and to articulate in an intelligible manner what he or she believes. The twenty-first century does not permit engaged persons to be without opinion or conviction about the most important questions. *Theology for the Layman* is a precious guide for those who wish to think through the fundamental principles directly relevant to the questions and disputes of our contemporary age.

The value of *Theology for the Layman*, thus, is the fact that it represents an initiative designed to meet one of the greatest needs in all generations: (1) a cohesive presentation of the Catholic faith, (2) in language that is accessible to readers from all backgrounds, and (3) according to the wise, ordered, and attentive structure of learning and teaching that St. Thomas Aquinas identified. The fact that these volumes were composed about seventy years ago should not cause us any chagrin. Because human nature never undergoes essential change, the most important questions of human existence are always the same—regardless of the century. Moreover, the Christian faith doesn't go out of style; It's never outdated. The essence of the Christian religion remains the same because Jesus remains the same.

Theology for the Layman explains, with great charm and clarity, the most important things about the human person and what happens when human persons meet the wise and loving God—in every generation.

The High Quest
Why Man Should Know God

Walter Farrell, O.P.

Introduction

This is the introduction to a series of pamphlets on the relationship between man and God—a series based on the *Summa Theologiae* and designed to meet the study club needs of Holy Name Societies throughout the country. Its aim is to cover the entire field of theology from the point of view of the layman and particularly for Holy Name men.

Why such a remarkable series is undertaken; why the project is so ambitious and systematic; why such an apparently unpopular subject as "theology" is treated in such flimsy and short-lived booklets as these; why such an erudite book as the *Summa* of St. Thomas Aquinas is used these questions and others which come to the mind are answered in this introductory pamphlet.

The Holy Name Society challenges its members to read this little book carefully. That's all we ask. For we know that if you read this you'll investigate the subsequent pamphlets, and if you follow through the series, you will discover new vistas, new relationships between God and man, new motivations for human conduct—all of which will be summed up in a new and revitalized society.

We firmly believe and sincerely hope that this little booklet will prove to you a pearl of great price.

Why?

The project which this pamphlet initiates cannot even be introduced without arousing a storm of questions. It is not quite accurate to picture this pamphlet as a hat tossed into the house to determine whether a social call is in order or whether the hat will come flying out as a prophecy of the coming fate of the unwary caller; for there is nothing tentative about the orderly series of pamphlets that will follow this one. But it does seem necessary to state the case of this, and the other pamphlets, bluntly; immediately arouse the questions; and get them answered at once. A clean-cut argument definitely settled or a proposition clearly stated has about it all the refreshing clarity of a bright sun after a sudden spring shower.

This pamphlet, then, introduces the project of a systematic education of all Catholic men, under the sponsorship of the Holy Name Society, in the relationship between God and man. Or, to put it more simply, the Holy Name Society is promoting a pamphlet course in theology for every Catholic man who can read.

Clearly, this kind of thing needs explanation. Why is the Holy Name Society mixed up in it? Why jump feet first into theology and drag all the defenseless Holy Name members along? Why attempt such an enormous job with the frail tools that are pamphlets? These questions need answering. They are honest questions, objections to be met before there can be any hope of the rousing welcome that these pamphlets may deserve and that the times demand. Let's look at the questions one by one.

High Hat

There seems to be much to be said against the Holy Name Society sponsoring so ambitious, and so obviously intellectual, a program. Holy Name men have traditionally worn badges, not caps and gowns. In a Holy Name gathering, it was expected that a man stood on the solid grounds of his Catholic manhood; there was no academic mummery, no deference to university degrees as such, no discussion of academic precedence. For the Holy Name Society has always existed, not for a learned few, but for the generality of Catholic men divided by parishes. It has always been true that with a particular society there were men who were completely at home in the most learned of discussions, lawyers, doctors, scientists and all the rest; but there were also men, plenty of them, who knew the taste of sweat and the ache of fatigue, men who had difficulty keeping their eyes open long enough to read a newspaper after the jar, the crash, the labor of a long day. It will be a tragedy if the Holy Name Society goes high-hat on men such as these. It has always existed to encourage frequent communion and to discourage profanity and blasphemy; are these to be abandoned as too petty a goal?

It has always been true, and still is, that the Society is designed for all Catholic men. Its Catholicity is like that of the Church. It must always remain the great goal of the Society to bring men to the Sacrament of the Altar. It must always remain a principal aim of the Society to instill a horror of blasphemy and profanity. The present series of pamphlets is no indication that the organization is departing from its specific work and getting into other fields. It is rather one of the preliminaries of the complete program which is so needed by the Catholic men of the United States.

Old Goals Remain

Holy Communion is a splendid climax, but it is also a firm foundation; it is a shining goal, but it is also an enthusiastic beginning. When the apostles had, one by one, accepted Christ's invitation to follow Him, they reached the highest point their lives had until then touched; they tasted of the sweetness of the goal of life with God; but they also laid the foundation for that incredible story of simple heroism that has fascinated the world ever since; they were but beginning that long trek along the roads of the world that had a common rendezvous with death. The embrace of the Son of Mary has never been the end of activity but the beginning of it;

to welcome Christ is to set out on the high road with Him in a journey that ends only on arrival at an eternal home.

The Holy Name man, receiving Holy Communion, has reached a high point in life; but only that he might go still higher. His life with Christ is not thereby finished; it has received a fresh start. This foundation of intense Christian life that is the intimate union of the soul with its Lord and Master must be amplified and lived during the hours and days that a man is not at the altar rail. Life in union with the Mystical Body of Christ is not something that is finished in an hour; it is a full time affair.

Obviously, the Catholic man must know what that life is about and the implications of it; the more deeply he knows, the more intensely can he live it, the more zealously can he share it with others. If the program of frequent Communion is to be complete, the knowledge of the life it begins must be available to every Catholic man. It is towards such a completion of the traditional Holy Name program that this series of pamphlets works.

His Name

Stress has indeed been laid on the avoidance of blasphemy and profanity in the past. That stress will not be removed because of the larger program. It is inconceivable that a soldier could long revile his Commander-in-Chief without finally being suspect of halfhearted lip-service, if not treason. Nor can a man habitually revile God without being suspect of just such lip-service, if not of a re-enactment of the role of Judas.

These bad habits of speech are often minimized because of the elements of human respect, carelessness, and indifference that enter into their formation and continuation. The task in this line is to sharpen our consciences and to evaluate that basic attack on the Second Commandment of God in its true light. Just what place has this preference for "human respect," this willingness to serve men rather than God, in a Catholic? What room is there for an excusable indifference or carelessness to the One the Catholic man professes to love above all things?

4

For a nation as professedly practical as we are, it is downright astounding that we can overlook the fact that unless divine authority is maintained there will be no basis for civil or religious authority. It is a peculiarly fatal type of blindness that prevents our seeing that the indifference shown Almighty God, by disrespect to His Name and that of His Divine Son, has immediate and tragic repercussions in respect for the President from a man who has no respect for God. On what do we base our expectations of sacrifice for the state from a man who is indifferent to divinity? Isn't it just a little stupid to expect devotion to men from one who is careless of God? Religious indifference may be decked out in the uniform of religious tolerance and have no need to parachute into the midst of us; but it is a most dangerous fifth column nonetheless.

However, it is not enough to go about saying "Don't say this" or "Don't say that." Our Catholic men must be offered the reason for the enormity of indifference and carelessness. Therefore a systematic education in the relationship between God and man, that is, in theology, is the intention of the Holy Name Society, and, indeed, its solemn duty. In no other way can the life based upon the Sacraments be completed; only in this way can sound reason be offered to awaken men from their careless and deplorable habits of speech. The Holy Name Society, in other words, is abandoning nothing of its traditional program by this series of pamphlets; rather it is rolling up its sleeves and getting at a job that is desperately urgent in our times.

Why Pamphlets

There is much to be said against attempting this systematic education through the medium of pamphlets. A pamphlet does allow a man who has nothing to say to look important in the process of saying it and to finish up before he can be challenged. It does make a man, who has something to say, swallow half his words in the hurry to get it said before the covers of the pamphlets close in and imprison him. Then, too, pamphlets have a way, once they are tossed on the living room table, of burrowing under newspapers and magazines like a puppy trying to keep warm. They are lost easier than one glove; since they seldom run much over five or ten cents, even a miserly man can see that more than a nickel's worth of effort would have to be put into the job of locating them.

Then again, by the very force of circumstances, pamphlets have to depend on their gaudy, almost vulgar, dress to attract attention as they skulk in the remote corners of the Church vestibule to which custom has relegated them. Quite naturally, they get not so much as a passing glance from the thousands who mill in and out of Church in solid columns on Sunday morning. Their appeal is to the man and woman with a little time to waste as they saunter out after a week-day Mass or drop in Church for a visit. Even here, to strike the eye and attention of prospective customers, the pamphlet must be attractive both in subject matter and in cover design. It has always been an "impulse-item"; an item, in fact, often regretted before it has been ushered into the home, for such selections are almost necessarily haphazard and such pamphlets are almost necessarily dated. In such desperate straits and with so much competition, of course much more money must be put into the appearance of the pamphlets.

Why Not Pamphlets

On the other hand, there is much to be said in favor of the pamphlet. In the first place, it doesn't cost much; and when pennies are bought with sinew and sweat, this is an item not to be disregarded. Then, too, they are small, inoffensive things with much more of the dachshund's eagerness for friendliness than the chow's bullying demand for respect; even the most timid of non-bookworms can hardly be frightened by a pamphlet.

The Holy Name series is designed to overcome most of the objections against the pamphlet. It is to be a progressive series, thereby giving the man with something to say plenty of time to say it in, and barring the wind-bag from all participation. It is based on the *Summa Theologiae* of St. Thomas Aquinas and, as such, promises to offer a complete picture of the field of man's relationship with

God. Moreover, it is to be done by experts, who are not rushed, since it is a long-term venture, and promises, from that quarter, to be thorough.

The pamphlet will not be picked up on a rack, but will be promoted through the Society and can be put out for a minimum price. Since the volumes will be numbered, it will not be difficult for men to add their back numbers together or to secure back numbers and build for themselves a popular compendium of theology. The pamphlets are to appear at the rate of one a month; which gives them little enough time to crawl into corners or burrow under newspapers, particularly since both the subject matter and the presentation are to be of an attractiveness calculated to forbid the pamphlet's being tossed aside within the first twenty-four hours of its purchase.

Indeed, given a fair chance, it is quite likely that the pamphlets will have to have time quotas put on their use as carefully as those tacked on the use of the family car. The pamphlets in this series are not for scholars, but they will not be despised or looked down on by scholars. They are for the men of the country who are trying to live fuller lives as Catholics, and it is the hope of the editors that they will bring Holy Name men closer to the God to whom they pledge reverence.

That Word "Theology"

The objection that arises from the subject matter of these pamphlets, that they deal with the relationship of man to God (the proper field of theology), is not so easy to brush off. Nor is this because the objection is difficult to answer; in fact there is nothing easier. The difficulty comes in the tremendous importance of both the objection and its answer.

It has only been by an extremely odd quirk of the history of thought and the abuse of words that men have come, in our time, to think of theology somewhat as they think of the language of ancient Egypt; an object of study for a handful of specialists for reasons known only to the specialists and God; certainly not an object of intense interest to the farmer or the laborer. The absurdity of this position begins to appear when it is realized that a Catholic starts to study theology his first day in school, or for that matter, with his first questions, and continues to talk about it until death has cancelled the wave-length on which he has done his broadcasting.

The Son of God came amongst men bearing two divine gifts, the gifts of grace and truth. It is the latter that theology engages itself with, savors, illustrates, penetrates, defends. No man, in his right senses, would imagine that the Son of God was made man to bring learnedly unimportant and obscure gifts for the few; He did not come to furnish a few learned men with intellectual playthings, but to bring life, a fuller, more abundant life, to *all* men. It is with Him and His divine truth that theology is busy.

Going Anywhere

Or, to look at it another way, a man's whole life is spent in thinking about, talking about, and working for the particular goal that gives it significance. When he becomes convinced that there is no goal, and hence no meaning to life, a man commits suicide, or hurls himself into a whirl of activity in the attempt to forget he is alive, or settles down to imitate the life of a plant by simply vegetating. Most men are not easy victims of so monstrous a lie about human life; so most men spend themselves in the man's size struggle for the goal of life. It is precisely the goal of life that is a center of theology's interest. Clearly, it is important that a man—every man—take his theology seriously, and that he know it is theology he is concentrating on.

As a matter of fact, there has never been a time in the history of the world when theological interest, theological thought, theological talk was in danger of disappearing among men. In our own time, for instance, there is no dearth of theological talk among truck-drivers, sand hogs,[1] and walking delegates. It couldn't be otherwise. For every man has a goal, a supreme value, the most

---

[1] Term used during this time for underground construction workers. —Ed.

important thing in his life. It may be money, or pleasure, or power, or even so prosaic a thing as sleep. Whatever it is, he talks about it as incessantly as he thinks about it and cheerfully subordinates everything else in his life to its service. This is his goal; and a man's goal is his god. In St. Paul's day it was noticeable that for some men their god was their belly; the phenomenon is still with us, strange as it may seem to see a man attempting to bow down in worship before such a deity. The point here is that all of man's considerations of his goal, which is his god, are theological considerations; such a theology may be a very bad one, a twisted, perverse, monstrous thing. But it is theological, for it has to do with the relationship of a man to his god.

Want a Map

The theology with which these pamphlets are concerned is the splendid, clear beauty of eternal wisdom. It brings man the truths that every man has to know to escape personal tragedy, the tragedy of draining his life both of its significance and of its successful issue. In the course of learning truth, a man can set out on the road either of discovery or of instruction, or both, since both lead in the same direction. So, for example, a man starting out on an automobile trip can discover the route to his destination by the rather exhaustive process of personally investigating every road until he hits the right one; or he can submit to the instruction involved in consulting a road map which will tell him the most direct route, though it won't keep him on the right road.

In a case like this, it is clear that instruction can well be a time-saver. Some truth can be discovered by personal investigation, but not without the expenditure of time that is often much too precious to be wasted. A medical student, bored with the routine of classes as he might well be, could start off on his own, brushing aside the long history of the past and its discoveries. Given time, he could discover very many of the principles of the art of medicine. Of course there would be quite a trail of corpses strewn along the path of his advance to knowledge; for such discoveries would be paid for not only in time but also in human life the human lives which were the object of his experimental studies

It is not hard to see, then, that instruction can be a life-saver as well as a time-saver. Some men must know some truths quickly that other men may not suffer. Thus a doctor must know the art of medicine at the beginning of his career, not only after years of practice; a lawyer must know the law when he walks into the court if his client is to escape the electric chair; the engineer must know his subject before he builds his first bridge, not after his fortieth. Moreover, this knowledge must be expert, if other men are not to suffer, not the hit and miss variety that is liberally sprinkled with errors.

You Too

But it is also true that *all* men must know some truths expertly and quickly, in fact at the beginning of their responsible lives, not primarily that other men might not suffer from their ignorance, but that they themselves might escape personal tragedy. If a man's life is really a walk towards a goal, he must know when he takes the first step just where that goal lies. Since a man's life is measured by the good he does and the evil he avoids, he must know at the beginning the difference between right and wrong; as he is to carry full responsibility for all his actions, he must know at the beginning wherein his control lies, how it is perfected and what threatens it. He must know what it is to be a man, to possess a spiritual soul, a free will and a mind that can grasp truth.

Given time, a wise man might learn all these things, allowing himself, since he is human, a generous margin for error in the course of his learning. One who was not so wise, might, in the course of years, pick up a pretty good percentage of these necessary truths, with a much wider margin of error. In both cases, we must suppose leisure enough for study and investigation, as well as an inclination for that sort of thing. The average man, who is not so deeply wise, who is desperately hurried and thoroughly fatigued by the labors of the day, the responsibilities of a family, and the other human burdens that perch on a man's shoulders, would come off pretty badly in the scramble for these truths that are absolutely necessary for the living of human life.

In these matters, theology acts primarily as a time-saver. Here, revelation and the theological investigations that flow from revelation are offered to men because it is not only the wise and leisured who must live human lives. All men must know these truths. They must know them at once, at the very beginning of life. Nor is there room for error in this desperately necessary knowledge, for error here is a guarantee of tragedy.

By saving time, theology and the revelation from which it flows obviously saves lives. In other words, even in the field of natural knowledge where a man's mind is, strictly speaking, adequate, theological instruction is necessary. Yet it is not here that the pre-eminent value of theology lies. It is precisely as a life-saver that theology operates in its own proper field, the field that is totally above the powers that are natural to man.

The High Quest

If a man lives for a goal that his mind cannot even suspect until told of it by God, obviously man needs instruction about that goal. The absolutely crucial point is that man does live for precisely such a goal, the goal of eternal union with God Himself. If a man can reach that goal only by tools of which he could not conceive, let alone manufacture, tools which must be given to him and in the use of which he must be instructed, clearly he cannot depend on his own efforts. The fact is that it is only by such supernatural tools, the sacraments and the supernatural virtues, that a man can make a success of his life and finally come home to eternal life with God. If fatal mistakes can be undone, man should know about it; if these mistakes can be undone in a way he could not suspect and by a power that is totally supernatural, these things should be told to a man.

The truth is that the only tragic mistakes in life, a man's own sins, can be undone but only by the saving power of the blood of God in the Sacrament of Penance. If there are truths about a man's

life, and about a man's God, that transform every instant of his
life from dull routine to high romance, from insignificance to the
point where every instant of that life is the most important thing
in the universe, from brass to precious gold, these things should
not be kept from a man; he should be told. The astounding thing
is that the alchemist's dream has become the accomplishment of
God; that from the base metal of human life, God has drawn the
infinitely precious sharing in divine life. Now, it is strictly true that
the stairs of a tenement can be a flight to divinity, that a moment
of agony can be a cause of supreme joy, that sacrifice can be a gay,
lilting thing, and the most abject failure in the human order, the
most sublime success in the eternal judgment of the wisdom of God.

Truths like these cannot be learned by discovery. No amount
of grubbing about the foundations of the world for any number
of years by the keenest of human minds can unearth a single one
of these things. Yet they are all absolutely necessary for every man
from the beginning of his life. Without them, life has lost its savor,
its meaning, its chance of success.

Truth

It is to be particularly noticed that all these things are *truths*. The
claim they make is on the mind of a man. This relationship of a man
to God is the basis of human life. That basis is not the frail, change-
able foundation of sense, even of religious sense. This supremely
important field of moral values is not the murkily mysterious field
of the emotions. Realizing this, the Holy Name man stands apart
from his contemporaries, even his most learned contemporaries
Many of them will cultivate an attitude of indifference, or, more
leniently, an attitude of tolerance towards the religious life of a man.
Some will take that relationship of man to God seriously indeed;
but insist that it is a matter of man's feelings, of his emotions, an
affair that is not subject to the searching light of his mind. To the
great majority of the really modern, then, the basis of a man's life is
not laid on convictions, but on emotions, opinions or sheer guesses.
To such as these, there is no possibility of theological instruction,

of systematic education in theological truth; for to them there is no such truth.

To us, on the contrary, this relationship to God is something a man can *think* about, and with profit. These essential prerequisites for successful human living are truths; indeed, they are the front page truths of life. These are the headlines that, day after day, stream across the whole space of a man's life. The editor who would glance through them hurriedly, then relegate them to an obscure corner of an inside page would have no sense of news value at all. These are sharp, vivid, personal truths seen as such, or they are hardly seen at all. It is precisely the task of a systematic education in the relationship of man to God to bring these front page truths up to the front page of the Catholic man's life; to underline their personal character, to sharpen the edge of them, renew their vividness and so inject them into the vital stream of human living.

It is these truths that give the whole flavor to human life. Wherever human life is lived, there these truths are to be seen at work: on the battlefield, in the office, in the bustle of a home, in the laborious worries of a child's homework, in the rough give and take of a man's life. For these are the things by which a man lives.

No Lost Horizons

It is this that must be seen beyond all shadow of doubt: it is by truth that a man lives big, divine, fundamental truths. Truths that open up the gates of the universe and let a man's mind wander out of that natural prison into the divine land of infinite horizons; that let his heart follow his mind, free to love without the specter of an inevitable end to that loving, without the haunting fear of a disillusionment inevitable in the embrace of what is unworthy of the love of a man, without the cautions, the conditions, the emergency escapes so characteristic of an age afraid of life and love and so degrading to all the high aspirations that mark the heart of a man off from the rest of the universe. These are truths which a man's mind can never exhaust, of which it cannot tire, with which it is never to be finished.

In handling these truths, man develops the science of theology. And it is a science; not in the narrow sense of experiment and sense observation, but in the larger, truer sense of completely certain knowledge come at through completely sure principles. In this case, the starting point is, of course, the truths that come directly from God Himself; these are the principles had, not through the uneasy filter of human reason and human discovery, but from the very source of truth itself. From them, the mind of man works to scientific conclusions which properly take their place at the head of all the findings of all the sciences.

The theology to which these pamphlets introduce you has about it all the joy of a science which searches for truth for truth's sake, and all the handiness of a science that exists simply and solely for the practical purposes of life. In other words, theology does not have to crash the gate of a gathering at which the guests are metaphysics, ethics, psychology, and the rest; it deserves the place of honor. In these things, where truth is sought, not that it might be put to work, but that it might nourish the mind, nobility is determined by the quality of the truth attained; theology has for its object the supreme truth, the source of all truth. If these things seek to learn the causes of things, theology concentrates on the first and last cause of all things, not as it is seen by the mind of a man, but as it is known in itself and of itself, as it is told to man by the first and last cause Who is God.

Glimpses of God

Aristotle, the peer of pagan philosophers, once said that the joy of the least knowledge of the highest things far outstrips the most detailed knowledge of the lowest or most particular of things. It sounds a little obscure, said just like that. In reality, it is incontrovertibly true and completely obvious. When you have learned that Brooklyn lost the world series, you are in possession of a single, concrete fact. That fact might have been the source of joy or sorrow. But now that you know the fact, what can you do with it; what more of truth is to be wrung from it; what significance has it for your mind and your heart through all the long length of the years? On the other hand, when you know that the soul of a man is a spirit, you have just begun to uncover the riches of personal immortality, the unlimited horizons of truth, the depths of love and the generosity of sacrifice. When you know that God is good, you have lifted a corner of the veil that hides the face of the infinite.

At a much humbler get-together, say of chemistry, biology, physics, and the rest of the sciences whose proper uniform is a pair of overalls because they search for truth for the sole purpose of putting it to work, theology would be right at home, even the life of the party. In such company, prestige is measured by practicality; because our times, and our nation, so esteem practicality, these sciences hold an extremely high place. They get things done, things that are worth doing because they do something to or for a man; in plain language, they enable a man to get the things done he has to do, they bring him to the places he has to get to. They serve the ends or goals of a man; the higher, wider, more extensive the end a particular science serves, the more it stands out in this company; so, for instance, the science of biology serves the end of the physical well-being of man, military science serves the end of defense of man's country, while political science serves the end of the well-being of the nation in both peace and war. In the scale of importance, then, politics (as a science, remember, not as a livelihood) ranks first, military science second, and biology third as far as these three go.

First Place

It does not take much imagination to visualize the practical importance of theology in these terms. It does not primarily serve the end of man's health, an end that is at best a matter of a few years and covers only a little corner of the interests of a man; it does not serve the end of a particular escape of the nation from an external enemy, an end that is by no means the summation of a man's interest and, in the historical view, is a matter of a few moments; it does not serve the end of the well being of a nation, an end that is a tool to the absolutely central interests of a man and is always bound within temporal limits. It serves the end of ends, the last end that gives worth to all the other ends of a man; the end that is as wide as his life, as high as his God, as extensive as eternity; the end that endures forever.

No, a systematic education in theology need make no apology in this or any time. If no other indication of its excellence were at hand, it would be enough, to be convinced of its being worthwhile, to glance at the fruits it produces. For surely there is nothing to surpass the sharper taste of God it brings through a deeper knowledge, and consequently deeper love of Him; this is the preview of heaven granted to men on earth, the foretaste summed up so divinely in the Eucharistic union of the soul with God. Outside of that miraculously generous divine gesture of Holy Communion, our union with God is by knowledge and love of Him; direct knowledge and the ecstasy of love that will flow from such immediate vision of God make up the essence of the happiness of heaven. With the foretaste of God comes, inevitably, the long, serene view of wisdom which should be the badge of the soul of a Holy Name man; that clear sightedness that, looking at life from the heights of its beginning and end, sees the hills and the valleys, the trivia and the essentials, and guides a man through them all patiently, calmly, prudently, wisely.

Thomas Aquinas

Let's suppose, for the sake of argument, that the Holy Name Society should have sponsored this project, that the medium of this systematic education of Holy Name men should be pamphlets, and that the subject matter of the teaching should have been the relationship of man to God, or theology. Why was it necessary to go to the *Summa Theologiae* of St. Thomas Aquinas for the material of this systematic study? What if it is the supreme theological book of all time? After all, theologically speaking, we are probably less embarrassed shopping at Klein's than at Macy's; we might do much better on Maxwell Street than on upper Michigan Avenue. Let's not be snooty about this thing; much has been done since St. Thomas' time, his work has been digested, made easier, the rough spots ironed out and the modern touches put to it. The *Summa* is a tremendous, seven hundred year old work that absolutely no one can read in slippers and an easy chair. Why not start with something easy; say a little bit of a book by a man who was neither a genius nor a saint? We could feel much more at home with such a man, for he would not be plunging us into the depths of truth or spurring us on to the heights of virtue. And there is much to be said for nice, flat, monotonous country.

Well, to understand why the *Summa Theologiae* was chosen, had to be chosen, as the groundwork of this series of pamphlets, it is not necessary to look at the book at all. But it is necessary to look at Aquinas, really look at him; not be satisfied with a mumbled introduction and the momentary glimpse which alone is possible when he is seen in the press of the thousands of theologians who have graced the pages of the history of the Church.

A Man's Man

First of all, Thomas Aquinas knew men. A good deal of the explanation of his knowledge is given when it is said that he travelled back and forth across Europe again and again and always on foot. The explanation, however, does not really sink in until, by a little trick of the imagination, Thomas is seen in a modern setting. Today that would mean that any truck-driver might, in the course of his run, come across Thomas standing by the side of the road thumbing a ride. He would look a little shabby, thoroughly fatigued, yet, in some mysterious fashion, as quietly happy, serenely content as a tenement mother smiling at the infant nursing at her breast. The prospect of miles of hot, lonely road, the slim chance of a handout somewhere along the way to keep him alive, and the obvious destitution of a man who had nothing with him but a book would not seem to bother Thomas at all.

In the course of the months, all company rules to the contrary, Thomas would ride in the sleek cabs of fast freight trucks, in prehistoric jalopies, in rattling but efficient flivver[2] trucks of farmers, in the tourist's crowded sedan, and, once in a very blue moon, even in a luxurious limousine. He would know the sting of fall rain, the numbness of cold, the relentlessly pursuing heat of the sun, and the smothering silence of snow's invitation to dreams and oblivion. On a raw night he would crowd into the stuffy heat of a hamburger stand and know the rich feeling of luxury; the smell of coffee would almost make a poet of him; and the jostle of many men would seem like a caress, so welcome was it. He'd stop in villages and towns; and when he put up in one of the thousand "big little cities" he would know soon enough not to talk about the way things were done in New York. He would have first hand knowledge of California fogs and Florida showers, of the rocky basis for New England's stubborn pride, the rich loam of the Midwest and the quiet, drifting lilt of the South.

A Saint

In his own time, Thomas and his brethren of the Dominican Order were the unqualified favorites of all classes of men. They belonged to the people, and the people were fiercely proud, possessively thoughtful, completely approving of them; though, at the same time, they were ruthless in their demands upon the friars. These priests were the confidants of the world of their time. Thomas himself was besieged by questions through the mail, on the high road, at inns, even on his death bed. To him all hearts were opened that the trouble and worries of the souls of men might be given to him who was so capable of carrying such huge burdens.

In our times, then, the truck-driver who had given Thomas a lift would reflect in astonishment, after he had set down his passenger, at the amount and the intimacy of the talking he had done. Thomas

---

[2] Flivver is early twentieth-century American slang for an automobile, frequently used for a poor quality or poorly maintained car. It may also refer to: Flivver, nickname for the Ford Model T, the first mass-produced automobile. —Ed.

would hear of the struggles of the girl behind the counter of the hamburger stand, the family worries of the burly State policeman, the sorrows of the destitute, and the gnawings of conscience that went on under the veneer of hardness assumed by the criminal. In this age, as in that, the hearts of the common people would swing their doors wide open for his sympathetic inspection.

For he would be the kind of man a person could and would talk to: interested, sympathetic, helpful in a common-sense sort of way with nothing of the sentimental about him. Being a saint, he would have the penetrating eyes of Christ to see down into the depths of courage, of hope, of remorse, of fighting strength that are to be found in a human heart. Being a saint, he would have the patience that springs from a profound understanding and love of men; being a saint his last thought would be for himself, his first for all these men and women who were so precious in the eyes of his greatest Friend as to merit the unspeakably generous sacrifice of Calvary on their behalf.

A Scholar

For all this closeness to the most humble of men and women, this Thomas could preach before Popes, argue brilliantly before the greatest minds of the greatest universities, be at home at the banquet table of kings. As a matter of fact he did all these things in an almost routine fashion. He had something to say to men, to all men, kings or paupers.

Thomas knew men; he was the sort men could and would talk to; he had something vitally important and vividly inspiring to say to all men. He spent himself for men. Why shouldn't the men of our time go to him for the time-saving and life-saving instruction that they need with a need above that of the men of any other age? There are no substitutes for a man like this and no one knows this better than the one who attempts the substitution; deliberately to choose the substitute would be totally unworthy of the hard-headed practicality of the America of the twentieth century.

Book for "Beginners"

The supreme work of this outstanding genius and saintly friend of men is the *Summa Theologiae*. Possessed of one of the greatest minds the world has known, working at a pace that puts our feverish hurry to shame, and with a consuming zeal explicable only in terms of the fire of his love for God and men, Thomas in the years of his religious life had plumbed the depths of wisdom amassed by men. The despairing philosophies of the East, the brilliant but stumbling thought of the philosophers of Greece, the wisdom of the Fathers, and the labors of the long thousand years that went into the making of scholasticism—all these went into the crucible of his mind. He wrote, argued, taught at the greatest universities of Europe; he struck sparks from the finely tempered minds of his time; he prayed and meditated on the word of the Scriptures he had by heart. When he had reached the peak of his powers, with only a few years of life left to him, he put the full force of his mature genius to work at "exposing the whole of Catholic doctrine, in as orderly, brief, and clear a fashion as the matter allowed, *for beginners*." The words are the words of Thomas; the italics are mine. This supreme work, whose completion was prevented by death, is the *Summa Theologiae*.

Why shouldn't the *Summa Theologiae* be the basis for the systematic education of beginners in our time in that relationship between man and God? It has never had an equal. In it Thomas goes to the depths open to the human mind aided by faith in his treatment of God, the world, angels and men. The moral, which is to say the human, life of a man is studied here in all its details: the prime importance and concrete character of the goal of that life, the mastery of action which distinguishes human life from all others, passion and habit, virtue and sin, law and grace are treated in an exposition that supposes nothing. Then, one by one, faith, hope, charity with all their allied virtues and bitterly opposed vices come under scrutiny; justice and the whole gamut of the virtues of social life with God and man, prudence, courage with its outstanding children of patience and perseverance, temperance in all the beauty of its human moderation. The road which a man's feet must travel in his journey home, the Way that is Christ, is handled sublimely: the life of the Savior, the beauty of His mother, the tragedy of His life and death, along with the continuation of both that life and death in the sacraments to the climax of living which is reached in death, judgment, heaven and hell.

No Easy Beginnings

We could, of course, go to a little bit of a book, a comfortable, easy book; but only if we were not in earnest. To look for a comfortable, easy beginning is to deny the desire to begin at all. There are no easy beginnings. If a child were to wait for an easy beginning of the habit of walking, it would crawl all its days on all fours; if a man waits for an easy beginning to learning, he will be forever ignorant; if a man waits for an easy beginning to living he will be dead before his time and will never have lived at all. It is not the heights of sanctity which represent difficulty, but the beginnings of it with their agonized struggle against sin. If we are to wait for an easy beginning of the study of God, we shall never begin. We must start the hard way, simply because there is no other way to start at all.

There was a time in this country when it might have been argued, with some plausibility, that the minimum education in the relationship of man to God offered by the penny catechism was enough for the average man; further study could be left to priests, nuns, and the very few outstanding leaders among the laity. There was a time in this country, too, when it might have been argued that the care and defense of the country could be left to a few politicians, some roughly organized police officers and a handful of poorly equipped soldiers. That the argument, in each case, was valid might now, in the light of present circumstances, be seriously questioned. At any rate, that time is now passed.

Holy Name Men Awaken!

The welfare of the country is now the worry of every citizen; the aim now is for coordinated effort, for mighty armaments and an army of millions. Perhaps that will be enough. The welfare of religion, the state of Catholicism in America, is now the serious obligation of every Catholic. There can no longer be any doubt that every individual faces a challenge, even a battle, that is constant; nor, in this day of ours, is the battle only one induced by external enemies; often enough it starts within the very heart of a Catholic in the form of a storm of doubting questions awakened by the very atmosphere of the times in which we live. The things the Catholic of the twentieth century stands to lose are the things that mark the difference between hopeless failure and brilliant success for every man; these are the things from which springs the hope of the world.

Is there an easy way of meeting the challenge? Can't it be left up to the priests? Can't it be accomplished by a little surface reading while we relax in slippers and an easy chair? The questions would be absurd if they were not indicative of so terrible a danger; for they could not even be asked if there was the slightest appreciation of the threat to the most important things in the lives of men.

The Holy Name Society, the Society that embraces the generality of Catholic men, proposes to complete the program implicit in the frequentation of the Sacrament of the Eucharist and the campaign against blasphemy and profanity. It proposes a systematic education in the relationship of man to God through the medium of a pamphlet a month based on the *Summa Theologiae* of St. Thomas. In view of the facts, such a proposal does not demand apology or explanation. It is a challenge to men who think there are things worth working for and worth fighting for. That challenge will be met by the men of the Society.

Study Club Outline

OBJECTIVES FOR DISCUSSION

The Holy Name Society has as its major objectives frequent Communion and the avoidance of sins of the tongue. Why a course in theology?

The Holy Name Society is not exclusively for scholars and the learned. Why a series which is not based on popular and timely topics?

St. Thomas must be outmoded. New problems have arisen. Why not seek a modern authority?

Those who want to study theology can find the proper books. Why drag it out in a pamphlet series?

With the world collapsing because of bad economic theories, selfish fanatics and a bewildered educational system, wouldn't it be wiser to concentrate on particular problems than to spend so much time on the entire relationship between man and God?

STUDY QUESTIONS

1) What is theology?

2) Who is St. Thomas Aquinas?

3) What is the *Summa Theologiae*?

4) Why is the Sacrament of the Eucharist called a beginning as well as a goal?

5) Is the attack on profanity losing its place in the Holy Name scheme of things?

6) Why not begin with an easier book than the *Summa*?

7) Is this an opportune time for such a study?

8) What determines the importance of a science?

9) How do you rate in importance the sciences mentioned in these pages?

10) What did Thomas Aquinas build on?

2

In the Beginning
Why God Exists

Reginald Coffey, O.P.

Introduction

This is the second in the series of pamphlets designed to acquaint the laity with the theology of the Church and published under the auspices of the Holy Name Society. It treats of the five arguments according to Saint Thomas Aquinas on the existence of God.

Since the pamphlets are prepared by different writers, the form of presentation may vary from one to another, but the editors will attempt to summarize the thesis simply, as is done in the letter at the end of this one.

Since the subject matter is necessarily exposed through very accurate and consequently rather technical terminology, a glossary of the most difficult terms and a brief biography of the philosophers who are mentioned is given at the end of the booklet.

The God Myth

Doctor Erasmus Q. Longhair, professor of psychology, surveyed his spell-bound class. Then adjusting his pince-nez upon his eagle-beak nose with a characteristic gesture of triumph he brought his lecture to a resounding close: "And so ladies and gentlemen," (the doctor was always most formal) "we have proved conclusively upon incontrovertible evidence that the god idea was begotten by the fear complex in man; fear of death, fear of the unknown, fear of his enemies. God is a fanciful myth, a myth that has done untold harm to humanity." His lecture ended, the doctor marched majestically out the door as though parading to the strains of *Hail to the Chief*.

But behind him in the classroom, the eminent professor and internationally known author of the famous book, *Think Man, Think*, had left at least one muddled mind. George Raymond Taggart, "Big Red" to the sportswriters and the guys and gals on the campus, sat in his front-row seat and reflectively rubbed his chin.

"Big Red" Taggart had come to Wheelock U. to play football, and, like most athletes, he could have gotten by on fresh air had he wanted to, but George Taggart was different. H knew that a guy was generally through in pro football at thirty, if he was nuts enough to play pro football, and so he wanted another trade to last him for the forty years, more or less, that came after. He decided to become a doctor, and in college he had studied hard to qualify for a good "med school."

He had taken subjects no Wheelock athlete had ever before attempted and had sat long hours in classrooms never before darkened by a football player's shadow. George Taggart was a good student—too good for his own good. He held books and learning in admiration if not awe. Somewhere in the dim past on the isle of saints and scholars there must have been in the Taggart ancestry a scholar if not a saint or two. How else could one explain this love of books in the big-headed grandson of brakeman Bill Taggart, who had never cracked a book.

Higher Education

When George Taggart first came to Wheelock he had been a professed and professing Catholic. But subjected to the eloquent persuasion of clever teachers he soon left that behind. During his first year his faith was shaken. During his second he became an agnostic. In the course of his junior year he convinced himself that he was an atheist. Now, in his last year at Wheelock, he didn't know what he was, where he was, or how he got there.

Longhair's attack on the "god myth" today was nothing new to Taggart. He had heard the same type of attack delivered countless times during the past four years. The onslaughts had all been of the same type, but somehow they were all different. For instance, Professor Skidmore, who taught philosophy, was in agreement with Longhair on one thing—that there was no God. But he did not agree with him on the point that the whole idea of God should be pitched out of the window. As he himself often said, "The idea of God is necessary to the human race. Man must have something to look up to." To the straightforward Taggart this kind of stuff was a lot of nonsense. He much preferred Longhair's honest rejection of God as a myth.

Then there was Doctor Dubenny, the renowned physicist. In comparison with most of the faculty Dubenny was practically a religious man. He thought that there was a "sort of a god" which he called "cosmic force." But Dubenny's god was a queer one, almost as queer as Dubenny himself. As defined by Dubenny it was "a blind force moving ever onward, whither it knows not but certainly to the best of all possible ends." According to the eminent doctor, who was something of a poet, this force had created the world and was itself perfected by the world. No one knew exactly what Dubenny meant—not even Dubenny himself.

Professor Klimsky, the prof. of chemistry, also had ideas about God. He called himself a pantheist. He thought that God was part of the world. "Why," he would say in moments when the stupendous import of the idea overcame him, "We are all of us part of God. Gentlemen, I ask you isn't that tremendous!" To Taggart's unpoetic mind that sounded anything but tremendous. In fact it sounded wacky. Reduced to common sense it meant: if everything is God, nothing is God. It was like everybody in a crowd being the best man.

Childish Superstition

Of all the opinions he had heard expressed, Taggart liked Longhair's the best. Up until today he had accepted it almost without question. Of course, once in a while a doubt would arise in his mind, but he had consulted Longhair about this and had been told not to worry. Longhair assured him that these doubts could be traced back to his childhood when his mother and the crafty priests had pounded the idea of a phony god into his poor little childish head. "Let us thank our lucky stars, Mr. Taggart," said Longhair, "that there is one country on this green earth, Russia, where parents are not allowed to practice such cruelty on their children. The new age is dawning. Utopia is just around the century."

But in class today, as he listened to Longhair's eloquent diatribe against the "god-myth," a horrible thought had suddenly struck him. As he expressed it to himself it was this: "These guys certainly spend a lot of time on something that ain't there. It reminds me of the pug who spent all his life shadow-boxing and never got into the ring." He tried to quiet his doubts by telling himself that they were due to the training of his childhood. Usually this method, which Longhair had recommended, worked. But today he could not dispel them. He was restless, uneasy, troubled. From out the depths of his consciousness came a sentence that old Father McNamara had used in a sermon back in the days when Taggart had been an altar boy at St Pat's. He was not sure why it had stuck in his memory—probably because it had a swing to it and was easy to remember. "Only the fool saith in his heart: 'There is no God.'"

With that terse sentence there came back to him memories of old Mac, the big florid harp; an Irish priest of the old school who could belt an altar boy, even the big ones, almost as far as he could belt a baseball; but who always made up for his disgraceful display of Irish temper (his only failing) by some open-hearted, generous act that made him your pal until the next time you were caught cutting up on the altar during Mass. Poor old Mac, the O'Connell of the pulpit. He had died before Taggart went to Wheelock.

The desire, almost vocally expressed, came to him: "Gee, I wish I could see Mac and talk things over with him. He'd probably slug me when I told him I didn't believe in God, but after he'd cooled down he'd have something to offer even if it was only a *creed for an atheist.*"

The thought of old Mac, combined with his own mental perturbation, made Taggart decide to talk the question over with some priest. "The priest may be all wet in his ideas," he thought, "but at least he'll have some definite ideas and he'll know where he stands and why. Maybe I can get my own creed straight if I can talk to a guy who doesn't spout gibberish about blind force and 'the flower in the crannied wall' being God."

The Quest

So impelled was he by his longing for mental peace that he cut the rest of his morning classes and went over to St. Mary's rectory which was a few blocks off the campus. A few minutes after he had made his decision he found himself in the rectory parlor waiting for the priest who was on "house-calls" whom the housekeeper had promised to send.

He didn't have long to wait. Almost immediately a tall, slim, youngish cleric entered the room. Taggart arose and extended his hand. "Hello, Father," he said. "My name is Taggart. I'm from the U."

"Sure," replied the priest, "I recognized you right off." He smiled. "You know I sometimes read the papers. But to tell you the truth I am surprised. I never expected to see you around here after these four long years. Well at any rate you're welcome, Red. My name is Father Seymour."

"Father," Taggart began abruptly, "we might just as well get our cases straight from the start. I don't believe in God. I lost my faith some time ago. What I came here for is not conversion or a sermon about the unhappy state of my soul, if any, but for a philosophical discussion."

"No one," interposed the priest quietly, "wants you to believe in God. That is one thing that a man of average intelligence can see.

Only half-wits and morons have to *believe* in God. You're not a half-wit, Taggart, and I don't believe that you are a genuine moron. You are only an example of a guy with a sabotaged mind. Some of these clever word-twisters like old man Longhair at the U. have sold you a bill of goods against your better judgment. Don't feel too bad about it. I used to go to the joint, and they did the same job on me. Kid, step right up and mitt the ex-chump. The only thing, Red . . ."

But Taggart interrupted. "What do you mean you don't have to believe in God? Personally, I can state without fear of contradiction that I never met Him and I never met anybody who did. Even the guys who haven't the guts to deny His existence really don't pretend to be as sure of Him as you do."

"I mean just what I say," replied the priest. "You don't have to see a thing with your eyes to know that it's present. I never saw an electric current, but I know such a thing exists. I never saw goodness but I know that there is such a thing . . ."

"That's a swell line of sophistry," put in Taggart. "Of course you never saw an electric current, but you can measure it, you can feel it, you can see what it does."

"I can also," interjected the priest quietly, "in a manner of speaking, measure God, feel Him, and see what He does."

Aquinas Speaks

"But, Red, if you want to go into this thing and have the patience to discuss it, I think I can prove it to you. It's almost time for dinner now, so come up to my room where you can scrape off a little of the classroom grime before we tie on the nose-bag."

When they reached the priest's study the older man took down one of the many volumes with which the shelves of his bookcase were stacked, and opened it on his desk.

"This," he announced, "is the first volume of the *Summa Theologiae* of Saint Thomas Aquinas. So you'll know I'm not grabbing the arguments I'm going to give you out of thin air. The question of God's existence is a very old one, and Saint Thomas treats it better than it has ever been treated before or since. He gives not one proof for the existence of God, but five."

Father Seymour was interrupted in his discourse by the dinner bell and so the discussion was continued in the dining room. Since the pastor and the other assistant were both out of the house on business, Father Seymour and the collegian had the place to themselves. After they had taken their places at the table the priest picked up the conversation where it had been interrupted.

"Saint Thomas doesn't seem to consider this a very important question, or rather let us say, he does not seem to think it a very difficult question because he handles it rather summarily. It is one of the short questions of the *Summa*—only three articles; for Thomas seems to take it for granted that the majority of men admit the possibility of proving God's existence. However, because Thomas is too careful a workman to skip the question entirely he treats it from three angles."

How Do We Know God

"In the first article of the question he inquires whether God is known immediately, the same way that we know that white is white and not black or that I am myself and you are yourself. These things need no proof; Thomas concludes that God is not in this category. To know God naturally, says Thomas, we must use our reason."

"Just a minute, Père," Red broke in. "How's about the arguments of the skeptics, such as Hume, who don't admit that first principles are self-evident, that you are yourself and I am myself?" "Personally," replied the priest, "I think that question is a bit beside the point. But I'll give it right back to you. What do you think of the arguments of the skeptics?"

"I think that they're a lot of hooey," retorted Red.

"Okay, then," went on the priest with a smile, "that's one point we're agreed on. Let's get on with the argument."

But they were not permitted to "get on with the argument" immediately because Norah Finnegan, the veteran housekeeper of the rectory, the truculent terror of the grocers of the neighborhood, who had served the good fathers, "God bless them", for twenty-five years, came in to remove the soup plates and discovered that the soup had not been touched. She roundly scolded Father Seymour for not eating his soup, and turning her warlike eye upon Taggart, she let it be known to all who cared to listen that as far as she, Norah Finnegan, was concerned, "the college bums and blather-skites" might find something better to do than to be bothering the good fathers at their meals. With the threat that if the soup wasn't finished in three minutes they wouldn't get any dinner at all, Miss Finnegan turned her broad back on the culprits and stalked back to her domain.

"Well, Red," laughed the priest, "if we expect to keep our health we'd better not ignore a Finnegan order. Let's call time on the discussion until after dinner."

Sedulously avoiding the absorbing topic of God's existence for the remainder of the meal they turned the conversation to small talk; football, the weather and, of course, the war. "The Finnegan had no further cause for complaint over unnecessary delay. Dinner finished, the couple adjourned to the priest's study were the topic uppermost in the minds of both was reopened. Red spoke first.

"So Saint Thomas says that God is not known instinctively as you might say. Why, I thought that everyone who held that God existed "knew Him" that way. I'm sure that my mother did. She always spoke of God as though He were the man next door. But if anybody asked her to prove that He existed he would have had her stumped."

"Your mother knew God from Faith, Red. She didn't need any arguments. She got her knowledge from God Himself. She believed. That was enough for her."

"Okay," said Red, "I agree with Thomas so far. Where does he go from here?"

God Known by Reason

"In the second article of the question," answered the priest, "Saint Thomas asks whether the existence of God can be proved by reason.

He concludes that it can be so proved. For, he argues, if God exists, there must be some trace of Him in the world, some effects of which He is cause. Now these effects can be traced down to their cause."

"Hold your horses, Father," interjected the younger man, "You can't just assume that there is such a thing as causality. After all, some of the greatest of modern thinkers deny it. William James and before him John Stuart Mill and Herbert Spencer have raised quite valid arguments against it."

"Yes, I know," the cleric replied, "and before James, Spencer, Mill, Hume, Berkely and Hobbes there was Ockham back in the Middle Ages. And long before Ockham there was Sextus Empiricus and the Greek Epicureans. That only goes to prove that most so-called modern errors are as old as the hills. It does not prove that they are true. Not even their age can make them venerable. If we go into all these sidetracks one by one we won't get anywhere for a year. So once more I'm going to shovel-pass the question back to you. What is your opinion on causality? Do you accept the general theory that Hume illustrates, in his *Essay on Human Understanding*, with the example of the billiard balls? If you recall, Hume says there that if one billiard ball is thrown against another the other one moves, but we can't positively say that the movement of the one was caused by the other hitting it. Do you honestly think that when your foot hits a football and the ball goes soaring for sixty yards down the field, your foot had nothing to do with its flight?"

"Well, to be frank, Father," answered the boy, "I always thought that example of Hume's and the theory itself was the old malarkey. There are some things that everybody knows to be true, no matter what or how clever the argument that may be raised against them. For instance, Hume has never been able to convince me that nothing exists in the world but myself, although he argues very cleverly on that point. I think that we know things like that from consciousness, without proof, and causality is one of them."

"Good," ejaculated the priest. "When a fellow hasn't lost all his common sense you can at least talk with him. We won't need to waste a lot of time on Hume's inanities, then. We will assume that causality, which is the common experience of mankind, is a fact."

"That's jake[1] with me," said Red, "I'll string along on those terms."

1st Proof: Motion

"Saint Thomas' first proof," began the priest with a smile, "is based upon the most common thing in the world—motion. Motion is the one thing that we can all see; it is going on around us all the time. Now, mind you, I am not referring to local motion, movement from place to place only, and neither was Thomas. In speaking of motion he means change of any sort, substantial change, which perpetually takes place in the world, the kind of change that occurs when hydrogen and oxygen become water; according to the decreasing or increasing intensity of a quality, the sort of change that takes place when a cold iron is heated; and even spiritual movements of the intellect and will. Motion has a god-like quality in that it is universal, and that quality may be one reason for the conception of the idea of pantheism.

"However, to get to the question: Thomas begins his argument by stating that everything that is in motion is moved by something else. Let us take an example from local motion. I take this book and move it from the desk to the chair. The book did not move itself; it was moved by my hand; my hand was the cause of the book's movement. Or to take an example that will better illustrate the proof, let us consider the motion of a train. What makes a train move? The engine pulling it. What moves the engine? The wheels of the engine turning move it. What makes the wheels turn? Well, not being a mechanic or an engineer, I can't say exactly, but the gears attached to the drive wheels move them. What moves the gears? The piston moves the gears. What moves the pistons? Steam under controlled pressure moves it. What controls the pressure? Well, ultimately that is controlled by the throttle which is moved by the engineer. So in tracing down the movement of a train we

---

[1] Slang used in the 20s equivalent to the word "cool."

finally come to the engineer. All of the other motions are essentially subordinate to him and, now get this, to each other. For instance, in the turning of the wheels the gears are absolutely necessary. Without them the wheels would not turn.

"Now, to get back to the argument. I think that it is a matter of common experience, a proposition that everybody will admit, that no motion occurs unless there is something to do the moving. The term "automobile" is a misnomer. Nothing moves by itself. Right?"

The big red-head who had held his peace to give the priest a chance to develop his argument without interruption reflected on the question for a while. Finally he nodded his head.

"I agree with you so far," he said.

Who Gives the First Push

"So in any series of movers," continued the priest, "which are subordinated one to another, you must finally come to one which is the principle of its own motion. Every train must have its engine, every hand capable of movement must belong to some living body. Somewhere you must come to a number one which is moved by nothing, a mover which is the cause of its own motion."

"Well," broke in Red, "in the example you just gave of the train that's easy. You finally come to the engineer who is the principle of his own motion."

"Are you really serious about that, Red?" asked the priest.

"Sure," replied the young man, "I don't see anybody in the picture pulling strings to make the engineer move. Do you?"

"Oh, yes there is someone pulling the strings, but he's behind the scenes as in a puppet show."

"You're kidding now, aren't you?" Taggart asked the priest in amazement.

"No, I'm not kidding," Father Seymour replied, "I told you to begin with that there is nothing that moves which moves itself. I also told you that local motion was only one kind of motion, there is also qualitative motion and spiritual motion. A thing that is cold becomes hot—that's qualitative motion. Remember? Why even your physicist will tell you that is motion. And how often have you read in novels: 'She was moved to tears.' That is a kind of spiritual motion. Now to get back to our engineer. Why does he pull the throttle?"

"Because he wants to, I guess," the younger man answered.

"Exactly," said his instructor, "or to put it more precisely, because he wills to. That movement of the engineer's will from passivity (the state of not acting) to act is real motion—more real than the motion of the engine. Now, since human experience knows no automatic motion the logical conclusion is that the engineer is no exception. He must have been moved—but by whom or what? The answer given by the modern materialistic psychologists, namely, that he was moved by external stimuli, is not enough, for it is also a matter of experience that motion can only be communicated to a thing by something that possesses motion or the power of motion. We all know that to move or knock over a stone wall which has a ten thousand pound resistance, we need a tractor that can muster at least that much power. The same principle holds true in this case. The external stimuli are not powerful enough to move the will of the engineer from passivity to act. That movement comes from God, the first mover and the only mover that does not depend on another for his motion.

"That, my boy," said the priest smiling, "is the first argument given by Saint Thomas. What do you think of it?"

"Personally," answered the young man, "I don't think it's so hot. It seems to me that it supposes too much. As a matter of fact it seems to me that it supposes a belief in God."

"Well," the priest replied, "I don't think so much of the popular appeal of the first proof either, although I don't agree with you when you say it presupposes a belief in God. I'd say rather that it presupposes a mind trained to metaphysical argument and speculation of a high order, an exercise which your materialistic education has hardly equipped you for. I only gave it to you because I thought I'd give you the whole works while I was about it. You know it is axiomatic among the scholastics that out of the five arguments there is always one which will convince the seeker after God, but it is not always the same one."

2nd Proof: Causality

"Judging by the argument you've just given I don't believe that you'll convince me," said the collegian with a smile that was a bit sardonic. "Metaphysics as far as I'm concerned is the philosophy of things that ain't."

"Well, just to keep the record straight we'll proceed in order. Thomas' second argument is also slightly metaphysical. It is really only the first proof taken from the opposite side, from the side of the causer of the motion rather than from the side of the thing moved. It is called the argument from efficient causality. Since you were entirely unimpressed by the first argument, this one will also probably leave you cold. I won't spend much time on it, then."

"If it's anything at all like the first," interrupted Red, "you needn't."

"Before we began this discussion," smiled the priest, "we both admitted that causality was a fact of experience. We both know that when we come down to breakfast in the morning and find an egg on the table, the very existence of the egg is proof that a hen exists or, at least existed, before that egg could be put upon the breakfast table."

"Elementary, my dear Watson," laughed the red-head.

Whodunit

"Okay, then," said the priest. "There we have a concise statement of Thomas' second

argument. Thomas says that we see in the world about us an order of efficient causes dependent on one another for their causality. We can find in the world nothing that is the cause of itself. Let us suppose, for example, that you are found dead on the street tomorrow. When the police find your body and determine that you are dead they immediately look about for the cause that suddenly turned Red Taggart from a football player into a corpse. Upon inspection the cause is found in your head. It is a bullet. The bullet then caused your death. But the police are smart. They do not arrest the poor little piece of lead. They know that although the bullet caused your death it did not get into your brain all by itself. So they conclude that the bullet that caused your death was able to do so because it was impelled into your brain by some exterior force.

"Upon the bullet they find marks of rifling and discoloration caused by heat, and it is immediately concluded that a pistol and not a sling-shot sent the bullet into your brain. They then know that its flight was caused by an explosion of powder. The powder, they are certain, did not explode by itself. It was exploded, they know from past experience, by the percussion of the hammer of the weapon. Being, as I said, smart cops, they know, too, that the hammer did not fall all by itself. The reason the hammer struck the cartridge was because a trigger was pulled. The mystery, then, is: Who pulled the trigger?

"There we have a long string of causes, each one essentially dependent upon a higher: the bullet, the powder, the hammer, the trigger, the finger, the man. Now back to Thomas. Thomas says that all the causes which are essentially dependent, one upon another, presuppose a first cause which is uncaused, a cause which depends on no other, because a procession of essentially subordinated causes into infinity is an impossibility. Also, adds Thomas, nothing can be the cause of itself."

Last Cause

"Now let's get back to our cops. They finally discover that Red Taggart was done in by Oliver the tramp, a low character about town. As far as the cops are concerned they have found the cause of the murder. But the end of the trail is not yet. Oliver's finger pulled the trigger, the muscles of the arm and hand tightened to crook the finger, the muscles were supplied with their power by the blood, which depends upon the heart for its circulation. And the muscles and the heart depend for their beating upon what?"

"Well, ultimately upon the principle of life itself, I suppose," answered Red.

"And what would you say that life depends upon?" asked the priest.

"Well, to skip a lot of intervening causes, ultimately upon the sun," replied the student.

"Exactly," said the older man, "that is why the ancients worshipped the sun as God. They believed, and modern scientific investigation upholds their belief, that the sun is the cause of all physical life. But, I ask you, must we go back to the worship of Ra, the sun-god? Is the sun the final cause? Whence came it?"

"Why, it always existed," answered Taggart.

"Well, suppose we grant that for the sake of argument, where does it get the power to give life? You can't give me a dollar if you haven't the dollar to give."

"Why," answered the boy, "life developed from the sun's action."

"I thought that we agreed," asked the priest, "that things don't just happen. They must be caused."

"We did," answered Red, "but this is different."

"How different?" snapped the priest.

"Well, I don't know exactly, but . . ."

"Neither does anybody else. That opinion, my boy, is Victorian. Spencer and Huxley could use it in their time, but it is out of date today. Today, Science, much against its will, is slowly but surely being driven back to God."

"I'm sure there's an answer to your objection somewhere, Father, and I'll try to find it," said the collegian, "but in the meantime I'll admit you have me stuck."

"Fine," said the priest. "We'll leave you stuck there for a while and go on to the third argument."

3rd Proof: Contingency

"'Thomas' third proof," continued Father Seymour, "is also of a highly metaphysical nature. I shall not spend much time upon it. It is based upon the fact that the world and its contents are all *contingent* beings, that is to say, they can exist or not exist. This means that they do not exist forever. Men and animals are born and die. Plants decompose. Minerals break down. The elements of all beings enter into new compositions. As Shakespeare put it:

> Imperial Caesar dead and turned to clay
> Might stop a hole to keep the wind away.

"As a matter of fact the world and its furnishings and the lord of creation—man—are so *contingent* that Science assures us that time was when none of these existed. Now the very fact that these beings are *contingent* points to the existence of a being that is necessary, that is a being whose existence does not depend upon circumstance or the causality of another; a being that is not subject to decomposition or corruption: a being whose existence, in short, is not subject to chance. Upon this being, all other existing beings must depend for their existence. It alone has within itself the cause of its own existence. The existence of this self-existing being is the only explanation that can be given for the existence of dependent beings.

"If you notice, this proof, too, is based upon causality. But this proof looks at causality from a different angle and considers it in a more general sense. This most general sense of the principle of causality is known to philosophers as 'the principle of sufficient reason.' The principle of sufficient reason might be defined as follows: That which has not sufficient reason for existence in itself must have this reason in something else. You, for instance, are aware that you did not, Minerva-like, appear upon this earth fully grown. Even tiny children, when reason first dawns, are anxious to know the cause of their existence. No reasoning child thinks, like Topsy, 'that it just growed.' The child sees a reason for existence, maybe not always the true reason, in everything about it and so it concludes that it, too, has a reason for being here. It was questions from lisping lips upon this great truth that caused the invention of the stork myth."

Spontaneous Generation

"This truth is one of the surest things we know. Either we are the reason for our existence, or someone else is responsible for it. You can present your father and mother as your credentials, and they can present their parents as theirs, but where does the line end? Does the line of insufficient beings extend to infinity? Even if it should, and it seems most unlikely that it does, its very insufficiency points to the fact that there is a sufficient being. Saint Thomas argues this point most skillfully. He says that if there were in existence only contingent beings there must have been a time when nothing at all existed, and from nothing, nothing comes. So he concludes that a necessary being must have existed, a being which cannot not be.

"The early evolutionists attempted to put over the insane principle that something can actually come out of nothing spontaneously. Talk about the mysteries of the Faith! Under the aegis of 'Science' these fanatics exacted from their blind devotees a faith that mocked reason. The later evolutionists, seeing the insanity of the principle and willing to postulate the existence of anything but God, endowed the sun with eternity, saying that here was the sufficient reason for all life. Let us grant for the sake of argument that the sun is sufficient reason for all life. The question still remains: Is it sufficient reason for its own existence? If it is, then those who believe it owe it some form of worship, for they have found their God.

"Well," queried the priest, "That is Thomas' third argument. What do you think of them so far?"

"So far," answered the boy, "he's pitched nothing but balls. One more and I walk."

"Come, come, Red," urged Father Seymour. "Do you mean to tell me that they've left you that cold?"

Sun Worship

"No Père," answered the collegian, "that would not be the strict truth. Here and there in the course of the exposition I had a glimmering of conviction, and I think that the three of them taken together at least challenge serious consideration, but I don't think that they have convinced me. However, don't forget that I did not come here to be convinced. I came here principally to find out which form of atheism was the most reasonable. Well I think I've settled that already. After all, why couldn't the sun be the necessary being that has always existed? Why couldn't it be the principle of all life? So far you've convinced me of one thing: There must be a first cause or a first mover, and as far as I'm concerned, the sun is it."

"At least," answered the priest, "you have followed the arguments intelligently. If you are still an atheist leaving here it won't be for lack of intelligence or sincerity. We will have to put the blame for it either upon my own ineptitude or your materialistic education. All of these arguments preclude the possibility of the sun being the first cause, the first mover, or the necessary being. I thought I brought out clearly in the first and third arguments that you can't give a dime if you haven't got it nor life if you do not possess it. But you, evidently, did not quite grasp the import of it. However, don't leave after the next argument, even if it is what you call 'a ball.' Swing at it anyway, and stay in there for the pitch that follows. I'd serve that one up immediately, only the last two like the first three really go together, and the fourth prepares the ground for the fifth."

"Okay," grinned Red. "Start your windup. I'd stay to please you anyway. I think you're swell people, Father, and I hope to become your friend if not a lamb of the flock."

The priest's grin was as broad as the boy's.

"Thanks for the compliment, Red," he said, "even though it only goes to prove how you fellows draw conclusions from insufficient evidence. However, back to the Angel of the Schools, who is impatiently standing on the mound waiting to hurl his sinker. This, the fourth argument, is supposed to have its greatest appeal to mystics. It will probably floor you."

4th Proof: Degrees of Perfection

"This proof brings out the perfection of the first cause, and it is aimed especially at people like you who might be inclined to see in the sun qualities that would deify it. Like all of the others it begins right down here on solid ground. In looking about us we see in the world what might be called a hierarchy of being. We see minerals, plants, animals and men, all of which have something in common—*being*; but all of which have differences—the perfection in which they possess that being.

Minerals just are. Plants are and in addition also live. Animals not only are and live but move about. Men not only are and live and move about but *think*. I believe that according to modern classification these different grades of being are called 'kingdoms.' Incidentally, in passing I would like to remark that it is the community of being possessed by all the so-called kingdoms that helped give rise to the error of Pantheism which is an argument that is somewhat appealing to a mind with a mystical turn. The Pantheist is a good example of the guy that just missed the boat. Instead of being so enamored with the idea of community of being, if he could see the terrific import of the distinction of being, it would be a sure road leading to God.

"This difference between the kingdoms is quite evident, so evident that only an insane man would deny it. I might call you a stick or a stone or a bump on a log. Or I might call you a pig or a lion or a bear. But you wouldn't have to be very smart to know that you are none of these things. However, you might get angry. You know well that you are not only none of these things, but you know that you are superior to any of them. The being you possess is superior to that of a stick or a stone; the life you have is far above that which an animal has. It possesses more goodness, it is more perfect. Will you admit the argument so far, Red?"

"There's no question about it, Father," answered the boy. "Carry on."

There Must Be An Absolute

"Okay, if you admit the varying degrees of perfection you must admit the existence of a perfect. If being can be found in various grades you must agree that there is an *ungraded* being. If goodness can be found differing in degree from other good, then we know that absolute goodness must exist. If we can find a true and a more true there has to be a supreme truth. This can be stated as an axiom: *If there is a more and a less there has to be a maximum.*

43

"Now this maximum of truth, life, goodness, and the rest is to be found only in the supreme being—that being which exists without the limitations which we see imposed upon the beings around us and which we know are imposed upon ourselves.

"This supreme being is the cause of all other existing beings because if the beings which we see around us were their own causes they would possess being to an unlimited degree. They would possess goodness to the absolute degree. But we are aware that no sensible being is unlimited, and it does not possess goodness to that extent, and we can conclude that the being that does possess it in that manner is the cause, not only of its own being, but of all other beings as well.

"Every imperfect being, then, is a caused being in which there is a mixture of good and evil, being and non-being. It is only the uncaused being that is utterly simple, entirely without mixture and possessed of complete perfection. We are driven to a knowledge of this being's existence, says Thomas, by the fact that the lower degrees exist.

"What," asked the priest pausing, "do you think of the argument?"

"It is the most appealing to me so far," answered the red-head. "Not, mind you, because I am a mystic but because I can grasp it better in terms of my favorite science, physics. Some modern physicists have tried to make a god out of space-time. It always seemed a foolish sort of a god to me and still does. But both are of such tremendous proportions, both approach, in a manner of speaking, the absolute, that the temptation to endow them with god-like powers must be hard to resist for a man who is looking for a god."

"My admiration for you grows apace, Red," smiled his instructor. "A man who can see where Eddington and Jeans got their cosmic god and who has enough common sense to reject it surely has intelligence enough to overcome the disadvantages of education and to see the God that is before him, around him and in him; the only God who is not blind but all seeing; who is not force but personality; who not only acts but knows the wherefore of his action. This is the God that Saint Thomas presents in the next argument. Do you want to go to confession now, or shall we wait until we finish with the last of the arguments?"

"I hope," smiled Taggart, falling in with the priest's mood, "you don't let your whiskers grow while you're waiting for me to go to confession. If you do, Rip Van Winkle rolling out after his Catskill cat-nap would look like a sub-deb[2] in comparison with you."

5th Proof: Design

"To proceed," said the priest, clearing his throat with mock severity, "where we left off in the last class—we will consider the fifth argument from the prolific pen of the "dumb ox" of Sicily. The fifth and final proof presented by Thomas is based upon the order prevailing in the universe.

"It is not surprising to find that men, who are rational beings, act for some intelligent end. But it certainly should be surprising to find animals and even inanimate beings acting for ends which also seem to be intelligent. What, for instance, causes the heavenly bodies to rotate and gyrate through space with such precision? Why do you suppose it is possible that countless huge worlds, all of them larger than our own, can hurtle through space and avoid cosmic collisions? Is your mind satisfied with attributing such a seeming miracle to the law of gravity and leaving it go with that? Granted, it is the law of gravity, then do you not ask yourself who instituted the law of gravity? Every law must have a maker. A law is the product of an intelligence, and the law of gravity is no exception. No blind force could so regulate the planets in their courses. Collision, without a directing intelligence, would be unavoidable. Leaving the near infinite for the infinitesimal we find the same wonderful order existing in miniature among the molecules and atoms. The mind that can observe the order of the universe and deny a directing intelligence is a mind that is woefully weak or distressingly dishonest."

---

[2] A type of high school sorority popular in the 40s.

Nature Not Haphazard

"We find the same marvelous intelligence exhibited by animals and insects. The ants have a system of government and of defense, the order of which would put human principalities to shame. The bees with their wonderfully constructed hives, their methods of developing a queen from the common eggs and the dispatch with which the extra queens are killed off after the birth of the first point to an intelligence beyond the bee. The carpenter wasp with its inexplicable aptitude for building; the wonderful order and skill displayed by birds in nest construction—all these things which are quite beyond animal 'intelligence' point to an intelligence working through the animal. There isn't a phase of nature where an intelligence working to a definite end cannot be found.

"We find the same intelligence exhibited in the design of the human body. Here the various parts, as you know, are so interconnected that they are, viewed from different angles, the causes of one another. Yet they concur in bringing about one complete effect. Let us consider by way of example the human eye. In this organic structure, the act of seeing presupposes the presence, simultaneously, of thirteen conditions. Each of the thirteen conditions presupposes many others. Scientists have proved that, according to the law of probabilities, without any designing cause, there are 9,999,985 chances against 15 for the possibility of these thirteen conditions meeting so as to make seeing possible.

Intelligence Presupposed

"And yet men can look at the stupendous miracle of the universe about them and then try to tell themselves that there is no God. This reluctance to deny the inevitable truth is one of the great mysteries of all time. If you were cast ashore on a desert isle, and while strolling the beach of your barren domain, you suddenly came across a watch you would not try to hood-wink yourself into believing that the watch just happened there. You would know, because you found an instrument which gave every evidence of order and design, that it had an intelligent maker. You would realize that no matter how often the seas agitated the sands of the beach they could never, by so doing, produce the instrument you had just discovered. Why then, when we see a universe, which throughout gives evidence of design and order far beyond that found in any man-made instrument, should we attribute it to chance. The only sufficient reason that can be given for the order and design existing in the universe is God."

The priest paused and looked at the boy who seemed lost in thought.

"Well," he asked, "what do you think of the five proofs as a whole? Do you find them just a bit convincing? Are you still at the plate swinging, or has the last pitch been too high and wide for you to hit?"

His companion, still sunk in a deep study, had evidently not heard his query. Suddenly he spoke.

"I would like, please Father, to borrow the book where you got all this dope. It sure sounds as though it would be worth looking into at any rate. What did you say the name of it was?"

"Here it is," said the priest taking it down from the shelf. "It's the first volume of the *Summa Theologiae* of Saint Thomas Aquinas. It's really a pretty fair job and I think you'll find a lot more there besides what I've told you."

"Okay, Père, thanks. Well I guess I'll have to beat it now. Don't bother coming downstairs. I guess I can find my way out all right."

Postscript

The next afternoon a letter addressed to Mr. George Taggart, Hadley Hall, Wheelock University, arrived at its destination. Opening the missive the addressee read the following:

Dear Red:

After you left my study, I began to think over the discussion we had, and it dawned upon me that I had fired great gobs of theology at you. So I am writing this letter for the purpose of putting our talk in nut-shell form. This summary will not only help you to remember the discussion but will give you a greater grasp of the arguments presented in the *Summa*. The way in which I am summarizing these arguments is known as syllogistic reasoning. Now you many never have heard of the syllogism, but it is really a very valuable tool and is the nearest approach we have to the actual functioning of the human mind. Here are the arguments for the existence of God in syllogistic form:

1) *The Argument from Motion*: That there is motion in the world is a certainty attested by experience.

    Now, everything which is in motion is moved by another.

    Moreover, there cannot be an infinite series of movers essentially and actually subordinated one to the other.

    Therefore we must conclude that there is a prime mover, who is not himself set in motion by a mover of a higher order, and whom we call God.

2) *Proof from Efficient Causes*: In the world there are efficient causes which are essentially subordinated to one another.

    Now, these efficient causes, which are thus subordinated to one another, presuppose a first cause which is not caused.

3) *Proof from the Contingency of Being*: There are beings in the world which are evidently contingent, i.e., indifferent to existence.

    Now contingent beings presuppose a necessary and self-existing being.

    Therefore, there must be an absolutely necessary Being, the cause of all other being.

4) *Proof from the degrees of Perfection*: The beings in the world form a hierarchy, i.e., some beings are more perfect than others.

Now, we speak of things being more or less perfect according to the degrees in which they approach that which is most perfect and the cause of all other things.

Therefore, in all these imperfect beings the varying degrees of perfection must be produced by a Supreme Cause that is absolute perfection.

5) *Proof from the Order Prevailing in the Universe*: We observe that irrational beings act for an end.

Now irrational beings cannot tend toward an end unless directed by an intelligence.

Therefore, there is a Supreme intelligence directing all things to their proper ends.

There are the nutshells, Red. Be careful you don't break a tooth.

Sincerely,
Father Seymour

Mr. George Taggart of Hadley Hall, after reading the letter, carefully folded it and placed it between the pages of the book he had been reading all that day. He closed the book to rest his eyes after his eight hour stretch since breakfast. Besides he was very hungry, for he had forgotten about lunch. He smoothed the volume with his big redhaired hand in a patting motion and in a thoughtful abstracted way. Then getting to his feet with a stiffness begotten by long inaction he left the room, leaving behind him on the desk the book which bore the title The *Summa Theologiae* of St. Thomas Aquinas.

Brief Biographies of Philosophers Mentioned in Text

1) *Saint Thomas Aquinas* was born at Rocca Secca, about fifty miles from the city of Naples, Italy, in 1225. Scion of the noble and proud family of the Counts of Aquino, he joined the mendicant Order of Preachers in 1243. He became a prolific writer in philosophy and theology and holds first rank among the world's great thinkers. His best known work is the *Summa Theologiae*, in which he examines

and defends the entire body of Catholic teaching. He died at Fossa Nova, near Maienza, Italy in 1274.

2) *William James* was born in New York City, January 11, 1842. He was educated at Harvard, where he later became a professor. He was a leader in America of the materialistic Neo-Hegelian Movement. A founder of the pragmatic school, James denied causality and maintained that the only true criterion of truth is the conduct it dictates or inspires. His best known philosophical works are: *The Will to Believe* and *The Varieties of Religious Experience.*

3) *John Stuart Mill* was born in London, England, in 1806. He was a government clerk until 1858, after which he spent the rest of his life in France, except for the years 1865–1868 when he was a member of Parliament. His most important works are: *System of Logic* and *Utilitarianism.* He taught that the aim of all human action should be the promotion of the greatest happiness for all sentient beings. For Mill, sensitive experience was the sole source of knowledge. He denied the principle of causality. He held that what we call causality is nothing but "invariable and unconditional sequence." He died in Avignon, France in 1873.

4) *Herbert Spencer* was born at Derby, England, in 1820 and became a civil engineer but abandoned the profession in 1845 to devote himself to writing. His best known works are: *Social Status, Principles of Psychology, Principles of Ethics* and *Progress: its Law and Cause.* In the last named work he anticipated Darwin by enunciating the principle of Evolution as a universal law. In philosophy Spencer was a syncretist, that is, he combined the teachings of philosophers who preceded him. His masters in thought were Kant, Comte, and Wolff. Thus he was an agnostic, a positivist, and an evolutionist. He died December 8, 1903.

5) *George Berkeley*, a bishop of the Church of England, was born in Ireland in 1685. His best known works are Principles of Knowledge and New Theory of Vision. Berkeley wrote on philosophical subjects with the intention of defending Christianity, and his book *Alciphron* or the *Minute Philosopher* was directed against free-thinkers, but his principles were false, and his writing

has harmed rather than helped Christianity. His doctrines led directly to skepticism and agnosticism, if not atheism. He died at Oxford, England, in 1753.

6) *Thomas Hobbes* was born at Westport, Wiltshire, England, 1588, and was educated at Oxford. His principle works are *Leviathan* and *Elementa Philosophiae*. He was the first of the English sensists. He taught that nothing is universal but name, and that the senses alone are to be trusted. Hobbes died in 1679.

7) *William of Ockham*, called the *Doctor Invincibilis* was born at Ockham in Surrey, England, about 1280. He taught at the University of Paris, and wrote his famous *Commentaries on Aristotle*. With Ockham began the decline of scholasticism from the heights to which it had risen at the times of St. Thomas and St. Albert the Great. Ockham was a nominalist and laid down principles that were contrary to the principles of Christianity. He died in 1394.

8) *Sextus Empiricus* was an obscure and minor Greek philosopher.

9) *Thomas Huxley*, defender of Darwinism, was born in Ealing, England, May 4, 1825. He died at Eastbourne, England, June 29, 1895. His best known works are *Evolution and Ethics* and *Gay Sermons*. As a philosopher he was a materialist and is not regarded too highly.

10) *Eddington* and *Jeans* are contemporary English physicists who have written much on time and space: Philosophically, they are materialists and evolutionists. They attribute to space-time god-like powers.

Glossary of Terms

1) A *skeptic* is one who holds for the unreality of the existing world and the impossibility of proving the existence of anything. A total skeptic believes that only the thinking subject (himself) exists. The rest of existence is, to him, an illusion. But not all skeptics hold this extreme view.

2) *Reason*—As a faculty is synonymous with intelligence and denotes the knowing faculty as proceeding by a discursive process.

3) *Cause*—Whatever something depends upon either for its being or for its becoming. There are four kinds of causes: a) *Efficient* cause, by which a thing comes to be what it is. For example—the carpenter is the efficient cause of a table. b) *Final* cause, for the sake of which something is made. By the final cause the efficient cause is drawn into action. For example, the carpenter makes the table because he doesn't want to eat his dinner off the floor. c) *Formal* cause is that by reason of which a thing is what it is. By virtue of the formal cause the article made by the carpenter is a table and not a chair or a piano. d) *Material* cause is that out of which a thing is made. In the example given the material cause of our carpenter's table, in this case, is wood.

4) The Epicurean school of thought is named after its founder Epicureus who was born at Samos, in the year 341 or 342 B.C., and died at Athens in 270 B.C. Philosophy was defined by Epicureus as "the art of making life happy." Hence he and his school were sensists who held that pleasure and pain were the only standards of truth. They denied the possibility of anything but sensitive knowledge and scoffed at speculation. For them things were not caused—they just happened.

5) For Hume's theory see sketch on Hume in *Brief Biographies*.

6) *Motion* or *Movement*—For a definition of motion an understanding of act is necessary. The word *Act* as used by the scholastics has several meanings. In its most general use it is the perfection which fulfills the

capacity of a perfectible being. In regard to motion it is the *terminus* of it. *Motion* is the transition from potentiality, or passivity of some kind, to act.

7) *Metaphysics* is that brand of philosophy that deals with the immaterial. It considers, principally, *being* as such. It strips the subject of all the things that are objects of the five senses and considers it with the intellect alone.

8) *Essential dependence* is used in the text in contradistinction to accidental dependence. The term as used might best be defined as the continuous exercise of causality by one thing on another in such a way that without that causality the thing could not exist.

9) *Infinity*—Without limitation.

10) *Contingent being* is a being that is not necessary. A necessary being is one that cannot not be.

11) *Evolution*, as commonly used today, refers to the development of the world from nothing without the action of any Supreme Being. "Evolution" in its correct usage means development. There is nothing illogical about the development of the world without the direct intervention of God, but for the world to come from nothing by itself is an impossibility. Many great theologians, particularly St. Augustine, taught evolution but an evolution which had God as its cause. This is the only kind of evolution that is not an insult to our reason.

12) *The principle of sufficient reason*, simply expressed, means that the cause must be capable of producing its effect. You can't make a silk purse out of a sow's ear, and mice do not give birth to elephants.

13) *Materialism* is the school of thought, so current today, which denies the existence of the spiritual and supra-sensible.

14) *Being*—Anything that actually has existence is a being.

15) *Pantheism* teaches that there is only one substance, God. The world and everything in it are parts of God (*substantialist pantheism*) or Manifestations of God (*dynamic pantheism*).

16) *Perfection* is the possession by a being of whatever is suitable to it.

17) *Absolute* perfection is that which contains all perfections in an infinite manner.

18) *Intelligence* or *Intellect* is the capability of understanding.

STUDY QUESTIONS

1) What is a first principle?

2) Is God known immediately?

3) Is God known only through Faith?

4) Can the existence of things unseen be proved?

5) Can the existence of God be proved?

6) Do first principles need demonstration?

7) Can causality be proved?

8) Why do the skeptics deny the possibility of proving causality?

9) What is a skeptic in the philosophical sense?

10) What for the skeptic is the only existing thing?

11) What is the basis of Thomas' first proof?

12) Is local motion the only kind of motion?

13) What other kinds of motion are there?

14) Is change synonymous with motion?

15) What is the difference between accidental and essential subordination?

16) What is meant by "infinity"?

17) Can essentially subordinated motion extend into infinity?

18) What is the basis of Thomas' second proof?

19) In what way does it differ from the first?

20) What is meant by causality?

21) What is the basis of the third proof?

22) How does it resemble the first two?

23) What do you mean by "a contingent being"?

24) What do you mean by a necessary being?

25) How many necessary beings are possible?

26) What is the basis of the fourth proof?

27) To what type of mind does it most strongly appeal?

28) What is meant by perfection?

29) What is meant by absolute?

30) Could the sun be the cause of the world?

31) Could the sun be the cause of itself?

32) What is the basis of the fourth argument?

33) Is there any connection between the fourth and fifth arguments?

34) What is meant by design?

35) Does design or order presuppose an intelligence?

36) On what are all five arguments given by Saint Thomas founded?

37) How does Father Seymour describe a syllogism?

38) Do you agree with his description?

39) What is meant by the word "act"?

40) Is evolution, as such, 'illogical'?

41) Was evolution taught before the time of Darwin?

42) What do you mean by the faculty of reason?

43) What do you mean by intelligence?

44) What is the science of metaphysics?

45) What is Pantheism?

46) What do you mean by the word "being"?

47) What is Materialism?

48) Is Materialism current today?

49) What is a "Sensist"?

50) Name a few philosophers who were sensists.

3

Looking Upward

The Simplicity, the Perfection and the Goodness of God

Richard T. Murphy, O.P.

Introduction

This is the third in the series of pamphlets designed to acquaint the laity with the theology of the Church, and published under the auspices of the Holy Name Society. It treats of the first three attributes of God.

Since the pamphlets are prepared by different writers the form of presentation will vary from one to another, but the editors will always attempt to assure a clarification of the subject matter in each pamphlet, as is done at the conclusion of this one.

Furthermore, since the subject matter is exposed through very accurate and at times technical terminology a glossary of the more difficult terms is given at the end of the pamphlet.

"A Beginner's Book"

"In this work we propose to expound, in a manner suited to beginners, those things which pertain to the Christian religion." Thus does Saint Thomas Aquinas begin his famous masterpiece of theology, the *Summa Theologiae*. Too long have men admired this work only from afar; Thomas never intended that! In fact, he intended it for the simple folk, for beginners, and not for a select group of experts! He had been a student himself, and had seen how difficult it was to find a brief, clear, respectable synthesis of theology, for in his day most of the textbooks were wordy, contradictory, or too subtle for the beginners who were to catch up the torch of Truth and carry it on, unextinguished, to future generations. Thomas decided to write his own text, ruling out such undesirable qualities, for the benefit of the all-important beginner.

The first thing to do was to rid his book of all intricate divisions, so he divided his work very simply into three great parts, one of which (the second) he divided into two on account of its length. Each part was then divided into *questions*, and these questions into *articles*. To tell the truth, if it were variety one were looking for, this division would soon become intolerably boring, for it is maintained throughout the whole of the *Summa*. However, its excellence compensates for possible boredom, and it is within such a framework that the mighty *Summa* is enclosed. Part, question, and article; and every single article is cut up into objections, argument, and the answers to the objections.

Thomas' work has often been compared to a cathedral, revealing unexpected delights where one would least expect to find them. To enter this cathedral, the only ticket required is a respectful trust in the power of human reason, and a reverent attitude towards the revelations which is stored up in the Catholic Church. Reason and revelation are like two brothers who meet with united front any onslaught or attack launched at either one of the two.

The Story Thus Far

Lack of clear-cut, precise ideas was something Saint Thomas never tolerated in himself, and something he disliked in others. That is why he began his huge work on theology with a discussion of the meaning of theology. The first pamphlet of this series, "The High Quest," has taken care of that discussion. Thomas then plunges into the heavens, and argues that man's knowledge of God is not something born with the man himself. Neither was the idea of God the result of some very heavy wishful-thinking on our part. Thomas himself was too solid and substantial a thinker to dally with such ideas. He proceeds to show in the very second chapter that his whole book is going to deal with a reality, with something reason need not feel ashamed of. In a word, Thomas lays down five different ways (*quinque viae*) in which human reason, even without the aid of revelation, could demonstrate the existence of God.

The "Five Ways" or proofs for the existence of God conclude to the actual existence of a First Unmoved Mover, a First Uncaused Cause, a First Necessary Being, A First Mind (from which alone Order can flow), and of Perfection itself. These are mouth-filling phrases. They are more than that: they are the cream of Reason's mightiest effort, for they contain, buried in much formal, scientific language, the answer to the eternal question: Is there a God? They answer the question: Yes, there is a God.

Then, strangely enough, we discover that we are not yet satisfied with such an answer. Even if God exists and is the First Unmoved Mover, and if He is the Cause of all beauty and order and perfection in the universe, still we are not going to let it go at that. We want to know more about Him. We want to know what sort of being God is, Who He is, what He does, and even if God is lonely! It is much to know that God exists, indeed. But reason cannot declare itself completely satisfied and proceed to settle down to a sluggish inactivity. It is one thing to deduce from creation the existence of a Creator, to argue from effect and motion to a Cause and a Mover, but after all, this is like learning of the existence of an inventor from his invention; or like being convinced of the existence of a boiler-maker from an examination of a boiler! Obviously, this knowledge is precious, but it is not enough. And precisely because of this lack of perfect knowledge, our minds remain unsatisfied, always seeking, always searching for greater knowledge of God.

Backing In

Yet here reason must bow its neck in humble submission to the "terrible" truth that it cannot grasp everything. This is a strange admission, and reason is tempted to rebel at the thought; but the fact remains that God is simply too great to fit into our minds all at once. The paths that lead to Him soon show that He grows larger and greater and mightier the closer we come to Him God, unlike the mountain at the end of the trail, does not dwindle and grow less majestic the closer we approach to Him; on the contrary, when finally reason deposits us at His feet after soaring flight, we realize with stunning force our own littleness, and above all, the puny strength of our vaunted intellects. But then, humility never hurt anyone; that is, the right kind of humility.

The fact that God is too great to fit into the mold of our finite human ideas should not turn us away from our high quest. We can know something about Him, but it is to be expected that there will be definite drawbacks to our knowledge. The first of these is that we must sometimes content ourselves with a knowledge, not of what God is in Himself, but with what He is not. It is a crab-like, back-door approach to God; not very flattering to be sure, but a perfectly valid procedure and one that produces good results. The highest recommendation we can give to this method is that it so admirably fits the requirements or limitations of the human mind. There are so many people who know so many things that are not so; we are going to direct our attention on some of the things that God is not.

We can know something about God; this is certain. But unfortunately this "something" must be garbed in the awkward garments of human words. We say awkward because no one word or group of words will adequately describe God—"We shall say much, and yet shall want words," says the inspired writer of Ecclesiasticus (43:29), but he goes on to say: "the sum of our words is: He is all." Yes, though words are like boxing-gloves on a man who tries to pick up a needle, or like a dozen thumbs on our fingers when we try to tie the universe and its Maker up in a verbal bundle, still we can know about God. Words are messages of thought; they have a meaning. But for us, talking about God, they will have more meaning if they are used negatively to tell what God is not. Luckily for us we do not have to talk this way all the time; only when we talk about God.

I. Simplicity

The Good Old Days

A great deal of the talk about town these days centers about "the good old days." Looking back over the years, we realize that the days of our childhood take on the air of enchantment. How tranquil and smooth and simple life was then! There was no radio to thrust its persuasive melodious tongue into our ear all day long and on through the evening until bedtime. Newspapers did not then scream so loudly. There were no automobiles to whisk Granddad and Grandma away to a round of social activities that never slackened its pace. And in those days there were hardly any movies with their flamboyant, extravagant claims to importance. The great Shakespearean actors and actresses came so seldom that it really didn't make much difference. Then were indeed the good old days of leisure and refinement. Small wonder if back in those times men were mountains of erudition, polished orators, finished statesmen, and these were gentlemen and gentle ladies. Small wonder that then there were authors of worth in greater number than at present. You see, in those days of Spartan simplicity, it was easier to do all those things. People had more time.

But today all this is changed. There is first of all the radio, which surrounds us with a babbling torrent of oratory, music, drama, comedy, and "information please." We cannot escape the radio; in fact it seems as if we cannot do without it. We even have radios in our automobiles so we may listen to something while speeding to our appointments and rendezvous. Then there are the movies, which now try to inveigle the unwary by double doses of doubtful qualities. There are more lectures being given today in most large cities than you could count on both hands; these take time to attend, even more time to prepare. Nothing seems less glamorous, or consumes more time, than taking care of a few children. Ask the Mother who owns two or three! Meanwhile Dad is worriedly working during the day to support a family, and spends his evenings at home planning and scheming for the future, even while he pursues the constant, deadening, soul-searing task of meeting deadlines, paying bills and the like. If only things were not so hectic!

Modern Complexity

The net result of our present manner of living is that we have no time left for anything. No time to visit the old folks as we know should be done. No time to read the new books lined up so colorfully on our shelves. No time to indulge that secret urge to do a bit of working, or painting, or model airplanes, radio-building, or the like. Even such an absolute necessity as sleep we have to catch when we can. For these reasons, all of them good, and capable of being multiplied forever, we sigh after the good old days.

The truth is that we are envious, not so much of the good old days, but of the apparent simplicity of those good old days. The fantastic pace of life in the city and the myriad interests of normal, intelligent man or woman make of life a complex thing, and in reality it is against such complexity that we rebel. Complexity we feel to be a drain, a terrible waste of energies and talents. If only things were more simple, then our day would be productive of more masterpieces, more statesmen, more geniuses, and more saints.

But human life cannot be simplified without being destroyed! Human life cannot be simplified without being stultified, without being less than human. We can never lead lives of simplicity because we are complex creatures, composed of body and soul. The body has thousands of parts, and has as its constant companion a human soul which in turn contains the faculties of intellect and will. Well, then, if a man's very make-up is complex, hardly anything else can be expected of his life than that it be complex, and if this is so, then we will have to reconstruct some of our ideas about those lamented good old days. Both Grandpa and Grandma were human beings, composed of body and soul, and were therefore highly complex individuals, with as many interests and duties as we have.

The "Good Old" Myth

Yes, it is high time the myth of the "good old days" was exploded. Even in those good old days life was a hustling business. If the old folk lived on a farm, there were never-ending chores to be tended to every day. Besides the heavier tasks in the fields, cows had to be taken care of; fire-wood chopped down and hauled to the farm, brought into the house day by day, to feed an ever hungry cook-stove. By night time Grandma had put oil into the lamps, fed the chickens, darned and mended clothes for all the family, baked bread, prepared the vegetables, set the table and gotten supper ready. After supper there was the quilting or more sewing; children had to be got ready for bed, and when the day was long since over, Grandma was ready for a well-earned rest. Both she and Grandpa were up before dawn the next day, and the daily task of living with all its thousands of details was begun again.

This was not the case only on the farm. Nowhere was there a forty-hour week or what we would call "hygienic" working conditions. There were no laws prohibiting child labor in mines and factories and sweatshops. Wherever we look, from Revolutionary days right down to the present, the picture is the same: human life is a complex thing. It always will be so, as long as man is man.

It may come as a shock to realize that some forty years from now our grandchildren will be looking back on our day with the same blend of envy, wistfulness and general misunderstanding, as we distil and through which we look at "the good old days." We have only to transpose the picture of our own day over that of some fifty years ago to hear the same complaints about the complexity of life, the same irritation over the hurry of life, and the same nostalgic longing for those good old days, when everything seemed to be so simple and easy, so leisurely and unhurried. Oh well, let us not feel too harshly about our grandchildren, and not too idyllic about the past; Adam and Eve started a fashion when they disobeyed God and ate of the fruit of the tree which He had forbidden them. The Devil, you remember, had suggested to them: Ye shall be like Gods, and then they took and ate. We all want to be like God, whether we know it or not, every time we complain irritably about the complexity of life and living. We would like to do away with such complexity and thus imitate God, Who is, supremely simple.

Simplicity

Now, a word about a word. The word is "Simple" or "Simplicity." In a sense, it was unfortunate that Saint Thomas proceeded to ask if God was Simple immediately after he had proved the fact of God's existence, because "simple" is one of those words which we ordinarily associate with a man named Simon. It has an unfortunate meaning which arises to mind each time we read about a person who has just bought the Brooklyn Bridge, or who got fooled with wooden nickels. "Isn't he simple?" can be a smiling, barbed comment.

Saint Thomas says God is simple. And he means, certainly, nothing belittling in making such a statement. The fact is that in scientific terms, "simple" signifies merely to lack parts, or not to be composite, and in the same breath (although this is overlooked in our everyday speech) to lack the imperfection of unrealized potentialities. Everything on this earth which we touch and handle is a composite thing, or something composed of parts.

Man is a compound of body and soul, which can be separated from one another sometimes on very short notice. A tree or building is made up of all sorts of parts; but the tree can be chopped down and up into thousands of pieces, and the building can be blown sky high by a nicely directed bit of dynamite. But once this has happened, the tree is a tree no longer, and the building is no longer a place for people to live. This is not to say anything against trees and buildings; they are both wonderful things, but the whole point is that they are *not* perfect simply because they are made up of parts, and are therefore material composite things. Being tangible and composite, they can be acted upon by something or someone in such a way as to be destroyed or perfected or used elsewhere. This is imperfection!

Any composite thing, especially if matter forms one of its parts, is imperfect; and since God is the First Unmoved Mover, He can never be acted upon and moved (willy nilly) by some agent outside of Himself. All that He has and is, is His from the very beginning. In God there is no imperfection or limitation, because He is simple and has no parts that go to make Him up. Furthermore, anything that is a composite can write its history in two words *before* and *after*, for this composite does not exist until all the parts are assembled. God knows no *before* or *after*. He is a pure spirit, having no material parts whatsoever in Him, and therefore always very much in motion. To sum it all up in one single word: God is simple.

High Tribute

On the other hand, we instinctively realize that simplicity is not a "fighting word"; it masks absolute perfection or power or skill or movement, and if our friends describe our living room as simple when it is filled with expensive furniture, none of us takes the remark as anything other than a compliment—which it is. Simplicity means order in the midst of complexity; or harmony where there might easily be discord, or beauty where ugliness has reigned. The word "simplicity" is often used to describe an austere gown which is unadorned by ribbons and fluffs, feathers and what not. Looking at such a gown, we appreciate its beauty and pay willing tribute to the master hand that created it. Simple though it may be, we know that no ordinary amateur had a hand in designing it. It takes skill to make a very complicated thing appear to be simple and gracious. Sonja Henie executes the most intricate pattern of figure-skating as if it were something she had just thought of for the first time, and so it appears to be delightfully spontaneous and natural. There seemed to be a sort of communion of tremendous brawn and keen brain in the artistic way Babe Ruth used to roll his bat around in the path of the oncoming ball, so simple did it seem. There are some New Yorkers who do not become particularly enthusiastic about the Radio City Rockettes, for they fail to perceive, beneath such perfect precision, the utter mastery of bewildering detail—and the simplicity! Any museum tells the same story. Wherever there hangs a masterpiece there hangs something not just thrown together in a hurry, but the careful work of a lifetime, the product of a thousand strokes of genius which combine to produce a picture which tells its story clearly, simply. Simplicity, always, is the trademark of the master craftsman.

God Is No Mere Superman

This doctrine is valuable not only because it gives us, negatively, some idea of the perfection of God, but also because it cuts the basis out from under any system of thought which tries, as the old Greeks tried, to make a God out of man, or as some of the moderns, a man out of God. God does not enter into composition with anything. It is true that He is everywhere by His essence, presence, and power, but this does not mean that he is a part of every tree, stone, blade of grass, or human being or animal in the universe. Such a system stultifies our notions of God, and if allowed would offend against the law of contradiction: God, absolute Being and Perfection, First Efficient Cause and Mover Unmoved, and at the same time entering into an unholy union with matter, with all that is limited, imperfect, and inert. All this Saint Thomas avoids very nicely at the outset of his work on God, by saying that God is simple.

As for ourselves, we need not be frightened by the complexity of our lives. As human beings we can expect nothing more. Complexity is what we expect from composite, limited beings. And complexity may be turned into simplicity. We admire the natural simplicity of a child, so full of naiveté and trust; but we admire and respect the splendor of a mature adult life whose acquired simplicity shines gloriously, in the midst of complexity. How, we wonder, can some people do so much or so many things and still face the world with unperturbed serenity. These people have instilled order into their working day; an order similar to the order a string instills into a handful of scattered pearls. As long as the pearls lie around unstrung, they will never form a beautiful necklace; once string them, and they are a thing of artless beauty, of sheer simplicity, or order in complexity. Life can be made like that, if we consciously realize that each step, each motion, and each human action is directed to one final goal of all living, to God Who is utterly simple, utterly beautiful, and perfection itself.

II. Perfection

The Age of Enlightenment

Every so often we are treated, we of 1942, to pictures which deal with the Gay Nineties, and such fun it is. Gales of laughter shake the theatre or living room where the styles of yesteryear are exhibited. All we have to do to prove how far we have progressed since those days is to look at our own clothes in the picture albums of just a few years ago.

To get into immediate contact with far-distant Europe or Asia or to chat with a friend at the other end of the city we need not stir from the comfort of our own living room. No more for us the slow, jolting journeys by horse and buggy, for we have a choice between slick, shining, streamlined trains, or equally slick, shining, streamlined and speedier air-liners. Yes, we are quite smug about our material comforts and achievements, and we wouldn't exchange this world of ours for anything; at least not for anything as outmoded and backward as the past century. We are not medievalists but moderns, living in a stream-lined age.

Modern achievement is an established fact, and gives unmistakable evidence of the genius of man. At the same time, however, up to the present most of the achievements of which we boast are limited to the scientific sphere. Of course they are good. There is no reason on God's earth why we should wish to renounce those good things that science has been able to contribute to human living. There is no call to return to the medical practices, for example, of the last century; we have indeed outgrown those, as we have a hundred other things. The only thing is, we must recognize the limits of the progress we so jealously defend.

Man, The Inquisitive

Amid all the material advances of science, there is one thing that has remained wholly unchanged and that is man himself. He is still a creature composed of body and soul; and his inquisitive mind is still never satisfied to let well enough alone; always he must be on the search, looking, experimenting, trying new ways. Apparently the depths of man's creative genius are inexhaustible. As a result, each year witnesses the creation of new things, new styles, new inventions, new applications of science to life. Who would have thought, a few years ago, that television was a practical possibility? Or that fluorescent lighting would replace the famous incandescent lamp? Who could imagine the revolutions that have taken place in the automobile and locomotive and airplane industries? No sooner does a new model appear than engineers—men with their inquisitive minds—are already devising new improvements which will be incorporated into a better model next year.

There is a reason for our dissatisfaction with even the best that our science can produce. Man is a bloodhound on the scent of absolute perfection and beauty and efficiency, and the trail blows hot and cold. Each advance, each thrilling exploit of electrical or mechanical engineers and inventors seems momentarily to afford us the perfection we crave until our inquisitive minds begin to ferret out imperfections; then the quest begins all over again. So it has always been. We refuse to be satisfied with anything less than perfection, and anything less than perfection can hold our minds captive only for a moment.

Insatiable Thirst

The inability of concrete, individual, tangible things to satisfy the instinctive desire of our minds for perfection is behind the dissatisfaction and much of the unhappiness of the present world. Without knowing exactly why, we persist in looking for the perfection that will give us happiness, not where we should look for it, but, rather stupidly, in persons, places, and things which all bear the trademark of limitation, and therefore imperfection.

Often we speak of a "perfect" thing. We speak of people we know as being perfect husbands or wives; last night there was a perfect moon which shone on a perfect garden containing perfect roses. News comes up from Florida that the golf professionals are playing in a tournament: the medalist has just shot perfect golf for a 72 (although in these days of perfection, no one with a 72 would ever be medalist). Perfect smiles, perfect teeth, perfect anything and everything! And yet, in each case, our use of the word perfect implies a limitation. If this lovely flower is a perfect rose, it cannot well be anything else but a rose. Its own beauty is only the beauty of a rose. A perfect provider or cook is not by this one fact necessarily a perfect husband or wife, a perfect business manager or mother. In a word, all the things of this earth which we call perfect can boast of their perfections in a limited sphere.

And yet in that limited sphere, the rose is perfect, and the smile and the teeth or the hair or sunset or anything may be perfect. Everything on earth has its own beauty: but the rose is not the only beautiful rose; the husband or wife are not the only husband and wife exhausting in themselves all the perfection of love. No, all earthly perfection is given only on trial. It is a borrowing, not a perfect actuality. For instance, the rose has beauty, the husband has the fine quality of affability and considerateness; but the rose is not Beauty, nor is the husband Affability or Considerateness, for everything except God is limited in its very being, and therefore in the perfection which is in proportion to this being. Created beings march to the ever-flowing, limitless fountain of existence. If they return from the visit made to this spring, with limited existence and perfection, the fault lies not in the spring itself, but in the containers dipped into it. That is why everything cannot satisfy us for long, for when it comes to spiritual matters, we want to drink deep and long, and not just sip without ever quenching our thirst.

Greater Than These

Beneath the stern, unyielding face of the mineral kingdom the beauty of perfection can be faintly seen. But beauty of crystals and the dull glitter of precious metals are as nothing when compared to the startling perfection of the new world which spreads out before him who scales the peaks of the vegetable and animal kingdoms, where perfection contains not only growth but also locomotion. Still higher up the ladder of being stands the lord of the world, man. In himself he contains all the perfections of the kingdoms lower than himself, but he is far greater than any of them because he can leap with his mind through countless leagues of space; he can explore the labyrinthine depths of material creation, and he can examine the workings of the stars; knowing something of man, he can know a little something of the joys of heaven or the pains of hell. But even higher in the scale of created being, mightier even than man are the angels: pure spirits, without bodies and much more perfect in their manner of being, thinking, moving, and loving than man, limited only in that they do not realize all their perfections at once. And finally, at the summit of the magnificent mountain of being, transcending all space and time, there sits the Ancient of Days, possessing in Himself all the perfections of creatures, but in such a way as to BE all perfection, instead of merely sharing it.

Divinity

The farther, then, we get from matter, the more we find of perfection. An investigation of created perfections starts us off on an exciting journey that leads us to God Who is all perfect, and perfection without limit, because He is absolutely simple, and free of any composition of material or spiritual parts. Fashions in the divinity do not change from one century to another! What God is now, He always was and always will be. Moreover, He is whatever He is. We speak of Him as being beautiful, but do not always remember that in His beauty there is nothing that will fade, nothing that will suddenly blossom forth; God is Beauty itself. He is whatever He is, simply because He is so far removed from the limitations of matter, and also from those undeniable limitations of spirit common to us and to the angels.

In other words, whenever we speak of God's perfections, we simply wipe away all limitations, smash down all barriers or fences that hem in human (and angelic) perfection. We do not say that God is truthful so much as God is Truth; and in the same way, God is Beauty, God is Love.

Because then, the human mind has been so persistently foiled in its quest for perfection in the daily things of life, it is never at rest. The styles in hats, happily enough, are constantly changing, because no one style pleases for long. All human fashions and styles change like the weather. Those that contain more perfection are tolerated, nay, welcomed, by a world hungry for perfection. But it is as difficult to cram into a limited being all the perfection we wish for, as it is to find a word which will adequately express God or His nature. In some case we try to enclose an ocean in a quart bottle, and in the other, just as futilely attempt to span infinity with a host of tiny bridges.

This urge for perfection, however, has resulted in much that is good. There is no point in minimizing the considerable perfection which man has been able to enclose in his own little creations or inventions. The pageantry of color and sound, of symmetry and orderly arrangement, are achievements of man's genius. Famous paintings, majestic symphonies, towering sky-scrapers, efficiency in all human endeavor, all are marked: signed with the sign of perfection. Unfortunately however, masterpieces can be shown in only one museum at a time, symphonies cannot be played all together, and there is only one New York; in a word, perfection mirrored in all these things is limited, singular, and we might say, individual. Their perfection is something borrowed, something possessed, but not an actuality of being, not absolute fullness, as true perfection is in God.

All our lovely perfections, though they speak with a thousand tongues of beauty and excellence, are unable to give a thorough account of themselves. The perfect rose is hemmed in by the walls of the garden and by its very self; therefore it is finite and not all-perfect. The perfect smile would certainly be a weird thing—like the smile of the vanishing Cheshire cat in *Alice in Wonderland*—if it lacked the stage of a face to appear upon! The charm and grace and beauty of perfect things on earth, in direct proportion to their distance from matter, are a faint echo, an inkling of the perfection of God Who is pure spirit. Therefore He is absolute. There are no limits to His existence, just as there are no limits to His perfection. Whatever He is, is His absolutely, and is identified with Himself.

Not Perfect But Perfection

God is the First Cause Uncaused. It was from His efficient fingers that the universe rolled on the day of Creation; and it is from those same beneficent fingers that we obtain our own existence. Were it not for the exercise of His causality this very moment, there is no one of us who could remain in existence. Beautiful things owe their existence to Beauty itself; but all beauty or perfection in the world, being limited and capable of further development, like a "farthing candle held to the sun," is a faint reflection of the surpassing fulness and completeness of the perfection that is God. He alone is the adequate explanation of whatever is true and perfect and beautiful in the world; being these things by His very essence, He can bestow them upon creatures: the cause contains in itself all the perfections of the effects.

No, there is no contradiction, although it does severely tax the imagination. How for example can God be said as the first efficient principle in the order of causes to possess in Himself all perfections of creatures, when those perfections of creatures include, beside the beauty of the rose and sunset and other fragile examples, the unde-niable perfections of a lion leaping at his prey, of the majesty and fury of a hurricane, of the resistless strength of a mighty wave which imperiously demands free passageway of all man-made obstructions? The perfection of one species of animal presents hazards to another species. We can imagine the poor defenseless metal or coal cringing from the miner's pick; the grass of the fields shrinking from con-tact with the beautiful white teeth of cows; the beasts of the field shuddering at the approach of man. Each of these species contains in itself many perfections, depending naturally upon the degree of being or actuality (as opposed to potentiality) it contains. These are specifically different perfections, and yet, since God is First Cause, and absolute act, He must possess them all.

At first sight this would appear to do away with the simplicity of Almighty God, but as Saint Thomas remarks, perfections which are numerically and specifically distinct in us, exist in a different way in God, so that they do not affect His simplicity (1, 4, 2, 1m). The best thing to do is not to labor the point. Everyone knows that the dainty tulip is contained somehow in an ugly looking root or bulb; that the breathtaking, finished statue somehow is contained in the uncut block of marble. To prove this we do not dream of fitting the flower back into the root, or the statue into the stone; we recognize and accept the fact that some perfections are virtually contained in principle, and owe their perfection to that principle. The father undeniably possesses all the perfections of the human nature of his son, and in the same way; *formally* there is no difference, but *numerically* there is. Lastly, the artist contains within himself all the dazzling perfection of his work, but since "hand and brain go ne'er paired" in a more perfect way. Eminently, a theologian would say, the artist possesses all the perfections of his work, and more. It is, then, possible that diverse and opposite. Things can preexist in God as one, without for all of that taking from Him that requisite for enduring perfection and actuality His simplicity.

Activity or Act

Preachers often complain about a constant diet of social activities. Some of them are adept at painting grim pictures of a life that is one constant party, and they are perfectly correct—at least in what they mean. What they mean is that such aimless activity is not fitting for intelligent people. That activity itself is good. In fact, St. Thomas calls God "Pure Act," and bases many of his conclusions on the principle that perfection is not passivity or potential greatness or mere possible goodness, but activity, actualness, completeness, and life. No wonder so many people shy away from religion or a search for perfection, when these things seem to consist in a mere negation, a *not*-doing of a great many nice things. This is of course arrant nonsense. Real perfection, as far as we are concerned, is human perfection: and human perfection consists in human activity, which in turn consists in using those faculties which distinguish a man from all the lower creation: the use, that is, of his intellect and will. The more *human* activity the better, then, for this means more thinking and more loving; thinking about soul as well as body, and loving objects worthy of our love. This kind of activity is real living. It is the only living worthwhile, and explains the steady flow of inventions, progress of Science and Potentialities; it is this active living which spells perfection.

Imperfection spells limitation; it is a star still out of reach. God is not limited. The only way He could be limited would be to limit His essence, and then He would be able to receive only a drop or two of existence as creatures do. But God would not then be God—at least not for us. In Him in whom existence is identified with essence there can be no imperfection or limitation; in Him there must be actuality. There are no limits to His being because there are no limits to His essence. In Him there is nothing that must be achieved; nothing to be laboriously worked out, nor anything caused by anything else: God is perfection because He is His own existence, He *is* goodness, truth, beauty itself.

Like to God

Faced with such staggering perfection, we are only mildly surprised that Saint Thomas bothers to ask the question if a creature can be like God. There have been some, Pantheists mostly, who declared men were gods. Thomas is concerned with a similarity between a perfect God and a perfect man, and in his reply he takes care to safeguard the utter uniqueness of God. Yes, he writes, man can resemble God: not as a son resembles his father (for then they would have the same nature), nor in the way the heat of a sun-lamp is like the heat of the sun (for while the formal effect of the heat is the same, it is produced in different ways and one is much greater than the other). The only way in which a creature may be said to be like God, then, is analogously.

A dog, for example, may do tricks which seem to demand a high degree of intelligence. Indeed, we may speak of the pup as a "smart dog," but the word "smart" is used analogously; for while being specifically different from one another, both man and dog seem to be alike in their use of reason. The same thing could be said of a robot going through human motions, or of an actor who takes on a famous character: analogously. The connection between the most perfect of creatures and God is, then, an analogous one; according as all things are beings, they are likened to God Who is the first and universal principle of their being. We are all like unto God by reason of the fact that we share in Being, whereas He is Being without limit; but we are all terribly distant from Him, too, in that His being contains no limitations but rather all perfection. In a single word, we are somewhat similar to God, but He does not resemble us.

In fact, in all that we do, we should try to imitate as lies with in our power the perfection of God. This means actuality, activity; it means the realization of thousands of hitherto uncapitalized talents, the infusing of life into our sluggish minds and hearts. Once this is done, our world will indeed be bettered. Inventions in all fields of Science will be continued as our restless minds attempt to sound the wells of being, and our hearts will become afire with the human joy of loving a known God.

III. Goodness

Delivering the Goods

Our age has seen the rise of a new and potent science which exerts an incalculable influence upon the lives of our citizens. The new science is called the Art of Advertising. It is a kind of propaganda that can invade the privacy of our homes via radio; it makes its appeal from between the covers of magazines and folders. It refuses to countenance for a minute the idea that a man likes to do his own thinking, sometimes!—so our roads are lined with billboards extolling the varied perfections of a thousand hotels, restaurants, and manufactured products.

A good advertising man makes a direct appeal to the curiosity of his prospective buyer; a very sound procedure incidentally, which the old Scholastics recognized when they crammed much truth into a few syllables: *Ignoti nulla cupido.* (Nothing is desired unless known). It is a waste of breath to praise something about which we know nothing; mink coats, diamond bracelets, cars, even much healthful food would be little in demand if the buying public knew nothing about the existence of such things. To solve this problem, to bridge this gap, acquisitive genius discovered a use for glass, and now it requires heroic willpower to walk past the shop-windows in the business district or department store without being tempted to stop, take a look, and eventually to listen and buy.

Along with this appeal to a man's curiosity, there are coupled others directed to his good judgment, to his discernment, his innate hankering for a bargain, but above all, to his sense of practical values. In a word, he is asked to pronounce sentence upon the unquestionable worth of the object in question. In most cases, the assurances of the goodness of these products are rather well founded, on the goodness of the object itself.

It hardly needs explaining that the goodness of which we now speak has nothing to do with generosity. The excellence of a car, of a play, or actor in a play, of an animal even, has no connection with giving. In fact prodigality in sharing with another what belongs to a person is not to be searched for in the lower worlds of animal, vegetable, or mineral nature. It takes a man to be able to forget himself and share with others.

Goody-Goody

Neither has goodness the sickening or disgusting characteristics which we ordinarily associate with an effeminate man or a clinging-vine type of woman. We admire manliness and strength as well as femininity, and turn away with feelings of displeasure from any man or woman who does not exhibit the strength of manhood or womanhood. That is why we condemn such people with the phrase: "They are the goody-goody type," and promptly proceed to strike them from our lists of friends. No, goodness is not a bed-fellow of a sickly, maudlin, negative temperament; it must be something more than this.

Goodness *is* more than this. When we come to analyze it, we find that the idea we have of the *being* of a thing, goodness adds only the note of *desirability*. In very technical language a philosopher says: goodness and being are convertible terms.

When we analyze this notion, it becomes clear why such an art or science as advertising ever came to be. No one ever advertises something that does not exist. We cannot be expected to become financially interested in a thing unless it *is*—another way of saying: unless it is a *being*, an "ens," and not simply a figment in the brain of our salesman. Once assured that a being here and now actually exists, we begin to take note of its good qualities and perfection. Now, we measure the metaphysical perfection of a thing by the degree of being or actuality (as opposed to potentiality, to unrealized capabilities, to unachieved goal) inherent in a thing. An angel is more perfect than a man, man in turn is more perfect than animals or plants and rocks and stones; and this perfection, based on the abstract notion of *more being* as opposed to *less*, of more excellence because of more spirituality, is responsible for the clarion call of desirability that penetrates all ears and all minds. We love things because they are, because they are perfect, which is only another way of saying: because they are good. There is no real distinction between being and goodness. The thing which has being has necessarily goodness, for goodness after all is only being which is attractive to us, or that which all things desire.

Goodness Attracts

We could put the whole argument backwards and say: we love things because they are perfect, and they are perfect because they have all the being that they are supposed to have. At any rate, what is certain is that desire on our part is connected with the perfection of the object of our affections.

But alas, it is so easy for us to err in this matter. Sad experience with nonexistent gold mines has taught us much! Many a product, extolled to the skies by the vibrant tones of a radio announcer, falls far short of the promise conveyed with perfect diction, studied intonation, persuasive appeals to buy a box *today*, to get a carton *now*, to try this product and forever renounce all rival products. But all these things are unworthy substitutes for real actual goodness, and men eventually turn away from anything that is not actual goodness.

So true is this fact—that only goodness is desirable—that the Devil with all his ingenuity and savage hatred for the goodness that is a reflection of God's beauty and truth and being can discover no better means of enticing men into sin than by throwing over sin and vice the borrowed veil of goodness. "Vice is a monster of so frightful a mien, as to be hated needs but be seen."[1] Yes, sin is ugliness. Worse still, it is as much a lack of goodness as a rumpled fender; it is a negation, a lack of positive, actual perfection.

No man wittingly—if in his right senses—eats or drinks anything he knows to be harmful; the cup that inebriates is attractive, not because it reduces an intelligent person to the mental level of a babbling baby, but because a man's taste is stimulated and mental activities momentarily quickened. The removal of an annoying rival by means of a tommy-gun at the end of a country road used to be a favorite pastime of some moronic individuals who considered such a removal to be good for their own business, but not because killing or murder for itself was good. Yes, evil of itself is incredibly unattractive, and would be utterly incapable of winning to itself devotees unless it appeared decked out in robes of goodness, for only goodness will men desire.

---

[1] Alexander Pope, *Essay on Man*, Epistle II.

All is Not Gold . . .

The fact that men err oftentimes in their choice of what seems good is sometimes discouraging. Many in fact have become discouraged in the search and have swung away, cynical and bitter, from the pursuit of good. Too many disappointments and failures on the part of created goods are enough to take the heart out of a man, if it were not for the fact that a man can turn his failure into victory by looking for happiness and the satisfaction of his desires in more genuine higher good, which will be absolutely free from imperfection. It must be remembered that all goodness on earth, all the excellence which so attracts us in things we see about us, all traces back to a supreme goodness and supreme perfection. What we seek in created things is actually an existing good—but it is like a drop of water to a thirsty man. A good supper, a quiet evening, an interesting book, these things *are* all perfect, in their own sphere, and therefore capable of arousing a desire for them. But none of these good things is able fully to quench that thirst for perfection rooted so deeply in human natures. The desirable things of the world do not try to coax a man into their arms with their smiles; they encourage him to keep going in the same direction, but far beyond them, until lifting his eyes heavenwards, he shall see his joy fulfilled in seeing God.

God is Goodness

Quite without realizing it, each time a man comes to a decision in favor of some particular good, he is taking a step towards a goal. Goodness is the goal of all our choice. The hope of goodness is like the happy ending of a story, or like the pot of gold at the end of the rainbow. Our minds cry out for it—demand it—are frustrated without it. It is realization, perfection, actuality, and all its perfections. Saint Thomas describes God as the *Summum Bonum*; the highest good is God. If He is the highest good, then He must likewise be not only the most perfect Being, but the most lovable and most desirable. It is God Who is responsible for the enchanting, lovely traces of goodness we find all about us. Having made all things as First Uncaused (Efficient) Cause, God is at the same time the ultimate target of all the arrows of human ambition. "Thou hast made us for Thyself, O God, and our hearts will not rest, till they rest in Thee." Saint Augustine had figured it all out. Yes, goodness is that which all desire. We seek God, the all-good, when we seek to preserve our lives, when we plunge forth looking for Truth and Beauty and Love and Knowledge. We seek God when we look for Peace and Leisure and Justice and Virtue. We may not realize that He is our goal. All things in seeking their own perfection seek God. We who are privileged to be among God's rational creatures seek Him with our reason, and cut our path to Him with the blade of that reason. All other creation, such as the animal kingdom, seeks God, not exactly as we seek Him (for in this kingdom there is nothing of rationality but simple appetite or desire), but in following its nature. Inanimate nature, trees, and mountains and such, desires goodness; not in the sense that these things apprehend goodness, but in the sense that they are directed to good by some intelligent being, and in case that being happens to be God Himself.

And thus we come to the conclusion of Saint Thomas that God is the first principle of all goodness. He is its exemplar, its cause and its end; its model, its maker, its goal. He is goodness itself, beauty itself, and perfection itself: not the kind of perfection that fears to move for fear of betraying imperfection, but rather all activity and power and goodness. Indeed, God is the end of the rainbow, the happy ending, for in Him and in Him alone can the heart of man hope to find all his desires for goodness fulfilled.

The Weakness of Words

So far in this series we have seen what theology is and what its aims are. We have witnessed that tremendous discovery of reason that there is a God Who is now and ever shall be, Who caused all things to be without being Himself the least bit caused, or moved either! On the heels of the breathtaking fact of an actual God, we saw (very sketchily, it is true) some of the attributes of God, or qualities which flow from His essence and manifest Him to us.

It grows more difficult to draw a breath, from wonder, for God's attributes clothe Him with vibrant life and beauty and perfection and desirability. Away then forever with the false conception of a faint, pale, wraith-like, sterile, abstract, evolving, impotent, and ineffectual type of God. We will have none of him.

At the beginning we remarked that one of man's most unhappy faculties is that of being able to speak much, and say little. Nowhere is this more apparent than when speaking about God. If any angels happen to be hovering 'round, they might (were it not for their great charity) be inclined to shake their heads and chuckle at our efforts. It is so very difficult to match one's thoughts with words! On the other hand, it is so very easy to create a wrong impression with them. Just a little bit of misplaced emphasis, and an error has reared its ugly head. It would be wrong (please God we have not committed this error) to focus so much attention and praise on the beauties of rich complexity, for example, that, when we turn our eyes to the rather plain-looking simplicity, we would find ourselves unmoved, uninterested, and unenthusiastic. This would be wrong, because God is not something that leaves a man unmoved, or uninterested; the lives of the Saints (those who thought much about Him) prove the contrary!

Simplicity

This much is true. In His simplicity, God is infinitely more graceful, infinitely richer, than any of His creatures singly or collectively in their complexity. All the wonderful things on earth, composed of various combinations of matter and form, of potency and act, or essence and existence—God surpasses in His simplicity. All else can fail, but not simplicity, or rather, not a simple God! Simplicity cannot fail because it lacks parts that can disintegrate.

Perfection

Our souls, then, and the angels, lacking parts also, cannot ever not be; such things are immortal. But souls and angels have this much in common: both are created beings, and therefore "borrowers" from God. They borrow some little bit of existence from Him, but do not possess it as a natural right. Their essence is that of created beings, which cannot help but be limited somehow. God alone, the First Unmoved Mover, the First Cause Uncaused, possesses such absolute fulness of Being that we must eventually fall back upon the description He gave of Himself to Moses: "I am He who is." Yes, God *is* all perfection.

Goodness

Finally, the supreme Being who is all perfection, is a natural target for men hungry for goodness. Being which is desired is goodness; and as God is absolute Being, He is absolutely desirable Hidden beneath and behind all finite, created goodness, giving it what goodness it has, there stands the *Summum Bonum*, the Good *par excellence*. There, hidden deep in the alluring, but earthly objects of men's desires, is the Divine Good of which all other good is merely a reflection—and—an invitation.

Obviously, it is impossible to crowd all we know about God into a few pages like these. Of course there is much more to be said, and will be said in further pamphlets. These will discuss God's other attributes, such as infinity, omnipresence, immensity, omnipotence, changelessness and eternity, to say nothing of His wisdom and mercy and justice.

At the beginning of this pamphlet we issued a sort of apologia for the scantiness of our knowledge about God. Having written all these pages, we still go issuing such apologias; but with the difference that we know something more about God than the mere fact of His existence. Now we know that in every truth God is all good and perfect in His simplicity. And we begin to say over again, this time with a mite more comprehension: "Eye hath not seen, nor ear heard, neither hath it entered into the heart of a man, what things God hath prepared for them that love him." (I Cor. 1:9) Heaven will consist in the eternal, joyful unravelling of the mysteries of God.

GLOSSARY OF TERMS

1) *Actuality* or *Act*—the intrinsic principle on account of which a thing possesses a certain degree of perfection.

2) *Analogy*—a likeness in one or more respects between two things which are otherwise different.

3) *Being*—confer 14. in glossary of pamphlet Nos. 2, "*In the Beginning.*"

4) *Efficient Cause*—confer 3. in glossary of pamphlet Nos. 2, "*In the Beginning.*"

5) *Ens*—the Latin word for *being*.

6) *Formality*—something affected by a determined manner.

7) *Metaphysics*—confer 7. in the glossary of pamphlet Nos. 2, "*In the Beginning.*"

8) *Potentiality*—capacity for being perfected by some form.

9) *Principle*—that in virtue of which something exists or is done.

10) *Pure Actuality*—a being whose perfection is limited by no potentiality.

STUDY QUESTIONS

1) Why is it not sufficient to know only that God exists?

2) Do we know what God is or what He is not?

3) Why must human life be complex?

4) What is the meaning of *simplicity*?

5) What is the meaning of *imperfection*?

6) How is God simple?

7) Why is God simple?

8) Why is there no absolute perfection upon earth?

9) What are the orders or kingdom of being?

10) In what does divine perfection consist?

11) Why do we say that God is not perfect but perfection?

12) In what does human perfection consist?

13) How is man like to God?

14) What is *goodness*?

15) What are some of the modern meanings of *goodness*?

16) What is the difference between *being* and *goodness*?

17) Do men really desire evil?

18) If men do not desire evil, why do they sin?

19) How are animals and plants attracted to what is good for them?

20) What is meant by *Summum Bonum*?

4

The Heights and Depths

A Consideration of the Infinity, the Immutability,
the Eternity and the Unity of God

James M. Egan, O.P.

Introduction

This is the fourth in the series of pamphlets designed to acquaint the laity with the theology of the Church, and published under the auspices of the Holy Name Society. It treats of the other attributes of God which Father Murphy did not consider in his pamphlet, "Looking Upward."

Since these pamphlets are prepared by different writers, the form of presentation will vary from one to another, but the editors will append a glossary of the more technical terms contained in each pamphlet so that the reader may be assisted in the study of its content.

An adequate appreciation of each pamphlet can only be obtained if a general knowledge of the preceding pamphlets is had, for each pamphlet is but a part of an integrated and systematic survey of the whole of Catholic theology.

Knowing the Unknowable

St. Thomas makes the following rather startling statement just before he starts to talk about God's nature: "We cannot know what God is but rather what He is not." That statement might be taken to mean that our search for knowledge about God is vain, a waste of effort, a looking for an extra fine needle in an extremely large haystack. Actually it means that no matter how long and thoroughly we study about God, the divine reality itself vastly outstrips our poor idea about it. In a few words St. Thomas reminds us that God by His very perfection is ever eluding our grasp.

There is really nothing very strange in this. Even about the objects of everyday experience we sometimes talk in negatives. The very small, the extremely large often enough go beyond our powers of expressing them. In trying to describe an experience or an object to a friend, we might say: "It was not this exactly, nor was it that," and so on, until the listener says: "I think I know what you mean." True enough, our friend does not have a perfect notion of what we mean; yet it is better to try to convey some sort of idea than to keep utter silence. There are many men today who insist that because you are unable to have a perfectly clear idea of what God is, it is better to keep quiet or simply accept Him as "Unknown and Unknowable." Yet, there is no reason why we should be so timid, for there is much more that we can say about God, even though it is only childish prattle when compared with what God actually is.

God Exists

In proving the statement, "God exists," in a previous pamphlet, "In the Beginning," we noticed how we had to back into the fact of that existence. It is not immediately obvious that God exists; but by a reasoning process from the character of the world around us we are forced to admit that the world is utterly meaningless without God. Things are always changing, which demands an unchanging source of all change, an Immobile Mover; things are caused not by themselves, but by others, which leads us to the Causeless Cause of everything; the things around us need not have been, or need not be just what they are, which demands the existence of a Necessary Being, who is the only reasonable explanation of a world that badly needs explanation. And so we go on from things that lie about us on every side, things that we see and touch and taste and smell, to God Who always remains above our sense perception.

When we look very closely at these familiar objects about us, we discover other characteristics that cannot belong to God. By denying these qualities to God, we get a clearer idea of what He is really like. Thus for example, we know that the objects of our experience are limited or finite, but God is infinite. Furthermore, space and change and time limit creatures of this world, but space cannot cramp God, because He is omnipresent, neither can change, because He is immutable, nor can time, for He is eternal. Finally, there can be no other gods but God, for two gods would make God absurd.

A word of warning. The reader should not become impatient if he discovers that some of the things we shall say here repeat what was said in previous pamphlets. Repetition is to be expected. Does a music lover become bored by hearing a favorite masterpiece played a second or a third time? No, for each time he hears something new, something that escaped him before. The music is so rich in meaning that it cannot be grasped in one hearing. The reality of God is so vast and profound, so far beyond our ken, that we keep circling around it, straining for a glimpse here, an insight there, coming back again to something we previously understood to see if it will not yield a bit more information about our God. In a sense, everything that we shall say about God in this pamphlet was said in the proofs for His existence. We are only uncovering perfections within the existence of God which were not explicitly discussed before.

I. The Infinity of God

Infinity

Did you ever get between two big mirrors in the barber-shop, for instance, and see yourself and the barber pictured dozens of times and growing smaller and smaller in each reproduction? Did you ever wonder where that series stopped? Of course it really doesn't stop; it's just that it grows so small, we can't see it anymore. Or did you ever see on a magazine cover a man or woman holding the same magazine? The same picture was reproduced in smaller scale, and on that little magazine, there was a smaller one. Did you ever wonder how far that went—at least theoretically. Well, that gives us an inadequate notion of "infinity"; something which doesn't stop—which has no limits.

God is infinite. What do we mean when we say that? Here we have an excellent example of "backing into an idea." If we could clearly grasp the infinity of God in a positive way, we would understand just what God is. "Infinite" warns us to be careful even though it only states that God is not finite. Breaking it down negatively makes it easier for our minds to seize, as cutting the meat makes it easier for the child to eat it. But what is finite? The finite is that which is in some way limited; the finite then has limits.

Let us consider this notion of "limits," or "limitations," for a moment. Sometimes a limit is an imperfection, sometimes it is a perfection. That a young lady have a waistline is a limitation, an imperfection (if she were an angel she would have no waistline, and to be an angel, even without a waistline, is more perfect than to be a woman with a perfect waistline): however, since she is a woman and has a waistline, it can be a perfection if her waistline satisfies the current decree of fashion. It is always true that a perfection has to remain within the limits of itself if it is to preserve its very perfection.

When we say, then, that God is infinite or not limited, do we mean that we can never admit any limits, or use the word "limited" at all in regard to Him? We do not, for though the perfections of God are pure perfections, they are limited by their very character as perfections. There are many, for instance, outside the Church who are unable to accept the Catholic doctrine of hell. As a reason they give this: "God is so infinitely loving and merciful that He couldn't condemn anyone to an eternity of punishment." They are unwilling, then, to place any limits to the love and mercy of God: but they forget that God is also infinitely just. Now if God were to allow His love and mercy to run away with Him, He would no longer be perfect, for perfect love and mercy must be limited by the demands of justice. Clearly, perfect mercy cannot involve injustice. Such limitation does not cause God any trouble; His action is a perfect blending of love, mercy, justice, and all the other perfections we attribute to Him. In reality, there is limitation only from our point of view, which is sometimes incapable of understanding that too much of a good thing is not good; we can see that it is no perfection to have too much of a waistline, but we are tempted to think that it would be more perfect to be infinitely merciful without being just.

No Limiting Imperfections

We can now return to our word "infinite." When we say that God is infinite, we mean simply that there are no limiting imperfections in Him. Anything that is a real perfection among creatures can be attributed to Him, as we saw in a previous pamphlet, "Looking Upward," and every perfection is present in Him to its fullest extent.

If you say that a woman is beautiful, you can bring the woman before your audience to prove it; if you tell a Chicagoan that New York is a better city to live in, you can bring him to New York for a visit and try to prove it to him. But when we say, "God is infinite," we cannot produce God before the audience and say: "There you are; see for yourselves." You also cannot say positively what it is like to be infinite, for only God can do that, and He would be understood perfectly only by Himself. What you can say is why God is infinite: in fact, you have already said it when you proved that God is the Immobile Mover, the Causeless Cause, the Only Necessary Being, Source of all being and truth and goodness, the Ruler of the World. Such a Being must be infinite, *simply because there is no way to limit Him.*

If you were pouring wine into a glass, there are two ways in which the amount of wine would be limited by the capacity of the glass or by the will of the one pouring, that is, you could stop at any point before the glass was filled. You cannot put more wine into a glass than it will hold; you can, if you wish, stop pouring at any moment. These are, in fact, the only two ways in which anything can be limited, by being received into a subject that limits it, or by the will of the thing's maker. Take, as another example, an artist who wishes to make a statue. Before he decides definitely on what sort of statue he wants to make, he has to decide what sort of material he is going to use; for his material definitely limits the type of statue he can produce. After he has chosen his material, then he puts limits to the statue he has in mind; thus, if he chooses to work in marble, he decides whether to produce a life-size image or one of heroic proportions.

But Not Infinite

We have already seen that God is so completely simple that there is no place for any distinction between receiver and received. There is no subject into which He has been received, and hence limited; He has not been made out of anything that could impose limits on Him. Moreover, He has no maker; He is; so there is no possibility of limitations coming from someone outside God. No matter how perfect a creature may be, there is always that profoundest of all limitations—he exists at the will of Another; no creature is the sufficient reason for its own existence. Of each creature we may ask, "Why?" And the answer is, because God wills it. But if we ask, "Why God?" there is no answer outside God Himself. He is the one completely independent and absolute Being in existence.

The reality expressed by the word "infinite" is difficult to grasp, because infinity is the mark of divinity. In its presence we might well lapse into silence and admiration. Yet in speaking of God we must always bear it in mind. It saves us from innumerable errors. Standing on your porch of a late summer afternoon watching the sun go down, you might think that it was setting in someone's backyard, if reason did not remind you that it was millions of miles away. Thinking of the goodness, the truth, the mercy, or the justice of God, one might be led to think of God as a very great man but for the constant recurrence of the word "infinite." "Infinitely good" means that God is good, yes, but not as creatures are good, but in a way that is proper to God alone, which, as yet, is beyond our grasp.

It will be one of the joys of heaven to find out what we really mean when we say that God is infinite, although even then we shall never completely understand its meaning.

Before leaving this notion of "infinite," there is a question we must ask. "Is God the only infinite Being in existence?" The answer, of course, is—yes, He is. Going a step further we may ask, "Is that simply a fact, or could God produce another God?"

And the answer to this is that it is impossible. At first glance it might seem that if God is infinite, of infinite power, He could produce a being that was also infinite. At second glance, however, we see that this is not possible, even to God. For as we pointed out above, a being that is produced, that comes into existence at the will of another, cannot be infinite, for it is limited by the fact that it is produced. Here again, we run into what might be called a limitation on God's power: even infinite power cannot produce the absurd, and an infinite creature is absurd.

There are instances where we can use the word infinite in regard to created things: the mathematicians speak of infinite numbers, or of infinite lines; in moments of enthusiasm we speak of an infinite number of people attending a rally. In these cases, we mean, not the infinite, but the indefinite; we are not saying that the number, the line, or the crowd actually have no limits, but that we cannot here and now assign limits to them.

High in the Sky

Once we begin to grasp the meaning of infinity, God seems to be receding far from us. There are those who flatly state that if God is infinitely perfect, He can have no concern for us, and to suppose that He is interested in us and in the workings of our insignificant universe is merely childish imagining. In reality to picture God as some magnificent eastern potentate hidden behind the walls of a far-off castle in the skies is childish fancy. There is no greater distinction possible than the one that lies between God and a creature; however, that does not make God distant and aloof, Who keeps far away from the common herd.

Infinity really brings God close to every creature, so close as to be awe-inspiring. For if God is without any limitation, space cannot limit Him. This means that God not only can be, but is, everywhere, and that He is in one place just as definitely and actually as He is everywhere else. To express this truth we say that God is *immense* and *omnipresent*. There is a difference between these two ideas that we should note in passing. Immensity signifies that God is capable of existing everywhere; this characteristic He possesses eternally, for it is an aspect of the infinity of God. Omnipresence is attributed to God only after creation; in other words, God is present to all things only when they exist. If tomorrow the whole of creation were to pass out of existence, God's immensity would remain; He would no longer be omnipresent, for there would be nothing for Him to be present to.

In trying to think of God as omnipresent we must avoid the error that St. Augustine confesses he made in his youth. "So I thought of Thee as stretched out through infinite spaces, interpenetrating the whole mass of the world, reaching out beyond to immensity without end." This is to conceive God as a shoreless ocean, somewhat as a spiritual ether, in which the world of creatures is immersed as fish in the sea. This is a very gross conception of God's omnipresence. If it were true, we should be passing our hand through God as we lifted it to scratch our heads. Moreover, there would be more of God in big things than in little things, more of Him in an elephant than a mouse, more in a mountain than in a man.

The first step, then, in conceiving God as omnipresent is to get away from our ordinary notions about the way things are present to one another. Practically everything we know is extended within space because of its length, its width, and its thickness. So those that are close to each other are present to one another. If one moves off to a distant place, it leaves the presence of the other. This is true, however, only of things that possess quantity; that are measurable by a yard stick.

Where Are Souls?

In order to rid ourselves of such notions, let us ask, "Where is a man's soul?" Have you ever thought of that? Is it concentrated at some one point in his body, some minute section of his brain, perhaps, whence it can direct all his activities? No, it is in the whole body, giving life to the whole. Is it then to be thought of as stretched out through the body, or as having shadowy hands and feet and other parts on the pattern of the body. Again, no! The soul has no dimensions; the whole soul is present to all the parts of the body, as much in the toe as in the head. How can this be so? Because the soul is a spirit, and that is the way a spirit operates. The soul pervades the whole extent of the body making each single part live and operate vitally. However, the human soul is limited in its functions: it does not go beyond the body that is its own. Yet, understanding the way it is present in the body helps us to understand to some extent how God, Who is the supreme Spirit, can be present to all things.

To understand further the way in which God is present to all the universe let us take another example. Let us suppose that one of the Holy Fathers is going to proclaim a doctrine of faith that has been traditionally accepted in the Church but never before formally defined. He is carried through the cheering throngs of the faithful in St. Peter's up to the Pontifical Throne behind the main altar. Having ascended the Throne he turns to read the dogmatic decree. That is the picture. Let us now see in what way or ways the Holy Father was present to various groups of people:

1) He himself is present in just one spot, the small amount of physical space that his body occupies.

2) As he reads the decree, his voice reaches the small group of people immediately around the throne. He is present to them in so far as he is operating upon them by the power of his voice.

3) Every so often, the Pontiff lifts his eyes from the text of the decree and gazes out on the vast throng in the main body of the basilica. They are beyond the range

of his voice, but he can see them all, and they are in the same building with him, and therefore we can say that they are present to him.

4) Lastly, the Holy Father, as the Supreme Teacher of Christendom, is proclaiming a doctrine of faith involving the infallibility of his office. He is by his authority imposing a doctrine to be believed on all the faithful throughout the world. In this widest sense, he is present throughout the world, present to every believer.

And so the Holy Father is, in our example, present to the entire world by His moral authority, to the faithful in St. Peter's by his view of them, to the few around him by the power of his voice, while he is physically present only at the Throne.

Does any of this apply to God? Yes, with two very important differences: first of all, nos. 1) and 2) above are not distinct in God, as we shall see in a moment; secondly, the extension of God's presence does not increase as we pass from one type to the next. So we can say that God is present to all creatures in three ways by His authority, by His knowledge, and by His essence and operation.

God is present to all creatures by His authority, for He rules all from even the tiniest mineral crystal to the highest angel. In His wisdom He has set the laws for all His creation, and all are subjected to these laws, some with complete necessity from which they cannot escape, others, like men and angels, with freedom, who can rebel against the laws of life only to fall under the laws of death. Moreover, the vast panorama of the universe from the dawn of time into the ever-widening vistas of eternity is ever before His eyes. He sees each action of every creature, and nothing can escape that penetrating gaze. "And there is no creature hidden from His sight; but all things are naked and open to the eyes of Him to whom we have to give account." (Heb. 4:13)

Always and Everywhere

Present to all creatures by His authority and His knowledge, God is also present in them by His operation; and *where God operates, He is.* This is the most important aspect of God's omnipresence, and we make a special effort to understand it. Let us go back to the example of the Holy Father. Clearly, he himself is present in just one spot, the Papal Throne; yet by the power of his voice he was acting on the ears and the minds of those about him. Through the medium of sound waves he was causing effects to happen where he himself was not.

This is not true of God; in Him there can be no separation of His operation from Himself, nor does He work through a medium. Wherever God acts, He is, the infinitely perfect divine essence, the "whole of God," we might say. The infinite God is present then in men, holding me in existence every moment, helping me to write down my thoughts about Him. God is present to the reader, keeping him in existence, helping him to read God is present to the and understand what has been written. God is present to the farthest star and to the smallest crystal in the earth's center. Wherever there is anything that exists and operates, there is God causing the existence and the operation. If He were not operating there, the thing would pass into nothingness, as the world would be engulfed in darkness were the sun to cease shining. In a sense, God is present even to nothingness, for by His creative power He can always people it with realities.

No one has expressed this truth of God's omnipresence more beautifully than the inspired Psalmist:

> Whither shall I go from thy spirit
> Or whither shall I fee from thy face?
> If I ascend into heaven, thou art there,
> If I descend into hell thou art present.
> If I take wings early in the morning
> And dwell in the uttermost parts of the sea,
> Even there also shall thy hand lead me

And thy right hand shall hold me.
And I said, perhaps darkness shall cover me,
And night shall be my light in my pleasures.
But darkness shall not be dark to thee,
And night shall be light as day,
The darkness thereof and the light thereof are
like to thee. (Ps. 138)

No matter where we turn there is God, for as St. Paul tells us: "He is not far from any of us. For in him we live and move and have our being." (Acts 16:27, 28)

There are other texts of Sacred Scripture that speak of God as present to the souls of men. We have heard them often, enough. There is, for example, the consoling farewell of Christ to His disciples: "If you love me, keep my commandments. And I will ask the Father and he shall give you another Paraclete, that he may abide with you forever. The spirit of truth, whom the world cannot receive, because it seeth him not, nor knoweth him, but you shall know him, because he shall abide with you and *shall be in you* ... He that loveth me, shall be loved by my Father, and I will love him, and will manifest myself to him. If any one love me, he will keep my word and my Father will love him and *we will come to him and will make our abode with him.*" (John 14:15, 16, 21, 23)

Here Christ promises that the Holy Trinity, Father, Son and Holy Ghost, will come and dwell in the soul of him who loves God. Is Christ indicating to us in these words a more perfect way in which God is present to certain of His creatures, or is this merely another way of expressing the general presence of God to all creatures? Catholic tradition teaches us that Our Lord is revealing the special presence of God in the souls of the just. We cannot leave the question of God's presence in the world without first pondering for a few moments this great truth.

God With Us

By His general presence God is intimately united to every creature as a cause is to an effect. In this way God is present to the trees and the flowers and all the animals in the world, that are quite incapable of knowing that He is there. In this way, too, God is present to countless men and women, who ignore Him, for they know Him not; and to countless others who, though knowing Him to be present, have recoiled from Him and His love by sin. To none of these is He present as an intimate and mutual Friend, as one with whom one can share the reciprocal joys of love. And it is as a Friend that Christ promises to come to us with the Father and the Holy Ghost.

Even within our own narrow experience we can find evidence of these two types of presence. If you have never done it, you can at least try to imagine yourself riding on a New York subway train during the rush hour. You are crushed on all sides by masses of humanity. The man on your right almost knocks your glasses off trying to manipulate his tabloid. Turning to avoid disaster, you find the ends of a young lady's hair in your mouth, her umbrella resting determinedly on your ribs. There are so many human beings physically present to you; yet they bring no response from you except an urgent desire to get out into the open-air. Then suddenly, you hear your name called out; looking around you see the face of a very dear friend. What a change takes place! All the other struggling humans fall back to the shadowy places of your consciousness and you are present to your friend, who is not closer to you physically than the lady with the umbrella and the flying hair-do.

If, now, we can look on God as a Friend, love Him with the mutual love of friendship, we can also say that God is present to His friends in a special way. In a sense, all creatures love God. In loving and desiring, unconsciously, their own perfection, they are loving and desiring a participation in the complete perfection of God. The plant that pushes its stem out of the dark earth into the sunshine and air, that continues to grow until it is crowned with a lovely blossom, is seeking in its own way God. Only intellectual creatures can know and love God in the strict sense. Yet men naturally know God only as an abstraction, a Being whose existence can be demonstrated by reason, Who is the Creator of all things, to Whom adoration and reverence are due. But there can be no intimacy between the natural man and God, for the difference is too great.

But God did not wish to be looked upon as an abstraction: "I have not called you servants but friends." God's love, therefore, raised man to an intimacy with Himself that surpasses all human friendship and love. He made man capable of loving Him with a friendly, intimate love, a love that is somehow worthy of an infinite object. When charity is poured forth in our hearts by the Holy Ghost, the cold and formal relations of creature to Creator, of servant to master, are suffused with the warmth of friendship.

Divine Kinship

What are the requirements of friendship? Whether the friendship be human or divine, it is a mutual love founded on some type of common interest. This common interest is the basis of all friendship. That is why we seldom see a great friendship between the very young and the very old. The interests of the child are too diverse from those of the man. Moreover, a difference of religious beliefs is a great handicap to true friendship. For while there may be union on many points, the most fundamental interests of each are diverse. When there is this fundamental union, mutual love can grow. One person may love another greatly, yet if there is no return of affection, there is no friendship. Even if two people loved each other and were unaware, each of the other's love, there would be no friendship. Friendship, then, is the conscious union of two beings who have similar interests.

It seems almost too audacious to talk of the relation of a creature to God as friendship. Yet the love of God knows no bounds. He has given us a share in His own life. The whole Catholic religion is a revelation such as no one would make except to a friend. The cardinal point of all revelation is that God has willed that we be happy by what makes Him happy, the eternal vision of His own infinite perfections. This sharing of the divine life, which we possess through grace and the virtues of faith, hope, and charity, is the community of interests that we possess with God.

Friendship is obtained and maintained in three ways. The first is the union that we just considered, the community of interests. This is the embryo of friendship, we might say. The union essential to friendship is the mutual agreement of personal wills which is another expression of love. The third union is the effect of friendship and its perfection the real physical presence of one friend to another. These last two forms of union are clearly distinct. Two people may be miles apart, separated by oceans and continents and still be friends. Nevertheless, they will ardently desire to meet, to see each other, to talk over the things that have been happening to each. If that is impossible, the union of wills keeps the friendship alive until opportunity for meeting presents itself.

Friend

All this is applicable to the soul's friendship with God. By grace and the virtues a fundamental community of interests is established. There is union of wills as long as the soul does not commit mortal sin. Divine Friendship, once established, is unchangeable on the part of God; He never fails us. Of course, we can and do fail Him all too frequently. Yet as long as the union of wills lasts, God is also physically present to His friends, for He is not far from any of us.

The truth of God's presence in our souls is one that we should never cease to ponder. A realization of it is a bulwark against temptation, a consolation in time of suffering. A temptation to sin is not merely an invitation to enjoy the pleasures that creatures can give us; it is also a demand that we destroy the bonds of friendship with God. To give in to temptation is not merely an injury to a far-off God, it is an insult to a Friend in whose Presence we always are. Is there anything more uncomfortable than to meet a friend whom we have greatly injured? By sin we are no longer friends of God, yet that does not destroy the realization that He is still close to us, hoping that we shall not resist His proffered grace to turn back to Him and be reestablished as His friend.

As we lie on a bed of sickness, doctors, nurses, relatives, and friends hover about us, hoping to be of service to us in some small way. They are a consolation. But there is also another Friend, closer to us than all the rest. Though it may seem as though He had forgotten us, had left us to suffer needlessly, we know that such is not the case. There He is, always, watching carefully to see whether or not we are simply His "good-weather" friends, who accept His Friendship only as long as He seems to have gifts to distribute. It is at moments of suffering and sorrow that God's presence is most precious for those that are truly His friends. Thought of His presence will make us realize that our suffering is, after all, the "shade of His hand, outstretched caressingly."

A clear understanding of the infinity and omnipresence of God saves Catholic thought from the errors of Pantheism. Pantheists believe that there is only one existing reality; all the apparently distinct objects that we see around us are merely parts of this one real being, which they call god. They simply cannot understand that though God is intimately present to all things, He does not cease to be infinitely perfect and they do not cease to be finite effects of God's causality. Though God is transcendently above us by the perfection of His nature, He is intimately with us by the care of His creative love. "Who shall separate us from the love of Christ? Shall tribulation, or distress, or persecution, or hunger, or nakedness, or danger, or the sword? I am sure that neither death, nor life, nor angels, nor principalities, nor things present, nor things to come, nor powers, nor height, nor depth, nor any other creature will be able to separate us from the love of God, which is in Christ Jesus our Lord." (Rom. 8:35, 38)

II. The Immutability of God

Change

St. James tells us that "every good gift and every perfect gift is from above, coming down from the Father of Lights, with whom there is no change, nor shadow of alteration." (James 1:17) Catholic tradition accepts this statement of the Apostle completely. God is absolutely changeless. Yet, this notion of an unchanging God is very unacceptable to many minds outside the Church. Such minds are truly provincial, confining their view to the world in which they live and are unduly impressed by the ever-changing aspect of created reality. At its worst, such minds establish change as the only reality, going so far as to erect change into a quasi-divine reality, as though the ultimately real were some divine force blindly striving to realize itself, ever seeking more and more perfect manifestations of itself on the moving screen of time. Overly impressed by the hypothesis of evolution, such men can accept no absolute beginning and no absolute end. The notion that the whole process of evolutionary development was started by a perfect God for a preordained end is simply an absurdity for them. If such were the case, there would be absolutes in the world, absolute truth, absolute goodness, absolute standards with which to measure the progress of the world. However, they cannot bring themselves to admit that anything is true before it has been tried; by methods of trial and error, they maintain, truth and goodness can be momentarily determined. Tomorrow one has to try the experiment over again, for tomorrow is another day. If they lived strictly according to their beliefs, such men would go through life like an American soldier trying to find his way through strange London in a blackout.

Even to men with no philosophical axe to grind, change seems to be a very precious treasure, changelessness a bore. Sitting in a dentist's anteroom, waiting at a street corner for a tardy friend, lying sleeplessly through hours of the night, other like experiences of doing nothing except waiting for something to happen are sufficiently annoying to make us shun immobility. Changelessness seems to imply stagnation, doing nothing, and human beings are not very happy when they are inactive; if forced into inactivity, they prefer to sleep so that at least they will not have to face it. Even activity becomes boring when actions are merely repeated over and over again with no change. The monotony of an assembly line may turn out products faster, but it stagnates the human beings who are subjected to it.

However enjoyable change may be to us, we would never be satisfied with a continually changing world. There must be a fundamental solidity, a changelessness to support the surface

changes of which we are, perhaps, more conscious. Would the housewife want her butcher to be in another store every time she went to buy provisions? Is the husband happy, if, on his return

home each evening, he finds that his easy chair is in a new spot? Do we find no value in the unchanging faithfulness of a friend, the steadily burning love of a wife, the unbroken doctrinal tradition of the Catholic Church?

Excess Change

Of course, the fact of the matter is that there are different kinds of change and of changelessness. Not all change is good; not all changelessness is good. To understand the unchanging character of God we must keep a number of distinctions in mind. Let us try to trace these distinctions in our own experience before we apply them to God.

We seem to be ever-changing from minute to minute, day to day, year to year. And yet beneath the change there is something permanent. How else could we perceive the change? If I, growing calm, are two entirely different beings, how can I know that I was angry and became calm? The man himself remains as a rock-bound coast over which dash the waves of change. The ruddy infant and the blanched oldster are one and the same man; he has been modified greatly by the changes that have taken place during the course of his life, but the fundamental core of his being has remained the same.

Change can be for better or for worse. No created being possesses all the perfection it is capable of from the first moment of its creation. This is rather obvious in the case of man. Starting out in life he is little more than a mass of undeveloped capacities. He can get off to a bad start and become progressively worse. He can start off right and keep going in the right direction. There can also be alternative periods of progress and regress. He can try to stand still, although he'll never succeed. The only kind of change we admire is change for the better.

Change, then, can be substantial, affecting the very core of being, as, for example, the change that takes place in a dog when he has been poisoned, or change can be accidental, affecting the surface, as it were, for example, the change in a dog when he has been shaved for the summer.

Imperfections of Change

Wherever we find a being that changes, we find that it also has other important trademarks—it is potential, it is composite, it is imperfect.

Change first of all demands potentiality. It is a transfer from one state to another. Local motion is a change of places; alteration is a change of quality, from hot to cold, for example; augmentation is a change of quantity, from greater to less or vice versa, from the virile slimness of twenty-five to the flabby heaviness of forty-five; substantial change has a fundamental effect upon anything, such as the passing from one type of being to another—from a live dog to a dead dog. In every case, though, the object in the first state of its being is not the object in the second state, yet is capable of passing to that state; it is, therefore, in potentiality. So a person in the basement is not in the attic, but he can be; hot water is not cold, but it can be; the slim youth is not the flabby middle-ager, but he can be; a live dog is not a dead dog, but he can be.

Secondly, change demands composition, for in passing from one state to another there is not a complete destruction of the first being and a re-creation of it in another state. There is never any annihilation, that is, total destruction of the whole reality of a thing. While passing from hot to cold, water remains, so there is composition between water and the opposite qualities of heat and coldness. This is true of every change; the subject remains intact, but it is united to two different elements that account for the changed condition of its existence.

Lastly, change involves imperfection. This is not difficult to understand. Change is, we said, for better or worse. Obviously, then, if a thing changes for the worse, it is imperfect, for perfect things do not deteriorate. If the change is for the better, then the thing was imperfect, for a perfect thing cannot be made better, at least in the respect in which it is perfect.

Not Nirvana

With all this in mind, we can see that God must be utterly unchangeable. In former pamphlets, "In the Beginning," and "Looking Upward," we have seen that God is Pure Act, without the slightest mixture of potentiality; moreover, He is both absolutely simple and utterly perfect. In God, then, "there is no change, or shadow of alteration."

Does this mean that after all our efforts we have arrived at an immobile, stagnant God, Who is a do-nothing? Of course not. We have arrived at a completely perfect, self-sufficient Being, Who has possessed His perfections without decrease or increase eternally. God's immutability is not easy for us to grasp, for we are inclined at least to think of Him as changing His mind or His attitudes towards creatures. Yet even such change must be excluded from God. By one infinite and eternal act of His intellect and will, He has taken into consideration all the possible happenings in the universe of created events. He has taken care of every circumstance, and nothing new can be brought to His attention that could make Him change His decisions.

This notion of God's immutability causes a number of difficulties, most of which will be treated at length in future pamphlets. Why, for example, should we pray, if we cannot change the will of God?

Then, there is the doctrine of the Incarnation: up to a certain time the second Person of the Blessed Trinity was not man; then at a definite moment in time He became man. Did this cause a change in God? We read in Sacred Scripture that God became angry with men, and even that He laughed at the attempts of secular rulers to overthrow His rule.

To all such difficulties there is one reply: the change takes place, not in God, but in creatures. We read in the Epistle of St. James this admonition: "Draw near to God, and he will draw near to you." (James 4:8) If God can be said to draw near to us, He can also be said to withdraw from us. Now we know from what we said above about God's presence in things, that

this drawing near or away does not apply to God, but to us. When we are in the state of grace, God is near us; when we sin, God departs, or rather we depart from God. Yet we know, too, that He is still present to us or we should cease to be. An example might help us. Why do we shiver in the winter and sweat in the summer? Has the heat emanating from the sun increased during the summer? No, there is no change in the sun's rays; the earth has changed its position in relation to the sun.

III. The Eternity of God

What is Time?

Closely connected with the notion of God's changelessness is the notion of eternity. We can never begin to grasp the meaning of eternity until we have understood something of immutability. We found that the difficulty of understanding God's changelessness was caused by our constant experience of change in our lives and our surroundings. Change seems to be so much a part of things that we cannot get away from it even in our thoughts. The idea of eternity is difficult to grasp because it is utterly opposed to time, and we are completely immersed in time. Moreover, it is almost as difficult to understand what time is. Just try to answer the question, "What is time?"

Nevertheless, if we are to have any realization of the meaning of eternity, we must first grapple with the idea of time. We get an inkling of the nature of time at a race. Who wins a race?

The man, or horse, or dog, or machine, that covers a certain space in the fastest time. Two men are running a hundred yards. One does it in 9.6 seconds, the other in 9.8. The first man wins because he did the hundred yards in the shorter time. Time, then, is a way to measure motion. The motion itself is the fundamental reality; the measuring of motion is the work of the human mind. How do we get this measure? By dividing up a certain fixed motion into numerable parts. The time we all use as a measure for every other motion is the measure of the earth's motion around its axis and the sun. This motion is relatively stable; it is continuous, and it is, like all motion, successive. So we divide it up into years, months, days, hours, minutes, seconds, fractions of a second. Even the scientist, who studies motions which are much faster than that of the earth, measures them in terms of the earth's motion.

If it were not for motion, we would not have any idea of time. A sleeping man is not conscious of the passing of time, and a reader absorbed in a detective story has the impression that time just flew by without his noticing it. On the other hand, to a sleepless sufferer time drags along second after slow second, because there is but little change, and he is acutely conscious of that fact.

Time has as slight an existence as motion itself. In our hundred yard dash, the two men are at the fifty yard mark. The motion that brought them there no longer exists, the motion that will take them to the goal does not yet exist. What does exist is the passing from one place to the next. The same is true of time. Philosophers say that all its reality lies in a "flowing now," which is a more technical way of saying that the present is the only part of time that really is. The past is no more, the future is not yet; the present bridges the past and the future. The basic reason for this is that change cannot take place in an instant; it has parts that come one after another as the runner's feet hit the ground successively.

I Am Who Am

Now if God does not come to be in successive steps, but simply is, then there is no question of time in God, but of eternity. We cannot say God was or will be. He is or as He Himself put it, "I am who am."

The classical definition of eternity is the following; "The simultaneously whole and perfect possession of interminable life." We cannot tell what a man is until he is dead and has received his reward or punishment from God. Then, in a sense, is his life complete. But that takes time. He has lived his life piecemeal, second by second. God always possessed the complete perfection of His infinite Being. Eternity is not something outside God, whereby we measure His duration, as the motion of the earth, whereby we number the years of our life, is outside us. Eternity is God, and God is eternity.

We must not think of the moments of God ticking of in synchronization with those of ours. Eternity embraces all of time in its own simplicity. To God there is no difference between our past, our present, and our future. All the moments of time from the beginning to the end are present to Him always. This is another difficult truth to grasp and will be treated extensively in another pamphlet. For the present let us be satisfied with an example. God is somewhat like an observer stationed on a hill around which a vast procession is going. To God all is clear; to those in the procession, their progress around the hill is made in successive phases. They do not know what is ahead, but God does.

Despite all the difficulties involved, we have reasons to accept the truth of God's eternity, the infinitely perfect, endless existence of the only truly independent Being.

IV. The Unity of God

God Alone

Lastly, we must maintain that this infinite, omnipresent, unchanging, and eternal Being is the one and only God in existence. In an earlier section of this pamphlet we saw that God could not produce another infinite being. Here the problem is slightly different. The question is, "Could two gods exist, independent one of the other, both infinitely perfect?" Again of course, the answer is " No; there is only one God."

Why can there be but one God? Let us suppose for a moment that there were two. One would not be the other. One would have to be distinctly different from the other. Thus one would have something the other one lacked. Consequently one would surpass the other. Then the two would not be all perfect, nor would they be gods either.

The doctrine of the unity of God is one of the most precious gifts of our inheritance as Christians. The story told in the Old Testament has as its plot, one might say, the struggle that God had with men to make them accept and live according to this truth. God fought the battle through His prophets. For some reason, deeply hidden in fallen human nature, man is always seeking the absolute of divinity and hesitating to find it in the Absolute Who is God. Time and again the Jewish people abandoned the one true God for the idols of their pagan neighbors. Though in the beginning monotheism was the general practice of mankind, it was not long before knowledge of one God was corrupted, and the mind of man turned to the sun, the moon, the stars, other creatures, to worship them as gods. From out of this welter of polytheism God rescued the Jewish people and trained them to worship Him alone. If this belief in one God had not been kept alive, Christ's reception in this world would have been worse than it actually was. In fact, there were enough believers in the true God to assure the acceptance of Christ as the Son of God, although many Jews betrayed the care God had lavished upon them by denying the divinity of Christ in the name of the unity of God. They did not see that they could hold to the truth of monotheism and admit a Trinity of divine Persons. No doubt, it is difficult to see how there are three Persons in one divine nature, but then Christ gave sufficient testimony to the truth of this doctrine to satisfy any reasonable human being.

Further discussion of the Trinity in relation to the unity of God must be left to a later pamphlet.

No Strange Gods

We have come to the end of our present task, a search for clearer knowledge about what our God is really like. True, we have had to back into this knowledge, finding out more perfectly what God is not. Yet, when we group our denials together and try to penetrate through them to the reality beyond, we are satisfied that the effort has been worthwhile. At least, we have had a glimpse of a Being that alone can be the intelligible reason for the world and ourselves.

We have not felt any primitive conscious states, as of fear, or terror, or ignorance, pushing us to create a god for ourselves, a god who would be purely subjective, or at best, an externalization of our needs and desires.

We have not been intellectually swamped by the evidence of continual change in the world and by the scattered testimonies to a possible evolutionary explanation of the universe; such evidence has not forced us to decide on an evolutionary god, one who can develop toward his proper perfection only as the universe develops.

Deeply impressed as we were by the fact of God's intimate presence in the world and in us, we were not tempted to confuse God with the world in a pantheistic mixture.

Above all we refuse to cast over any state, or nation, or race the holy mantle of divinity; we shall never take humanity (which, by the way, does not exist) as the proper object of our religious allegiance.

Rather will we continue to express the sentiments of the great prophet of divine unity, Isaias: "Praise ye the Lord, and call upon his name: make his works known among the people: remember that his name is high. Sing ye to the Lord, for he hath done great things: shew this forth in all the earth. Rejoice and praise, O thou habitation of Sion: for great is he that is in the midst of thee, the Holy One of Israel." (Isaias 12:4–6)

Glossary of Terms

1) *Change*—is a transition from one state to another. There are many kinds of changes: substantial change involves the corruption of one kind of being and the generation of another. Accidental changes may be quantitative, qualitative, or local. Creation and annihilation are changes only in a broad sense, for there is no permanent subject of change in them. In creation the whole being is produced from nothingness; in annihilation the whole being is reduced to nothingness.

2) *Eternity*—is the simultaneously whole and perfect possession of endless life.

3) *Friendship*—is a mutual love between two intellectual creatures. Founded in likeness, it is essentially a union of wills (affective union), always seeks its perfection in real presence of friend to friend (effective union).

4) *Immensity*—an attribute of God expressing the fact that He is not confined within the limits of space.

5) *Immutability*—an attribute of God, whereby He is said to be absolutely changeless. This does not imply that creatures cannot change in relation to God.

6) *Infinite*—that which lacks limits; the absolutely infinite lacks all limits, is the plenitude of Being, God Himself; the relatively infinite lacks limits in a certain direction.

7) *Monotheism*—the doctrine that there is only one God Who is distinct from the world by His infinite Being, present intimately to it by His creative love.

8) *Omnipresence*—an attribute of God expressing the fact that God is present to all His creatures as the cause of their being and operating.

9) *Pantheism*—a doctrine that maintains no distinction between God and the world.

10) *Perfection*—a thing is perfect when it lacks nothing that is demanded by its nature. The absolutely perfect is that which possesses all perfections without the slightest taint of imperfection.

11) *Polytheism*—worship of many gods.

12) *Spirit*—is a being that has no matter or quantity in its makeup.

13) *Time*—is the measure of motion and is essentially successive. Hence it is directly opposed to eternity.

Some of the terms which have been used in previous pamphlets as well as this one, and are not contained in this glossary can be found in either "In the Beginning," or "Looking Upward."

Study Club Outline

In the preceding pamphlet in this series (LOOKING UPWARD by Richard Murphy, O.P.), we have discussed the first three attributes of God according to the order chosen by St. Thomas Aquinas. These are (1) Simplicity, (2) Perfection, and (3) Goodness.

The present pamphlet takes up the rest in the following order (1) Infinity, with the corollaries of Immensity and Omnipresence, (2) Immutability, (3) Eternity, and (4) Unity.

Suggestions have been made to break the pamphlets into chapters for the use of study clubs which meet weekly. However, authors who are preparing future pamphlets feel that such divisions would in some instances be arbitrary, and have preferred to leave to the editors the task of indicating logical divisions. In the present instance, the editors suggest that the four major topics lend themselves readily to distinct consideration. Consequently, the questions will be grouped under those four main headings.

STUDY QUESTIONS

I. The Infinity of God

1) What is the meaning of infinity?

2) Is the word "infinite" ever applied to created things?

3) Is God infinite because to His perfections or because of His essence?

4) Why does not God's infinite mercy conflict with His infinite justice?

5) Describe two ways by which creatures are limited.

6) Why could God not create another God?

7) How does immensity differ from omnipresence?

8) Where does the human soul reside?

9) In how many ways is God present to us?

10) How does the presence of God differ from the friendship of God?

11) What are the requirements of friendship?

II. The Immutability of God

1) What is the meaning of change?

2) What are the kinds of change?

3) What is substantial change? Give examples.

4) What is accidental change? Give examples.

5) What is local motion?

6) What is alteration?

7) What is augmentation?

8) Why does change demand potentiality?

9) Why does change demand composition?

10) Why does change demand imperfection?

11) Why cannot God change in any way?

III. The Eternity of God

1) What is time?

2) What is eternity?

3) Why must God be eternal?

4) Is God alone eternal?

5) Is eternity in God or something outside of Him by which He is measured?

6) Is the expression "I Am Who Am" a definition of God?

7) Does God see the past, present, and future at once?

IV. The Unity of God

1) Does this proof include uniqueness or unicity as well as unity as commonly understood?

2) Why can there be but one God?

3) What is the difference between monotheism and polytheism?

4) Who is the prophet of divine unity?

5) How did the monotheism of the Jews affect the acceptance of Christ?

6) Why could not two gods be each perfect?

7) Is pantheism opposed to the unity of God?

"Eyes Hath Not Seen"
A Consideration of our Knowledge of God

Philip F. Mulhern, O.P.

Introduction

This is the fifth in the series of pamphlets designed to acquaint the laity with the theology of the Church, and published under the auspices of the Holy Name Society. It treats of our knowledge of God and has as its source the twelfth question of the *Prima Pars* of the *Summa Theologiae* of St. Thomas Aquinas.

"God made me to know Him, to love Him and to serve Him in this world, and to be happy with Him forever in heaven" is a familiar answer in the catechism. These pages are an effort to tell how we know God.

If you are interested in this series, may we urge you to obtain the former numbers because while each pamphlet is complete in itself, it is part of an integrated and systematic survey of the whole of Catholic theology.

Footprints

Stories of the weak confounding the strong seem to have a universal appeal. In the forefront of these histories should go the tale of the Prince Edward Island farmer who met a learned, and talkative, visitor at his neighbor's home. One bright winter evening, the islander sat quietly in the neighbor's kitchen, attentively listening to a brilliant discourse on the nonexistence of God. He sucked his pipe contentedly, said nothing. As the hour grew late, he drew on his boots and prepared for the cold walk home. Just before the farmer turned to the door, the visiting monopolist of the conversation brought his extensive soliloquy to a close with a question which was intended to clinch the argument: "Who ever saw God, anyway?" The hardy potato planter, who had seen much of the island's good earth and its hard-won fruits, but had seen little more, knocked the ashes from his pipe as he made his longest speech for the evening: "Right, right! Who ever did? But I saw His tracks on the snow tonight, on my way over here."

The unspoiled eyes of the farmer had seen what books could not have taught him, for in his struggle with the rich soil of his native isle he had learned to read the signs of the footsteps of God. The moonlight on the snow, the green sprout in the dark loam, the golden corn in the summer sun were but markings in the sand. Their Maker he had not seen, indeed, but that they had a Maker Who might be seen, never did he doubt. In the answer made to the superficial pedant, simple as it was, he had summed up the wisdom which men have gathered who, with a clear vision of man himself, faced the question of how man could know God.

Little Man

In the wordiness with which the enlightened intellectual protests that this God cannot be seen, nor felt, nor heard, there is hidden a strutting pompousness which says, emphatically if silently, "Here we are—men! We are intelligent. We have discovered the secrets of nature. If there is a God, why can we not know Him, see Him? We know everything else. Where is He?" This attitude makes a very big and a very bright person out of man; it gives him the piercing vision of a bird who might fly right into the rays of the sun and never blink. It loses sight, however, of the countless testimonies to the inadequacy, the weakness, the nearsightedness of the human mind.

Not the vision of a bird who might fly unblinkingly into the rays of the sun, but the sight of the weak-eyed who must shut out light lest he be blinded such a vision has the human mind. How much, after all, have human beings been able to learn? How far can they penetrate into the forces behind the world they see, and hear, and touch? How much, to become quite concrete, have science and medicine learned about the human body so close at hand? Not much. Medical practice today, with all its white hospitals and all its gleaming instruments, with its X-ray equipment and its elaborate diets, still works as much by guesswork as by knowledge. Today's widely heralded discovery is tomorrow's outmoded theory, and what was jettisoned centuries ago as false is accepted again under a new name. Thus far the human mind has not been able to analyze completely the frame it calls a body, and yet men cry that there can be no God because they do not see Him. It is like denying the existence of love because it cannot be put in a paper bag.

Dark Glasses

Great, indeed, have been the differences of opinion on God and His nature. Thousands, and perhaps even millions, of works have been written on the subject, and many are the disagreements among them. The authors have been scholarly, studious men who gave the better part of a lifetime to the pursuit of God. At the end, what did any one of them have? At best, many of them had only another theory which might be knocked down before his own bones were cold. This seems to back up the contentions of many modern teachers that there is no point in discussing God, because it is impossible to arrive at any sensible conclusion about Him. Of course, it does not back them up at all. The failure of men of learning to arrive at definite and common conclusions about God and His nature is but further testimony to the weakness of the human mind. Men disagree because they see only incompletely, and like several people asked to describe a car which passed them in the dark, they describe imperfectly what they see imperfectly.

Because an unfortunate householder cannot draw a picture of the burglar he caught sight of fleeing through the shadows of his orchard, it does not mean that he has no knowledge of him. He has an idea of his height, and perhaps some notion of his features; even though he and his wife disagree on the size of his shoes, it is probable that they will recognize him if he is caught. It is much the same with the vision we have of God through the shadows cast by the material world. Were His brightness to shine through that darkness, we would be blinded indeed, for the lenses of our eyes are ground only to see the material world; His is a brilliance those lenses could not stand. But that does not mean we do not see Him at all. We can see His tracks in the snow, hear the rustle of His passing, feel—sometimes—the ever so gentle touch of His hand.

Face to Face

This is a disturbing, an irritating kind of knowledge which, nevertheless, urges on the impatient spirit of man. Men wish to see, not alone the letters which, in grace, and beauty, write the name of God across the universe; they would see the Writer whose greatness is mirrored in what He has penned. Men see the wild torrent of the waterfall; they see the wheeling and screaming gulls, who sweep downward into the frothing whiteness stirred up by a passing ship with breathtaking poise and accuracy; they see the loftiness of a human heart which can pour out the rich tide of love and sacrifice without asking reward. All these bear the marks of divine hands; it is the hands we would see, and not their works. But this desire to pluck aside the curtain which hides all mystery, to have the answer to all questions, to look at Him whose footprints cross our path at all points, is a thirst which will never be quenched in this life. Human eyes are too weak; they could not stand the splendid brilliance of Him from whom all life's beauties have come, as sparks from a fire.

Chesterton somewhere tells the story of a little girl who, questioned as to the picture over which she was laboring, answered that it was a picture of God. With much seriousness, it was explained to her that nobody had ever seen God, and therefore no one knew how

God looks. "They'll know when I get finished," was her answer. But she and the rest of us must wait until the veils of human flesh have dropped from our spirits. Even if an angel from Heaven had visited the little girl, and guided her hand in the drawing of her picture, it would still be inadequate, for while we "live in the body of this death" we must remain as owls blinking in the light of God's face. That blinking, however, is the forerunner of a true and sure vision that is to come, the preface to the story of our knowledge of God.

Lifting the Veil

While it is true that, in this life, we must be satisfied with a vision of God which is only a straining of our eyes in the darkness, in the next life we will be able to know Him as He is. It has to be so, and it is a mistake to think that the poor vision we have on earth will follow us into eternity. Our happiness, when the limitations of this life are laid aside for the garments of eternal life, will come to us through our highest, most noble powers. Here on earth, unfortunately, that very often is not so. Because we have bodies and live in a bodily sort of world, it is generally through the body that men find happiness, and to find it through the mind—the highest power human beings have—is left for the few, the scholars, the "longhairs" of the race. So true is this that most people think of Heaven in terms of temporal, earthly pleasure if indeed they think about it at all. Many, if not most, people shy away from any thinking of what they are to find in the land beyond the stars, even though they are very careful about getting there. The idea of knowing God and being completely happy is difficult to put over, simply because "just knowing something" is not considered much fun.

Here, on earth, it would be worthy of headlines if everyone decided to enjoy life by dipping into deep study and profound thought. In a boogie-woogie conscious world, it is rather hard to sell the idea that the greatest happiness human beings can have will come to them through their minds. Boogie-woogie, and like amusements, have the edge on thinking because here the body has the edge on the mind.

Mind's Eye

Hereafter, when the mind is in complete charge all the time, the principal source of happiness will be through the mind, through knowing. It might sound like a tame sort of happiness, but if it seems tame that is because our rubbing elbows with things which can be seen, and tasted, and handled has dulled appreciation of finer things. Because it is easier to live principally by the senses, the way to the top in human happiness on earth, that is, the way to the contemplation of truth, is disdained by the majority. The gay high-liver who counts that hour a weighted yoke which must be spent alone, without noise and excitement, might look with disdain at the round-shouldered scholar who reckons as lost the time in which the noise and goings-on of the world keep him from his studies. The even pace of the scholar's life seems dull beside the varying whirl of the gigolo. Yet, it is possible that the violent pleasures of life are as nothing compared to the "gentle happiness of the lonely student, who, cut away from the world, and in the sublime aloofness of intellectual exercise, follows the magnificent processes of thought" in philosophy or theology. Because the mind is the highest power man has, it is by the mind that he must find his highest pleasures here, and his highest happiness in the here. after. Here it is not so evident because the body blocks the light; hereafter, the body will be so well governed that it will not be able to block the light.

Thirst for Knowledge

It is said that when the fever for money lays hold of a man, it wastes, not his body, but his soul. It kindles in him a thirst which never dies, and the more he attempts to quench that thirst the more fiery it becomes. The fever to know, to learn, once it is aroused, is just as fierce, just as fiery, just as unquenchable. Once the mind of man has experienced the thrill of learning, once his curiosity has reared its insatiable head, not a world, but many worlds, would be required to satisfy it. The thirst for gold has driven men across the sea and across the world; it is a thirst that dies with death. The thirst for knowledge, too, has urged men across the world, to the tops of mountains and to the bottom of the sea, into the bowels of the earth and above the clouds; but at death it does not die. It goes on forever, this human thirst for knowledge, and can be satisfied not with all the mountains and seas and earth and clouds in a streaming milky way of worlds.

It is not necessary to appeal to "the gentle happiness of the lonely student" for proof that man's highest happiness, even in this life, comes through the mind, through knowledge. The common experience of people whose lives seem a fight from knowledge testifies to this truth, although they might be the very last to recognize it. A gangster king, whose reading ability is limited to the numbers on greenbacks, probably does not derive a great deal of pleasure from the actual shooting of people. His aim in life has been the leadership of a big gang; his happiness is based on the knowledge that he is the boss.

Much of the joy in human life springs from the knowledge of achievement, not from the achievement itself. In all the long roster of experiences which bring warmth to human life, there can be few which surpass, for pure joy, the dawning knowledge of a newly born love. And, in the growth and nourishment of love, it is the increased knowledge of the personality and life of the beloved which plays such a great part. The comfort and courage of a valuable friendship are reinforced and supported by the knowledge of the unfailing heart which always understands and helps. The drudgery, the weariness, the positive suffering of a mother's life are transmuted into a wondrous light kindled by the knowledge of the young characters which are unfolding under her busy fingers. In every phase of life, it is the same; it is through knowledge that we experience love's ecstasy, through knowledge that we appreciate a goal achieved.

Happiness in Knowledge

Man's greatest happiness, then, is found in his highest achievement—in knowing; the perfection of that happiness can be had only in the most perfect exercise of his highest achievement, that is, in knowing God. In the vision of God, the fever to know does not die, but the thirst it enkindles is quenched throughout eternity with the joy of knowing. In this life we know God, not as we know our own homes—by the green blinds, the three floors, the wide front door. We see Him, not through the colors which flash upon the eye, but through that which the mind makes of those colors, even as the art student knows the great painter, not in the colors splashed upon the canvas, but through the marks of his personality which the mind sees in the splashed colors.

So for this life. What of the life to come? How are we to know God, how are we to see Him when we have "shuffled off this mortal coil"?

On earth, the mind of man must be satisfied with the marks which the divine hands have left on their handiwork, for the windows by which he looks out on the whole world are glazed with matter. An eye sees only a material thing; it sees color. It does not see the beauty of colors; it sees only the colors themselves. The mind alone can piece together, from the material impressions which filter through the material avenues of perception, the ideas and conceptions which are immaterial. The eye sees the splendor of color with which prodigal nature splashes an evening sky, but only the mind sees the beauty in that chaotic brightness. The mind can fashion out of the fragments of sense information a mosaic of knowledge far superior to any of its pieces. Yet the mind cannot know God as He is. Even when the dark hampering panes of the windows are taken away, the mind, face to face with God without barrier or window of any kind, could not see Him, by its own power.

Sight Unseen

In this life, everything is seen through an image of some sort. The sunset cannot be in the eye and in the sky at the same time; it is in the sky, and its image in the eye. The mind depends upon this image of the thing in order to know it. But God cannot be framed within an image any more than the little girl Chesterton wrote about could put His image on paper.

No image, no picture can contain Him, and so the mind which is built to know things by means of images, cannot know God that way. To see God as He is, to see the God for whose vision the sights of earth have been but the remote preparation, man needs something more than his natural mental powers.

The eyes of a man's soul are too weak to gaze unaided into the Face of God; it is not that God's Face is something which is not easily seen in Itself, but only that eyes which would look at It are not strong enough.

The printed page of a book lying open upon a table is visible enough in itself; it can be seen. Not so for one who is near-sighted. His eyesight must be fortified, strengthened, built up, if he is to see that which others of strong eyesight can already see. Of course, no creature is able, by his nature, to see the Face of God. Even the angels, spiritual as they are, need a fortifying power which will lift them up so that they can see God in His own intimate life. Unlike us, the angels see God in themselves, inasmuch as the angelic nature is an image of God, and knowing their own natures the angels know God. This is natural to them, but it is only parallel, on a higher plane, to the knowledge we have of God on earth. The knowledge of God that we acquire naturally on earth is much less perfect than that of the angels, but even their knowledge is far from perfect. We see God in His effects; they see God in the reflection cast by Him in their own natures. Because no nature can reflect Him perfectly, the angels, even as ourselves, need something more than their own natural power to see God as He is, in His own intimate life. Compared to the angels, our poor vision of God is like the sight of a mole compared to the swift, unerring eye of the eagle. Yet, the angelic vision, even as our own, must be sharpened and enlarged, in order to penetrate into the glowing brilliance of the divine essence.

Light of Glory

This improvement or enlargement of man's vision cannot be wrought by natural powers. It is a gift of strength and discernment which does not belong to the soul. When the eyes of a child are proved too weak for the normal work required of school children, the doctor probably will prescribe glasses. These will aid the vision of the child, giving the eyes a wider field than they had before, but there is nothing supernatural about them. They merely give wider scope to a natural faculty, by giving it an external help. The "light of glory," the supernatural gift which raises the soul up to a higher level is in an altogether different class from the glasses prescribed for weak eyes. Glasses but strengthen the vision along natural lines; the light of glory imparts to the soul a power of vision quite above its own natural powers. If it were possible to inject into the eye muscles a vitamin, or some kind of substance, which would give the eye a sort of X-ray vision, we would have a closer, but not perfect example of what the light of glory does with regard to the soul. To see through and beyond material substances is, quite obviously, above the power of the eye. The doctor who could give the eye the penetrating power of the X-ray would give the eye a permanent gift of sight which nature did not grant to it. It is something like this, but on a higher, nobler plane, that the light of glory does for the soul; it infuses into the soul a permanent, lasting vigor and strength by which it is able to know God. Calling it a "light of glory" may lead to a misunderstanding. This supernatural help given by God is not like a flashlight put into the hand of the soul by which we chase away the darkness which surrounds God. Rather, it is a treatment which puts a kind of new muscle into the eyes of the soul so that now the eyes can remain open and not be dazzled by the tremendous brilliance of the divine essence.

Unfailing Light

Here on earth, the soul is given a superior kind of power by which it is able to reach up, out of its earthly sphere, to perform works in another world. It is as if a child without musical education reached his tiny fingers to the piano and played a difficult concerto. Divine grace does that; it gives a man who is on the earth, who is surrounded by earthly things, the knack of doing things which are completely unearthly. It is just this sort of thing, on a much higher plane, that the light of glory does for the man who has left the earth behind. One great difference between them is that the light of glory brings a person nearer to God, makes him more like God. Grace makes some of the greatness and power of God shine in the soul; the light of glory deepens and extends the divine likeness causing a share of God's power in the human soul. Grace, which gives the faculty of doing works which have eternal value, can be lost; the light of glory, the crown of all gifts, cannot be lost. The soul which shares the friendship of God by grace can throw away the unearthly faculty by which it does so; it can give up its supernatural strength. Not so the light of glory. Once obtained, it is enjoyed forever; once a man's soul has been "'lifted" to gaze into the face of God, never can it turn away.

Different Candle-Power

At first sight, it seems that everyone in Heaven will have the same vision of God, that those just inside the gate will have just as good a view as those who have a high place. There is only one God, and there is no way of splitting Him up. The vision of Him, the knowledge of Him means the very greatest happiness anyone can have. When that joy is reached, no more can be desired. But if there were different degrees of this vision of God, would there not be room for dissatisfaction? The repentant sinner who just slipped into the kingdom of Heaven through a last-moment act of perfect contrition after a lifetime of offending God—might he not be less than entirely happy just inside the gate? Looking up, would he not sigh a bit with envy at the sight of those whom he probably mocked in life, now drinking more deeply than will ever be permitted him of the fount to all joys? How, after all, can one be completely happy, happy to the fullest extent possible, when there is something higher, better, that one could want? Indeed, it seems that there can be no difference, there in the heavenly country; it seems that fortunes must be distributed alike to the sinless and the one-time sinners.

Were this the way things are done, it would not seem exactly just. Is a hard-working missionary who burned out his life thinking up ways of helping others to have an eternity identical with that of the fat parasite who only at the end forgot himself? A Little Sister of the Poor who in every dirty and diseased face she met on earth saw the image of God—can she see no more in God's face in Heaven than the woman who never thought of God until shortly before she came to face Him? Indeed, it would not seem just. Nor is it. Truly enough, all the workers in the Lord's vineyard even though they come in, not alone at the eleventh hour, but as late as the last moment before the whistle blows, at the very twelfth hour itself, they receive—all of them—the same wage, the penny of eternal life. He who was apostle, and he who was parasite, she who gave her life for God's poor, and she who ground her living out of them—are they absolutely alike once they have passed the pearly gates?

To Each a Penny

Alike they are in the wages presented them, however long—or short—each might have worked to obtain those wages. They are not alike in their ability to enjoy those wages, to spend them, so to speak. There will be no difference in the penny all receive; to each will be given the soul satisfying vision of the Eternal Light. The penny will be the same; the face of God will be shown to all, but not all—and here the likeness stops—not all will be able to see that face with the same clarity, the same penetration.

One's intelligence, or braininess, has nothing to do with it, strangely enough. The knowledge of God which makes the happiness of Heaven does not depend on keenness of mind, and places in Heaven are not handed out in classroom order. Very often, that order will probably be badly scrambled. Indeed, it could turn out that people, who, while on earth, had sifted to the last grain all human knowledge of God, will see Him less clearly in Heaven than those who had little time for the earthly study of theology. The reason is that what we see of God's face in Heaven depends, not upon what we knew of Him on earth, but rather on how we loved Him on earth. So the different places in Heaven, the different degrees of happiness are decided by the degrees in which God was loved when He was seen but darkly and indistinctly. That is why the Maid of Nazareth, called Mary, has a place above all the doctors. They might have spun fine arguments about the divine nature which she never heard; none of them came near the devotion she had for her Maker.

To Learned and Unlearned

When life's short dream is over and the day of eternity has entered upon its never-ending round, the keenness of mind which made a child prodigy on earth will be quite useless for seeing the face of God. All that knowledge, all that brilliance are natural, human powers, and natural powers but face a wall of blinding light before the presence of God. Mind alone, as a matter of fact, is no more an assurance of eternal happiness than is muscle alone. Well-fed minds and well-fed bodies are of a like coinage at the counter of eternity; they are both natural. Something more than the natural is demanded—that something, the elevating, supernatural, divinely-given faculty of seeing, which we call the light of glory. It is the light of glory alone that opens up the eyes of the soul to see God; upon that light, its strength, its intensity, in each case, will depend the clarity, the penetration, with which one can see the features of the divine countenance. Not alone does it give the vision of God; it supports the vision and controls it as well.

Godliness

The force and the strength built up in the soul by the light of glory depends, in no way, upon natural talents of body or soul. So one's place in Heaven can have nothing to do with them. In raising up the human soul so that it may be able to withstand the light of God's face and so see Him, the light of glory makes the soul like to God, to some degree. It is quite necessary that this happen, for to see and understand God completely would require infinite understanding, since God Himself is infinite. While the light of glory certainly does not make gods of men, it does give an added quality of godliness to the soul, and so it must. This quality of godliness alone gives a limited, finite being the power to lift himself up to see and know God. It will be greater in some than in others, because some come to it with a greater inclination, a greater disposition toward God. Eyes, which, by habit, have developed a certain tendency to see better at night than ordinary eyes do, will probably react better to the substances which promote "night vision" than will ordinary eyes. It is much the same in the vision of God. Because a man has been directing the eyes of his soul toward God throughout his life, he is a more apt receptacle for the light of glory than the chap who may have looked at a lot of books about God, but rarely tried to look at God Himself.

To make one step in loving God requires divine grace. Grace, too, gives a certain measure of godliness, a likeness to God. The person who, across a lifetime, has been given to living by that grace, has developed God's likeness in himself. He, because he has desired God and has looked for Him, is, as he enters eternity, better prepared for the vision of God because he has desired it, than is his neighbor who looked at God only at the last, desperate moment. Each may go to Heaven, each may go to receive the vision of God; one—by divine grace—is a more fit, a more apt, receptacle for that vision than the other. It is loving God on earth that leads to seeing Him in Heaven, and it is that love on earth which is the measure of the vision in Heaven. This love of God is not natural, a gift some people are born with and others denied. It is not a liking for church music, nor an interest in parish social affairs. Simply, concretely, love of God means living in divine grace, obeying God's law. The most ordinary, common life can be a through way to one of the highest spots in the heavenly kingdom. Not what is done, but how it is done, matters. Each act of the day, from shutting off the morning alarm to putting the cat out at night, if lifted up by the grace of God, is building in the soul a greater capacity for the vision of God and the happiness of Heaven.

Different Sized Bottles

Capacity has a great deal to do with the question. While the vision of God granted to one may be less than the vision of another, it is not because one has less of God than the other; it is because one cannot hold as much as the next one. There is not any possibility that the last minute penitents who were fortunate to get inside Heaven's gate will begrudge Our Blessed Lady her high place. The chap inside the gate will be quite content with his lot, for he will know very well that there is nothing left for him to desire. His happiness with the vision of God granted him will be complete, for his capacity will be filled. On earth, as long as life lasts, one can grow even greater, can increase in the capacity for happiness. When life's term is reached, there is no adding to the capacity; it has been fixed by one's own use of God's grace. So to each one is given all the light of glory which he can have and hold. To think of a larger measure would be to think of pouring wine into a glass long after the glass is filled. Admiration for the higher saints, as they reflect the glory of God, will be the joy of the lower ones, even as a buttercup might admire a lily. But the buttercup, too, will be admired by the lily, and each will be too filled with its own beauty to envy the other.

This teaching on the different degrees of reward attained by God's friends is strictly Catholic doctrine. It is not something we may hold, or not, just as we wish, for it has been solemnly defined by the Church as belonging to the matters of faith. Those Protestants who deny to man any part in his own salvation naturally deny this Christian teaching which makes the place each attains in Heaven depend, in some measure, upon his own efforts. Luther's idea that everything human beings did was useless, and even wicked, led him to teach that all salvation depends completely upon Christ to the exclusion of any participation in it by men. In other words, whether one tried to obey God's law, or not, made no difference at all, so far as the next life is concerned. Those who were going to be saved had nothing to do with it at all; they would be saved, if at all, only by the merits of Christ. Hence, according to Luther, the reward of all would be exactly the same, since each receives his reward from one source. This teaching, in effect, empties of meaning Christ's own words which encourage and stimulate His followers so to live that they may be worthy to enter the kingdom of Heaven.

Not by Faith Alone

No Catholic could ever believe that men are saved by their own efforts alone, that one can walk into eternal bliss completely on his own power. That is as wrong as Luther's teaching. To be capable of seeing God, human beings, weak and finite as they are, need the elevating and strengthening assistance of God. Merely to begin here on earth the preparation for that vision of God, we need the special support of divine power, and every effort which is to build a person's capacity for the happiness of knowing God must be reinforced with the help of God's hand, which is called divine grace. The absolute necessity of God's outstretched hand is beyond question, but that does not mean that God walks for us too. Truly enough, it is He, and He alone, Who places our feet upon the path of eternal life. He gives us even the strength to move them, but it is we, not He, who must do the walking, and our efforts under the impulse of His grace will decide our eternity. The Church recognizes clearly the evident place man holds in God's plan, when she sees his inability to see the face of God unless God lifts him up. Luther and his associates but debase man and make him little more than a machine in denying him any part in reaching his destiny beyond the stars.

The destiny which awaits man beyond the stars, the happiness which is a crown of godly life, remains, and must ever remain, a human destiny, a human happiness. To reach it, a man is raised up to a stature he would never achieve by his own efforts, or through his own nature. In water, the hydrogen attains a new, a high form of existence; it is no longer hydrogen, it is part of water. Eternal life in the vision of God does not do this to man. In the next life, just as in this one, we remain creatures, imperfect, limited; never, regardless of place in Heaven, can a human being reach to the stature of God. The vision of God granted in Heaven will be, and will remain always, a human vision of God; that is, it will be limited, incomplete. To think of a human being, or, for that matter, an angel, who could see and know God as He is, in all His limitless perfection, is like thinking of a human eye which could see all of a million pictures at once. God's special help lifts up the natural powers of men so that they might stand tip-toe to see the divine essence. He could not lift us up so high that we could see all, without exception, for only God can know Himself perfectly.

Finite Vision

God is infinite. The beauties, the joys, the fine things we come to know in life, if all rolled together, are but the pale reflection, cast on a distant sky, of the eternal sun that is God. Even when we have exhausted mind and brain multiplying these things by days, and years, and all the numbers we know, still we fall short. We are finite, limited; the entire Atlantic Ocean could be more easily filmed by one shot of a pocket camera than God could be seen by a human, or by a created, mind. Even the supernatural vitamin, the light of glory, which stimulates us to a feat of seeing that which is above our eyes, could not strengthen us to see God as He is, clearly, completely. It alone—this supernatural vigor—can strengthen human eyes to look into the face of God. To know God completely would be to know Him infinitely, but human powers can do nothing infinitely. Only God is infinite, and only God can act, or do something infinitely; only God, then, can know Himself perfectly, for that is to know Him infinitely.

In all this talk of seeing God perfectly, completely, it must be borne in mind that there is no question of dividing God into sections. The light of glory, which corresponds to the degree of love the soul had for God on earth, is not doled out with a mathematical precision so that each one can know a certain, prescribed part of God, and no more. Any person's achievement in glory determines not how much of God will be known, but how well, how clearly, how distinctly the divine essence itself will be known. This difference in the degrees of knowledge is common enough. It is quite probable that a college student knows all of the multiplication table, so that he could recite it backwards and forwards. But he may know almost nothing of the many applications and extensions which the same table may have in the realms of higher mathematics. Both professor and student know the table, all of it, but the one knows it far more profoundly, completely, than his junior. So it is with the divine vision. No one of the saints knows any more of God than the others, but there can be an almost infinite variety in the degrees of knowing Him. How poorly, in relation to his betters, one of the lesser saints may penetrate into the knowledge of God will depend entirely upon the elevating power given to him by the light of glory. God will be visible to Him even as to the highest, but he will see Him less perfectly than the highest simply because his supernatural eyesight will be weaker.

Knowledge Not Vision

In this life, many men derive their greatest satisfaction and joy from the pursuit of knowledge, and it is very doubtful that people who depend for their pleasure on less important things can approach the happiness a scholar knows. Yet all the knowledge and wisdom an industrious student can amass across a long lifetime is a very small spot on all there is to know. In one moment of eternal life, one glimpse of the majesty of God, all the wisdom of the world will be surpassed.

St. Thomas, toward the close of a life of study, turned from his books and left them. Some special heavenly light seems to have been given him, for, when he was pressed to go on with his work, he responded, "After what I have seen, all that I have written seems as straw!" To us that writing represents one of the highest achievements of the human mind; to him, after some vision granted him even before he could have seen the face of God, what he had written was insignificant, futile. He must have had a foretaste of eternal life; all his hard won wisdom grew suddenly unimportant, and he would write no more. The great goals reached by the first minds of the human race during all its history will be crowded into obscurity in the beatific vision. Of all that has been learned, of all that can be learned or known, God is the beginning and the end. When we come to see God, we are at the center, the source of all wisdom, and the great feats of genius will be as nothing in comparison.

What will we know of that infinite store of knowledge, of which all man can know on earth is but a pale and scarcely discernible reflection? Principally, we will know God Himself, the source of all that is and of all that can be known. To know Him alone will quiet every desire, will fulfill every wish, will satisfy every longing will leave us at rest, asking no more, seeking no more. Still, in knowing God we will know much else besides.

All in God

Everything that ever was or ever can be is contained in God, for everything—flowers and trees, animal kingdom and heavenly bodies—is a reflection, in some often distant way, of the divine essence. The problems which vex us here have their solution there; the questions we would like to ask are answered there; the sights we want to see, the personalities we desire to know, are contained there. Added to our knowledge of God Himself, there will be a vision of these other things, far in excess of the knowledge that even the greatest genius could gather on earth. All the things God has made, or could make, we certainly will not know. To have that wisdom would be to know God perfectly, completely, which is above human powers even when aided by supernatural help. But the knowledge granted to us in the vision of God will surpass anything we can imagine here. In Him we shall see, not only his own essential perfection, but all the beauty and order of the universe as it mirrors and witnesses to the beauty and perfection of its Maker.

Keenness of Soul

To each one who reaches the kingdom of God will be given this knowledge of far-flung creation, for in seeing God each one will see the manifold things which proceed from the eternal mind. The clarity and the extent of this knowledge, in particular, will depend upon the light of glory each one possesses. The sight of details in a picture always depend upon keenness of vision; a grasp of details in a story or in an argument depends upon keenness of mind; the vision of the details of God's essence depends upon keenness of soul, and only the light of glory gives that keenness. No one, seeing God, will be denied some knowledge of the things God makes; no one, seeing him, can know all that He makes; everyone, seeing God, will be given some knowledge of the divine accomplishments, the extent of that vision depending upon the individual's merits.

So it will be for the general illumination given to the blessed on the workmanship of God. Aside from that, there will be particular interests each one will have. The young mother who was called away from the home she was making to the home God had made will wonder about the little ones she left behind. A Catholic leader who has spent years building up a charity organization in his parish will be concerned with the fortunes of his work. He who has cast aside interests of family and business to take up the affairs of a larger family and a more important business—the priest—will be anxious about the flock he has left, about the marriage he has been trying to save, about the boys he has been trying to influence, about the vocation he has been directing. Examples could be multiplied many times. Each one who goes out to his eternal home keeps ties, very often strong ties, with the land he is leaving behind. What of those things? Must we be reconciled, in death, to losing sight, until the judgment day, of those whose every day has been our concern in life? Not at all. In the face of God we shall see and know about those things which pertain to us. The mother will watch her little brood growing up; the charity worker will keep posted on the progress of his society; the priest will follow the fortunes of his people. Face to face with God, we shall know those we have a right to know, and we shall know them better, more clearly, more effectively than we knew them in life. Their prayers for us will be known to us; their prayers even to us will not be hidden from our sight. In knowing God as He is, the blessed in Heaven will be closer to those they love on earth; truly, they will know them as they are.

The Trail is There

There are times and events in every life which seem to bring us right onto the heels of God, moments in which the heart seems to stand still awaiting the vision of God in the sky. Sometimes, He seems so near that we expect to hear His voice. Other times, and perhaps most of the time, blurred, almost to extinction, His footprints seem to indicate that they were made by a very distant, very indefinable sort of God. Indeed, in life's lowlands of weariness and trouble, those footprints may seem to disappear entirely. But, the marks of God's presence, of His beauty and power, are impressed on every element of life. They do not blur or recede; we lose the track, because so many things within ourselves can disturb our vision of the world about us. Our faulty eyesight, not the markings of God on the snows of life, must be blamed for our failures to keep on the trail that leads to Him.

When the glory of the blue firmament has rolled away and given place to the greater, eternal glory, the reflection of God in His creation will stand out clear and firm. Here, we see only one sign at a time; there, the vast record of his journey in creation will be read at a glance. Here, with our poor myopic eyes, we straggle across life, missing many of the footprints He has left; there, with a vision which the bounty of God has made supernatural, we shall look across from the everlasting hills to the path we have cut through life. Then, we shall see, more clearly than the island farmer saw, the tracks of God marking every foot of our journey to eternal life.

GLOSSARY OF TERMS

(Many of the terms used in this pamphlet have been defined in the glossaries of the preceding pamphlets. However, the following may require a word of explanation.)

1) *Angel*—a created pure spirit. They are between God and man in the hierarchy of being.

2) *Grace*—a supernatural help given us by God. This will be treated extensively in subsequent pamphlets.

3) *Heaven*—the state and place where the good are rewarded after death.

4) *Image*—(Psychology) the mental reproduction or similitude of that which is perceived by the senses.

5) *Mind*—(although the term is generally loosely used, for our purpose it may be defined as) the soul as the subject of some and the primary principle of all the powers by whose activity consciousness is produced.

6) *Nature*—that which makes a thing what it is; its essence.

STUDY CLUB OUTLINE

The content of this pamphlet is based on the thirteen articles in question 12 of the first part of the *Summa*. For the use of discussion groups who divide their study of the pamphlet into four weeks, using but a quarter of the pamphlet at each discussion, the following question plan is devised:

STUDY QUESTIONS

I. The Instrument of Our Knowledge of God

1) Why cannot we not describe God adequately?

2) Why cannot even great scholars and thinkers do so?

3) What does the mind perceive?

4) What is our natural knowledge of God?

5) Why must we work out our own salvation?

II. The Aids to Our Knowledge of God

1) In what does human happiness consist?

2) Why is knowledge greater than achievement?

3) What is meant by light of glory?

4) What is the difference between light of glory and grace?

5) What is required for complete understanding of God?

III. The Limits of Our Knowledge of God

1) When will we know God as He really is?

2) What does the author mean when he says the body is more powerful than the mind?

3) What is the measure of the vision of God in Heaven?

4) Why will we be content with our degree of happiness in Heaven?

5) Will we know anything else but God in Heaven?

IV. The Manner of Knowing God

1) How do the angels see God?

2) How can there be degrees of happiness in Heaven?

3) How is the soul like to God?

4) Is it our knowledge or our love of God which will determine the degree of our happiness in Heaven?

5) When is one's capacity for happiness in Heaven increased?

6

Riches of Wisdom
A Consideration of God's Knowledge

Philip F. Mulhern, O.P.

"Oh, the depth of the riches of the wisdom
and of the knowledge of God!"
Romans 11:33

Introduction

This is the sixth of the series of pamphlets which are designed to acquaint the laity with the systematized and organized theology of the Church. Since it is but one of an integrated survey of Catholic theology, it is hardly complete in itself and should be read and studied in relation to the preceding pamphlets of the series.

In this pamphlet Father Mulhern did not have to resort to any technical theological terminology, and consequently the usual glossary appended by the editors is missing, for obviously it is not necessary in this instance.

Up in the Air

Lightness in the head—which is not permanent—is sometimes described as being "up in the air." And the expression has its foundation in reality, for high places make some people dizzy. Air travel can have the same effect. Recently, a very well known writer, who has a couple of ultra-best sellers to his credit, demonstrated the baneful influence flying can have on the intelligence. In a popular magazine, he recorded some thoughts a plane trip provoked in him. They went something like this: "The earth and men and human problems looked very small from way up there. One city looked much the same as the other. Streets and houses merged into one pattern. Men were smaller than fly specks on a high ceiling. I thought to myself that, if God saw things from His Heaven as I saw them from the plane, a laboring man has about just as much value in His sight as a bishop has."

There certainly was not anything light-headed in the writer's evaluation of a bishop and a coal-heaver. Nobody in his right mind would ever deny that a coal-heaver could be closer to God than the bishop whose coal he delivered. This seemed like a big point to the air passenger. Really, it was not much of a point at all, but he made a very pointed mistake in arriving at it. Because the plane took him a good distance off the earth, and much closer to the blue vaults of Heaven, he evidently thought that he was seeing things in much the same way God sees them. Air travel caused him to make the brilliant discovery that a man above the earth does not see the earth very clearly. Hence, God must be a bit near-sighted, too, since He looks down from a level even above the airways.

It is common enough for human beings to put up their own experiences as the measure of everything else in the universe. Only popular writers have the opportunity of imposing upon an easily-led world their self-mirroring interpretations of everything that is. From a plane window men looked smaller than ants; therefore, God, peeking around a mountain of clouds and sometimes through a thick layer of clouds would not know very much, if anything, about men's hearts. God's nature is measured by man's nature, the divine eyesight is no better than human vision; God's knowledge is very much the same as ours limited, groping, erring; this the writer of best sellers concluded from his view of the earth from the air.

Beyond the Clouds

If God is really God, and not just a kind superman who has to live in the discomforts of the upper air, He must have a higher way of knowing things than men have. How much, in fact, do people know about themselves? After a lifetime of getting acquainted with himself, a person can still discover new things in his heart. It has to be that way because of the way knowledge gets into our heads. Even ourselves we know by images, by images which—one at a time—reflect to us our actions. Every human being is surprised, at some time of his life, by discovering an unsuspected quality in himself. What we know of our hearts, our own reasons for acting, the real foundations of our loves, our fears, what—in a word—we know *of ourselves* is sketchy, haphazard, imperfect.

Were that true of God, He just would not be God. He does not learn by slowly, laboriously, putting together images He has gathered together. He does not judge His nature by the way He finds Himself acting. Our knowledge is gathered in time; His must be eternal. Our own very selves are barred from our eyes by the barriers of size and shape and color; He needs no round about way of knowing Himself, for He is present to His own eyes always. Only by sifting our actions, our words, our emotions, through the material sieve of a brain, can we know ourselves. No material brain blocks or twists the divine knowledge; God *is* His knowledge. While He exists that eternal wisdom is before Him.

To understand this is not easy for us. Much of the information we gather about ourselves becomes lost in the hazy shadows of memory. All that we know of self is blotted out, almost completely, in sleep. Sometimes, disease creeps over a man's mind so that he is robbed of all knowledge he had of himself. In God, this is not so. There is no head-scratching, no combing of the divine mind to recall part of His past history. Never is there any wonder about how He might act next year, or next century. All that He is, all the infinite, limitless detail of the divine essence is known to Him in luminous clarity, always. We have to come to conclusions about ourselves. That is not His way of knowing. Our step-by-step knowledge, gathering this bit of data, hoarding it and adding it to the next, is a very imperfect way of knowing things. In one keen, penetrating glance, we cannot plunge to the very depths of our own souls and see all that we are, all that we ever shall be. Slowly, painfully, we build our knowledge. Through the ageless moments of the eternal years, God's infinite self is known to Him. By one never suspended glance of piercing, complete accuracy, He knows all that He is.

Below the Clouds

Sometime ago, in one of our state universities, a group of very learned young people spent an evening together. The subject under discussion was God and His nature. Each of the very learned young people, in turn, expressed personal views about what God should be like. It was all very blasphemous. Each one plastered onto God the ideas *he* had spun, and a delightful time was had by all, chipping off some of the other fellow's contributions to make room for one's own. These educated people probably thought it most interesting and clever thus to swap their ideas about God. One is tempted to wonder how smart they would have thought themselves if they could have heard God unfold His ideas about them. From the limited experiences of very short human lives, these people were setting up standards to which God was expected to conform. With all the cocksureness of modern wisdom, they were elaborating on God and His qualities with a dogmatic certainty. It must be amusing to God, thus to see His creatures cutting patterns to which He must measure up.

There is so much in life which we can never hope to understand. If it is true that human beings have but an imperfect knowledge of themselves, what can be said of the information they gather about things outside themselves? Poets have sung a great deal about the powers and accomplishments of man's mind. Truly enough, it is one of earth's great marvels. With it all the comforts and achievements of our civilization have been won. But, how truly incomplete and imperfect is the knowledge which human beings gather of many things which they meet in life. Most of the things which we know, we know only on the outside; we see the shell; of the fruit inside much is mystery. Electricity lights our lamps, runs our machines. *What it is* escapes us.

There is not anything that escapes the mind of God—not the what, the how, the why, or the when. We know that the snowflake which falls in to the river and is lost forever was more finely formed than the chiseled gracefulness of a Greek statue. What forces so fashioned it, what long journey through the heavens blew it into a crystal so rare as to be unlike all others? That we do not know. Nor do we know why this bit of elusive beauty, which all man's efforts could not duplicate, should be wafted across the world for a moment and then be lost. The snowflake, even as the electric current, is known to us as an effect, something that has been caused. To some of the qualities of these and myriad other things, we may penetrate; none of them do we know perfectly, completely.

Man and Mystery

God's knowledge is so different. Every tiny cross bar of the flimsy snowflake, every charge of electricity is known to Him. The grain of dust which stops a watch, the fine web of dampness which is the morning dew, the crash of lightning in the sky, the heart of a man—all these things the eternal mind knows, and no detail escapes Him. What we know as effects, things that have been made, God knows as their Maker. What we see from the outside the law of gravity which pulls all things to earth, the perfect timing and coordination with which the heavenly bodies move–God sees from the inside. He sees these and all other things from the inside, for He sees them in Himself.

A person who knows his own strength knows just how much he can do, what he can lift, how long he can work. A cook who knows her own powers knows just what she can make, and how well she can make it; if she is good on pastries and bad on meats, she knows it. God knows His own powers, knows how far they extend, what they can do. To take this knowledge away from Him would be to make Him less than God, for it would be to take away from Him the perfection of His knowledge. Even as the cook knows what goes into each thing she can make, so the uniting mind of God knows in each smallest line and shade everything that falls from His hands.

It seems very difficult for some people to understand this doctrine of the completeness of God's knowledge. Why, they would ask, should God be bothered about such things as grains of sand? Or, how is it to be explained that the divine mind is concerned with things like snails, and beetles, and reptiles? It seems undignified, unworthy of God. These things seem difficult, unworthy of God, only because they are looked at upside down. God does not have to gain His knowledge of tadpoles by rooting around in the mud, any more than He gains His knowledge of sunsets by poking His head out of the clouds to have a look at the colors splashed across an April sky. Saint Augustine wisely says, "God contacts nothing that is outside of Himself." He was a long way from meaning that God does not know what is going on in the world, or that He gets out of touch with things. The point is that by knowing Himself He knows everything outside of Himself, for His essence contains an image of all things which are not Himself. Everything that may be—a beautiful face, a noble heart, an ugly duckling, the beasts of the forests—is a reflection of the divine essence. Knowing that essence, God knows all things that reflect it. That some of those things do not seem beautiful to us does not affect the perfection of God. Everything that is has something of beauty, of perfection, about it by the very fact that it exists. For everything that is mirrors, in a poor way perhaps, but in some way, the beauty and perfection of God.

Self Knowledge

This relation of things to the mind of God has a sort of parallel in human experience. It is not a perfect parallel, for it is impossible to find perfect parallels for anything that has to do with God. The things an artist makes are a certain reflection of himself. They are reflections of his mind, or perhaps it would be better to say they are endeavors to reflect in color, or in stone, or in sound, something of his mind. So, an artist, too, knows the picture he has painted, knows it in all its details, for it found its source within his mind. But, the parallel breaks down. There can be a sunset, because a sunset reflects God's essence. A painting does not reflect a painter's essence; it but reflects something that is in his mind. In human beings, mind and essence are not identical as they are in God. What a man knows changes, is developed; the picture he painted last year may not represent at all what he thinks this year.

Too, with human handiwork, once it has progressed from the mind of the maker into the stone or wooden reality, it is beyond the control of its producer. Many alterations of which the architect does not approve can be made in a house; certainly, many will be made that he will not know of. With the divine architect this is not possible. Nothing can be which is not contained in the divine mind. A young face, once alight with the joyous beauty of youth, when molded and mellowed by sorrow takes on the gentle beauty of maturity; in both beauties, the beauty of the divine face shines. Like a rare stone turned in the sunlight, each facet of creation shines with a different shade of color thrown by the rays of God's brilliance.

Immutable Creation

Every slightest variation which takes place in the things which He has made is known to God. All the knowledge He has of the world outside Himself, He gathers from His own essence. This does not mean that He knows flowers, and trees, and men only in the way they existed in the eternal mind from eternity. He knows them as they are. All the wonders described in "Believe It Or Not!"—the almost infinite variety of abnormal ways created things can develop—these are known to God in each stage of their warped existence. They are known to Him so, for in each moment of existence they deflect the divine essence. In the course of its life, a potato will take on many shapes; each change is a phase of God's silhouette thrown on the screen of the universe. God knows each change, not by looking at the potato, but by looking at Himself.

Many of our very learned young people, who make the nature of God the subject of arm-chair philosophizing, would be revolted by this idea of God. Surely, they would say, you would not load God down with all this useless detail of the world's creatures. But, it is not a question of loading God down. It is all very well to say, glibly, that God wound the world up as a boy winds up a top and all He cares is that it keeps spinning around. That explanation does not meet the facts.

In our own human experience, we know that a general knowledge of a thing is imperfect knowledge. The school boy who has a "general idea" of the day's lesson gets a low mark for his carelessness about details. A machinist who has a general—or vague—notion about the structure of his machine will soon be out of a job. It is not very complimentary to God—although some people think it is—to credit Him with only a very sweeping, but indefinite notion of the universe He has made. The perfectly learned man is the perfectly posted man. A perfectly intelligent God must be a perfectly posted God. It is not shrinking Him to say that He knows the number of one's hairs, or that He knows the size of the tear drop that stains the freshness of a child's cheek.

Both Great and Small

To argue that any slightest detail, however small, escaped Him, would be to remove that much perfection from His eternal mind. A mind with even that slightest imperfection is an imperfect mind. God could not be that imperfect and still be God. Our intelligent young people, who might accuse us of making God's brain a sack to stuff with useless hay, are only letting their feelings run away with them. Because they do not like toads, it is not a sign that toads are no good. A toad has life, a perfection. A toad grows, takes on new perfections. If the toad's horny skin escaped God's eye, it would be because God had not made it.

People in being emotional sometimes think they are being intelligent. It is pure emotion to argue that God's mind can not be overloaded with the things which we do not like. Such an attitude

146

makes of God a mechanic stamping out creatures with a big machine, and neither understanding the machine nor knowing the creatures. God is not a mechanic; He is an artist who knows every line and contour of the creatures He has fashioned. Everything that is, and all that it is—whether we happen to like it or not—has something of perfection in it, and perfection, even when mixed with imperfection, is of God.

Much of the difficulty we encounter in trying to understand something of God's knowledge arises from our own way of knowing things. Our knowledge and God's knowledge have very little in common. In all our knowing, we proceed very slowly. As a child learns to speak his language word by word, so we think by taking one idea after the other. It is not that way with God, but because it is the only road of knowledge of which we have experience, we find it difficult to conceive of any other. God is beyond time and above time: His mind is not limited as ours are. We know one thing *after* another; He knows all things in one sweeping glance. This thought rather cripples the imagination.

To see all the long array of men who have ever lived, to know every leaf of every tree, every wave of oceans and lakes, every thought and intention and desire of every man—to do all this in one infinitely rapid, yet continued, glance is more than we can picture. Yet, this is God's knowledge. A man sweats away a lifetime to gather a few obscure facts, to store up in his mind a mere bit of the world's knowledge. Even when he has gathered it, he can use but a little at a time. God has known it all, always; He knew it a million years ago, He knows it today, He will know it a century from now in the same way—instantaneously, completely, with one glance.

Limited and Unlimited

The mental life of a human being might be called a rather halting journey from complete darkness to light. All the reasoning which we do, all the real thinking, is made up of jumps, jumps from something known before to something which was unknown. We cross the gap of ignorance by joining together things we have known; we learn by uniting bits of knowledge. God's mental life is altogether different. He does not learn of tomorrow's weather by joining together His knowledge that a red sunset means a fair dawn. That is man's way, hopping along tediously with the help of the information he can gather.

Knowing in God is not a continual progress from ignorance to knowledge, with the ever present danger that false steps leading to error, instead of to truth, will slow up the journey. With God, knowledge is not a process; it does not advance; it can make no errors. Merely being Himself, God knows all truth, for He is all truth. He has no reason to speculate about sunsets to know tomorrow's weather, because tomorrow and all about it is already known to Him. We advance in knowledge very slowly and seldom very far; He does not advance, for there is nothing unknown towards which He could advance. There are no blind spots in the divine mind, no pools of ignorance to be filled with light.

From the depthless expanse of light which is the divine mind, streams the endless procession of God's creatures. Of the world, and the uncounted number of worlds which reach out into space, God is the Maker. No part of the wondrous work can escape His intelligence, for His knowledge has caused it all. Each ray of light, each current of air, each river, each mountain, each human heart, each bit of the architect's work finds its principle, its source, its fountainhead in the mind of God.

Knowledge, at first sight, seems to be far from a cause of anything; in fact, it is the cause of everything. Mind alone does not erect skyscrapers, but it is the vision of the skyscraper in the mind of the designer that makes the building a possibility. Ideas have caused the evil things in the world, as well as the good things. Before a great and powerful army is put in the field to impose the yoke of slavery upon whole peoples, the plan of that army, the dream of conquest, has lived in the mind of some leader. It is the same with fine things. The sombre majesty of Velasquez's *Crucifixion*, the serene dignity of Murillo's *Immaculate Conception* were caused by the minds of their creators.

Infinite Art

In like manner, the artistry of all creation finds its cause in the mind, the knowledge of God. The ideas, stored from eternity in the mind of the eternal Architect, are the source whence flow all things. Ideas, of course, while the root cause, are not the only cause of things that are made. A painter might paint the most exquisite pictures upon the canvas of his mind, a manufacturer might build a flying fortress with imaginary steel and aluminum. Before the picture can thrill others, or the plane kill others, the ideas have to be put to work.

The world is full of people with ideas. Ideas are a necessary, but not sufficient, cause for the production of ships, or for the correction of a bad situation. Ideas are the blueprints, but the blueprints cannot put themselves to work. Just as a painter, or a writer, can keep stored in his mind the "blueprints" of a painting or of a novel, so the First of the artists can keep stored in His mind the plans not yet put into execution. From eternity, He saw His Church in all its organization, in all its history. Only when the divine will chose to bring that plan into execution was the plan of the Church put to work.

The sculptor who envisions a monumental statue of Christ on the top of a mountain can go on seeing it, in all its beautiful detail, for a lifetime. So long as he only sees it, it will remain in his mind. When there is a point of putting it up there on the mountain, the will must come into play and *decide* that this idea is to become a reality. A long series of events will intervene between the joining of the will to the idea and the anchoring of the statue to the mountain. Stone must be found and cut, a mountain must be prepared, and money must be obtained to finance the entire process.

But, in God, the ideas are more causes than they are in men. No idea which rests in the simple intelligence of God will exist outside that intelligence until God so wills. Once He has willed it, there will be no long process to go through, no arrangements to be made, no bargains to be driven. In us, the mere thought of going across the street backed up by the intention of going across the street will never get us to the other side. God, however, because He is His intelligence, does not have to go through a process of putting things to work as we do. His mind is identical with His essence; His mind, therefore, *is* His infinite power, and there can be no gap, as there is in us, between what His mind envisions to be done and the actual doing of it.

So God Wills It

So much for the things which God has made; He knows them, for they are reflections of Himself, and His knowledge of them, joined to His will, causes them to exist as they are. What of things which do not exist? God's knowledge is infinite, without limit. Is it possible that His knowledge extends even to things that are not? Youngsters sometimes like to try "sticking" their religion teachers with the question, "Can God make a stone too large for Himself to lift?" Our question may seem to be of the same sort—"Can God know things that are not?" Actually our question is of a very different sort; it may seem to contain a contradiction, but it does not.

Everything that exists, from mud puddles to the milky way, is known by God because it mirrors Himself, because it came forth from His mind. Many other things will one day exist on earth which are not here now. One hundred years from now we might be more out of place in the world of that time than someone who died a century ago would be in ours. Changes multiply daily. All the new inventions of the 1960s are known to God with the same clarity, the same preciseness, with which He knows the gadgets of today. The articles yet unmade never could be were they not contained in the mind of God. Down to the texture of the pilot's seat, the slim airship which is not even yet a dream in its inventor's mind is present to the wisdom of God as it will be when it rolls off the assembly line. Even though the machines of tomorrow, as the men and women of tomorrow, do not yet exist on earth, they exist in the mind of God. Whatever a creature can make or think, or talk about, or whatever can be made by any means whatsoever—those things God knows. And so, the question "Can God know things that are not?" is not so foolish.

There is a sense in which it can be a very foolish question indeed. Tomorrow's inventions, which to our "modern" minds might seem rank impossibilities, were in His mind from the beginning. But, there is another class of non-existent things, the kind involved in the youngster's question to the catechism teacher. The square circles, the four cornered triangles, the stones too big to lift, all belong to this class. God does not have knowledge of them except as they are the toys of man's imagination. Indeed, God is not alone in His ignorance. Nobody knows such things, for they are unknowable, made up of ideas which contradict each other. They belong in the same class with the project which occupied a night watchman's spare moments: the manufacture of a light which would give *black light*.

Knowledge and Intelligence

The world and all in it will change; we change, our ideas change. In God there is no change; His knowledge is eternal, immutable, yesterday, today, and forever. Because our data on things are so poor, so incomplete, it is necessary that our knowledge change. What we knew of our friends in the beginning, we must revise and adjust as time goes on, for in the beginning we knew only a part. Always, God has all there was to be known on any subject; his store of information cannot be added to, cannot be improved. If next year, the world changes its shape from round to oblong, it will not cause God to raise His eyebrows in surprise. He knew it in the beginning.

As His knowledge is unchangeable as the everlasting hills, so it is one, indivisible, undivided. It is not a flowing stream of which He has limited glimpses from time to time. Yet, because we know things in different ways, on different levels so to speak, it is customary to speak of different kinds of knowledge in God. This is merely a matter of convenience. Actually, God's knowledge is God's substance and His substance is one, undivided; so too, then, must be His knowledge. In human beings, we speak of a person's intelligence, and mean an altogether different thing when we speak of the same person's knowledge, wisdom, or prudence.

Many men with little knowledge are gifted with extraordinary intelligence, and very learned people can be almost completely lacking in prudence. These variations are not found in God, for to split His knowledge would be to split His essence, since they are identical. Wisdom, counsel, understanding, whatever we may wish to call it, God's knowledge is all one. For our own benefit, to match our own way of thinking, we apply different names to His knowledge, in accordance with the objects of that knowledge.

In time, events march on, one after the other. All the things that exist follow on each other's footsteps. What was yesterday, tomorrow is seen no more. The achievements of next year are unknown today. The existence of created things, as we see it, is a procession, to be recorded on a film of continuous exposures. As the mind of God sees the works of His hand, from the first ages of history to its twilight—they are not a procession. They are one. As if all the figures on the film of time were merged into one composite, complete picture of the whole, He takes them in at a glance. They represent change, succession in time, but the ebb and flow of the temporal tide are the unmoving *now* to the eternal gaze of God. The marching events of the ages are spread before His unblinking eyes. This knowledge is called the knowledge of vision, for it is present to God through all eternity.

Innocence and Ignorance

Another name is given to His acquaintance with the many things which could be made, but which will never be. For example, we may suppose that there will never be a chain of gold mountains spread across the middle of our country; it could be, but it probably will not be. Too, we can think of—and some people dream of—a world without war, without quarreling, without meanness. That sort of a world is possible. Men *could* live together in harmony; Christ has pointed out the way to it. It is not pessimistic, however, to conclude that this is a possibility which will never be realized.

These possibilities, of which there are examples without number, possibilities which will never exist, are known to God. This knowledge is called the knowledge of "simple intelligence." The meaning is not simple intelligence in the sense of sub-normal or second-rate intelligence; it means only that these things are only *known*. They are not known with a view to being made to exist.

Whenever the question is raised on how far the knowledge of God goes, someone is bound to bring up the point of evil. It is always urged, not so much on the point of His *knowledge* of evil, but rather His allowing evil if He knows it. That particular aspect of the question belongs in another place. It is only the precise point of God's acquaintance with evil that can concern us here.

Knowledge of evil is often enough considered to be evil, but this notion is far from the truth. "Good" people are expected not to "know too much," and if young people display a knowledge of certain moral points, their elders are liable to cluck disapprovingly. Virtue and ignorance are somehow joined together in some minds; a priest, for example, because of his holy calling is conceived of as utterly removed from all acquaintance with man's lowly side. Actually, ignorance of man's lowly side would be an imperfection in a priest, for it is his business to know all about man. It is not possible to know all about a thing if only the fine points of it are known. An automobile mechanic does not know the car he is asked to pass judgment on if he only knows that it has new tires, a good coat of paint, and strong lights, but does not know that it has a perfectly miserable clutch. Perfect knowledge of a perfect thing means knowing all its perfections. A young man knows the perfectly formed face of his love, if he is acquainted with each fine feature, each contour, each perfection. But, he certainly would not know his sweetheart if he knew only these lovely looks, yet did not realize she was toothless and deaf in one ear.

Whence Evil

This kind of knowledge cannot be attributed to God. People often enough act as if God somehow could not see the imperfections in His creatures. He must be able to see them, for He would not know the good in them unless He could see where the good stops and the bad begins. Evil, of course, is not a *being*; it is the absence of something which ought to exist in a being but does not. A piece of cloth is bad—evil—because it does not have the proper weave. A newly baked cake can be bad because it does not have baking powder in it. People can be bad because they do not have the goodness, the virtues, which they should have. To act as if God did not know all the bad points we have is just the same as saying that He does not know what we could be. Good people sometimes become terribly depressed when they discover all the imperfections they have. They almost say, "What will God think of me?" as if God somehow expected them to be angels. God knows the imperfections, because He knows the perfections; He knows the bad because He knows how far the good goes. The principal thing is not to lament the bad; it is to increase the good.

An obvious objection immediately comes to the fore. If God knows evil things, if He is so perfectly acquainted with all the sad deficiencies in the world and in men, why did He make these evil things? In another study, this subject will be treated thoroughly. Here it is enough to state briefly how God knows existing evil. He knows the evil because He knows where good is lacking, as one knows darkness because it is the absence of light. Evil in itself is not something to know. It is a lack, a defect, something missing rather than something present. So, while we show that God's knowledge is the cause of all that is made in the universe, we cannot say that God's knowledge is the cause of the evil in the universe. Evil does not reflect the divine essence; it is a defect whereby the reflection of God's own self is rendered incomplete. Evil is something missing in the reflections of the divine essence. Gods' knowledge, indeed, is the cause of those reflections; it is the cause of everything that is good. Divine knowledge of those reflections cannot overlook the defections of goodness, which are evil. It is only in and through the knowledge of good, therefore, that the divine mind understands evil.

Immeasurable Measures

All this discussion of what God knows was begun with the question of what God knows about man. Obviously, that is our primary interest. Men, in their concern to discover how human affairs appear to divine eyes, often try to look through God's mind with their own eyes. That is what the man in the airplane was doing; because—to him—men seen from the sky were seen very indistinctly, he thought that God should adopt a human judgment of mankind. He forgot that God was not enclosed in a plane. The group of university students we have already mentioned were but imposing human measures upon God, summing up on human grounds the kind of God they wanted. But, what God knows about the affairs of men, what He knows about human hearts, and the value of laborers as compared to bishops, certainly cannot be measured as we measure what we know.

What, after all, does God know of men? Does He look down, in great confusion, upon the world He has made and wonder what it is all about? Does the bishop on the altar look any different to a distant God than the carpenter at his bench? Men look at things from the outside in. They see color, size, shape, they hear sounds, they touch surfaces, and then they conclude to intentions, to principles, to character. Unfortunately, for the infallibility of man, size, color, shape, sound are not sufficient data for a judgment. Even in the material world, experience has taught us that all men's' senses are not capable of getting the entire story. Despite all the information our scientists can gather on some of nature's doings, they cannot forecast what she will do. All the fine instruments of the weather experts do not assure us of having the correct report. If God's knowledge were not better than this, why do we call Him God? He would be only a slightly overgrown man.

God is not distant. He does not peer out at man from the window of an airplane. Nor does He look at the outside and come to conclusions about the inside. He sees inside as inside, and outside as outside. Not by looking at clothes, or car, or money does he make up His mind about people. His mind does not need to be made up; that mind knows what of bad there is in a human heart, for He knows what of good is there. If the laborer is a good laborer, and the bishop is a bad bishop, God knows it. If it is the other way round, God knows it. But, He knows, too, that, whether the bishop be good or bad, the bishop is His own representative before the people. When the bishop appears before God in the name of the people, because He has commissioned him to care for the people, the divine ear is bent to the bishop's words.

Within and Without

Hearts are not hid by clothes—from God. Nobody in his right mind ever said they are. Everything one bishop will ever do God sees in His knowledge of vision; everything he could do—and perhaps should do—but will not do, God knows in His simple intelligence. He does not have to learn these things about bishops from the kind of cars they drive, nor from the size of their waist-lines. Human hearts and human lives are spread before Him with their pages open, and He needs no reading glasses to understand them. He does not see things as an air traveler sees them, and so a bishop does not look the same to him as a laborer. The bishop has a high office and high responsibilities; so God sees him, and so God will judge him. The laborer, in a lower place, with less responsibilities, will be judged accordingly.

Some centuries ago, one of the great Cardinal statesmen of Spain sat through a sermon in which a fervent monk lashed him with fevered rhetoric for his worldly life. The Cardinal was Prime Minister; he kept a great house, was surrounded by a guard fit for a king, and entertained with a lavish hand. In lurid colors the monk painted all these extremes of living, and dipped into the pit of hell to warn the prelate of what awaited him unless he changed his ways. When the service was over prince of the church and preacher met face to face. The Cardinal drew the monk into a side room. Without speaking, he unbuttoned the flaming scarlet of his robe, pulled aside the purple shirt within and showed the monk—a coarse hair-shirt.

All Knowing

We need never fear that the God of the universe is missing anything that goes on in the world He has made. Each person, each thing, each act is mirrored in Him; as the flame of existence burns, each dip of its fire shines on the screen of His eternal wisdom. Not alone through the snowy cloud banks of a June sky or through the leaden layers of March mist, but as well through the purple and denim which may cover a man's heart, His eyes find their unerring way. If a bishop's soul is swathed in sack cloth, the purple of his mantle will not shut out the divine eye. If a bricklayer's overalls hide a spirit which is greedy for the soft garments of this world, the mind of God will not be deceived. The things He has made He knows, and there is nothing hidden from Him.

Study Club Outline

This outline of questions comprises twenty so that the subject matter may be divided for those discussion groups which meet weekly and allow five questions for each discussion meeting. Because of the particular content of this pamphlet, being concerned with but one subject and allowing no definite fourfold division as was done in some of the previous pamphlets, the study of this pamphlet will involve a progressive procedure.

STUDY QUESTIONS

1) Can God's nature be measured by man's nature?

2) Is our knowledge of ourselves perfect?

3) Does God accumulate knowledge?

4) Is our knowledge based on causes or effects for the most part?

5) How does God know things outside Himself?

6) Is there any parallel between God's knowledge and man's knowledge of things?

7) Does God know things as they are within His mind or outside His mind?

8) Is God's knowledge general or particular?

9) Is there any limitation on God's knowledge?

10) Is there any progress or advance in God's knowledge of things?

11) Is knowledge the cause of anything or the cause of everything?

12) What besides knowledge is necessary to cause anything?

13) Does God know things which are not?

14) Does God know things which cannot be?

15) What is the difference between knowledge and intelligence?

16) What is meant by the knowledge of vision?

17) What is meant by the knowledge of simple intelligence?

18) Can God know evil?

19) What is the difference between God's knowledge of things and man's knowledge of things?

20) Does God ever make conclusions from His knowledge?

7

BEYOND LIES GOD

A Consideration of Truth and the Life of God

REGINALD COFFEY, O.P.

"My thought speeds, lightning shod. It
comes to a place where checking pace it
cries, 'Beyond lies God.'"
—Cale Young Rice

Introduction

This is the seventh in a series of pamphlets designed to acquaint the laity with the theology of the Church, and published under the auspices of the Holy Name Society.

The present pamphlet treats of truth, falsity and the life of God as presented in the sixteenth, seventeenth, and eighteenth questions of the *Summa Theologiae* (*Prima Pars*) of Saint Thomas Aquinas.

An adequate appreciation of each pamphlet can be had only if one has a general knowledge of the preceding pamphlets, because each one, while complete, is but part of an integrated and systematic survey of the whole of Catholic theology.

I. Truth

What is Truth?

In the judgment hall of the Roman Procurator stood the handsome young Jew—tall, calm, and dignified. His long, curly, chestnut-red hair was damp with perspiration, and upon the arresting face, with its finely chiseled features and aquiline nose characteristic of His race, purple lumps showed that He had received a man-handling. Yet in spite of the ordeal which He had evidently been through the previous night the man's composure was supreme. He stood and spoke like a king in his own court, not like a criminal in the shadow of the gibbet. All this the keen black eyes of the Procurator noted as he surveyed his Prisoner.

The Procurator spoke. "Art thou the king of the Jews?" he asked.

And the Prisoner, instead of answering the question, countered the crafty Roman's query with one of His own.

"Sayest this of thyself," He demanded, "or have others told it thee of me?"

Caesar's administrator, slightly irked at this regal composure where he had expected abject fear, replied tartly. "Am I a Jew? Thy own nation and chief priests have delivered thee up to me. What hast thou done?"

The Jew again ignored the question. "My kingdom," He retorted, "is not of this world. If my kingdom were of this world my servants would certainly strive that I should not be delivered up to the Jews. But my kingdom is not from hence."

The Roman, quick to take advantage of any opportunity to extract a confession, shot a leading question at his Prisoner. "Art thou a king then?"

The Jew answered, "Thou sayest that I am a king. For this was I born and for this came I into the world; that I should give testimony to the truth. Every one that is of the truth heareth my voice."

And Pilate asked, "What is truth?"

We do not know what reply Christ gave to this stupendous question or whether He gave any. All the evangelist tells us is that after

Pilate had asked this question "he went out again to the Jews." Probably Pilate did not wait for an answer. After having proposed the question, it is very likely that he considered it would be impossible to get, from this untutored Jew, and opinion worth hearing. The brilliant philosopher of Greece and Rome could reach no accord upon the question. What could be expected from a Jewish laborer?

Wait, Pilate!

What answer would Christ have given had Pilate waited? No doubt He would have given the answer that had been the theme of His preaching for the three years before His meeting with Pilate, namely, that God is truth. It is hardly probable that our divine Lord would have gone into a detailed philosophical discussion upon the nature of truth and this is possibly what Pilate had in mind. Maybe that is the reason why Pilate, on second thought, decided to skip the discussion. Or perhaps Pilate, the product of an age when both Greek and Roman philosophies were tinged with skepticism, was convinced that truth could not be defined.

But Pilate, with his unanswered question upon his lips, stands as a symbol of mankind. "What is truth?" is the question that has formed upon the lips of man from the time man has appeared upon the earth. Equipped with an intellect that has truth for its object and needing truth just as surely as a stomach needs food, man is engaged upon a constant and never-ending search for truth. The search for truth is the basis of rational existence. The attempt to discover its nature is the principal object of philosophy. Yet, despite the fundamental importance of this vital question and the utter impossibility of rightly evaluating any single truth without a correct conception of the nature of truth, there is no question upon which there is more disagreement upon this most important point that is responsible, to a large degree, for disagreement upon all others.

Where?

To Pilate's question "What is truth?" philosophers have given every possible answer. Some have said that truth is God alone and has no existence elsewhere. Others have replied that truth has no existence anywhere—that it is a vain illusion. Still others have replied that it exists but in an ideal world, that it does not exist in this world of ours. At this solution to the problem greybeards with serious mien have scoffed, saying that it exists nowhere *but* in this world. Some have declared with serious air that they themselves were the only truth. One school says it can be found only in the intellect; another declares that the intellect is the one place where it isn't. Some say it exists only in the senses. A. declares that it is absolute. B. affirms that it is relative. C. advances the opinion that it is non-existent. Much, much more elusive than the Scarlet Pimpernel is this thing called truth. But the reason why truth is apparently elusive is because it is so palpably evident. It is within us, without us, and all about us. It is so evident that the philosopher who keeps his nose to the ground like a dog on a faint trail passes it right by and never sees it. With these few brief words of assurance and encouragement I now turn the class over to Saint Thomas Aquinas who, they tell me, is a killer-diller on this particular subject.

Aquinas treats the question at this point in his *Summa* because here it naturally falls into place. It would be impossible for him to treat of God's knowledge without treating the question of truth, because any discussion of knowledge involves a discussion of the object of knowledge which is truth. It would be a much easier task to hold forth on the subject of barking without mentioning a dog or to debate about shooting with no reference to a weapon than to talk and write about knowledge and make no mention of truth.

So, although Thomas chose the logical place in the *Summa* to introduce the question of truth, the question is much more fundamental than any that has been treated thus far. It can be treated to far better advantage for the student in a preface to the *Summa* and that is exactly what is done today. Men who are preparing to study the *Summa* are subjected to an intensive course of philosophy for three years before they are introduced to Saint Thomas. In taking up the question in the *Summa* Saint Thomas is not there treating the subject of truth for the first time. No indeed! Long before he started to write the *Summa* he had written and talked much on the nature of truth. One of his greatest works, *De Veritate*, runs for some 770 pages or about 380,000 words in its modern printed form on this subject alone.

First Things First

In saying that the question of truth is more fundamental than that of God no blasphemy was intended. As a matter of fact a study of the question is more fundamental. It is impossible to prove the existence of God to a man who does not believe in the existence of truth. And this is an error that is widespread today. Your typical modern philosopher holds either one of two errors, namely, either that truth does not exist or that it is relative.

Both opinions mean the same thing for the holding of the second is tantamount to holding the first. From this philosophical error (which far from being modern was in vogue in the time of Saint Thomas) comes the doctrine of indifferentism so current today, which is often expressed by the phrase: "Well, after all one religion is as true as another." This sentence denies the existence of truth. If a thing is true, its contrary cannot be true. If I should make a statement and you should deny its major premise without equivocation or condition, then it stands to reason that at least one of us is in error. We cannot, *ceteris paribus*, both be stating an objective truth.

If one doctrine is true, its opposite is false. If one religion is true, it is utterly impossible for any other to be equally true. That, incidentally, is one reason for the great popularity of indifferentism today. All of the religions outside of the one taught by the Catholic Church have been proven false so often and so conclusively that there is not other haven to which the non-Catholic can fly except to the shelter of a philosophy of indifferentism.

But in spite of the modern dread of truth and the reluctance of the modern savant to admit its existence, nevertheless, truth, like God, does exist, and it, like God, cannot be legislated out of existence nor conjured into non-existence by catch-phrases, fancy words, fast talking, or sophistical thinking. "What," asks Pilate, dreading to hear the answer, "is truth?"

Truth Exists

But despite the efforts of modern philosophers to talk both truth and God into non-existence, man knows in his heart that both exist. The word truth and its synonyms are among the commonest terms in any language. Everyone knows that truth exists. All men instinctively know what it is. The untutored laborer needs no course in philosophy to be able to distinguish ordinary truth from falsity nor does he require an Aristotle or a Saint Thomas to tell him that there are different kinds of truth. If he were asked for a definition of truth he might not be able to give glibly the answer of the scholastics and tell you that *veritas est adaequatio rei cum mente* (truth is conformity of a thing with the mind), but he could give you a description that would amount to the same thing. He would tell you that truth is something real and that a thing is true when it is supposed to be. "For instance," he might say, "take gold for example. There is such a thing as true gold, and there is such a thing as false gold. Everything that glitters is not gold. A thing may look like gold and feel like gold and yet might be only a gold brick. In certain cases it would take an expert to distinguish the true from the false gold. But just because I may think that a so-called gold brick is gold does not make it gold. It is either gold or it isn't gold."

Our friend has here given us a pretty fair description of that truth that was known to Thomas Aquinas as "ontological truth." However, it is impossible to consider truth apart from an intellect. Our friend, the common man, if pushed for an explanation of just what made true gold true, might tell you that gold is true insofar as it measures up to its nature. This would be correct as far as it goes. But it would not be complete. In order that the note of truth be added to that of being, its relation to an intellect is necessary.

Certain cases can be postulated which make this necessity of the relation of a being seem strange. For example a stone buried in the earth is a true stone whether you or I or an created being is aware of its existence or not. Yet that stone depends for its existence, as shown in a previous pamphlet, upon the Divine intellect. And it is from its relation to that intellect that it derives not only its being but its truth. In the same way a house is true insofar as it measures up to itself as it exists in the mind of its architect. Consequently, although creation is defined as making something out of nothing, it is not entirely wrong to call an architect the creator of a house. For the house depends essentially upon the mind of the architect for its existence. So it is that even things that have not yet been discovered, things that are known to no man, are true despite the fact that a thing is true only as considered in its relation to an intellect. Everything that is or will be has such a relation to the Divine mind.

Conformity with the Mind of God

So in the consideration of truth the knowing intellect is the more important factor to be considered. This is the point developed by Saint Thomas in the first article of the sixteenth question which deals with truth. Thus it is not too hard to see why those philosophers who being with a denial of the existence of truth end with a denial of the existence of God. It becomes evident, too, why those who begin with a denial of God must end with a denial of truth. Because without God there can be no knowledge of truth and without truth there can be no knowledge of God. Yet in their hearts these fancy Dans of the world of thought know that they are sounding brass and tinkling cymbals. In their case this attempt to get rid of both the truth of God and the God of truth is wishful thinking based upon pride and yen for moral license. Pride—because they would make the mind of man rather than that of God the yardstick of existence. Immoral yearning—because once truth is destroyed responsibility ceases. To satisfy their pride and make man bigger than God they make man a brute. To fulfill their amoral yearnings they free man—free him from his humanity. But the truth of God persists, not only in time and in eternity, not only in heaven and upon earth, but in their hearts. They may shout that nothing is truth, but reason whispers that everything that is is true.

Inextricably mixed up with the mystery of iniquity is the why and wherefore that while animals which cannot know truth always act in conformity with it, man—who alone of all mundane creation can know it—alone denies it.

"Logical Truth"

In addition to the truth of things that exist apart from intellect but not independent of it and which is called "ontological truth," Thomas considers that truth which exists in the mind of man, apart from external existing things but not independent of them. For as the mind of God is the cause of all existence, these things in turn are the causes of the truth that exists in the mind of man. This truth the schoolmen called "logical." Logical truth is a view of truth from the opposite side. For as ontological truth is the conformity of an existing thing to the intellect, logical truth is the conformity of the intellect to the existing thing. For the creation of logical truth the operation of the human mind is necessary, as the operation of the Divine mind is necessary for the creation of ontological truth.

There is one error that must be carefully avoided if truth is to be kept pure. And that is the error that holds that truth exists in the intellect alone. Because of the important role played by the intellect in the conception of truth this error is one into which many philosophers, with the best of intentions, have fallen. Some have held that truth exists in the divine intellect alone. If that were so, it would lead to a philosophy of unreality—either Pantheism or Idealism. It would be impossible for man to know truth except by divine revelation. Such an error would bring its proponents to Skepticism, either total or partial.

Equally vicious is the doctrine that all truth exists in the human intellect alone. From this error as a jumping-off place, philosophy, since the time of Descartes who laid the groundwork for the error, has run the whole gamut of false doctrine from idealism to crass materialism.

False Prophets

From one extreme to the other, the philosophers have gone. Those who rejected idealism and subjectivism adopted the opposite view, namely, that truth exists in the outside world alone. That it is impossible for the mind to know truth. This group succeeded in avoiding the grasping claws of Scylla only to sail into the gaping maw of Charybdis. Even those who fell into neither error adopted as their teaching the worst theories of both schools, avoiding, in a manner little short of miraculous, the only true teaching. Some of these false prophets have taught that while truth cannot be known by the intellect, it can be known by the senses, and from this unholy union, without the benefit of reason, was born sensualism, the philosophy so current today, with all its shades of attendant evils. Another offspring of this marriage of the son of the intellectual god with the daughter of materialistic man is the monster, dialectical materialism, developed by Hegel and Feuerbach and utilized by Karl Marx as the "intellectual" basis for his Communism.

The only legitimate union and the sole conjunction from which the fair and beautiful Truth can be born is the moderate realism of the Schoolmen. This is the doctrine Saint Thomas exposed in Question Sixteen. Truth, he teaches, is neither in the intellect alone nor in the material world. It is produced by the mutual action of each. The method whereby this conjunction is made is not treated in this question. That subject has its proper and full treatment in a later question. What concerns Thomas here is the existence of truth, not the method of knowing it.

Is God Truth?

After establishing the existence and the mode of existence of truth, Thomas next proposes a question that seems likely to upset the whole apple cart and scatter the nicely polished fruit of his mind into the gutter. In the fourth article he inquires whether God is Truth. It has just been established that truth is conceived from the action of the intellect upon the world outside the mind. The answer to the question of whether God is Truth seems, at first blush, to be, "Certainly not. If He were, He would be the product of an intellect acting upon existence apart from itself." However, let us approach the question from a different angle. "Does God know truth?" The obvious answer to this question is that He does. Well, since God's understanding is His essence, as was proved in a previous pamphlet, it follows that God not only understands truth, but must, of necessity, be Truth.

However, it is necessary to avoid the pitfall that lurks in this answer. Just because God is Truth we must not fall into the error of saying that He is the sole truth and that truth cannot exist apart from Him. If there were true, we would be led directly into Pantheism.

But created truth, as we have discovered in other pamphlets, is not identical with the essence of God. Therefore created truths are neither immutable nor eternal as they exist here and now. But they do enjoy a kind of eternity as they exist in species in the divine mind. Everything that is or will be exists, in species, in God's mind, and since God is eternal, so are His ideas. He *never* forgets. Also, since God is unchanging, so His ideas never change. He never changes His mind as men do because God knows the truth, the whole truth and nothing but the truth—forever.

Another snare lurking in the answer that God is Truth might be expressed as follows: If God is Truth, and God is one, therefore truth is one. "In one sense," replies Thomas, "truth whereby all things are true is one. In another sense, it is not." We know from experience, for instance, that there are many truths. You and I are truths, but we are individual truths. Just because I know the individual truth, one times one equals one, is no reason for making the somewhat rash judgment that I know everything. Or the fact that I know both you and your uncle's wife does not make you identical with your uncle's wife. But all these things have one thing in common, namely, truth. And they are true only because they are in conformity with the divine intellect. So from this aspect all truth is one, because in the divine intellect truth is one.

Is Truth Everywhere?

In the Thomistic teaching on truth, there is one difficulty that stands out like a sore thumb. It is the teaching that everything that is is true. O happy day! We are thereby rid of all the world's patent falsity because falsity just does not exist. The immense fabric of lies that forms the propaganda of warring nations; the falsity and double-dealing that bring about wars; the cheating, stealing, lying of the business world; the so-called false philosophies; even the false face of the woman just out of the cosmetician's chair—all these things are either true and right, or they are just figments of the imagination. Because everything that is is true. What says the sage of Sicily to that? Does he reason the world's patent and evident falsity out of existence like a wishful magician, or does he just lightly skip the difficulty as being insuperable and not fitting in with his otherwise complete theory? Let us see. Let us see.

Despite the truth of the axiom that everything that is is true, Thomas finds that everything that is can also be false. He goes on to explain this paradox. We must look for falsity in that faculty in which truth primarily resides, the intellect. For as truth is produced by the action of the intellect upon things, falsity is produced in exactly the same way. All things depend upon some intellect insofar as they may be called true. The whole of natural creation, as we have seen, depends upon the intellect of God. Artificial beings, the products of the skill of man, depend upon the intellect of the craftsman.

Now this dependence of things upon an intellect is two-fold. To be simply or essentially false a thing must be false in respect to the intellect upon which it depends. To be relatively or accidentally false it is false to another intellect. For example, although we call fool's gold false gold it is essentially not at all false. In respect to the Divine intellect upon which it depends *per se* fool's gold is true iron pyrites. God did not intend iron pyrites to be true gold, and so He is not being fooled by fool's gold. It is only when considered in relation to the human intellect that the note of falsity becomes attached to fool's gold. It looks very much like gold, so much so that the early colonists in Virginia sent a ship load of it back to England. So in relation to their intellects it was false gold.

Only Man Can Be False

Now in things that depend directly upon the intellect of God no essential falsity can be found, except, perhaps, in the case of one type of being. Voluntary agents, to be precise, angels and men, have it in their power to withdraw themselves from what God ordained for them. These beings alone of all creation can be false to the Creator. That is why every sinner, even the most open and unabashed, is a liar, a cheat and a sneak.

In artificial things, things that depend upon the human intellect, falsity is to be found not only accidentally but essentially. Thus, a house that does not measure up in the minutest of details to the dream of its designer is false.

It should be pointed out that when falsity occurs regarding natural things the blame must be placed where it belongs—on the intellect. There is a great temptation, and a temptation in which many philosophers have fallen, to spare the god-like faculty, the intellect, and place the blame for the error upon the senses. But the senses are not to blame. They are no more capable of creating falsity than they are of creating truth—and that capability is nil. For while the senses are the agents of truth they do not know it. Their role in the conception of truth might be compared to that played by the dispatch riders between the front lines and the headquarters of the commander-in-chief. Their dispatch cases are crammed with the information upon which the commander bases his battle plans, but they never know what the information is. If the plans go awry, the general, not the riders, get the blame. Now of course the couriers may be made to share the blame. They may get their cases mixed up and give the wrong case to the right general. Or they may lose their cases now and then. Or, again, they may be tardy in bringing the necessary information.

In much the same way the senses get the blame for the intellect's conception of falsity. They may not get the facts straight, they may be tardy in reporting the facts, they may, through injury, be inca-pable of reporting the facts, but it is the intellect that makes the judgment and, therefore, it is the intellect that creates the falsity.

II. The Life of God

Vitality in God

Religious persons who meditate much about God are fond of pic-turing him as an old man with a kind face and a long, flowing beard. This method, which is not without its value in bringing souls closer to God is, nevertheless, somewhat misleading. The picture is a composite formed from the more staid attributes of God, such as immutability and eternity; the emotionally appealing attributes such as love and mercy; the patriarchal attributes, justice and prov-idence—with the conglomeration thrown against the truth of the fatherhood of God, a doctrine so consoling and inspiring to pious souls. But there is one thing wrong with the picture. It is difficult to reconcile it with God's more dynamic attributes. For example, some incongruity would be entailed in using this picture as the imaginative basis for a consideration of God's overflowing vitality. Of course you could take the old gentleman out of his patriarchal role, endow him with a second spring, put a swing orchestra in the background and have him trip a few lively measures. But that would be definitely taking him out of character. No, it were better in meditating upon the vitality of God to get a new player upon the stage of our phantasms.

And it is quite necessary to meditate upon God's vitality. That spirituality unnourished by contemplation of the life of God would be barren indeed. For God is the life as well as the way and the truth. The reason why we seldom consider God as being lively is often because false concepts of eternity and immutability have become fixed in our minds. We too often conceive of an eternal being as static, and we are too prone to regard an immutable being as something inert. But far from having such a meaning, eternity and immutability really mean the opposite. "When we say that God is immutable," says Garrigou-Lagrange, "we do not mean that He is therefore inert. We affirm on the contrary that He is the plenitude of being or pure act, He is essentially activity itself and has no need of transition to act that He may act." And eternity means that in God life is so abundant that it had no beginning and will have no end.

Although the eighteenth question is entitled *The Life of God* Thomas concerns himself in the first two of the four articles in considering the question of life in general—what it is and where it is to be found. We, who talk so much about life and place such a high value upon it, know little enough about it. It might be well to accompany the Angelic Doctor upon the examination he makes of life in general before we go to discussing life in its highest form—life as it is to be found in the source of all life—God.

What Is Life?

However, before beginning any investigation of this thing called life it is necessary, in order that we do not get on the wrong track at the very start, to disabuse our minds of any ideas we may have picked up in public school biology classes. The method of teaching biology and explaining vital functions by using the machine as an example has become increasingly popular in these later years. This is only one result of the influence of materialistic philosophers upon our education system. It would seem to be much more logical to explain the human body and its operations in the terms of itself and its maker and demonstrate the workings of a machine in the terms of the human body.

The body is, after all, so much older and should be, by this time, better known. However, the process was reversed because the materialistic philosophers of education were determined to engrave upon young minds the materialistic source of life. And so a few years ago, in the days before every moppet was a mechanic and cut his teeth on a monkey wrench, in every classroom of the nation there occurred daily the strange situation of the example that was supposed to clarify finding itself in need of clarification in the terms of the supposedly obscure object upon which the badly chosen analogy was guaranteed to shed floods of light. So before beginning our examination of the subject of life let us rid ourselves of any such materialistic notions that we may have absorbed from constant exposure to them. Life is not AT ALL like the action of a machine.

> Life is real, life is earnest and the grave is not
>   its goal
> Your heart is not a piston rod, your stomach is
>   no fire hole.

There is only one faint likeness between things that live and machines, and that is that they both move. But a stone given the proper impetus will move, and a cigar store Indian, given the proper conditions, might jump upon you from behind and lay you low with a powerful blow from his extended fist with its handful of cheroots. So motion, you see, is a rather shadowy relationship. It does not make you a chip off the old rock or a blood brother to a cigar store Indian. The important thing about motion is not the motion itself but whence it comes. No non-living thing is "automotive" and the machine gets its power of motion from the same general source that the rolling and mossless portion of granite and the *el ropo* sachem get theirs, namely, from some agent outside of themselves.

Immanent Activity

But this real and earnest quality that is called life comes from no such outside agency. It is a strictly homemade product, that is, insofar as the eye can see. It comes from within the thing that is alive, and herewith we have the best definition of it. The boys who make a business of formulating definitions really got off a classic when they defined life. "Life," they tell us, "is immanent activity." When they have said that they have said about all that they know concerning its physical origin. They might and do go on to give long disquisitions upon it—where it is found, how it operates, who has it, under how many forms it manifests itself, etc., etc., but what the quality itself is has baffled them all. It is one of the common phenomena of the universe, so common that it is cheap. But in spite of its cheapness money cannot buy the most infinitesimal quantity. It is possessed by very lowly, extremely simple organisms; every living creature has it; the ant, the amoeba and the blade of grass, creatures which are incapable of guarding the secret of their precious possession, creatures that can be taken apart bit by bit, almost atom by atom, to see what makes them tick—but the source of the tick has eluded the most powerful microscopes, the most patient observation and the sharpest intellects.

Organisms have been patiently constructed in the laboratory under the best possible conditions, and every now and again some sensational journal or publicity hungry scholar will announce that life has at least been produced in the lab only to have the next edition inform a world waiting with bated breath that the report was exaggerated (which is a big word the journals like to use for a much simpler three letter word because it is harder to spell and makes them look like educated guys). And so the waiting public once more disappointed at the debut of the test-tube baby can unbait its breath and enjoy the funnies.

But even if some fine day life should be "manufactured" in the lab, which is not an impossibility, it would not be such an achievement after the immense expenditure of money and time and work. That bit of not-too-thickened water called the amoeba has been producing it for some time now at considerably less labor and expense. And it would prove only one thing—that the scientist by patiently copying nature's patent, one of the cruder patents, had succeeded in getting a shadow of nature's results. He still would not know where, from the physical standpoint, exactly it was. In explaining the origin and the nature of life the physical scientist has met and always will meet an unscalable and impenetrable stone-wall. The most reasonable explanation of it, and that is anything but definitive, is that formulated by Aristotle and revised and clarified by Saint Thomas Aquinas, both metaphysicians—the theory of hylomorphism. But that does not concern us here. The theory will form the subject of a later pamphlet.

Forms of Life

We will have to be content, then, with the brief definition of life for the while we examine it in the physical world. And "immanent activity," while it is but a scanty definition, is a gigantic dividing line. It, like the equator, separates the world into two parts; yea, it goes even farther and puts up a wall throughout the entire universe between the haves and the have-nots. And where is this immanent activity to be found? Investigation shows us that it can be found only in those creatures that are organic. Rocks and minerals do not possess it. Although rocks can grow by the accretion of crystals from without, no one ever made the mistake of thinking a rock a living thing; no one, I should have said who possesses his full quota of sanity and common sense, because the theory has been advanced. So these things that have motion and growth from within we call living.

Now there are many beings which possess such activity and they differ to such an extent that really the only relationship they seem to share in common is being and life. For example, the gap between an ant and an elephant is immense. And no one would be liable to classify even the shyest of men as a species of violet. Yet the distance between Saint Peter and Peter Rabbit is nowhere near as tremendous as the unbridgeable gap that separates Ambrose Amoeba and the water wherein he was spawned. But all things that live have two things in common. They grow and reproduce. These two conditions are the minimum requirements. These mysterious powers are possessed by the lowest form of life, plants. From this point the life scale rises to God Himself.

There is one thing that is to be observed as life goes up the scale because this observation composes, with the definition of life, one of the most important characteristics of living beings. Saint Thomas expresses it in the axiom: "The greater the immanent activity of a being the higher is the life it possesses." The truth of the principle is readily evident. The animal, which can move about in search of food, is obviously a more perfect being than the plant which is anchored. One need not be a genius to understand that the horse is a better being than the grass that it eats and the bird more perfect than bird-seed. The animal, then, is better off and more perfect because he has greater immanent activity. And in addition to such activity the animal also has sense perception. The dog can hear his master's whistle, he can feel heat and cold, for he is a sensitive being. This power does not come from outside the dog but from within. It is the result of immanent activity. And so on up the scale to man who, in addition to being sensitive, possesses the further capability, the result of immanent activity, of thinking.

Living God

Thus we come to the real point of the question, to which all we have so far said has been preface. Does God really have life or do we attribute life to Him as we attribute it to a stream when we speak of "the living water." Waters do not live, as any child knows, and when we use the term "living waters" we are but speaking in figures. Is the term "living God" likewise a figure of speech? Is Saint John also using figurative language when he writes "In Him was life?" It certainly seems as though there can be no life in God. Life, as we can see by just looking about us, exists only in organic beings. But God has no organism. How then can He have life? We have also seen that only those things have life that move about. But certainly there can be no motion in God because motion is change and change spells corruption.

On this point of life in God, Saint Thomas gets right down to business. Often in treating a problem Thomas clears the way for the solution with one or more distinctions and delays the statement of his doctrine until the middle or the end of the article. Here he comes out flatly in the very first line with the uncompromising assertion, minus any qualifying *videtur:* "Life is in the highest degree properly in God."

We have seen that life is immanent activity. That and that alone constitutes the quality known as life. There is nothing in that phrase to suggest that an organism is absolutely necessary for the existence of life. Of course there is the argument that all the life that we know by means of our senses works through an organism. But that still is no argument that life cannot exist without such an organism. As a matter of fact, if the organism were an essential condition for the existence of life, the more organism a creature had the more perfect it would be. But this is not the case. If it were, a tree would be a higher form of life than some animals, and such is not the fact. If organism were the all important thing an elephant would be superior to a man.

No, it is activity, of the immanent variety, that constitutes life, and beings are graded according to the quality of that activity through which life operates. If the organism itself created life, life could not have remained the mysterious thing it is. But, as we have seen, the laboratory and the dissecting room have failed to trace down the origin of life in even the most simple organism.

Another proof of the instrumental rather than efficient role played by the organism in the causation of life is the fact that spiritual life operates through a material organism. The brain of man is not composed of a super-special kind of material. The brain of man contains no rare chemicals that can be found nowhere else on earth. From the standpoint of material there is no reason why the brain of a horse or the brain of an elephant should not be as capable of producing thought as the human brain. But they are not. Matter, then, cannot be the *sine qua non* for the existence of life.

Material Not Required

It is necessary, too, that we remember a point that has been developed in previous pamphlets, namely, that activity does not necessarily mean change. We have seen that change, far from being necessary for activity, is an imperfection connected with it. It has been demonstrated previously that the higher the activity the less the change involved in it, until we come to God, who being pure act, suffers no change. The lion, to get his dinner, must indulge in a considerable amount of activity, physical activity that involves continual change. However, there is far less "motion" and physical change in and for the poet writing a sonnet. Yet which is the superior activity?

A further indication of superior activity is the amount of self-determination possessed by the agent. A plant has no choice as to the form of its activity. If it does not fancy one particular spot it cannot pull up its roots and move on. (As a matter of fact it cannot even "fancy," so limited is its activity.) The tendency of its nature towards good, of course, will cause a plant to do some remarkable things. It will sink its roots to a remarkable depth to find water. It will become a "creeper" to obtain food. But this is not self-determination. The animal's self-determination is much greater. It can move about after its food and seek the shade for its siestas. But here again the self-determination is rigidly limited. As a matter of fact, it is not really self-determination but only a closer approach to it, for the animal is determined by its external stimuli. Man possesses self-determination of a much higher order. He has free will and can choose his own activity. But here too the self-determination to activity is limited. Man has free will, that is true. But man's free will is moved by God. And even below the direct action of God man is restrained in his self-determination by nature. Man must will his last end. The basis of his knowledge, first principles, are supplied him from the same source. Man is unable to declare himself free of the principle of contradiction.

These limitations to life decrease the higher we go up the scale. Finally, we arrive at God in whom there are no limitations of any sort. His activity is not limited because He is pure act. His intelligence is not retrained because He is all intellect. He is "that being whose act of understand is its very nature, and which, in what it naturally possesses, is not determined by another." And so, Thomas concludes, he must have life in its most perfect degree.

We Live in Him

And not only is God life but all life is from Him. He is the source of all life, and the trail left by life leads directly to Him. Not in the carcass of a cat or the microscopic residue of a desiccated oyster nor yet in the brain of man will the scientist find the secret of life because these, though they use life do not possess its secret. The secret of life can be found in God Who alone is life. Not only the man whose days are numbered by his doctor is living on borrowed time. We all live on borrowed time—and borrowed life. We are in reality destitute creatures who possess nothing, not even what we euphemistically refer to as "our own lives." Our lives most certainly are not "our own." What life we have God has loaned us for the duration. Those mystics in reverse, the thinkers who laid the foundation for communism, came very close to the mark when they, without the help of revelation, decreed that man is entitled to nothing, not even "his own" life. They missed the truth by an infinity, however, when they neglected to assign the ownership of man and all that he is to that being to whom it properly belongs— God. For it is in Him, through Him, and with Him that we live, are, and have our being.

Philosophers Mentioned in Text

René Descartes was born at La Haye, Touraine, France, in 1596. He received his education from the Jesuits at La Flèche. Upon leaving La Flèche in 1612 he went to Paris where he remained until 1617 when he became a soldier in the army of Prince Maurice of Nassau. Upon leaving the army he took up residence in Holland in 1629 and began to write extensively on philosophy and mathematics. In 1637 he published the *Discours de la méthode* and this was followed by *Meditationes de Prima Philosophia* in 1641 and *Principia Philosophiae* in 1644. At the invitation of Queen Christina of Sweden he went to Stockholm in 1649. But life in the court of that Amazon was too strenuous for Descartes, and he died early the following year.

Although Descartes, the father of modern philosophy, by his writings laid the foundations for practically ever vicious philosophical error of the modern world, he himself always remained a sincere and devout Catholic, and he died firmly believing that his work had advanced the cause of truth.

Basing his philosophic system upon the principle of methodic doubt, that is the refusal to accept any of the principles or doctrines taught by previous philosophers, Descartes finally arrived at the principle which he considered must be the foundation for all philosophy, his famous and ridiculous *"Cogito, ergo sum"*—I think, therefore I am. Having thus proved his own existence Descartes proceeded to prove the existence of God and finally of the external world.

Having got off to a flying start on the road to unreality, the French mathematician continued his headlong course. He decided that God was the only true substance. However, he reasoned, since mind and matter need only the cooperation of God for their existence, they too, for want of a better term, might be called substances. But they are substances that are totally different because thought is essence of mind and extension the essence of matter. By this reasoning he evolved his doctrine of the dualism of substance.

In psychology the teachings of Descartes were equally vicious. It was he who first popularized the teaching that the body is a machine, carrying into operation impulses received from the soul. For Descartes there was no union between the body and soul of man. The soul had its residence in the pineal gland from which it directs the operations of the body. In this "angelism" of Descartes is the foundation for extreme subjectivism and idealism on the one hand and crass materialism on the other. As a matter of fact his whole system reads like a compendium of modern errors. The influence of this studious Frenchman, indeed, has probably been more pernicious than that of the majority of false philosophers in the history of thought.

Georg Wilhelm Friedrich Hegel, an intellectual descendant of Descartes through Kant, was born at Stuttgart in 1770. At the age of eighteen he entered the theological seminary (Protestant) of Tubingen where he devoted himself to a study of Kant and Rousseau. Leaving the seminary he earned his living as a private tutor from 1793–1800; these years he read extensively in Greek literature. In 1801 he entered the University of Jena where he was made professor extraordinary in 1805. In 1807 he published his *Phänomenologie des Geistes,* his first important philosophical work.

In 1816 appeared his *Logik*. Before his death in 1831 he taught both at Heidelberg and Berlin. Hegel was an absolute idealist. His "greatest" contribution to thought and the achievement with which his name is linked is the development of the principle of dialectic. The dialectic of Hegel simply stated is this: Not only thought, as maintained by Kant, but everything that exists must be in conformity with and develop according to the triad of thesis, antithesis and synthesis. This, in non-technical language means that from the clash of a being with its opposite a new being is developed. The classic example of this, according to Hegel, is the Holy Trinity (which, however, was not holy to Hegel) The Father (thesis), the Son (antithesis) and the Holy Ghost (synthesis). Another basic example of the universal application of the law is sexual generation wherein the clash of the male (thesis) with the female (antithesis) produces the offspring (synthesis).

Ludwig Feuerbach, a minor German philosopher (1804–1872), owes his fame to his contribution in applying the dialectic of Hegel to the materialistic philosophy of his day and thus preparing the way for

Karl Marx (1818–1883) who as a philosopher was a pigmy but was of some importance as a propagandist. Marx, intrigued with Dialectic Materialism, used the theory to explain class struggle and the inevitable triumph of the proletariat.

STUDY QUESTIONS

I. Truth

1) Does truth exist only in the ideal world?

2) What is the object of knowledge?

3) What does the author mean when he says that the question of truth is more fundamental than that of God?

4) What is the doctrine of indifferentism?

5) What is the scholastics' definition of truth?

6) How does a denial of the existence of truth lead to a denial of the existence of God?

7) What is "ontological" truth?

8) What is "logical" truth?

9) Can we say "God knows truth"? or "God is truth"?

10) Is falsity imputed to the intellect or the senses?

II. Life of God

1) Does not immutability make God inert?

2) Is it reasonable to describe life after the example of a machine?

3) Define life.

4) Can man create life?

5) What is the difference between plants, animals and men?

6) Is there really life in God?

7) Does life need an organism?

8) Does free will make man free from the principle of contradiction?

9) Who was Descartes?

10) Who was Hegel?

Beyond Lies God

A Consideration of the Divine Will

REGINALD COFFEY, O.P.

Introduction

This is the eighth in a series of pamphlets designed to acquaint the laity with the theology of the Church, and published under the auspices of the Holy Name Society. It is based upon the *Summa Theologiae* of Saint Thomas and treats of the Divine Will.

If you are interested in the series, we urge you to obtain the preceding numbers because while each pamphlet is complete in itself, it is part of an integrated and systematic survey of the whole of Catholic theology.

THE WILL OF GOD

God Through Human Eyes

Voltaire, the French cynic, once declared that if God made man in His image, man has certainly returned the favor, because men have been making God in man's image ever since. Voltaire can be credited with few remarks in which there is more truth.

Man in describing God has been forced, so to speak, to make God in the image of man—anthropomorphize is the two-bit word—because of the limitations of human language. Man has made God, who has no face, to smile. He has made Him, who has no arms, to wield the sword of justice. He has described the Deity, who can have no passions, as a God of wrath. The Almighty Creator, we are told, made the world with His hands. In the old days, we read in Holy Scripture, God walked upon the earth. And even Our Blessed Lord has Him speaking in human language at the last judgment when He will say, "Depart from me, ye cursed, into everlasting fire which was prepared for the devil and his angels from all eternity."

To describe God in such terms is necessary if we are to describe Him at all. We must, in a manner of speaking, cut Him down to our size. The necessity of this anthropomorphization (take a deep breath on that one) will be made clearer to the reader if he will notice that we have used the words "He" and "Him" in reference to God several times thus far in this pamphlet. And yet God has no sex.

Now the error that has arisen by this necessity of referring to God in human terms is this: Some say that man has created a god in his own mind and endowed that deity with human traits. Every attribute of God, they say, is some human quality raised to the *nth* degree to fit the deity. This is the claim of the deists who admit the existence of some force but deny it personality, and this is the real meaning of Voltaire's remark with which we opened this discussion. The reasonable interpretation which we put upon this remark was not intended by its author who was a deist.

Rationalists

Among the faculties with which man has endowed God, say these smart boys, are the peculiarly human faculties of intelligence and will. Now the reader who has followed this series thus far knows that Catholic theology attributes nothing to God merely out of the urge to make Him man-like. As a matter of fact the reader has witnessed Saint Thomas, following truth like a hound on a scent, attribute to God qualities that were decidedly un-human such as simplicity, eternity, immutability and infinity—attributes that, from the emotional standpoint, remove Him farther from us. But the big difference between Thomas and fellows of the stripe of Voltaire, who, incidentally, had the brass to call themselves "rationalists," was that Thomas used his reason. Thomas was a real rationalist. It is a pity that many who assumed that title as their own during the eighteenth and nineteenth centuries threw the word into disrepute by adopting it.

We do not even have to rely upon the negative approach to prove that God has intelligence and will. As a matter of fact the reader who has been following this series from the beginning will probably wonder why it is necessary to devote two whole pamphlets of the series to proving intelligence and will in God because in the second pamphlet, wherein the existence of God was demonstrated, His very existence was proved by the fact of His intelligence, and the fact that he possesses a will is inseparable from the fact that He is intelligent. An intelligent being must have a will as surely as a smile must have a face or that water to be water must have the *H2* as well as the *0*. The pamphlets devoted to the intelligence and will of God are not intended to establish the tact or God's intelligence and will. They are concerned primarily with a discussion of the nature of the Divine intelligence and will. Is God's intelligence and will like ours? If not, why not? What are they like? How do they operate? These questions and others concerning the Divine intelligence were answered in a previous pamphlet. The same questions concerning the Divine will form the subject matter of the present.

Poor God

Before entering upon a discussion of God's will, it is necessary to clarify a matter of terminology. Throughout this paper we shall refer to God's having this or having that for the purpose of convenience or to avoid circumlocution. But strictly speaking the possessive case can never be correctly applied to God. In a sense God is the poor man of the universe. He possesses nothing. He has no mercy. He has no justice. He has no truth. God *has* nothing. He IS mercy. He IS justice. He IS truth. God is everything. "Having" implies potentiality, and in God there is no potency as in our terminology. Potency means something unfulfilled or unrealized. Being all perfect He is entirely in act. And since this is the case, everything attributed to Him is attributed to His essence, and since in His essence there can be no imperfection, the qualities attributed to Him are His essence.

There is in every creature a tendency toward the good, good which is desirable and which will perfect the creatures' being. The river, its channel blocked, will gouge a new channel. The flower unfolds its petals to the sun because to it the sun means life. The bee will literally fly its wings off to collect nectar. The dog goes sniffing after the butcher-cart. All of these creatures are propelled to the desirable good by an urge which they cannot resist; drawn to that which will benefit their natures as irresistibly as the needle is drawn to the pole. Only man, of all creatures in the cosmos, can choose the good he desires and the means to obtain it. Of course, the dog can be conditioned not to go loping after the butcher's wagon. The toe of the butcher's boot, for instance, would be an excellent conditioner. The bee may even be conditioned not to rob the flowers of their sweetness. But this tendency to the good in man is conditioned only by the reasoning faculty.

The Will of God

So God, being intelligent, must be attracted to the good as an intelligent being is attracted, not in the blind way in which the animal's appetite is drawn; and this wide-eyed tendency to good we call will. Now, although the tendency of moderns is to deny free will, there are still those who, while they admit it in man, would deny it to God. These say that if God is perfect He cannot have a will because a will seeks after good and since God is all good He cannot seek after that which He already has.

These people labor under a false idea of the nature of the will. The will tends to good that is possessed as well as to good for which we are striving. The will of man is not always hard at work striving; sometimes it can sit back and revel in the good it already has. Otherwise how could we explain love. In God, unlike man, the will never strives after absent good. God's will is like a man in retirement. It is always enjoying the good it possesses. Unlike man God finds all good in Himself, and therefore the fact that God has a will does not imply that He is mutable and changing, for His will can be "moved" only by His own goodness, and this is not motion at all, strictly speaking, because the whole action, which occurs within the Divine essence, is eternal.

The fact that God finds all goodness in Himself, and that His will is His essence, naturally brings to the mind another question. Such being the case, it would not seem possible for God to will things apart from Himself which, to all practical effects, would make Him feeble rather than omnipotent. If God is concerned with willing His own goodness how can His will act upon things outside of Himself? How, for instance, can God will anything concerning us? Surely we are not part of the Divine essence. And if we are, that makes us all gods which, by the way, smacks of pantheism. However Thomas considers this angle of the problem. In answer to the question proposed, Aquinas responds that God can will things apart from Himself. In defending this stand he points out that all natural things in tending to good are concerned not only with their own proper good, ". . . to acquire it if not possessed, and, if possessed, to rest therein; but also to spread abroad their own good amongst others, so far as possible."

Goodness Diffuses Itself

The tree for instance sends its seeds abroad upon the wings of the wind. The bee with his insatiable appetite for nectar is not only enjoying itself but is gathering the materials to make honey which will feed the young bees during the winter after its own brief life is spent, worn out by work. The blossom where the bee sucks his sweets deposits upon his hairy legs pollen wherewith other blossoms are fertilized and so it, too, spreads its good abroad. And in man this tendency to diffuse the good he possesses is almost irresistible. It pertains to the nature of the will to communicate to others as far as possible the good possessed.

This desire to communicate good possessed is characteristic of the Divine will also. Indeed it pertains especially to the Divine will because such a tendency or characteristic is a perfection, and this like every other perfection is possessed to the full by God alone. God is the only goodness, and were He not to diffuse His goodness, it would be impossible to find this quality outside of Him. Or, if you would reduce the question to stark reality, if God did not communicate His goodness there would be nothing else existing in which goodness could be found for the simple reason that there would be nothing else in existence. Not only the universe and all the creatures thereof are examples of God's ability and desire to communicate His goodness, but Heaven and its population also bear witness to the truth. As far as God Himself was concerned He could have gotten along without the universe and all it contains. He could very easily have dispensed with the caroling and harp playing of the angelic choirs. He was perfectly happy all by Himself. He needed nothing to increase His contentment. He created angels and men not for His own sake but for theirs. He wanted others to share His own goodness.

What God Cannot Do

This consideration of God's willing His own goodness and willing things outside of Himself to share in that goodness brings us to a very interesting point. Paradoxical as it may seem, there are some things that almighty God cannot do. And one of these things that God is unable to do is to refrain from willing His own goodness. This inability on the part of God is no contradiction of His omnipotence. God can still do anything that can be done. The goodness of God is the one object that is adequate to His infinite perfection. He must will it. It is God's happiness and He is as much bound to will it as man is bound to will his own happiness, for the will, whether that will be Divine or human, has as necessary a relation to its proper object which is happiness as any other faculty has a necessary relation to its proper object. Just as the eye to see must see color which is its proper object, so the will must will happiness—even the Divine will.

But things apart from Himself God is not bound to will. They are ordained to the Divine goodness as to an end and in willing an end even we can pick and choose the means. So why not God? For instance, to preserve life we must eat but we do not have to eat spinach all the time. We can vary our diet at the dictate of our wills. To get from Washington to New York we have to make a journey. We cannot get there by just wishing we were there. But in making the journey we are not restricted to taking a train. We can fly or we can go by water or, if we so will and are of a rugged constitution or a member of a hiking group, we can walk. "Hence," says Saint Thomas, "the goodness of God since it is perfect, and can exist without other things inasmuch as no perfection can accrue to Him from them, it follows that He is not bound to will things apart from Himself."

Let Us Pray

But there is an exception to this rule. There is one case where God must will things which are apart from Himself. Once God has willed a thing apart from Himself, then that thing must stay willed, for God's will cannot change. When spiritual writers call God "the unchanging friend" they are not guilty of exaggeration, or of too free use of the imagination. God is the one being in which there is absolutely no change. Which, incidentally, brings up another interesting point. If this be so, if God cannot change His will, once having willed, what about prayer? What good is it? If God's will be immutable then, Sir, or Madame (as the case may be), when you spend time on your knees in prayer, time that you would much rather spend doing something else, mayhap, what are you doing besides wearing out your pants at the knees or encouraging the appearance of runs in your new silk stockings? What is the use of wasting all of this time in trying to get God to change His mind and His will? Then, too, what is the use of going to Church at all to worship Christ Who was evidently a false prophet, for He Himself told us to pray. "If you ask the Father anything in My name," said Jesus, "He will give it to you."

This is an old objection. If you and I had a nickel for every time it has been uttered or written, our income tax would be about the size of Henry's Ford's. The complete answer to the objection does not pertain to this pamphlet. According to the outline and the schedule of publication that has been drawn up you will receive the full answer to the objection about ten years hence. But since the Holy Name Bureau has no intention of employing the tactics of the serial movie and since it is not our intention to have people stop praying until the publication of the pamphlet treating that excellent exercise, we will clarify the point briefly here.

What Is To Be

First, let us state the objection as it most commonly occurs. We cannot change the will of God, and so prayer is a foolish thing. If God has willed that I am going to get killed crossing the street, there is no use to pray to Him for protection in crossing the street. I can pray until I am blue in the face, and I will still be killed. For God has willed it and His will does not change. Before answering the objection positively let us reduce it to its utter absurdity. Following the same line of argumentation, it is just as reasonable to say that no activity is necessary upon our part. If God has willed that we go to the store to buy dinner for the family we don't have to move a muscle. Just let us stay where we are, and God will see to it that we are whisked off to the store in our rocking chairs. As a matter of fact, if God has willed the family to have dinner He will see to it that they have dinner. It won't even be necessary for you to go to the store. It won't even be necessary for you to cook the dinner. In fact, the members of the family won't even have to eat the dinner! God has willed for them to have dinner. They will have dinner whether or not they cooperate. However, if Pop sits in all dignity at the table waiting for the lamb chop that ain't there to jump into his mouth he is surely, before long, to experience a very open and evident hunger.

The fundamental reason why we pray is identical with the reason why we help God carry out His will in the business of eating. God has granted to us a share in the Divine causality. He has made us His helpers in the business of running the universe. God is the first cause, but it is not His intention to be the whole show. He has granted to secondary causes the power to act and share the spotlight. Now man is a secondary cause not only in the physical but in the moral order. The action of bringing the lamb chop to our mouths enables us, acting as God's agents, to sustain life in our bodies. Prayer plays a similar role in the moral order. When we pray we are not changing the will of God; we are fulfilling it. God has willed from all eternity that Jane Jones will save her soul by praying salvation. From away back when time was not He saw Tommy Smith, and He decreed that Tommy would receive the grace to overcome the temptation to commit adultery by praying. And like the world which He created God saw that it was good and He said "Let it be done."

God Wills It!

The will of God is as important a part of the divine nature as the will of man is of human nature. Without a will, supposing that God could be God without a will, there would be nothing in existence outside of God. If God were merely a force or an intelligence without a will, as some philosophers have said, the world and man and everything else existing apart from Him could not be. For God's causality is to be found in His will as man's causality is to be found in his.

Then Saint Thomas considers the Divine Will as the cause of things. The treatise is aimed principally at those who claim that God acts by necessity, that He has no control over the things He does. Those who argue after this fashion would reduce God to the level of the animal, which, lacking intelligence, acts without choice but rather from instinct. This, of course, is absurd and once intelligence and will have been established in God the objection is already answered. The only reason why Thomas devotes any attention to the objection at all is because it was a rather popular one in his time and was argued very cleverly from the dialectic standpoint and "proved" by some fancy metaphysics. In addition to this the proponents of the theory found a quotation or two from Saint Augustine and Saint Denis which seemed to back them up.

Strange as it may seem to the modern mind the argument which was advanced by the Averroists caught on at the University of Paris where the intellectual atmosphere had been somewhat polluted by Arabian philosophy. We would just be tilting with windmills in going into a discussion of the point. We merely note it in passing for the sake of the record, just to inform the reader that there were people who conceded to God not only existence but intelligence and will and denied causality to the Divine will. If there is an Averroist in the crowd the author will be willing argue the point by mail.

Free Will

However, there is a point concerning the Divine will which is quite as important a question in our day as it was in the time of Aquinas—the apparent clash that occurs between the will of God and the will of man. Reduced to its simplest terms the problem, and it is a problem, might be stated as follows: If God is all powerful and if every created thing is moved by Him, how is it possible for the will of man to be free? The will of man is created by God and as a created being it comes under His power. Where then is its freedom? Or stated in another way: If the will of man is free, how can God possibly be called omnipotent since here is one created being not subject to His power? Here is one being exempt from the direction and causality of the Divine will.

It is not within the province of the present writer to prove human freedom; that comes within the scope of another treatise. So for the present the reader will presume, as he always has presumed, that the human will is free. He knows that he can lay down this pamphlet or not just as he chooses; he realizes that he is free to remain seated or go out for a walk. So asking the reader to presume the freedom of the will is not subjecting his good nature to too much of a strain.

Handled With Care

The point to be proved here is that freedom does not exempt the will from God's eternal and all pervading power. Freedom does not take the will out of the class of creatures. It does, to be sure, put it into a special class and label it SPECIAL HANDLING but it still remains an inert article in the baggage depot of the universe and cannot move until it is moved by the eternal station master. Of course the station master always takes cognizance of the label which He himself pasted upon this invaluable article that is the human will, and in moving it He always moves it in a very special way. He may "smash" the other baggage in the station in an off-hand sort of way, but when He comes to moving this special article, He puts on a white pair of kid gloves; for this article, the human will, must always be moved in one precise way. It must be and can only be moved FREELY. So the Divine station master always respects the rights which He himself has granted to the human will. He never moves it otherwise than freely. He has the greatest respect for this precious article.

The omnipotence of the will of God has already been established; the freedom of man's will is presupposed. The question to be treated here, then, is how to reconcile the apparent contradiction. How can God be omnipotent if man is free? How can man be free if God is omnipotent? It is necessary to warn the reader before beginning this discussion that a complete and satisfactory solution to the problem will not be found in this pamphlet. Such a solution cannot be found in the *Opera Omnia* of Saint Thomas Aquinas or the theological or philosophical works of any other great writer.

Answered in Heaven

Do not expect, after reading this treatise to be able to solve all the questions the insurance man, the ice-man, or your stenographer may have on the subject the next time you see them. Don't be like Abelard or Alain de Lille who were two very smart men, so smart in their own estimation in fact, that they thought that they could prove the Trinity. Like the Trinity, the exact way in which God moves the free will of man is a mystery, and like the Trinity we will discover the answer only on that day when we pass through the pearly gates and behold the vision of God. But since the reason for studying theology is not so we can go home and stump grandpa with some tough questions and make him gaze and make his wonder grow that such a tiny head could carry all we know, but rather to learn a few inside facts about God for our own good, speculation upon the reasonability of a mystery is not taboo.

It is quite legitimate to try to figure out how it is possible for one nature to contain three persons and so too is it all on the up and up to try to find a reasonable explanation for a free will being moved by a force outside itself. Maybe the explanation will be above our heads and we will be tempted to characterize it as "just a lot of stuff." It is quite human to label things beyond our grasp as "a lot of stuff." But whether or not we so characterize the explanation offered for this problem, let us remember that these two facts are true and incontrovertible; depending upon nobody's opinion and needing nobody's explanation, for they are eternal truths revealed by God Himself—*God is all powerful; and the human will is free.*

The Way of Freedom

The word "freedom" as it refers to the will means choice, devoid of necessity, of the means to an end. For instance, I can go from Washington to New York by plane, train, water, horseback, ox-cart, automobile, or on foot. Suppose I choose to go by train. I can take the *B & O* or the *Pennsylvania* and between these two lines I can pick any one of twenty-five or so trains a day. But I am really not compelled to go to New York at all. If I choose, I can stay in Washington. Now this act of the will in choosing is a change or motion from capacity to choose to actual choice, from indetermination to determination. It is evident that the capacity remains under its determination; that is to say, I can leave Washington and start out for New York anytime I wish. But I cannot be determined to a choice and free to choose at the same time. In other words, I cannot leave Washington and stay there at the same time. Now any attempt ever made to explain the fact of human freedom on grounds other than divine action have succeeded only in destroying that freedom and establishing fatalism. And some very clever lads have taken a crack at the problem. Descartes, Spinoza, William James, Kant, and Bergson, to mention only a few, have tried it. Their efforts ended only in confusion, intellectual nihilism, fatalism—in a word, chaos.

Let us examine the possibility of the will moving itself from capacity for action to act with no other agent having any part in the motion. If such were the case three courses, all fatalistic, are open to us. The first dilemma: The will in this case is at the same time undetermined (as the fact of freedom demands) and determined (as the fact of choice requires). The will is potentially choosing and actually choosing all at the same time. This leaves the will right in the middle between the devil and the deep blue sea. It leads directly to nihilism. It is the same mistake that is made by those who claim that the world came out of nothing all by itself. It is a denial of causality or the possibility of causality, for if determination comes from indetermination without causality, then something can come from nothing the same way; because that is precisely what we admit if we admit a self-moving will.

The second course offers you a will that is always determined. Man is moved by some necessary instinct, and so all possibility of freedom is ruled out. There is no such thing as morality because man can be lord of his actions no more than the dog who follows the butcher-cart or the steel which is drawn to the magnet.

The third course gives us a will that is never determined. Action is impossible. Existence is impossible. Beginning is impossible. You're impossible. I'm impossible. In fact everything is impossible. Nothing is everything. Everything is nothing. We are impossibly living impossible lives in the most impossible of impossible worlds. Sounds like Gertrude Stein. If the will moves itself, it must move in one of these three ways. If you wish to hold that the will does move itself you may pick what seems to you to be the most logical or illogical. But you may not have your cake and eat it. You cannot have a self-moving will and have freedom too. Name your poison, chum. But remember that in making your choice a free will cannot be self-moving.

Now let us consider another possibility. Let us suppose that the will is moved by an outside force but not by God. In this supposition we have the will being changed from capacity to choice by some external object or set of circumstances. When acted upon by a particular object or by such and such a chain of circumstances the will must act. But such action cannot be free, for these movers force it into acting. If this is what you want, then take it, but don't claim that you are a free agent. You are bound in a slavery that is worse than annihilation for an intelligent being. This alternative is no better than that offered by a self-moving will.

Only God Can Make One Free

Now since the will cannot move itself and retain its freedom, since it cannot be moved by anything outside itself but God and possess liberty, then God must move the will. And being God, the omnipotent, He can move the will and move it so that it moves freely. But this is not a direct proof, and the case is of too much importance to let it go with indirect proof if a direct proof can be produced. The frontal attack is always more satisfying than a flanking maneuver, even though the latter may suffice for victory. The direct proof of God's movement of the human will runneth thus: Since God Is the first cause, every being, every movement in creation depends upon Him. The birds of the air, the lilies of the field, the hairs of your head, yes, and even the wink of your eye depends upon the prime mover.

Let us consider this last movement, the wink, as illustrative of that motion. This slight movement that closes the eye for a split second can be completely under our control or completely beyond it. The eye winks involuntarily many times an hour to rest the organ of sight. The lids of your eye will close spontaneously when a blow is aimed at the delicate mechanism they protect. But these lids can be deliberately closed. They can veil the eye of a practical joker as he warns his audience of his victim's approach to the trap. Lowered teasingly over the provocative eyes of a coquette they assume a different meaning. It is clear then that one can wink either from necessity or from choice. One type of wink you can't control; for the other you are directly and fully responsible. Now in the case of the controlled wink, not only the wink but its freedom came from God, the first cause, for both freedom and necessity are realities and therefore fall under His causality. So, not only the act but the mode of the act; that is, its necessity or freedom, must come from Him. For these modes, freedom and necessity, being realities, cannot come of themselves from nothingness. And, in the case of the free act, unless that freedom be caused by God, it cannot exist.

So to summarize what has been said of the motion exercised by God on the will: the universal efficacy of the divine motion is not destructive of human liberty. It is, in fact, the only factor which preserves it. Just as it is the only explanation of the existence of the world, the facts that night must fall and the moon must rise; so too, it is the sole adequate reason that can be given for the freedom that belongs by divine decree to the race of sub-angels known as men. God is the cause of all existing natures and the cause, likewise, of every act produced by those natures. He, the First Mover, moves all things according to the natures with which He endowed them. The river flows of necessity, the bee flies because it has to, and, man wills freely. But God moves them all. How can man move freely? Well, that is another question—one that cannot be answered on this side of the Great Divide. We know He does move freely, and we know that God moves him. The secret of how it is done you will learn on that day when you will see Him not now as in a glass darkly but face to face.

Problem of Evil

There is another point on the causality of God that seems to perturb a great many people. If God is the cause of everything, then He must be the cause of the evil existing in the world. Take, for instance, the example cited above: the wink of the coquette's eye. That wink could be an invitation to sin. That wink could be an evil thing. God caused the wink. Then He must also be the cause of the sin. The murderer would not be able to pull the trigger of his gun if God did not move him to it. God moves the will in every sin as in every good act. Therefore God is the cause of sin. It is God who guides the hand that signs the declaration of unjust wars. Therefore God is responsible for all the heartaches visited upon sorrowing mothers. It is He who must be blamed for all the woes visited upon afflicted peoples. And finally since God is the cause of all things He quite deliberately plunges the lost soul, a soul lost through the sin committed by God, into Hell. Where, then, is your merciful God, the Father of all? Is not this Being who is the cause of all sin and evil rather a sadistic monster than a benign protector? The objections are not new. Saint Thomas away back in the thirteenth century had heard them all.

The answer can be given in a short sentence. It is impossible for God, who is all good, to will evil. But listen to this. It is even more revealing. It is impossible for man to will evil as such. And not only the will of God and the will of man cannot tend to evil but even the brutes of the fields are unable to tend to evil as such. But (and here's the sad side of the picture), "Nevertheless evil may be sought accidentally, so far as it accompanies a good, as appears in each of the appetites . . . when a lion kills a stag, his object is food, to obtain which the killing of the animal is only the means."

Whence Sin?

Now since no one can question the fact that evil exists, let us see if we can find where it comes from, since nobody seems to will it, neither God, nor man, nor beast. But first it will be necessary to get a clear idea of what evil is. You have heard this before, but it will bear repeating. The only evil that exists is sin. Do not think from that statement that I am laboring under the delusion that a cancer of the stomach is a delight to be sought after, but it is not essentially evil. However, we will give consideration to physical evil after we have disposed of the important part of this question which is the problem of God seemingly willing and man willing sin.

It is almost as hard to understand how man can will sin (which he does) as it is to grasp how God could will sin (which He doesn't and can't). All through this essay we have stressed that fact that the will can incline only towards good. Where, then, is the possibility of sin? Well, as a matter of fact, in the question of sin itself the will does not tend toward evil. When the will chooses evil it is because it has been duped by the intellect. The will is infallible in its choice of the good but it is a blind faculty which can only follow the directions of the intellect. It can never pick its own course. A great philosopher has compared the intellect and the will to two men, one, the intellect, riding on the shoulders of the other. Now the intellect can see, but it cannot walk; the lower man, the will, can walk, but it cannot see. Together they can get places with the intellect doing the steering and the will furnishing the motive power. The will has complete trust in the honesty of the intellect and will go unquestioning where it guides. So in the case of sin the blame must fall upon the dishonesty of the intellect. The intellect realizes that the action is evil, yet, smooth persuader that it is, it convinces the will that it is good.

Blind Will

To use the example of the two men to illustrate the point. Let us imagine that they are resting in the shade on their journey through life. Suddenly the intellect sees the woman, Sin. Now this gal has her points, and she immediately catches the intellect's eye. He sees that she has regular features and is well formed, and from the distance she appears very fair. But as she comes closer, her bad points show up. As she approaches, the intellect sees that her hair is not hair at all but is made up of live and very poisonous snakes; that her eyes are not blue or brown or grey but a bright and vivid red.

Yet, in spite of this, the intellect still feels himself attracted, so he wants to be near her. Being unable to walk he knows that he must sell his proposition to his blind companion. He also knows that this companion would be nauseated if he knew about the red eyes and the snakes, so in his description he omits these two rather unattractive features and describes only the lady's good features. The will, hearing the description, feels himself decidedly attracted and being a man of action he says to his trusted partner, "Well, pal, she sure sounds as though she would be a charming companion on this long dull day. Time's a-wastin'. What are we waiting for?" And hoisting the dishonest cripple upon his shoulders off he goes. That short drama might be entitled THE BIRTH OF SIN.

Freedom Permits Sin

These are the parts played by the will and the intellect in sin. Now where does God come in? We know that no matter what good or apparent good the intellect holds up to the will, the will cannot move unless moved by God. God moves the will to action but He does not choose the object of that action. When He created man He gave him an intellect to take care of this detail. He endowed that intellect with the power of knowing truth. In selecting the false the intellect does so deliberately. No fault can be imputed to God if the intellect betrays its creator.

The danger that lies in this attempt to explain the roles played by the intellect and will is that of over-simplification. In this description we have separated entirely the parts they act. As a matter of fact they are mutually very much dependent one upon the other, and it is difficult to discern where the action of one leaves off and the other begins. But what we have said here is a generally accurate account of the part played by each and detours us around a very long and very metaphysical discourse dealing with their mutual interdependence. Also while we are picking up the loose threads there is this point to be understood. In assigning the role of director to the intellect we do not intend to attribute to it independence of the divine motion. The intellect is, of course, not independent of it. It might best be put this way: God gives the intellect the power to see, but He does not do its seeing.

Now that we have proved that God's skirts are clean of all the dirt that is the evil of sin, let us see if we can determine what is His responsibility for the existence of physical evil. "The evil of natural defect, or of punishment," says Saint Thomas, "He does will by willing the good to which such evils are attached. Thus in willing justice He wills punishment; and in willing the preservation of the natural order, He wills some things to be naturally corrupted."

The Evil in Evil

By way of illustration of this teaching, let us take the case of John Jones. John Jones is walking by a precipice one day when a rock which has been loosened from its moorings by the recent spring rains falls upon him and breaks his back. Poor Mr. Jones finds himself a helpless cripple for the rest of his life, suffering great agony. Jones begins to believe that he is the special object of God's vengeance. Because had he walked north instead of south on that fateful day he never would have been struck down—or would he? He is not sure on that last point. If he had walked south God would have hit him with something else. Jones begins to hate God, who, he believes, has treated him so unjustly. What about this case? Is Jones right in believing that God has unjustly afflicted him with great evil?

Now, it cannot be denied that what has happened to Jones is, from the natural standpoint, an evil. Neither can it be denied that the evil was willed by God who wills everything that happens. This is a case where God wills accidental evil to preserve substantial good. Let us examine more closely the events of the case. On that afternoon Mr. Jones chose, of his own free will, to walk north. Just as he was passing the cliff the rock fell upon him. Being there was Jones' doing; not God's. God moved the rock to fall, but He did not move it for the precise purpose of hitting Jones. God moved the rock according to its nature. The movement was good, not evil. God also moved Jones to walk north instead of south, but He also moved Jones according to his nature—freely. Nothing forced Jones to walk north. He could just as easily have walked south. Jones chose to walk north. The fact that the rock hit Jones was an unfortunate evil effect of God's good action. But, and note this, that effect was also willed by God, but it was not willed for itself. It was willed as the inevitable accompaniment of the good acts of moving Jones and the rock each according to its nature.

Salvation of John Jones

However, while the breaking of Jones' back was unquestionably a physical evil, it was not necessarily bad for Jones. Let us proceed with the untold part of the story. The reason why Jones decided to walk north instead of south that day was because he was carrying on an affair with Jane Doe, the wife of John Doe, and since John was out of town for the afternoon, Jones decided that it would be a good opportunity for him and his partner in sin to put one over on the old man. The falling rock stopped Jones not only that day but forever. Confined to his bed of pain, Jones, after his first useless cursing of God, began to think. Lying there helplessly in bed, cared for by his faithful wife who, incidentally, knew all about his affair with Mrs. Doe, Jones had plenty of time to review his life. The result was that he forgot his bitterness and began to thank God for the opportunity He had given him for repentance. Before he died Jones, by making use of the evil with which he had been afflicted, became a very holy man. You see the falling rock and the evil that accompanied it was only a minor incident in a long story with many intertwined plots, the story which we will call THE SALVATION OF JOHN JONES. God had predestined Jones to eternal salvation. The falling was only a significant incident in the unfolding of the major plot.

That's okay, you may say, for men who can turn physical evil into moral good. But what about the poor animals upon which God inflicts pain and suffering seemingly for no other end? Well, the best reply to that difficulty is that that is one of the advantages in being a man and not a brute. The accidental evil of which they are victims for the preservation of substantial good cannot be turned into spiritual good by them as it can by man. That is unfortunately but necessarily so. However, even their evils can be turned into spiritual good for you. Because kindness to animals, when practiced for the right intention and not carried to irrational extremes (such, for instance, as neglecting your sick baby to take care of your sick cat) can be a virtue.

How Willing?

In the last article of the question Thomas picks up the loose threads. In it he considers whether or not the five expressions of will, namely, *prohibition, precept, counsel, operation,* and *permission,* can be assigned to the divine will. Because God's will is universal and efficacious, it might seem that it can be only the second of these two, i.e., preceptive or positive. It is easy to see how man wills in the other four ways. "A man may show that he wills something," says Saint Thomas, "either by himself or by means of another. He may show it by himself, by doing something directly, or indirectly." For example he directly wills to punch you in the nose when he does it himself. He indirectly wills it when he has his bodyguard punch you in the nose for him. He may not have told the bodyguard to let you have one, but the guard realizes that his boss has no use for you. And he was right. The boss gives him a twenty-five dollar bonus. Such an action of the will is called permissive will. However, if he told his bodyguard to do the job, that is more than permissive will. That would be preceptive will. If he said to the guard, "I'd like to have you punch this guy in the nose," that would be the will of counsel. But if the guard wants to punch you in the nose and his boss forbids it, that is the will of prohibition. In the first instance cited, where the man lands the punch himself, that, of course, is the will of operation.

Thy Will Be Done

Saint Thomas says that it is evident that God also works by these methods and not always by operation. "That permission, and operation are called the will of God is clear from the teaching of Saint Augustine who says, 'Nothing is done unless the Almighty will is to be done, either by permitting it or by actually doing it.'" Evil exists by the permissive will of God. "That precept, counsel and prohibition are called the will of God," says Thomas, "is clear from the words of the Our Father: Thy will be done on earth as it is in Heaven." But in God, Thomas teaches, the will of permission and operation refer to the present time, such as permission with respect to evil, and operation with regard to good. And as to the future time, prohibition is referred to evil, precept to good that is necessary, and counsel to good that is of supererogation.

This question has a bearing upon a thought that often crosses the minds of Catholics, and that is the will of God as regards their salvation. If God's will is always efficacious, then if you lose your soul it is because God has willed it. This makes God out to be a monster who creates souls only for the pleasure of plunging them into hell. Of course you cannot lose your soul against God's will. But it will be by the permissive will of God who will not rob man of his free will even for that thing He most desires—the salvation of souls. If you insist upon going to Hell you are, in a sense, tying God's hands. He will not destroy your free will, and He permits your damnation by an act of His permissive will. But always remember that "THIS IS THE WILL OF GOD—YOUR SANCTIFICATION."

STUDY QUESTIONS

I. Introduction

1) How does man make God to his own image and likeness?

2) How was Saint Thomas a rationalist?

3) Can God really possess anything?

4) How can God will anything concerning us?

5) Is it natural for the will to communicate goodness?

II. The Will of God

1) Why did God create anything?

2) Can God's will change?

3) Is prayer in vain?

4) Does God act by necessity?

5) How can the human will be free?

III. *The Divine and the Human Will*

1) What is the apparent contradiction between the divine and the human will?

2) What is meant by *freedom?*

3) What are the three possibilities of an independent free will?

4) Can freedom exist without God's causality?

5) Is God the cause of evil?

IV. *Good and Evil*

1) Whence comes evil?

2) What is the function of the intellect with the will?

3) How is God responsible for physical evil?

4) What are the five expressions of the will?

5) Does God will the soul's damnation?

9

When Mercy Seasons Justice
A Consideration of the Love, Justice and Mercy of God

Richard T. Murphy, O.P.

Introduction

This is the ninth in a series of pamphlets designed to acquaint the laity with the theology of the Church and the mercy of God as expounded in the twentieth and twenty-first questions of the Prima Pars of the *Summa Theologiae* of Saint Thomas Aquinas.

If you are interested in the series, we urge you to obtain the preceding numbers because while each pamphlet is complete in itself, it is part of an integrated and systematic survey of the whole of Catholic theology.

I. The Love of God

Eternal Quiz Program

Once upon a time there lived a boy by the name of Thomas Aquinas. One day, with all the unexpectedness of a child, he asked his mother an extraordinary question: "What is God?" Doubtless his mother gave him one of those all-satisfying answers mothers know how to give their children; perhaps her reply intrigued the young boy, for as he grew to manhood he became more and more interested in the question, instead of forgetting about it. Eventually his inquisitiveness blossomed out into the great *Summa Theologiae*. Few innocent questions have led to richer results.

The first important thing to be settled was the query of his youth, and Thomas disposes of this in the second question of his *Summa*, where he establishes the existence of the First Unmoved Mover, the First Cause Uncaused, the Orderer of the Universe, and Source of all perfection. Thereafter he simply expands each of these cryptic phrases, drawing each one out, explaining, unfolding, until bit by bit, from a hundred distinctions, as from so many strokes of the brush, there emerges a clear picture of God.

What sort of person is God? Is He like us? Really, this second question is putting the cart before the horse, for God is not like us; we are like Him and made in His image and likeness, resembling Him most through the spiritual side of our nature, through our intellect and will. But it must always be remembered that we are only very faint and imperfect copies of Him.

God has a will. As in many a forbidding looking hill, there is gold in this prosaic statement; all we have to do is dig for it, or rather follow Thomas as he mines the expression. If God has a will, then He has that something which makes Him dynamic and active. Many of our acquaintances, intelligent and capable, never seem to get anywhere or live up to their possibilities, because they lack the driving force of will. It is the will that gets things done, and there is no substitute for it—not even in God.

The fact of God's having a will makes it certain that He will do many things. We cannot even begin to treat of them all now; Divine Providence, Predestination, and others will have to wait until later, but there are immediate consequences of God's possessing a will that are tremendously interesting.

The first of these is that God can live. The next is that He is absolutely just; and the third is that He is all merciful. We may well be amazed at the careful treatment Thomas gives to each of these points.

Love

It is important to have a correct notion of love because our world is filled with many ridiculous ideas about this tender passion. The word itself is now weighed down with associations from the most trifling to the most tremendous, that it is rather difficult to single out the essential note of love and convey it to anybody. The reason for such confusion is not hard to find. Love is so very common; everyone has experienced its twinges or pangs at some time or another. It has been described in glowing colors by great poets and artists; and it has had to sit for its portrait by rank amateurs. As a result, since amateurs far outnumber great artists, love has come to mean a sort of sticky, sentimental emotion that steals over men and women like a sudden rash, and after a time as unaccountably steals away. At least, this type of love is slobbered all over the pages of those pulp magazines that specialize in "romance" and "confessions." The fact that the circulation of these magazines reaches astronomical proportions suggests that a great part of the reading public is content to accept this picture of love. Partly to blame for this outlook are some of the professors on the big circuits, that is, in public universities.

St. Thomas was a university professor himself, and when we pass from the modern treatment of love to the Saint's treatment of love in God, it is somewhat like coming into the fresh, bracing air after a long session in a smoky room. The way Thomas proceeds is simplicity itself: Love is the first movement of the will or of any appetite. Simple, isn't it? There is the "sweet mystery of life" in a nutshell! Wherever you have an intellect you have a will. The will is an appetite; and wherever you have an appetite you have love.

Hunger of God

God has an intellect, and so He must have a will. The statement that He has an appetite might pass the censor unchallenged, and again it might not. It seems that "appetite" is not quite genteel; baser notions concerning food, drink, and sex cluster around it. It is considered to be a bit vulgar, or at least "unrefined," as for

example in the fable that history has somehow collected and pre-
served about St. Thomas himself. So huge was his appetite, as the
tale goes, that it produced great frontal results; so great in fact that
he was forced to cut out a semi-circle in the table so that he could
get within reaching distance of the food! In this connection, the
meaning of appetite is certainly uncomplimentary, and cannot be
applied to God.

It would be a shame to ruin Thomas' argument by misunderstanding his terms. The "appetite" is a very broad word. It may indeed
signify an inclination towards food and drink and sex, but that
is not all. There is also such a thing as an appetite for knowledge,
for fame, for glory, for goodness, for friends, for a thousand other
things, which deserve approval and imply no defect. The word
"appetite," then, need not be sent around to the servant's entrance.

And yet .... it is true that we do not parade our appetites, and it
is a rare day indeed that we boast about them. This seems to suggest
that if they are not vulgar or unrefined, still there is something
suspicious about them; they do not fare so well in the light of day,
and should best be kept where we keep the family skeletons. Should
we use this dubious word about God?

Well, there is a reason why we do not walk through life with our
appetites prominently displayed on our shoulders. Our path through
this valley of tears is beset by too many flying fists; things might
get knocked off shoulders. We shrink from the pitiless scrutiny to
which all of our actions and motives are subjected. We hesitate
to step forward in a crowd and take command, and we hide our
desires and inclinations, because we know from sad experience that
our ambitions and likes and dislikes, etc., are far from perfect. Too
close examination of things we flaunt in other peoples' eyes is only
too apt to disclose flaws that had escaped us.

But this has nothing to do with God, who is utterly perfect.
He deserves a close examination, the closer the better. Appetite as
such, and above all, appetite as found in God, will never be tried
and found wanting. Appetite, especially God's, is a good thing in
every way.

Not Intellect Alone

Is it necessary that God have an appetite? How would it be if He were some giant Intelligence, or simply Mind. Thrillers in the days of my youth used to weave fantastic plots around a monstrous Brain, which had to be fed constantly, as I remember, with more brain. It spent its time working out mathematical formulae, calculus, plans for ray-guns and machines, and such. Of course, the hero and heroine from the Earth managed to destroy this "thing" before the end of the story. The only justification for bringing it in here is that it serves as a contrast for a correct notion of God, and, incidentally, of ourselves. God has an Intellect, and along with it a Will. Were it not for that Will, there would be absolutely no activity anywhere. If we could conceive of such a thing as a plain, unadulterated Intelligence, nothing would ever happen, for intellect must be wed to appetite or will to ensure activity. Purposeless activity is as unworthy of God as it is of us.

Of course there are great differences between God's appetite and ours. Without going into matter here which will be treated later on, note that we are composite creatures, and God is a pure spirit. We are made up of body and soul, and of the two, the noisier of the partners is the body. It is the seat of two appetites: one natural and the other sensitive; and over and above these the spiritual side of man is endowed with a single appetite called the will. Every man therefore has three appetites. This is only another way of saying that man is a creature of desires; that he has inclinations and tendencies towards good and pleasing things; that he is inclined by nature, senses and reason away from anything that might harm or displease him. The tendency towards what is good and pleasing is called, in strictly technical language, love; the tendency away from some evil is just as technically called hate.

Passionless

As far as God is concerned, there can be no question of a sensitive appetite, for He is simple and has no body. This means also that He is undisturbed by passions, which are movements of the sensitive appetite accompanied by some corporal change. But we might as well not waste any sympathy on God on this account, since His lack of passions is not a defect but rather points to the perfection of His simplicity. He is more perfect without a body than we can ever be with one. He can love and hate and rejoice by an act of His will, without being bothered, as we sometimes are, by the voice raised by the body in these affairs.

Love is a passion. A modern writer would say "Love is an emotion," and mean the same thing as Aquinas. But notice how different this is from saying: Love is passion. Between these two statements there yawns the great abyss which separates Catholics from pagans. If love is only passion, then it is necessarily an act of the sensitive appetite; and then God is a stranger to love. But if love is *one* of the passions, then it is not so tightly bound up with the sensitive appetite, but may also be an act of the rational appetite which is the will, and in this case, there is no reason why we cannot say that God can love.

Can God hate, or become angry, or be filled with sadness, or even be pleased? Both the Old and New Testament abound in such expressions as applied to the Almighty; but they are to be understood as metaphorical expressions. Actually we do not conceive of God becoming red in the face and blustering whenever a sinner offends Him. That would be the passion of anger, and God is perpetually free from all passions involving the play of the sensitive appetite. But an angry man punishes another; so God is metaphorically said to be angry when He punishes anyone. There is a similitude of effect between God's action and man's.

In a word, we are forced to make one word do the work of two. Love sometimes signifies acts of the sensitive appetite, and sometimes exclusively the acts on the superior appetite, the will. We restrict our use of the word to the latter sense whenever we are talking about God and His love.

God Love You!

Love therefore is more than passion; it is one of the passions. Human love may be the inclination of the sensitive appetite towards something which attracts it through the medium of the senses. Human love at its best is the inclination of a man's will towards something his mind tells him is good and fitting, and it is this type of human love that affords us some grasp of the love of God. This grasp is precarious; we hold on by our finger tips, but still we do hold on to something. God's love is likewise that inclination of His will toward what is altogether good, fitting, agreeable.

Of course this must be understood properly. God did not discover, on one of those long days of eternity, that He was all good and deserving of all love. If He did He would have betrayed Himself as something imperfect, something not entirely in actuality, something evolving from less to more, and more than somewhat stupid. Once admit God's hypothetical discovery of His own lovableness, and, as the Scholastics used to say: "*Ruitur thesis.* The case (for God) falls."

From all eternity God exists in a state of absolute actuality and perfection. From all eternity He has a will which from all eternity is inclined towards the greatest good. This can only be Himself. This inclination of His will towards His own goodness is called "love." Does God love, asks St. Thomas, and replies with what must have been a magnificent flourish of the pen: God is love.

How interesting! God not only loves, He is Love personified. What next? Where does that get us? Not only does this get us into Article Two of the Twentieth Question of the First Part, but farther than that. It is important to remember that no one can love that which does not exist; whatever does exist, is lovable, for a thing is good in proportion as it has existence.

Falling in Love

Why do you love your wife? Why did you love her in the first place? Because almost from the first moment you met, you saw in her some wonderful qualities and perfections. You were attracted by the way she walked into the room, by her beauty, by the way she danced, or by her laugh, by her talk, by the way she looked at you, and by a thousand and one things. In her you saw, or thought you did, all perfection. Gradually the conviction arose in your mind that she was the only woman for you. You wanted to make her your own to take care of forever; all of which led logically to your popping the question. When she said "Yes," you were catapulted into the skies and walked on the clouds, for this creature of perfection and goodness incarnate had consented to be yours! How you would protect her in all her perfection; and how you would strive to supply her with all she desired and needed.

There is your old, old story. Can we fit God into it? There is something utterly fantastic in the notion that He could fall in love. What sort of creature *could* captivate Him and bring Him to its feet? A fall implies a motion of subjection, or downward direction. Could God fall in love?

The answer reveals the astonishing difference between our love and God's. Ours is awakened and set into motion by the goodness we discover in things and people—and sometimes we can make grave mistakes about the goodness of things. But *God's love does not presuppose* anything. God's love is *creative*. It creates the goodness in things which makes them lovable by anyone.

So that answers our question. God does not fall in love; he creates it. He cannot take a single thing from anybody or anything, but must continually give Himself away, must continually spend the inexhaustible treasures of His goodness for all eternity, and we fall in love with the faint reflections of the divine goodness which we see mirrored in those we love. If a thing is good, the reason is that God gave it existence; and as it is good, it is lovable.

Occasionally, oftener than we think, men and women catch such a view of the generosity of God who gives Himself away that they themselves try in a human way to imitate Him. It is not long before they are known as Saints.

Human Imitations

Briefly let us peep at the vision of loveliness that this idea evokes. There can be and is a love that seeks all for itself, that looks upon all others as objects of legitimate plunder. Selfishness is a kind of love, but it is love of self. On the other hand there is rational, truly human love, which in imitation of the divine love seeks not its own, but rather the beloved's pleasure. It consists in throwing life away, and—unlike selfish love—finding both it and happiness. Imitation of divine love? Yes, for God's life is a giving or diffusing of Himself; we might describe it as consecration to another—all creation being that other.

Love then is doing something for another, or at least wishing to do things for another. Paradoxically, this giving away of one's self perfects a man, makes him more truly human. It just happens to be the way the will works. It grows to its fullest stature and attains its greatest beauty when it goes out towards something else. Thus love—to wish good to another—is a safeguard against intellectual pride; it is a counterbalance to the workings of the intellect. The mind draws all things to itself. It can absorb an infinite number of things: God, nature, sand, a grand piano, a flash of lightning. No matter what it is, whether mountain or molecule, the intellect can draw into itself all things not itself. But the will works the other way around. By its nature it is destined to go outside itself, to wrap itself around something outside itself, which is one reason why we should be careful to love things above ourselves, otherwise our loves drag us down. We might almost say that a man is inclined by his very nature to love and serve another. The baneful results of Original Sin interfere with the ideal working out of this picture, but it remains true that in proportion as a man goes outside of himself and does good to another, in like proportion he becomes more and more truly human and more and more like unto God.

How do we know God loves us? Easily enough. All we have to do is to look at the gifts He has showered on us. It is a pity so many people think God does not love them because He does not remove all struggle from their lives. Because He does not send them luxury, fur-coats, limousines, and the like, they act as pouting, petulant children. But what they overlook entirely are such unbelievable gifts as our very existence, our daily bread, the air we breathe, the colors that delight our eye, friends, family, home, and so on down the long list. These things are not in the habit of simply materializing around us by chance; God gave them to us, one by one. They are the gifts of a loving God to each of His creatures.

God's gifts to us are a fairly certain indication of His genuine interest and love for us. Some earthly presents make us suspicious—that "ulterior motive" business—but God's gifts are above all suspicion; they are effectual proofs of His love.

All Things?

But where does it stop? After all, there are limits to a good thing. Is it not absurd to say that God loves all things? What would happen to the divine dignity if it stooped to pet a Pekinese puppy, a kitten, or a colt, or any irrational creature? It seems that God's love must have some limits.

Our amazingly well-informed guide, St. Thomas, replies that the love God has for animals is not the kind of love He extends to His rational children. Love of friendship demands a return of love as well as similarity of life. The love of friends must be able to withstand the shock of battle, the bitterness of defeat, discouragement, as well as rejoicing and happiness in victory. In a word, love between human beings, or love between God and man, is something that persistently refuses to fit into the world of irrational creation. The world of irrational creation, wonderful though it be, cannot love God, because it lacks the means of participating in His life of spirit and truth. No matter how much his tail wags our dog does not love us, nor do we love him. Without communication of thoughts and desires plus a return of affection, true love cannot exist.

Of course we would not say that God hates irrational creatures. As a matter of fact He loves them, since He makes a place for them in existence. It is not the highest place: they bear mute, lowly witness to His wisdom and goodness, and are useful to the lord of the universe—man.

Now then, if God loves all things, does He love them all with the same degree of love? In other words, does a man rate more love than a mouse, a gnat than an elephant or redwood, and so on?

Equality to All?

In times past there were certain men who held that God loved all things equally. (They also held that all men were equally just, and in their passion for equality they taught that all were destined for equal glory in Heaven or equal punishment in Hell. The Church condemned all such teachings.) St. Thomas with characteristic common sense says simply that whenever God wills, He wills with all His power; His will does not bear traces of fatigue towards the end of a week of creation! There is no gradation in the intensity of the will to create; this was the same for all. However, the objects of God's willing indicate some difference. Love means the wishing of good to another, and there is no reason why. God could not and did not wish a greater good to this creature than to another. Nobody dreams of denying the inequality of things. Animals have less value than men, more than plants; and man surpasses the whole animal and plant kingdom, but is inferior to the least being in the angelic kingdom. Yes, inequality is a fact realized and felt all too keenly.

Things are of unequal goodness, then, because God willed to some creatures a greater good than others. This fact reveals that He loves some more than others, for love is simply: to wish good to another; and the definition of love is the means of gauging love.

By this standard, then, that God loves more those to whom He gives a greater degree of existence, it is safe for us to conclude that God loves Christ and His human assumed nature infinitely more than mankind or the universe. Then He loves the Blessed Virgin more than saints or angels; and in general He loves angels more than men. But it is useless prying into the divine mind to try to settle whether God loved Peter more than John, or whether He loves the sinner who does penance more than the innocent who never offends Him. The only thing absolutely certain is that God loves those more than others who have a greater abundance of grace—for grace too is a gift and indicates the degree of divine love.

II. The Justice of God

Men are notoriously inclined to take the easy way out of difficulties. Here in America they boast especially of being tolerant, liberal, and broadminded. But there is a point beyond which no man may safely go with any one of us, and that is the point marking the boundary between justice and injustice. This is a very real boundary, and infringements on it have led to great violence. If this were merely an imaginary border, history would never have witnessed so many revolutions. If it were indisputably true that men always were given just wages, if widows and orphans were always protected from robbers and thieves who wore the badge of respectability in the community, if minorities were given the rights of self-expression, and so on, then there would never have been violence and bloodshed. Mark that this violence and bloodshed is aroused in the magic name of justice. Justice is something men and women really want more than anything else in the world.

God of Thunder

But when it comes to applying our desire for justice to almighty God, there is a great deal of throat-clearing, hemming and hawing. By some strange mental process, it is much more fashionable to consider God as the very essence of goodness and all-forgiving mercy than as a just God. It is thus possible to do away with the disagreeable notion of Hell, and the moral code loses its sting and coercive power. The vindictive God of the Hebrews, we are assured with bland confidence, has been replaced forever by the benevolent God of Jesus Christ, whose chief characteristic seems to have been forgiveness of the sinner, with or without sorrow. At any rate He simply could not be vindictive.

If God is not just, we might just as successfully try to pluck the stars from the heavens as to expect to find justice in the world, for in such a case there would be no way of accounting for the order that exists in the world, and no reason for living in conformity with that order.

We all have some notion of what divine and human justice is. We do not want God to reward us only for the good we do, and entirely neglect the evil we have done in our lifetime; that would not be just. Nor would we feel flattered if He rewarded us only for the evil that mars our record in the book of life, while the good so laboriously done was brushed aside as of no account; neither would this be just.

We abhor the thought that God merely cloaks over our sins with His loving kindness, thus hiding them from the face of the world much as a curtain hides a dirty window. We want our sins destroyed and forever done away with, and along with this we desire keenly that God will remember the good we have done. Keeping the just proportion, we feel, is justice. Justice is the refusal to deny anyone what is his due.

Justice

There are many kinds of justice. One is called *commutative,* and concerns the affairs of men. It is the justice which should regulate the affairs of the marketplace, buyings and sellings, and the like. But God is not a merchant; He has no equals to bargain with. As a matter of fact, Aristotle thought that the idea of the gods haggling and arguing over merchandise on sale was utterly ridiculous and destructive of divine dignity. What he said of the gods, we say of God. Commutative justice is not for Him.

Another type of justice is social justice, otherwise called *distributive* justice, since it regulates the distribution of benefits and duties necessary for any operation. Only a superior, a governor, for instance, can exercise distributive justice; and this ensures a man's receiving what is proper to him according to his place in society.

A good many years ago a French explorer returning home was asked by a reporter what was the most wonderful thing he had seen in his many years of travel. He had seen hundreds of ports in all the seven seas: some of them in the bleak north, others in the reek-ing jungle, still others over which hung the mysterious noises and odors of the Near and Far East; surely he had seen many wonderful and striking things. But after a moment's thought he replied: "In all my travels, the most wonderful thing I ever saw was the proof everywhere that God exists."

What he meant was that everywhere he saw evidence of order. He saw the regularity of the seasons, the marvelous adaptation of man to different climates and circumstances, the astonishing perfec-tions of strange creatures from the sea, of beautiful but dangerous creatures of the jungle, and all this pointed in the direction of God, who planned it all. The order of the universe, whether of the mighty planets and stars that wheel so majestically in the heavens, or of the delicate mechanism of a butterfly's wing, simply had to come from somewhere and from someone. This wonderful order is one of the greatest masterpieces of the Architect of the universe. God it is who forms and preserves this order giving to every creature what is proper to it according to its place in the plan. In so doing He manifests His divine justice.

No Man's Debtor

The seemingly insurmountable objection that is unfailingly hurled at the heads of the defenders of God's justice is that justice renders to everything what is its due. But God cannot be considered as another's debtor. Nothing can be superior to God. There is noth-ing which in His sight demands absolutely that He render unto it its due. God cannot be constrained. Better by far to sacrifice the notion of justice in God, than to make God inferior.

Yet there must be some misunderstanding of the justice in God if we feel forced to such a drastic decision. Thomas replies: God is no man's debtor; He pays no debt in order to win for Himself the title of "the Just." He gives without owing anyone a thing, but it would be false to suppose that He gives without rhyme or reason or with the same generosity and lack of order as is displayed by an uncontrolled oil-gusher or broken water-main. Everything God does is perfectly conformable to His Intellect and is regulated by it. This is another way of saying that He makes all things according to the plan existing in His mind for all eternity. In that plan nothing is missing; everything is there and in its proper place.

God owes it to Himself to endow His creatures with everything His intellect and wisdom indicate they should have. If He makes a man, He does it in accordance with the idea of man; if He makes a star or a starfish, this too is done in accordance with His eternal wisdom and intelligence.

Having therefore determined to make certain natures, such as animal and rational natures, God manifests His justice in giving to each nature what it needs to be that particular type of nature. Making things according to His plan, He both follows the plan and successfully carries it out. Call this a debt if you will; it is a debt to Himself alone, and in so acting God is just.

III. The Mercy of God

Mercy is not always a popular quality. Modern ears perk up, modern eyebrows go skywards, when someone casually remarks that mercy and justice can walk hand in hand, through the tangled web of human affairs. "Incredible," murmurs one; "Fantastic," says another; "God should be merciful, yes; a man should let justice rule his affairs, yes. But that God (to say nothing of man) should be simultaneously just and merciful, is impossible."

Behind such statements is the feeling that mercy is sissified, smacks of weakness, and implies a defect of manliness. In times of national excitement the suggestion that our enemies be treated with anything but the strictest vindictive justice is frowned upon; revenge is the order of the day. And in preparation for that future revenge, the minds of soldiers are deliberately brutalized and stripped of such impediments as mercy or kindness. Hate kills more enemies than mercy, so hatred is cultivated while mercy is driven from the training and fighting fields. All this, mind you, in total forgetfulness that God said: "Vengeance is mine (not merely forgiveness) I will repay, saith the Lord."

The Quality of Mercy

What is mercy? Mercy is a strong quality of soul; it means that I am saddened by the sight of your misery and attempt to do something to alleviate it; it is a virtue inclining a person to remove some distressing defect in another. A merciful man regards another's misery as his own (for the other is in some way considered to be another self), sorrows over it as if it were his own, and tries to relieve the suffering or misery.

Mercy, friend of sadness, is the foe of another's misery. How can God be merciful? He has no sensitive appetite; He does not therefore experience sadness at the sight of another's misery. But out of the treasures of His creative goodness He does give to His creatures whatever perfection they possess. In doing this He removes a defect—that of non-existence; as far as the effect of His action is concerned, God does what a merciful man does, and so we account Him merciful.

It is a stupid blunder to suppose that when God, or anyone else for that matter, is merciful, He cannot be at the same time just. Mercy is not a relaxation of justice. It is, surprisingly enough, the plenitude of justice; it adds something over and above justice, and fills the cup of justice to overflowing. God is just because He gives perfection to all created things in proportion to their natures, and in so far as this gift expels the defects found in the creature, He is merciful.

The work of divine justice always presupposes the work of mercy and is founded in it, says St. Thomas. Reason declares that all created things come from God; the fact that they were made at all must be traced back to the goodness of God. That they are what they are is an indication that they were made according to some plan, i.e., were given all that they needed to be what they are. They were made according to the divine plan or wisdom. But even here, creatures received from God much more than they had any right to expect; more than the mere fulfillment of the plan demanded, and it is precisely here that we see, tempering the divine justice; the mercy of God. Everything comes from God endowed with all that it needs, actually much wealthier in perfection than was absolutely necessary. Two eyes instead of one, two hands, two legs to carry us places, varieties of foods to nourish us, all acclaim the goodness of God, His justice, and especially, His mercy.

Just Mercy

Is God weak because He is merciful? Is a man a coward and weakling because he does not bully, brow-beat, and persecute those who need his help and ask for it? To identify manliness with strength and lack of pity would ultimately lead to the destruction of hospitals, centers of education, churches and all society. In less time than it takes to tell, dispensaries of mercy would be objects of official disapproval, and the only approved surgeons would be those who preferred brass-knuckles to scalpels. No, mercy is not for sissies. Mercy demands a strong and human heart, along with a human soul overflowing with perfections that can be of help to others. A merciful man is one who has something to give.

Too often the notion of God's justice is associated only with the words: "Depart from Me, ye cursed, into the fire that was prepared for Satan and his angels." Justice ordinarily wears a stern face. But we have seen that in God justice is never alone, but is always accompanied by mercy. These two are as it were the two arms of God, preventing any successful flouting of the divine plan, on the one hand, and, on the other, tempering the severity of absolute justice.

Stock objection number one: God must be unmerciful and cruel, since He condemns to eternal fire all those who die in the state of mortal sin. Can He send to hell a poor, weak human being who found the call of revenge, or pride, or lust, too strong for his fallen human nature? Can God be merciful in inflicting perpetual suffering upon such an one?

In the first place, note that God does not send people to hell. The only people who are in hell are those who deliberately chose to go there. One mortal sin can do this; it is a turning away from God and toward creatures; it implies at least confusedly a deliberate choice of *this* creature in preference to the friendship of God. If a person in this condition, God with all His omnipotence cannot save him from hell. And since death cuts short all chances of changing one's mind, for all eternity those who are in hell want to stay there. They have made their bed and must lie in it.

Punishment

But it is a crude mistake to picture God as gloating over the horrible sufferings of the halls of hell. God does not gloat over suffering. He is actually merciful even to those who are condemned to hate Him for all eternity, for these enemies of God are not punished nearly as much as they could be, and should be. Mercy tempers divine justice even in the damnation of the reprobate, says St. Thomas, not because it remits but because it lessens somewhat the punishment due to them, as God punishes them less than they deserve. "When thou art angry, O Lord, thou wilt remember mercy."

The problem of harmonizing God's justice with His mercy is sometimes exceedingly painful. When death snatches a child from the arms of his parents, when married people have to put up with worthless partners, or when war strips a nation of its youth and home life and all sanity, when the innocent are shamefully robbed, tricked, and exploited by unscrupulous politicians or business-men—then, especially if these things happen to us, we feel surging up from rebellious hearts the mighty complaint; God cannot be just, He cannot be merciful. If He were just He would not permit His laws to be so lightly set aside and abused; if He were merciful He would not permit these things to happen to me.

These are dangerous thoughts. Despite the racking grief and savage resentment such events arouse, we must always remember the truths about God: He is just, merciful, and loving. Once let go of these truths, and cynicism, pessimism, despair let loose their dark floods into the soul.

He Chastiseth

The fact that we suffer cruelly does not mean that all our suffering is just an accident, a painful interlude which must be terminated at once at all costs. It is possible that God deliberately permits suffering to walk a few steps with us. We certainly are not His step-children; He loves us, and permits these things to happen to us, much as a loving, just, and merciful father will permit some slight inconveniences to touch his children.

God who is all-merciful and all-just permits us to suffer for two reasons. Suffering serves as a flame which purges away from our souls all those light faults which are the inevitable result of human living. Suffering also serves the excellent purpose of making a man fall on his knees in humble supplication before the throne of God. When we suffer, we pray, we admit we need His help; and this we do in the conviction that God not only can but will help us, if it is for our own good.

Love, justice, and mercy, like three lovely sisters, lend grace and beauty to the life of us all. Banish them from our minds and hearts, and life at once becomes a barren desert, a cynical, brutal, dreary trail leading to darkness and despair.

Fortunately for us all, love, justice, and mercy cannot be banished from human living, because all three exist irrevocably, eternally, in God. They exist because God has a will. Indispensable to God, they are a necessity for men and women of every age and time. They are the first-fruits of God's will.

STUDY QUESTIONS

I. Introduction

1) What was the most dominant question in Saint Thomas' mind?

2) Is God like us, or are we like God? How?

3) What does it mean to have a will?

4) Is there any substitute for the will?

II. The Love of God

1) What is the first result of God's will?

2) What is love?

3) What is appetite?

4) What is the relationship between perception and appetite?

5) What is the difference between love in God and love in us?

6) How does God love His creatures?

III. The Justice of God

1) Can God be just?

2) What is commutative justice?

3) What is social justice?

4) Why does God owe nothing?

5) How does God manifest His justice?

IV. The Mercy of God

1) What is mercy?

2) Does divine justice presuppose mercy?

3) How are mercy and justice compatible?

4) Why does God permit suffering?

5) What are the first fruits of God's will?

10

In God We Trust

*A Consideration of the Providence
and Predestination of God*

Hyacinth Conway, O.P.

Introduction

This is the tenth in a series of pamphlets designed to acquaint the laity with the theology of the Church. This particular pamphlet treats of the providence and predestination of God as explained in twenty-second, twenty-third, and twenty-fourth questions of the *Prima Pars* of the *Summa Theologiae* of Saint Thomas Aquinas.

If you are interested in this series, we urge you to obtain the preceding pamphlets of the series, for though each is complete in itself, each pamphlet is also a part of an integrated and systematic survey of the whole of Catholic theology.

Does God Care?

As the East Side subway goes careening through the murky caverns of underground New York carrying its evening cargo of tired humanity home to the Bronx and repose, a conversation ensues that might just as well take place in Tokyo, London, Moscow or Berlin. Herman, who flattens rivets at the Brooklyn Navy Yard, leans over to Izzie who stitches uniforms for the Army on lower Broadway and murmurs below the high-pitched din of the subway symphony: "Izzie, do you really think God cares about us any more?" Three thousand years ago, Epaminander[1] might have said much the same thing to Aristarchus as they sat in the shade of a Greek portico looking out over the blue Aegean Sea. It possibly would have gone something like this: "O Aristarchus, thinkest thou that mighty Zeus, basking in the celestial splendors of Olympus, surrounded as he is by that happy company of gods and goddesses who roam the Elysian Fields, who drink the heavenly nectar and enjoy the harmony of the spheres, hath any care for mortals, weak and groping creatures loaded with infirmities and foibles?" Well, it's the same question.

Many men find it convenient to journey through this existence ignoring the presence of any God. After all, the sun rises and sets, winter follows summer, the trees grow, men are born and live and die without any apparent divine intervention. Why invoke a God when the universe seems to run itself quite well? However, the admission of some supreme Ruler is so universal and enduring among the denizens of this earth that it has never been effectively questioned.[2] Where opinion really varies is on the question of God's attitude towards the universe. What does God think about these little human creatures who grope about on the knotty skull of Mother Earth? Does He care about them? Has He plans for them? Or does He sit in lofty invisible eminence, contemplating their joys and sorrows with indifference, as we would contemplate the insignificant activity of an ant-hill, forgetting it entirely or throwing its minute complexity into chaos and destruction with a casual sweep of the toe?

---

[1] This may have been an error by the author. There was a Greek statesman named Epaminondas who lived during this time but we are unsure if this is who the author meant. —Ed.

[2] See Chapter 2 in this series concerning the existence of a supreme Ruler: "In The Beginning" by Reginald Coffey, O.P.

"A Mismanaged World"

Those who lean towards a belief in divine indifference have many arguments at their command. If God really cared about the world, how could He possibly mismanage it so terribly? While men are dying for want of a few drops of water in the Sahara Desert, others die from mountains of water which crash over dikes and carry themselves, their houses and their cattle to a watery grave. The Eskimos don't progress because they have to spend most of their time keeping warm. On the other hand, the tropical islanders fail in some achievements because of the opposite need for keeping cool. In a world apparently left to itself it is interesting to note that men themselves seem intent upon confirming the world's misman-agement. Men starve in Greece while granaries burst in America. Huge fertile portions of the globe remain untouched by man while armies battle over a few sterile acres of Europe. The powerful who sneer at God grind the poor and the weak into the dust; brilliant minds and noble ideals are consigned to nameless graves while thugs in uniform swagger over the face of the earth. And never a thunderbolt comes from heaven to right these wrongs. Thus, many arrive at the conclusion that there is no God, for if there were, how could He tolerate such horrors? If He is not indifferent, then He must be powerless.

But is God really so indifferent and is His government of the universe as chaotic as it seems? Perhaps God's care of us is so inti-mate, so unnoticed, so constant that we no longer recognize it, as the child often overlooks the years of patient, unobtrusive devotion of a mother, while swooning with delight at the casual affection of a friend. Perhaps we do not see His order because we are too small to comprehend, as the eye which can gaze unblinking at the flame of a match is blinded by the dazzling glory of the sun.

What Is Care?

What is this "care" which we expect of God? The word suggests a great a many things. It makes us think of green fields laid out in neat patterns around a sturdy farmhouse, or of a little boy in a well-brushed suit with glossy shoes and shining morning face, hair miraculously plastered down by a maternal hand, or again of the golden notes of a harp, poised in the air with faultless harmony. Care is a certain plan whose execution keeps things as they should be and leads them to the end they should attain. The carpenter cares for the chair he makes when he selects the wood from which it is to be built, planes and measures the parts in keeping with the plan he has in his mind, glues and joins them until finally there stands before him the glistening, sturdy image of what he has conceived. He fashions this chair for a certain purpose. Perhaps it is to be a fine, willowy chair to grace milady's salon, or an erect noble chair to stand at the end of a long dining table, or a well-stuffed chair in red leather, broad and low to invite repose in some smoke-filled study.

With such a certain purpose in mind, the carpenter sets to work. The purpose dictates the existence of the chair, and dictates the very form of its existence, for why should he make it tall or low, broad or narrow, straight or curved but to suit it to its purpose? The more he suits it to his purpose, the more careful he is. And lo, when all is done, the careful carpenter has provided a chair.

Providence

In the same sense, our Heavenly Father has providence over us. By a single act of His omnipotent will the world springs into being from nothing. But it is not a haphazard world that fell into shape without rhyme or reason. Its very heart-throb is purpose. The chair did not make itself, the only reason it came into being, that it assumed one form or the other was the purpose of the carpenter. So with the world. The only reason it came into being from nothing, that it assumed one form or the other was the purpose of God. This purpose, this ordering of things to an end is called *providence*. The providence of the carpenter over the chair extended only to shaping the wood that was already there, but the providence of God extends over the very being of the world, down to the smallest atom, since before He started to work there did not exist wood or chisels or glue, but nothing.

Hence, how strange it is to hear people speak as though God did not care for the world, as though He could not rule it once men set their wills against His, or as though the world with its earthquakes, its hurricanes, its droughts and floods was some huge machine running wild out of the control of its Maker! Far more wise were the statesmen who caused to be stamped on the currency of the United States the motto: "In God we trust," in itself a translation of the Latin motto: *Deus providebit*— "God will provide." Just as the chair would not exist but for the deliberate will of the carpenter, so the world would not exist but for the deliberate will of God.

From Nothing . . .

But the chair once made goes its way, supporting the weight of the humble and the mighty without further help of the carpenter. Why could God not have made the world, given it a push into space and then left it to shift for itself? Such an hypothesis would certainly explain the mess things get into, why justice goes a-begging, pain goes unhealed and poverty unrelieved. But while the carpenter can turn his back on the chair, God cannot turn His back on the world. The carpenter merely imprinted a certain shape on previously existing matter, matter which existed quite independently of him, and which remains independent of him. The shape remains as long as no destructive force such as a raging fire or a malicious axe comes along to alter it. But before God made the world, nothing existed. Consequently the very innermost being of things depends upon Him. Every single atom of matter depends upon Him, every possibility that every atom has is placed in it by God. The carpenter could go and select the lumber for his chair from the woodpile, but there is no storage-house of universes from which this one could have been selected and molded. Its antecedents were exactly nothing. Consequently everything it has comes from God. The carpenter made the chair, but God made the carpenter, gave him a brain, put strength in his arm, provided material for him to work with and on. Men build skyscrapers and bridges but God gives them the ore, the stone, the strength and the brains.

This supplying of being, both matter and life, is not something that is begun by God and then left alone, like winding a clock or filling a tank. The world came into being because God willed it to be. It is His will which retains it in existence. Should He for an instant cease to care for it, it would collapse into the abyss of nothingness. Everything we see in the world has some supply to draw on: the carpenter has lumber for his chair, the automobile engine has gasoline, the flowers have water, the heart has the bloodstream. But take the universe as a whole. It has nothing to fall back on but the nothingness from which it came. It has nothing to draw from. It is supported in the palm of God, and by the will of God alone.

. . . Back To Nothing

If one removes the total cause[3] of a thing it ceases to exist. The total cause of a chair is both the wood which enters into it and the carpenter who fashions it. Remove the wood and the work of the carpenter and the chair is annihilated. Turn off the faucet which allows a flow of water and the stream ceases to be. The will of God is the total cause of the universe, since before and beyond that there is nothing. Should God cease to will the universe to exist, there would once again be nothing except God.

Should God turn His back on you and me for an instant we should be nothing, since our whole existence is traceable directly to Him. He is the whole source of our being. We draw existence from none but Him, and just as the motor stops when no more fuel is supplied, just as the plant withers away without air and water, just as the man dies without food and drink, just as anything disintegrates and disappears unless it is supplied with what it needs to be,

---

[3] Scholastics teach that there are four types of cause in things: the *material cause,* or that out of which it is made; the *formal cause,* or that form into which it is made; the *efficient cause,* or the one who makes it and the *final cause,* or the purpose for which it is made. By *total cause* the author means all four combined.

so the entire universe would vanish if God ceased to furnish it with that existence which is all that stands between it and nothingness.

Purpose

But there is further evidence of God's everlasting care of the universe. This is found in the fact that all things are directed to an end. The most casual happening and the most subtle plotting, the wildest hurricane and the most serene sunset, the wilderness and the garden of Versailles, the geometric petals of the flower and the jagged explosion, the eyes of the potato and the eyes of the fair, all betray a deep, innate and irresistible direction towards an end by One other than themselves. The now familiar carpenter did not construct his tiresome chair by merely sitting down to a pile of wood and hacking and hammering merrily away. The result of such a proceeding would have been nothing more than a pile of shavings and a few bent nails. He had a plan, a clever little plan, which he executed. There was nothing in the pile of lumber before him to evoke a chair. He could have used the wood to stoke his furnace just as well. He could have made of it a table, or a back-door step whereon to sit on a stuffy summer's eve, he could have sent it to the mill and seen it turn into a newspaper or an *ersatz* dress. As he gazed upon the wood with a canny and knowing glance, no one else could tell what was going to happen, least of all the wood. Why did he saw off three inches instead of two and a half? Why did he gouge out here and not there? Why did a chair and not a flower-box appear? The wood, with supreme deference, was willing to become anything. It became what it was precisely because the stoop old man with gnarled hands, a battered cap upon his head, a pencil stuck behind his ear and a white canvas apron tied about his bony frame, had in his gentle, peaceful mind an image of a chair, the chair which he had decided to make, the prototype of the graceful four-legged object which was soon to spring into being through the deft machinations of his nimble hands.

Why The Carpenter Didn't Make a Layer-Cake

Our fascinating friend was of course not entirely free as to what he would evoke with the magic strokes of saw and chisel. The nature of his materials placed certain limitations upon him. He could not construct a gas-range or a bicycle, he could not metamorphose the wood into a chocolate layer cake, or fashion it into an electric light-bulb. But in the realm of furniture, he is undisputed master and the wood is there to do his bidding with never a whimper or protest, ready to be whatever he wills; and whatever it becomes, that it will be solely through the master's pleasure. The pot does not talk back to the potter, nor does the wood give sly little hints to the carpenter. The shape it takes depends wholly upon the craftsman's purpose.

As with our little makings, so also with God's omnipotent makings. With this difference. When our true and loyal friend the carpenter embarked upon his making, he was limited in his making by the wood. He could make anything within the realm of wood. But when God embarked upon His making, He was limited by nothing. There lay before Him the abyss of nothingness that was not God. It was so much nothing that it was not even there. There was only God, infinitely, boundlessly and eternally present, God so unspeakably infinite that the finite mind cannot begin to conceive of Him, utterly limitless in goodness, wisdom and power. When God made the world every atom of its being, every contour of its shape could only come from His divine power and wisdom, because only God was. Do not try to conceive His infinity, because the mind must limit to conceive and infinity consists in the denial of all and every limit.[4] But God was and God is, eternally. And He made the world as He would have it, limited in His plan by nothing but His own unlimited and infinite wisdom. The world sprang into being in the shape it has solely because God wanted it to be that way. He was not limited like the carpenter who could only make furniture;

---

[4] See Chapter 4 on Infinity: "The Heights and Depths" by James M. Egan, O.P.

He could make anything. And He did not start from wood; He started from nothing.

"Goodbye, Mr. Chips"

But just as the completely obliging wood became a chair rather than a table, because it was the carpenter's purpose to make a chair, so this world became what it is and not some other world because God wished it to be precisely this kind of world. Thus everything is done for a purpose. If the carpenter had had no purpose, the chair would never have come into being. If God had had no purpose, the world would never have come into being. Because the whole world and its continued existence in being is dependent upon God's purpose, every happening no matter how trivial and fortuitous it may appear, insofar as it is a part of the world's existence, is also dependent upon God's purpose. Without troubling to analyze any individual happening in order to detect in it some indication of God's purpose and solicitude, it is sufficient to analyze the existence of the world itself which by its very nature is inseparably identified with purpose. How thoughtless and near-sighted it is to think that even the smallest event in this world, the falling of a leaf, a bird's song, the ant crawling across the window-sill can escape God's providence, God's doing all things for an end, when it is purpose and purpose alone which maintains in existence the whole mighty universe, from grains of sand to the satellite-crowned planets!

Having detected God's omnipresent care for this great universe with its stars and suns milling through space, its nights and days, its mountains and seas, its trees and animals and people, its joys and sorrows, its loves and hates, it is proper to try to trace the loving hand of God through the various complexities which we know as life. But before doing so, let us bid a last *adieu* to our faithful carpenter and stand reverently as the kind and useful old gentleman picks up his various chairs and piles of lumber and staggers wearily off the stage, nevermore to reappear in these pages.

Soapbox Opera

If on a hot Sunday afternoon an ardent young Christian clambered upon a box in the city park and proclaimed to sundry nursemaids, old gentlemen, young lovers, and hoboes that all things are subjected to the providence of God (granting he were not promptly dislodged by an unimaginative constable), discussion would possibly ensue and he might well receive the following objections.

Nursemaid: "If God really foresees all things, then there couldn't be any luck, but if you ask me, everything depends on luck in this world, like bumping into the right man or landing a good job. You can pound the pavements all day doing your best to find a job, yet if you ever get one, it'll probably be somebody calling you on the phone when you're soaking your feet at home."

Old Gentleman: "Young man, ahem, I have lived long and I haven't seen the good prosper very much. If God ran this world, do you think He would let the politicians and profiteers have all the plums? If you ask me, either He can't stop them or He doesn't care."

Young Atheist: "Everything happens by necessity, according to law. If you use a certain chemical formula, you know you're going to get a certain result. When we know all the laws, we shall be able to foresee everything and there won't be any God."

Hobo: "If God takes care of everything, He doesn't take very good care of me. I do what I feel like and no one seems to worry, except to run me out of town now and then. Where does God come in?"

Ardent young man, what do you say to all that? Gentle reader, what would you say?

Answers For Hecklers

You would promptly turn back a few pages and remember the very nature of things, then say: "All things act for an end. And God's action, since all being comes from Him, extends over everything in this world. Therefore everything in this world is ordained by God to an end, known at least to Himself."

To the fair young nursemaid: "Miss, what is luck but one cause stepping in to block another cause? A good horse's legs are causing him to win a race, then a bee flits in and stings him on the ear, causing him to jump the fence and lose the race. One cause impedes another cause and you have luck good or bad. But all these little causes are subject to God's great, all-extensive causality. Luck to us it may seem, but foreseen by Him, like a master who sends two servants to the same place by different routes. When they get there they are surprised to meet each other, but it was all foreseen by the master."

To *old gentleman*: "Sir, God allows the wicked to prosper, and evil to occur, not because He is powerless, but because He is so powerful. Controlling all things, He allows minor evils for the good of the whole. If the lion could not kill, there would be no lions. If tyrants were not allowed to persecute the good, we should never have the glorious triumphs of the martyrs."

To *young atheist*: "True, my friend, when we know the laws of nature, we can foresee their necessary effects. But whose providence made and maintained these laws upon whose regularity we rely to make our own little providings?"

To the uncared-for knight of the road: "My friend, you are a very prince of the universe all unknown to yourself. You mistake your wandering life for a shortcoming of providence, whereas it is an indication of the special providence which cares for you. All other things are directed by God to their end without choice, but God shows you the way and asks you to direct yourself, treating you like a friend and a son, rather than a slave. He guides you, but He guides you freely, asking your cooperation, promising you: 'All things work unto good to him who loves God.' It's a long term promise, but worth suffering for."

With this we leave the park, leaving the young orator to further convince his listeners.

Let God Do It

As one becomes more and more aware of the ever-present hand of God in all the happenings of the universe, one may be perhaps tempted to visualize God as directly operating in all things in such a way as to exclude the reality of secondary causes. By secondary causes are meant causes subject to the divine causality which is the primary cause. For instance, one might visualize God as pushing the train along the track in such a way as to make the apparent action of the steam upon the pistons something purely illusory. Since God works in all, one might suppose it is His invisible hand and not the wings which support the bird in flight. One might suppose that our ideas came directly from Him and not through diligent concentration over books, keen observation of nature and laborious exercise of the grey matter. Such a conviction begets the tendency to sit in a corner and twiddle one's thumbs since, after all, God does everything. Then one would not take care of the beggar at the door because God will provide for him. One need not toil by the sweat of one's brow to overcome the slings and arrows of outrageous fortune because what will be, will be. One might be careless at one's duties since, after all, everything is in the hand of God and He can make it work out if He wants to.

This wrong, if convenient, attitude is engendered by confusing God's direction of all things which is providence, and God's execution of His direction, which is government. While He directs all things, He does not govern them immediately, but deputes His causality and power to creatures. If the President approving an act of Congress made a law that everyone should drive under forty miles an hour, he would not then leap upon a motorcycle and start patrolling the country's roads. He deputes that to the police, who leave nothing to be desired. If a king declares war, he does not take on the opposing army himself, but deputes that to his generals and the armed forces of the nation. So with God, while being omnipotent Himself and needing no help from any creature, He nevertheless shares His supreme power with creatures and allows them to take a part in His government. Realizing this, and while recognizing that all power comes from God, one should put one's back to the wheel and strive with all one's strength to put to use the power God has allotted to each to do his share in the work of the world.

What Will Be Will Be—But

These powers which God has conferred upon His creatures are of two sorts. Some operate with necessity, such as a man's desire for food and drink, the urge that drives him to seek happiness, and that instinct that causes him to protect his life. Others operate not with necessity but contingently upon circumstances, such as a man's power to turn to the right or to the left, contingent upon the decision of his free will. Thus while God guides the universe unerringly and infallibly towards the end He has decreed, it is plain He does not do so with necessity, but rather according to the laws of nature which operate sometimes necessarily, sometimes contingently.

An accident is the perfect example of the contingent side of nature. While it happens inevitably in God's plan, nevertheless, it does not come from a necessary cause. If Aloysius Jones had chosen to stay home, one wintry day, he would not have broken his leg on the icy doorstep outside his house. If Cuthbert Smith had decided to take another road to Syracuse, he would not have met the train at the level crossing.

Thus what God has planned will happen inevitably, but according to the laws of nature. If these laws are controllable by man, the events will happen in a way controllable by man. Hence the folly of a fatalism that supposes destiny is always riding roughshod and implacably over human activity. Those things that God has decreed to happen through human activity, will happen through human activity. If you drive a car at ninety miles an hour along a slippery road, saying sweetly to yourself: "If it's my time, I'll get it, if not, what fun!" the bystanders will probably be sadly picking you up in little pieces some moments later. By all the laws of nature you were due to leave the road and God usually governs the world by those secondary causes which are the laws of nature.

To expect God to govern the universe by constantly forestalling the laws of nature is to expect Him to work miracles at every instant. Now miracles are happenings which God reserves to Himself as a special indication of His own immediate intervention. Prophecies likewise fall into this category of special events which take place in distinct proof of divine intervention. Thus the grizzled fisherman, Peter, stepped from the tossing fishing-boat and strode towards his Master on the Sea of Galilee. Thus Jerusalem was levelled in keeping with Christ's prophecy despite the freedom of Titus to lift the siege. But ordinarily God rules the world according to its laws, which are ultimately His laws. So do not step from a tenth-story window with the consoling thought that if your time has not run out you will float gently somewhere above the street. We are advised to pray as though everything depended upon God, and to act as though everything depended upon ourselves. In this way, we recognize the unchanging and infallible decrees of divine providence on the one hand, and do our full share in fulfilling those acts which God has decreed to be executed by us on the other.

Predestination

Within the majestic scope of providence, there is a very special care devoted to certain creatures. The destiny of the flower is short, blooming today and tomorrow lying withered by the roadside, the short-lived fly and the long-lived elephant make their bow and eventually disappear. Even the world itself, if we may believe the scientists, is running down. But there is one of God's creations which is destined to go on forever, and live with God. That is man. Because man has such a lofty destiny, God has a special providence over him. God's providence over man, leading him from the first moment of his existence and to his ultimate goal with God, is called predestination.

Man has this special providence over him not only because he is a creature made in the image and likeness of God, destined to live eternally, but also because he has a destiny which surpasses his natural powers to fulfill. Man who toils and sweats on Earth, who weeps and suffers, who is bruised and crushed by the forces of nature, nevertheless, by the mercy of God, has been called to share the divine happiness of God Himself. To this divine goal only God can raise him up. This raising up is the effect of predestination by which God grants a man the grace which makes him pleasing in His sight and causes him to do good works through his own free will to be eventually rewarded with eternal happiness in the divine society.

What's The Use?

The fact of predestination, outstanding sign of God's infinite goodness that it is, has been, nevertheless, in the hands of those who measure God by puny minds an excuse for much gloomy cogitation. Considering that God's certain predestination of some—how many we do not know—to eternal glory, will be inescapably accomplished, whereas others will not attain Heaven, many have felt that it was useless for man to try to do good in this world. God commands all men to obey Him and promises eternal life to those who do, eternal damnation to those who do not, yet from all eternity He has determined who shall be saved and who shall not. What good is there in trying, if one's fate has already been sealed? Such is the somber music of Calvinism. The only course would be to enjoy oneself while one might, since the future is out of one's power to alter or avoid.

This outlook, which makes God unjust, since He would command a man to do His will and then prevent him by His own preordination from doing it, is due to a misconception of God's governing. God does not destroy His own laws. It is the law of God that a man shall work out his salvation freely. Those who fall away from Him are only those who do so freely. God is the primary cause, guiding the universe towards the end He has ordained for it. In executing His ordination He uses secondary causes; some necessary, such as the inescapable drive which causes animals to desire food and drink, or a stone to fall towards the center of gravity; some free, such as the human will which can determine itself to either good or evil. How God can determine all things and yet leave us free, is a mystery, a truth we cannot fully understand. Yet the fact remains: God has predetermined all things, yet we are free. God is infinitely just. This we know. Yet if He were to judge us as having by our own free will obeyed Him or turned away from Him when we were really not free, that would be unjust. And since He is going to judge us as having chosen our lot, we must indeed be free.

"Mercy Seasons Justice"

Yet it is a mistake to visualize God essentially as a God of unrelenting justice, indifferently contemplating the struggles of men, and once the contest over, coldly awarding them glory or damnation. God's mercy overshadows His justice. First of all, while He deliberately gives grace and strength to the just and confirms them in their righteousness, He does not deliberately condemn the wicked. The only action that can cut a man off from God and bar to him the gates of Heaven is grave sin. And God is in no way the cause of sin, has no part in it. Thus if a man is lost, it is through his own malice alone, while if he is saved, it is through the mercy of God.

The whole story of the human race is one of God's mercy superseding the claims of His rightful justice. God promised eternal death to our first parents if they disobeyed, yet when they did, He sent His only-begotten Son to redeem them and all men. No matter how often a man turns his back on God, rebels against Him, as long as he lives there will remain within him the voice of God—his conscience—telling him to turn back to God and be saved. If he repents only at his last gasp, God will forgive. No matter how hardened his heart, the Church of God will pursue him to the ends of the earth pleading with him in the name of the loving Savior to return to his Father's house. What love could be greater than that of Him who shed His divine blood and allowed Himself, God, to be killed, in order that *all* men, both those who would love Him and those who would hate Him for all eternity, might be saved. Sometimes we think that we are inclined to be more merciful, more forgiving than God, but let us remember that every feeling of love and mercy towards another, every good thought we have, comes from God, and He who puts these feelings of mercy in our hearts, is infinitely more merciful than we. He has *paid* a ransom of divine blood for every single human being. How often do we go beyond the stage of *feeling* sorry for others?

We are not deceived when the beauty and gladness of nature sometimes fill us with a bursting feeling of joy. The warmth of the sun, the tender blue of the sky, the laughing flowers, the green leaves of the trees swaying gently in the breeze, the caress of music, the enchantment of the human face, all are the smile of a loving Father upon the creatures He made to share in His own unbounded happiness. God had no need to make the world. His happiness is infinite and unperturbed and will always remain so. He created the world because of that characteristic of His own divine goodness which we ourselves inherit, the desire to share happiness. This world is the result of God's goodness and when all is over we will see it to be a perfect example of infinite goodness, since all that God does is perfect and fully satisfying to His own divine determination.

Errors

From the knowledge of the absolute dependence of all things upon God, it is not hard to determine the cause of predestination. Some, erring, have taught that it was because of the merits human souls acquired before their births, gratuitously supposing that the soul was created long before being infused in the body; but predestination is from all eternity, before any souls were created. Others, stressing human freedom to the exclusion of the divine guidance of all things, said that first we determine to serve God and then He rewards us with predestination, but since all our power comes from God, this very determination is a result of His ordination. Others maintain that because God foresees that we will freely follow Him, He gives us the grace to accomplish this purpose, as though our following Him, free as it is, was not in itself a result of His deliberate ordination directing all things to the end He has designed. Thus we must conclude, that although our attaining to glory is caused, as far as we are concerned, by our meritorious strivings to do God's will, nevertheless the ultimate reason that we decide to strive, strive, and succeed, is none other than God's own goodness, the cause of the world and all that occurs in it.

Why does God choose this man and not that man for predestination? This, too, is a question whose answer is traceable only to God's own will. St. Augustine says: "As to why God draws this man and does not draw that man, do not try to judge if you do not wish to err." Predestination, like the world itself, is the result of God's will, in no way coerced or acted upon. Since all things come from Him, including ourselves, He owes us nothing. To say that one has a greater claim upon His benevolence than another, through some merit other than that conferred by God Himself, is absurd. God, having freely made the world, has also freely determined the number of those to be saved, a number that is absolutely certain, and that no action of men, wild, rebellious or unruly as they may be, can possibly change.

Why Suffering?

This world, then, is a representation of God's goodness. But how can the sight of men starving other men to death, of brother killing brother, of so much mass suffering caused by mass selfishness be a representation of divine good? We must remember that no injustice will escape retribution on the one hand, and on the other, that, despite all appearances of abandonment, the oppressed of this world are watched over by God, who does not allow a hair of their heads to fall but for their good, since He wishes the good of all. The goodness of God is so infinite that no one aspect of the world can represent it completely. Hence the diversity of things about us, each aspect representing some facet of God's goodness: God's justice is shown by His punishment of the wicked and God's mercy is shown by His sparing of the justified.

What should be our attitude as we stand in the shadow of God's mighty and inescapable will? Should we say: "Oh, what's the use?"

and give up? If we must think of predestination, and worry over that about which we have no power, at least we should take a fair idea of God. Is He a cruel, hard God? No, He is a God who sent His Son not to call the just but sinners. His own Son described Him as a Father who forgot all the ingratitude shown to Him when His erring child returned. He is the God who wept over Jerusalem, the God who died on the cross for those who hated Him, the God who forgave where other men despised, who saved the adulteress from stoning, the God whom the most gentle and upright saints loved with all their hearts. Instead of feeling sorry for ourselves because our destiny is in the hands of God, how happy we should be that no matter how wicked or undeserving we are, our outcome still depends on a God who is merciful. How consoled we should feel that no matter how much a failure of things we make, no matter how powerless we are to help those we love, all events are in the hands of God who will bring the world to a good end, who loves those we love far more than we and who can help them with infinite power!

Confident in God's goodness, we should strive to make our predestination to heaven certain by obtaining those things through prayer, and accomplishing those things by work, which God has decreed that we should. While it is always true that God can save the most obdurate sinner if He so wishes, nevertheless, we dare not presume on Him to change the destiny man makes for himself. Yet we know from experience that a man can fall into mortal sin time and time again and still repent. Each time God gives the sinner the grace to repent, it is an act of complete mercy, a greater miracle than the raising of the dead, since here it is a dead soul and not a dead body which is raised to life. Thus we have an inkling of how God's mercy overshadows His justice.

Love Is The Answer

Need we worry about predestination? God does not command us to serve Him only that we be not lost. His command is : "Thou shalt love the Lord thy God with thy whole heart and thy whole soul and thy whole mind and thy whole strength." We should do what we have to do principally because we love God. Love is a disinterested thing, although the word receives some strange meanings. It consists in wishing the good of another for his own sake. We are supposed to wish the good of God with all our hearts for His sake, put ourselves entirely in His hands, make His will our will. Then what have we to fear, because all that happens is within the will of God, a will that is good and perfect, and our wills are united to His?

By reflecting on the omnipotent will of God we can find a source of consolation rather than gloomy dejection. What did God will in creating the world? We know that it was good, since the will always seeks something good for itself. And what is good to God? Certainly nothing outside Himself, since God is both the beginning and end of all things. The only good that God can wish is His own infinite goodness, from which every good we know proceeds and to which every good is ordained. The world came into being to satisfy the goodness of God. No matter how wicked, how brutal, how hopeless it may seem, we know that God will turn it all to good, to a goodness infinitely more than we. With the world in the hands of a good and omnipotent God, all is well. He is the Friend who never fails, the Father who always loves. Whom else shall we trust to give us strength, to bring imperishable joy out of sorrow? This is our motto: "In God we trust."

STUDY QUESTIONS

1) What is providence?

2) How do we know that God cares for the world?

3) Does God's providence extend only to directing events or to the very being of the world?

4) Does God govern all things directly?

5) What is a primary and a secondary cause?

6) How would you reconcile chance with the infallible plan of God?

7) Why does God allow evil?

8) Does human freedom contradict God's preordinations?

9) How would you reconcile them?

10) Does God's government impose a necessity upon events?

11) What is predestination?

12) Is predestination a part of providence?

13) Does predestination imply a denial of free will?

14) Does God predestine anyone to damnation?

15) Is predestination certain?

16) What does predestination depend upon?

17) What part do our prayers and actions play in predestination?

18) Why does God predestine some and not others?

19) God is both just and merciful, which attribute is predominant in human destiny?

20) To what end is the world ordained?

11

"STRENGTH OF HIS ARM"
A Consideration of the Power and Happiness of God

FERRER SMITH, O.P.

"For great power always belonged to Thee
alone; And who shall resist the strength of
Thy arm? For the whole before Thee is as the
least grain of the balance, and as a drop of
the morning dew that falleth down upon the
earth." (Wisdom 2:22–23)

Introduction

This is the eleventh in a series of pamphlets designed to acquaint
the laity with the theology of the Church. This particular
pamphlet treats of the power of God, with a brief consideration
of the happiness of God, as explained in the twenty-fifth and
twenty-sixth questions of the *Prima Pars* of the *Summa Theologiae*
of Saint Thomas Aquinas.

If you are interested in this series, we urge you to obtain the
preceding pamphlets of the series, for though each is complete in
itself, each pamphlet is also a part of an integrated and systematic
survey of the whole of Catholic theology.

"STRENGTH OF HIS ARMS"

Power

Five foot Johnny wants to be at least six feet, two—no less than that will suit him. Mary whose facial blemishes are an agony to her sixteen year old soul, has dreams of herself as a beautiful bride beside a nebulous but undoubtedly handsome groom. Mrs. O'Toole wants the war to end. So Johnny and Mary and Mrs. O'Toole pray—pray to God. Why? Because they are convinced that God can overcome their difficulties, that He is powerful.

So in treating of God's power—and, later, of His happiness—the problem is one chiefly of clarification. God is powerful. That can be readily established as fact, both from faith and from reason, but the ink will flow as we try to discover the nature, the extent, the restrictions and the actual use of that power. There are those who would have God square a circle and those again for whom His existence is one long and not too successful fight against tremendous odds. The truth of the matter will require precise, but not overly difficult, definition and division. A smattering of argumentation will complete the picture.

Words

The story is told that an American colonel, overlooking linguistic differences and using his best tone of command, ordered two Chinese to bring shovels. One returned with a murderous-looking knife, the other with a bowl of rice. He could only conclude that to one he appeared on the verge of wrath, and to the other as gnawed by hunger. Lest we arrive at a similar impasse, we must first agree on the meanings of the words we use.

Left to play with the word "power," memory and imagination might conjure up images of the plunging deluge of water that is Niagara Falls, or of the magnificently muscled torso of Joe Louis, or even of a dictator directing vast armies in their work of destruction and conquest. Power is the principle, the source from which some action, some effect proceeds: the electrification of a city, a jolting punch, the capture of Paris.

While we more commonly think of power in this way, there is yet a further meaning. Power is the ability to do—to plunge, to punch, to conquer; it is also the capacity to be done unto—to be hurled downward, to be jolted by the punch, to be overcome. The sculptor has power to chisel the stone, and the stone has the power to be chiseled. The hunter's bullet is lethal and the stag is mortal. Fire burns and the wood is combustible.

Both are powers—to give and to receive—but evidently of a different sort. The street car's ability to be moved will never send it down Main Street in search of customers. Its power is passive, a possibility of further perfection, a lack to be fulfilled. The stag, too, is passive, capable of losing a perfection, of being deprived of life. Just so the waters of the Niagara could be dammed. Flowing unimpeded, their power is that the dictator; the sculptor, the boxer, is active, productive, a perfection to be imparted; it is activating, fulfilling.

Power, then, is a principle, a source either of action itself or of receiving action. As originating action it is *active* power; as suffering or sustaining it is *passive* power.

Give and Take

Einstein solving a problem of the fourth dimension and Raphael painting a Madonna are both using active powers. Einstein uses his intellect; he thinks. Raphael does also, but more proximately and immediately he uses his hands; his fingers, his brushes and paints. The solution of the fourth dimensional problem is an activity of Einstein's understanding and like that understanding, remains within Einstein. Of course, he can make it known in speech or in writing, but that is a further process involving further activities and further powers. As a thought it is in the thinker, completing and perfecting him. Raphael's Madonna, however, is on canvas or plaster or wood; certainly outside Raphael. The first type of operation (the effect of which remains within the operator) is called by the Thomists *immanent;* the second (whose effect passes without) is called *transitive.*

Now there is a difference between digging a ditch and composing a sonnet, because there is a difference between a shovel and a mind. The powers involved in a transitive operation are in some sense imperfect; at least, they require something other than themselves to terminate their activity. The powers involved in an immanent operation are self-contained.

Power then is a principle of activity. It is passive or receiving, active or accomplishing. Active powers achieve their effect either within the user and are immanent or outside the user and are transitive.

Could Be

The ancient king of Babylon was hailed by his subjects as "Omnipotent One." Among the numerous and awesome titles of the modern Haile Selassie, the same phrase finds a place. The word itself means all-powerful and would seem self-explanatory. However, such usages as already given show that the word's face value has suffered some plastic surgery. Even to the Euphrates' fisherman or to the Ethiopian tribesman, the "all" in the word "all-powerful" did not mean quite everything.

Omnipotence, say the theologians (and Webster concurs), is the power of doing all possible things. The trick lies in understanding what is meant by possible. We can call Nebuchadnezzar or Haile Selassie omnipotent if we convey the meaning that they could do all things possible to a ruler. No Constitution or Bill of Rights placed any restricting fingers on their regal authority. So a plenipotentiary at a peace conference is omnipotent; he has unlimited faculties for treaty-making. Such omnipotence is relative, boxed in by the nature of the power in question.

Absolute omnipotence takes its "possible" in a different sense. Not what is possible to emperor or ambassador, but what is possible in itself is its concern. The objects of absolute omnipotence are restricted only by the limits of being, of existing at all. If it can be done, the omnipotent one can do it. It may be impossible to nature as, for example, the restoration of life; it may be impossible to man, as is the reading of another's secret heart. But, as secrets are intelligible and man can live, omnipotence in the strict sense can accomplish these things.

The simplest way to determine the possible and the impossible in their absolute sense is to examine the terms defining the proposed being. If the terms are not self-contradictory, the thing is possible. "The man without a soul" may be an eye-catching title for the mystery story, but a man without a soul isn't man and never can be. The terms contradict one another. A gold mountain may be equally rare as far as experience goes, but there is nothing in the nature of gold that precludes its assuming mountainous proportions; nor does a mountain find it self-destructive to be of gold. A flying ship was once only a mere possibility. A square circle never was and never will be.

Faith to the Fore

If we were uncertain whether God could do many possible things, or even any, such doubts would considerably alter our outlook on life. Our trust and confidence might be undermined; our prayers might be lacking in hope. After all, we might be just the ones to get entangled in a situation where God could only wring His hands and anxiously await developments. Unsure of God's power or the extent of God's power, we would find our position precarious, our ultimate state frightening. If we had to depend solely upon reason to discover God's omnipotence, that frightening state, that precarious position, might easily be the lot of a large number of us. God's omnipotence is not so evident as the sum of two and two.

So God Himself provides. He Who can neither deceive nor be deceived tells us plainly that He is powerful, in fact, that He is omnipotent. The inspired Virgin Mary sings in the *Magnificat*: "He Who is mighty, has done great things to me" (Lk. 1:49). The Apostle Paul, guided by the Holy Spirit, announced that God "alone is powerful, king of kings, and lord of lords" (I Tim. 6:15). The angel advising Mary reassures her: "Nothing is impossible to God" (Lk. 1:37). Jesus Christ, the Son of God, makes it clear and final: "With God all things are possible" (Mt. 19:26).

Thus God proclaimed and thus has the Church believed. At every solemn baptism since the days of Peter have been uttered the words: "I believe in God, the Father Almighty." Every Council of the Church from Nicea to the Vatican has reiterated: "I believe in one God, omnipotent." In Mass, in professions of faith—at all times and in all places has God been acknowledged almighty.

We believe God to be omnipotent by divine faith, the most certain of certainties. It is truth infallible, resting on authority supreme.

Reason Repeating

Yet, as the Vatican Council points out, it is possible for human reason unaided to arrive at the same conclusion: God is omnipotent. God in His mercy revealed it; man by his talents can know it. He could never have known the Trinity by unaided reason; even knowing that truth, he can't understand it. But whatever excuses for ignorance of God's power may be given, defect of intelligence or intelligibility cannot be alleged.

Our understanding of the terms immediately eliminates from God any presence of passive power. God cannot suffer change, either for better or for worse. No perfection can be added to the All-Perfect; absolute simplicity allows no loophole for corruption. He Who is pure activity cannot be further activated. He Who is without composition cannot decompose; there are no parts to break asunder. Water which contained all possible heat could not be heated, by so much as a degree. God in reality can become no more perfect, no more God-like, no more divine than He already is.

The question, then, is one of active power, and of active power to produce an effect outside the agent, not power of immanent activity. We knew before we began that there is immanent action in the divine essence. To know and to will are immanent activities, and God's knowledge and His volition have been treated at length in previous pamphlets. He knows and loves Himself; He knows and loves us.

Now it is obvious that the waters of Niagara Falls do not electrify the surrounding countryside; those waters plunging and harnessed do. The sulfur in a match will not light a cigarette; that sulfur burning will. Only insofar as a thing is acting will it be the principle of another activity or perfection.

Has God such active power? The principle of activity must be active. God is pure act. The principle of perfection must be perfect. God is all perfect. To deny active power to God would be tantamount to denying the existence of active power. It would be like saying: "To wet is to moisten; water is moisture; but it isn't wet."

Outside Activities

God can, then, produce an effect outside Himself. In that production all imperfection must be eliminated, for imperfection cannot flow from the all-perfect. With us, the same is not true, for in our transitive activity there is imperfection. The ball player cannot hit a home run by will alone. The bat, his hand, his muscles, indeed his whole body come into play. No sculptor fashions a statue merely by thinking about it. Between the will to do and the effect done many factors intervene. With God such is not the case. He needs no shovel to dig a ditch, even though that ditch be the Grand Canyon. He needs no hands to fashion either man or the universe. His intellect and will are immediately efficacious, productive of the effect desired. His "Fiat" alone suffices.

In God there are immanent activities: knowing and willing. In God there is active power to attain external results. Those immanent activities and that active power are one and the same. While immanent in themselves, those activities have the virtue the fruitfulness, the productivity of transitive powers. At the same time, they lack the imperfection and dependence of such power. All transitive power is imperfect at least in its dependence upon an object outside itself to terminate, to complete its operation. God's action depends upon no object. All objects depend upon it.

To go down the same road a little more slowly, we may compare our action with the action of God. We are men, essentially composed of body and soul. That essence of ours does not operate of itself but by means of its powers: the intellect, the will, the imagination, the passions, hands, feet, etc. Even those powers are not continually in a whirl of activity. We are not always walking or willing or suffering. We have George Bernard Shaw's word for it that most of us do not think more than once or twice a week.

Nor is our simplest accomplishment a really simple process. To write a letter involves the intellect, will, imagination, executive faculties of soul and body besides the pen and paper. Some of us seem to have experienced this complexity so fully that it is impossible to get us to write. In any event, there it is: a man writes a letter. Easy to say, but we know some of the steps required to do it: essence, powers, operations, and effects.

In God, however, there are not all these different things. In fact all in God is one, except the effect produced. God's essence *is* His power. His power *is* His operation. Essence, power and operation—all are God and God is one and simple. We make distinctions, of course, but solely for our own sakes that we may grasp bit by bit what we cannot comprehend all at once. Our distinctions are not unreasonable. They are founded in the fecundity of being that is God. Each expresses some further perfection found in Him and uncontained in any other attribute. The power of God is truly the operation of His intellect and will, but that power is His intellect and will operating in a special manner—to produce effects extrinsic to God.

"Almighty"

If we recall to mind what has already been said of the nature of omnipotence, it will not be necessary to dwell very long on that attribute as applied to God. Certainly, the omnipotence of God is not merely relative. To say that God is able to do all things possible to God, may represent the truth but it will not constitute progress in this discussion.

God is almighty in the absolute sense. He can do all things possible, i.e., capable of being or of existing. The scope of any active power depends upon the nature of that perfection which is the foundation of the power. A fire can heat because it is itself hot. Its power to heat extends to everything capable of becoming hot. The number and profundity of the intelligible things a man can understand depends on the degree of his intelligence. The cutting ability of a knife and the limits of its range in regard to the objects it can cut arise from the sharpness of that knife and the material of its composition. The power of God is founded upon, and *is* the being of God. That being is infinite, the plenitude of existence. Hence such a power so constituted can be thwarted only by that which cannot have being, cannot exist. A fire is limited by the things which can be hot. God's power is limited only by the things which can be.

Wrong or Right

The gods and goddesses of ancient Greece and Rome were certainly not above the green of envy, the deceptions of intrigue, or even a bit of downright stealing now and then. But those who enjoyed that classical civilization fashioned their own gods, patterned after their own ideals and failings. That urge perseveres in us and might lead us to conclude that God can sin. After all, we can sin. Can we do something which God cannot? It is something, isn't it? We can't maintain that God cannot sin because sin cannot be. Sin only too obviously exists.

If we have ever been perplexed by the problem and put it to question, we have probably heard this answer: "Well, you see, if God did it, it wouldn't be a sin." There is something not quite satisfactory about the solution. Nothing would be wrong or right in itself. The morality of every action would depend arbitrarily upon the whim and mood, or more exactly, upon the purpose of the lawmaker.

No doubt, some actions are sins solely because God forbids them, as, to profane the Sabbath. But a lie is a lie whether it be uttered by Almighty God or little Tommy Tucker, and a lie is a sin. If we say that God's utterance is not a lie, that it only so appears to us, that it is really a mystery, then we have departed from the original point. True, God can take life, for life and death are in His hands, and such a taking of life can only be apparent murder. True, God can take property, for all things are His, and we are but His stewards and such taking is only stealing in appearance. But can God sin? Can He perform a sinful act precisely as sinful?

We can answer that sin is an offense against God and that God cannot offend Himself. We can answer that sin is the preference of a finite good to God and that God cannot love anything more than Himself. We can answer that God cannot sin, because He is omnipotent.

Sin is a finite, imperfect action that can only proceed from a finite, imperfect power. Only an intellect imperfectly grasping truth, only a will groping after good can produce sin. To sin is not to be strong but to be weak; not to be efficient but to be deficient. The divine will loves and embraces all good. The divine power is infinite and all perfect. From such a power, from such an intellect and will, no sin could proceed. Sin exists, that is true, but it isn't an effect. It is an action. The sin is not the property unlawfully taken; it is the unlawful taking. It is not the murdered man but the killing. In God, however, His action is His Being. Sin is impossible to God, not as something He cannot effect, but as something He cannot be.

Can God Do More?

Forgive us for shaking the dust off this one: You remember the little colored boy who asked for "'lasses." "Not 'lasses, but molasses," his mother corrected him. To which the boy rejoined: "How can I ask for more 'lasses, when I haven't had any yet?" Similarly here, how can we ask "Can God do more?" when, so far, we have not spoken directly of His doing anything. We are taking the existence of the present order of things—the world, the universe, even the spiritual domain of grace—rather for granted either as the object of everyday experience or of faith. After all, as an irate professor of philosophy once pointed out to a constantly questioning student, if we try to prove everything at once we'll never prove anything.

In asking "Can God do more?", we have our inquiring gaze turned upon divinity itself. There are still some particular objects for us to judge as to possibility. But first we must discover whether there is some further restriction of God's power on the part of God Himself. He cannot sin as sin is contrary to the perfection of the action that is omnipotence. Could not His nature or wisdom or goodness exercise a deterrent influence? Since He has created the present order and remained God and wise and good, these attributes could only impede, if anything, a more extended exercise of divine power.

Must These Things Be?

The pessimist and the fatalist deny emphatically the extension of God's activity. God can't do more, they say, because what He does, He is compelled to do by the necessity of His nature. God can't do more, because He isn't free. Throw a stone in the lake and it sinks. Plant an acorn and produce an oak. Given God, the world results inevitably and necessarily. But we must remember that God is not a blind force, a sort of infinite seedling. God is the Supreme Intelligence. He is a person, possessed of intellect and will. His will, not His nature, is the principle of His actions. Things are because He wills them to be. Otherwise He would not be God but a beggarly substitute, less perfect than His creatures, without wisdom, without love.

Also, God's will is free. True, He cannot help knowing and loving Himself—infinite truth possessed and infinite good embraced. In the choice of lesser goods, however, He is completely and perfectly free. The finite, at best, can only imperfectly satisfy the infinite. The acorn into a mighty oak doth grow, never into an elm or beech; such is its nature, such its determination. That God wills the acorn or the oak is not because of His nature but His free determination. As far as the divine will is concerned, God can do more. His power is not the mere execution of a necessitated nature but the efficacious exercise of liberty. Given God, the world can be or not be, can be this world or any other.

Wisdom and Goodness

But not only are the divine nature and divine will implicated in the use of God's power. The will operates under the guidance of eternal wisdom and always towards supreme goodness. Have these the effect of tying God's hands to the present order of things?

The two—wisdom and goodness—are bound together. Wisdom deals with order and order is a question of objective. The end and the means to the end are the wise man's preoccupation. This ordering of things sets him apart from the aimless scatterbrain and the ineffectual dreamer. He knows his goal and sets about systematically to achieve it. God's goal is already determined: He seeks and must seek His own goodness in everything. Whatever means wisdom may dictate, they must be towards that goal. In a somewhat similar fashion, man's goal is his own happiness, and while wisdom may not always be the guide, that happiness must be the objective of everything man does.

Divine goodness could restrict the power of God only on the basis of the relationship between end and means, means and end. Between these, among created things, there is a proportion always observed. Fire heats in proportion as it is hot, and the hotter we want the soup, the hotter we make the fire. If we wish to break down the door, we have to exert a pressure against it superior to the force maintained by the lock. Sometimes, the end admits a variety of means. Thus, we can obtain food by stealing, making, buying, begging or growing it. Yet, always there is a limit, a limit determined by the limits of the end itself. Wishing has never kept anyone from starvation. There may be many ways of getting water out of a well besides drawing it up in a bucket, but the very fact that it is water and is in a well keeps down definitely the number of possibilities.

Between infinite goodness and finite creation there is no proportion. The end to be attained is without limit and the means to the end limitless. No universe or collection of universes could exhaust the possible reflections of divine goodness. It is a bottomless well never to be drained. It is like a masterpiece of art to be admired by artist and disciple, critic and ignoramus, to be photographed and imitated, copied and reproduced, yet always retaining a further beauty unperceived and unappreciated.

Bigger and Better Worlds

The question is: "Can God do more?"—that is, more than He has done, more than the present world as we know it. The answer is far more sweeping than the mere affirmation of possible other worlds. It is not merely saying that another world yet unmade in which men are blue, horses have green tails and fishes walk can also reflect the goodness of God. It is saying that not this world nor the actualization of innumerable possible worlds could exhaust the goodness of God.

We can never exhaust the goodness of God. We can never reach the point where it can be said: "Well, that's all. That's all that God can do, because He has done everything. There isn't anything more to be done." Such a condition would mean that the external works of God, in themselves finite and limited, had become as infinite and limited as the infinite power that produced them and the infinite good they reflected. God would have produced another God outside Himself, and the absurdity of that we exploded long ago.

Like the end-table to end end-tables, it would be the contradiction ending all contradiction. The contradiction, however, makes vivid our response: God can do more unless we presuppose that what He has done is infinite in itself and therefore also God.

Yet, it is well to note that this reply with all its dizzying talk of a myriad of universes really only settles one aspect of the problem. By it we are assured that God is not in the position of the man who wants to live and has to eat to do so. To God's objective, His goodness, there is more than one means. It remains to be seen whether God, confronted with this variety of possibilities, can choose any one or, in point of fact, is obligated by His wisdom to choose the best.

Can God Do Better?

Before charging into this question, a cautious reining-in and a care-ful scrutiny of the terrain ahead will not be a sign of over-timidity. Not one, but several difficulties are involved here, all turning about the central—perhaps insoluble—difficulty of harmonizing the per-fections of divinity. The delicate balance of that divine multiplicity which is, at the same time, the most perfect unity; of the divine complexity which is, at the same time, the most pure simplicity will ever elude our grasp. To fully comprehend it would be itself divine. We gaze successively at each facet of God's brilliance and find each one blinding in itself. We see and in the seeing know there is yet an infinity undreamed. Each step of reasoning with its attendant puzzles tends to emphasize the more that this is God we study.

The contention that divine wisdom places definite limits on the exercise of God's power is no straw man, set up only to be demol-ished. It is the conclusion of serious thinkers, seriously defended and, in some aspects, not entirely soluble. According to these authorities, God's omnipotence is limited to the present order of things, not precisely in that He is necessitated by His nature, or that His will in itself is not free, or that the present order is the only possible means to reflect His goodness, but that this order is the only possible means divine wisdom will allow.

Put it this way: from the point of view of the things He does, God has a chance, for these things are finite. But from the very fact that it is He Who is doing, there is no choice. Out of all the possibilities, He must choose the best, for only the best is wisest and, in God, not to be wisest is not to be wise. Since, then, this is the world He did make, as a sort of corollary we have it that this must be the best of all possible worlds.

Note that wisdom dictating this world as the only means is not in question. Of that we have already disposed. But the point here is that God can do no more because He has already done His best.

The Jansenists, a heretical sect who flourished especially in the 18th century, make a facile distinction to elude the difficulty. God's power, they say, is twofold; His ordinary power and His absolute power. His ordinary power is guided by His wisdom, directed by His justice, and in accord with His sanctity. His absolute power, on the other hand, suffers no such restrictions. It is His omnipotence in itself, unhampered by the dictates of justice, the order of wisdom or the necessity of holiness. Hence, God can do no more by His ordinary power. His wisdom has ordained the best. But His absolute power extends to other worlds and better ones.

Good, Better, Best?

St. Thomas would scorn the absurdity of such a reply. God's power is God. God's power acting independently of His wisdom and justice is not God but an unthinkable monstrosity. For St. Thomas, the present objection and all the preceeding ones are of a piece, strips from the same doth, cut from the same misunderstanding. That misunderstanding, radically, is the failure to appreciate the tremendous difference between God and creature, between the finite and the infinite. No universe is best in the sense employed. Infinity has no top or bottom. You see, we are not merely comparing universe with universe in themselves but in relation to the divine goodness. That goodness, we reiterate, is infinite.

Things are good, better, best from a definite point of view. A snapshot, a portrait, a wood carving all represent a man. One is good, one is better, one is best—with respect to one another. But for any one to be the absolute best, it must exhaust all the representativeness on the part of the man depicted. It must leave nothing to be represented or represented better. Thus, for any universe to be best, it must not only reflect the divine goodness but exhaust its reflectivity. It would have to be infinite.

Yes, we are back again harping on the same note. The reasons we have given for everything are really one and the same reason: no universe can be best, no universe can be unique, no universe can necessitate God's will, because such a universe would have to be infinite. That inherent impossibility has been the key to all the locks.

In answer to the original query, God can do better. He always can, not from the weakness of His action but from the plenitude of

His power, not because He has not done enough, but because He can never do too much or even all. The effects that He produces can never equal His power to produce them nor drain the goodness for which they are produced.

Can God Do Less?

Many, assured of the foregoing, have only found in it a cause for further unrest. What, they ask of the unused power of God? To make it concrete, what of the eternity that preceded time? Was God then less powerful? Should we imagine Him mustering strength, sort of in training for the mighty effort of creation? Like Poe's raven repeating "Nevermore," we must repeat that God is free. He is free not only to make this world or that but to make any or no world. To say He can't is but another way of saying that He is constrained by His nature, a seedling that must flower, a force that must expand.

Nor is His power thereby useless because unused. A thing is useless when it exists for an end it never attains: a chair in which nobody ever sits, a pen that never scratches a line. God's power, however, is not ordained to His external effects as to an end or purpose. Rather God Himself is the end of His effects. So we make a chair not for the wood's sake but for our own. Gene Tunney constantly squeezed a rubber ball, not for the sake of the rubber but to strengthen his own grip. If we choose to sit on the floor or Tunney foregoes ambitions of strength, the unused powers are not useless but simply not called upon to make their contribution.

During the eighteenth century, the German philosopher, Leibniz, called by his admirers "the most learned man of his age," lent the weight of his authority to the best-of-all-possible-worlds theory. He promoted its truth in the absolute and wrong sense we have just denied. But the theory in any sense irritated Voltaire, the great French skeptic. His own difficulties in securing money, his not over-robust health, the miseries of pre-revolutionary France convinced him, if anything, of the opposite. He vented his disapproval generally and ridiculed the notion that a world as replete with evils as this one could be the "best."

Relatively Best

Yet best it is, not indeed absolutely but relatively—relative to the end God has in creating it. What that end is we do not know entirely. In general, of course, it is God's goodness. The precise aspect of that infinite goodness, remains inscrutable. We cannot learn any more about it by studying the nature of God, for in His choosing, He was completely free. Nor is our knowledge of the world we live in sufficiently comprehensive to reveal its end.

We do know that there is an end. God could not create aimlessly. We also know that what He has done is most perfectly suited to that end. Given that end, God couldn't do better. To say otherwise would contravene His wisdom and His power. God not only chooses the means, and these most wisely, but upon Him the means depend for being. You and I want to get to Washington, and it seems everybody does. We can take our choice of the means at hand: plane, train or the strain of walking. Each has its good points and its drawbacks. God not only makes the choice but the things chosen. Certainly we can't imagine Him throwing the world together and then, like a bride with her first cake, standing outside the oven anxiously awaiting the outcome. Nor can He, like Edison, conduct a series of experiments to determine which process will obtain the best results.

There are difficulties, of course, in understanding the perfection of the universe. The difficulties do not arise from any uncertainty about God's wisdom and power but from the insufficiency of our knowledge of the plan and order imposed by that wisdom. Our eyes are filled with evil in the world, because we take too close and limited a view. We cannot hear the harmony of an orchestra if we hold our ear too close to the beating of the bass drum. The most beautiful of paintings is but a blotch on canvas unless we stand at the proper distance. There is order and harmony in the world,—but we cannot appreciate that harmony in its entirety until we see with the eyes of God, until we know even as we are known.

That Better World

This universe is the best possible for the purposes decreed by God. Yet that other better universe for other unknowable purposes remains intriguing. Once assured of its possibility, there is a tendency to construct a sort of Christmas list of the improvements we would find desirable. We might subtract all the evils in the world unless we realized that in so doing we were eliminating pity and sacrifice, compassion and mercy at the same time.

However, without getting entangled in that endless argument, we should know that there are certain restrictions to our imaginary "better creation." In a word, the essences of things escape our ameliorating hands. We could make a better mouse-trap, but we couldn't make a better mouse, as mouse. We couldn't make a better man, as such. Essences are right little, tight little sufficiencies which cannot suffer change without destruction. Man essentially is a rational animal, and if you try to add anything on a par with either his rationality or animality, you no longer have man but some other being. If you give a stone life, it is no longer a stone. As St. Thomas points out, essences are like numbers; if you add anything to four, "it would no longer be four, but another number."

Don't let that dampen your creative spirit. We couldn't better things essentially, but we could make essentially better things. We couldn't make a better man, but we could make something better than man. We couldn't make a better mouse, but we could make something better than a mouse. Then, too, not everything that is has this immutable nature of an essence. Virtues and qualities and quantities admit of degrees. A horse could run more swiftly and remain a horse; a tree could be bigger, a man more prudent. In our campaign of betterment, we could make Johnny wiser, Judy more beautiful and old Mr. Jones more inclined to temperance.

Before becoming dissatisfied with our lot, we should mull over the following passage from St. Thomas and remember that he is speaking of this our world: "The humanity of Christ, from the fact that it is united to the Godhead; and created happiness from the fact that it is the fruition of God; and the Blessed Virgin from the fact that she is the Mother of God; all these have all a certain infinite dignity from the Infinite Good, who is God. And on this account there cannot be anything better than these; just as there cannot be anything better than God."

Plenipotent

Orthodox theologians speak of God's absolute and ordinary power although their meaning is in no way Jansenistic. The power of God can never be independent of His wisdom. It is His wisdom. By "ordinary" they mean that divine power of executing the things which God freely elected in accord with His wisdom from the infinite possible orders of things and decreed to be done. Such power embraces the order of nature, the order of grace, the order of glory. It includes the accustomed order of nature and the miracles performed outside that order. Under God's ordinary power, Joanna Guzman gave birth to Dominic; Dominic became a saint; was to raise the young nephew of Cardinal Orsini to life, and now enjoys the beatific vision.

God's absolute power extends to all those things which He has not decreed but which, since they are possibles, He could decree conformably to His wisdom. It is His omnipotence in its total latitude. It includes the objects of those worlds that might be but are not. A previous pamphlet explained that the object of God's ordinary power is what He knows by the knowledge of approbation, and the object of His absolute power is what He knows by the knowledge of simple intelligence.

The usefulness of the distinction will only unfold gradually. Certainly this is evident that, since we cannot here know the full extent of God's actual operation, we can at least place all possibilities under the sway of power either ordinary or absolute, and thus we acknowledge His sovereignty.

No Undoing

Most of us are continually making new beginnings. Successive resolutions have fallen into successive failures. These, in turn, have begotten new resolutions. "I begin tomorrow"—to reduce, to study, to become a saint. Accompanying the yearning for tomorrow is the wish that yesterday had never been. We can only wish; wish that we had not been there, had not read that book, committed that sin. Can God fulfill our wish? Can He make it so we were not there, did not read, committed no sin? Can He make the past not to have existed?

Before the fact God certainly could have prevented that occurrence. He could have struck me dead before I got there or blind before I read. He did not, so I did. He can nullify the bad effects. He can make my sorrow for the doing the starting point of greater love, but the doing, even God cannot undo.

Remember our definition of the intrinsically possible: it must not imply a contradiction. That the past should not have been does imply a contradiction. I read the book. If it happened, it happened and it cannot be equally and simultaneously true that it did not happen. Once done, it stands as done for all eternity.

The thought of the everlasting aspect of our actions has aided many saints in avoiding sin. Baptismal innocence becomes an even more precious treasure when we realize that once lost it can never be regained. Charity can be restored but it must be as restored precisely as something which was lost. At the same time, the same realization makes us more appreciative of the mercy of God and the power of that mercy. Indeed, says St. Thomas: "It is in His mercy that God's omnipotence is particularly shown." Only infinite power, bound by no superior nor higher law, could so freely forgive, so more than fully restore.

Miracles

The complete and *ex professo* consideration of miracles does not pertain here. It lies ahead. Nevertheless, we can assure ourselves that they are in God's power. Not natural impossibility but sheer absolute impossibility alone can balk Him. To an incredulous Zola denying the miraculous happening before his eyes at Lourdes, we may say that God not only can but does perform miracles and that, by the very fact He does, He does so wisely. He is not plugging up the holes in His creation; rectifying earlier mistaken judgments. Both the nature He departs from and the departure are elements in His plan, parts of the order He has established, foreseen and decreed. To the mocking one who sneers: "Let God make me an angel and I will believe," we can reply that some proposals are not to miracles but to impossibilities. Knowing God's power, we do not say: "God can't do that," but, "That can't be done."

Power is the ability to do and to suffer. God can suffer no change nor shadow of alteration, but He can do to the fullest extent of doing. In the doing He is completely free. He cannot do His all, for there is no all. He cannot do His best, for there is no best. In what He does He acts with perfect wisdom. This world He made could be no better world and still be this. Intrinsic impossibility alone forestalls Him. He cannot sin, undo the past, or do a foolish thing.

Perhaps, we do not appreciate what it means to have a God Whose infinite power is subject to wisdom. The captious gods of superstitious creeds kept their devotees in a constant dither of uncertainty. Think of a god who could in the midst of uncontrolled rage tear the universe apart to vent his wrath, or a god led to abandon his creation from sheer boredom with it. "Whatever God does is for the best" is no mere wish on pious lips: It is the eternal truth.

St. Thomas observes that with the power of God we have treated the last of those things which pertain to the unity of the divine essence. By that attribute of omnipotence, God stands forth to us a majestic figure, commanding our respect and awe, exciting admiration. By that power, because we know that He loves us, we are filled with high trust, supreme confidence. So we pray. So we say with the Psalmist: "Who is the King of Glory? The Lord Who is strong and mighty, the Lord of Hosts: He is the King of Glory." (Ps. 23)

Can God Be Unhappy?

The little old lady from Ipwich crowded down in the protecting shelter for the duration of the air raid, and the girl beside her could hear her murmur over and over in perplexed tones: "But 'e isn't 'appy." She was referring, of course, to Adolf Hitler whose sudden rise to vast power seemed only to make him hungry for more. Indeed, in this vale of tears, power and happiness are rarely found together in the same man; somehow, they seem to conflict. Power of any consequence always carries with it a proportionate burden of responsibility. "Uneasy lies the head that wears the crown"—so goes the old saying and its truth history seems to corroborate.

The powerful man must contend with the envy of others alertly prepared to seize on any weakness. There is the constant stream of petitions for this and that to be dealt with. In the days of Bourbons, the Hapsburgs and the Stuarts, when men believed themselves "born to rule," they looked upon the exercise of authority as a duty and a care. Our democratic upbringing, nurtured by the fictional wont of portraying great men, causes us to be convinced that anyone possessed of power longs to "get away from it all" and be himself.

Turning to God and His happiness, we might conceive that power to be again an obstacle. We could be happy knowing all there is to know. We could be happy with no body to care for, no breakable arms to safeguard, no head to ache. We could be happy with no worries for the future, no contingencies to provide against. But could we be happy with all God's power to wield? Well, we shall see. Certainly, a gloomy God seems no incongruity to some religious people, if we are to judge by the perpetual length of their own countenances.

Beatitude

The object of happiness is good. No one can be happy over evil as evil. When Mrs. Smith rejoices over Mrs. Brown's social downfall, it is rather the rosy future of her own ambitions that moves her to joy. In some way, she sees a deflated Mrs. Brown as good either for herself, or, perhaps, for Mrs. Brown. After all, we should view her motives charitably. Evil of itself repels; possessing it causes misery. Only good attracts. Even Satan promotes the offense of God as redounding to his own pride.

The good of happiness must be possessed. Henry Ford's money does not give me the happiness of wealth. Justice Stone's dignity does not give me the happiness of honor. To one starving in China, the bananas growing in New Guinea are no particular source of happiness. In fact, the phrase, "I am happy for your sake" is used to express the close identity achieved by friendship and love.

Happiness is the result of the conscious possession of a good. Hence, to be happy requires an intellect capable of reflecting upon itself, of knowing good as good. The mere possession of good does not suffice. The cup of water is not made happier by being emptied and refilled with wine, nor is Rover really happy with his bone, but rather satisfied. He does not know himself nor perceive relationships. His possession of a good is not a conscious one. Thus, happiness is a prerogative of the intellectual being, of men and angels and God.

Beatitude, at least in the modern usage, is supreme happiness, happiness without alloy. It is the conscious possession of perfect good. A good may be perfect in its own order, as sufficient wealth, or the highest dignity or the greatest pleasure. The possession of such goods affords beatitude after a fashion. That good alone which is perfect in every way can cause complete beatitude.

Beatitude in God

A happiness constituted by the conscious possession of a good cannot be denied the God we have come to know. In Him, intelligence finds its purest meaning. Of us it may be said, and often, that we don't know when we are well off. We can see in retrospect our failure to appreciate good fortune when we had it and sigh, "Those were the happy days." No such weaknesses can find a place in God's understanding. No preoccupation, no unfulfilled desire can blind Him, cause Him to forget or to be unaware of the good that He possesses.

His good is perfect. We may be mistaken about the good that constitutes our happiness. A starving hobo in his "jungle" may dream of a heaven of rock candy mountains, coffee rivers and sandwich trees.

Yet, like the tramp in O. Henry's story of one Thanksgiving Day, the realization of his dreams may place him in a hospital painfully aware of overeating. A lovesick maiden may foresee ecstasy in a moment with her ideal, but the moment having come may bring only bitterness. The good of God cannot fall short. It is not part but the whole of goodness.

God's possession of His good is unchanging and unending. For us, happiness may be a transitory thing, a moment snatched in the face of destiny. We awake to find the highest joy become only a memory or even turned to tasteless ashes in our mouths. We may change and the object of intense longing become a commonplace. The tearful child sent off to bed consoles himself to sleep with thoughts of future adult privileges, and yet, one day, the corner candy store will draw him only for a newspaper and the social events which keep him up too late will make him wish his wife would send him to bed when the children are sent. The lowly clerk, become a financier, is oblivious of the rich appointments of his business office. Yet, once he dreamed of such appointments and thought of them as very real parts of happiness. He has changed; God cannot change, become mature or prosperous. His hold on good contains no possibility of weakening or loss.

The beatitude of God is perfect and unique. It is the unalterable possession of the incorruptible, all-embracing good. It is the divine complacency in divine perfection. That God is happy and supremely so cannot be denied without denying God.

Heart or Head

The poet asks: "Tell me where is fancy bred. Or in the heart or in the head?" For centuries, theologians have been asking: where is beatitude? in the intellect or in the will? Not that they deny happiness to be a matter of both faculties, but they seek which does it pertain to *primarily* and *properly*. Since beatitude is the perfection of the intellectual nature, it should be the perfect operation of that nature and certainly the perfect operation will be the highest of the most perfect faculty. For St. Thomas, this faculty is clearly the intellect. It is by the intellect that the object is grasped, possessed. The activity of the will is merely consequent, dependent. It is the intellect that achieves the union with the good, and that is beatitude: The will rests in the good attained.

A full discussion is out of place here. We seek only to put in order our understanding of the fruitful simplicity of God. In God, will, intellect, power and happiness are one with a unity ineffable. Our concepts of that unity are multiple with a unity of order to promote intelligibility. Just as we maintained God's power to be the execution of His wisely directed will, so we hold His happiness to be essentially and primarily an activity of His intellect.

To claim God is our happiness, that we are not only capable of grasping the perfect good but are ordained to do so would take us far afield. It suffices here to note that, if man is to attain perfect beatitude, the object of that happiness must be God, the only perfect good. Nor would we thereby be God, for our possession of Him, however elevated, must inevitably fall short of His infinite possession of Himself.

While our beatitude, even the most perfect, must fall infinitely short of God's, His in no way lacks in anything that earthly joy can bring. The self-sufficiency that riches promise, and so often do not give, is His. The power that men seek with such untiring energy is but a participation of His omnipotence. No pleasure can equal His joy in Himself. No dignity surpasses that of the King of Kings. Fame testifies to an excellence achieved. The whole universe reflects His goodness and His glory. The exalted ecstasies of thought and contemplation are His continually, without strain or weariness. Whatever of happiness created things can give, only by the goodness of God can they give it, as a faint image of His own beatitude.

God of Sinai

Happiness is so obviously an attribute of divinity that there are no reasonable denials of God's beatitude. Such doubts and questionings that do arise are more in the nature of popular misconceptions. A sad-eyed God, sorrowing over our wrong-doing, is a common imagining of childhood. Often, unconsciously, we carry the implication, if not the vivid picture, into maturity. The wrath of God, called down on us by preachers, might intensify the conviction that God has His unhappy moments. We are making God to our own image and likeness. Wrath, in God, is not a choleric passion of hot and racing blood. "It is His most wise justice. There are no absent goods for God to sorrow over. He has no need of us, but rather we have need of Him and our actions will always accomplish His will whether to reflect His mercy or His justice.

Yet, that God needed the world to make Him happy is a very widespread belief. As if God, like a child with his toys, coos and chortles over the swift paced courses of the planets and turns the stars on and off. Or perhaps, like the retired banker, tired of idleness He created the universe to occupy Himself. Besides being contrary to the infinite sufficiency of God's goodness, we can see the error of a necessitated divine nature lurking behind such amiable camouflage.

Lonely God

Our initial reflections on power's seeming conflict with happiness are on the opposite tack. God did not create the world to be happy; rather, in creating the world He destroyed Hishappiness—so runs this contention. The vastness of the responsibility God assumed in creating has Him worried as it were. Something might get out of place and out of hand, and God might find He had made a Frankenstein, a monster He couldn't control. Once again, any one of the divine attributes suffices in response. God's wisdom is at stake as is also His infinity. Particularly, our consideration of God's power removes the harried gleam and the anxious squint from the divine eye.

The resolution of one lingering suspicion will bring our pamphlet to an end, at the same time, constitute an introduction to the next. Possibly, there are tenderly thoughtful souls who pity God all alone way up there in Heaven. He has everything, is everything worth being in an eminent degree, but still He has no one to share in His happiness. Is that loneliness a shadow on His happiness? No doubt, some will soon answer that He has the angels and the saints to dispel any depressing feeling of seclusion. Is this real companionship? Angels and saints no matter how high their perfection are still infinitely below God—the distance separating them is greater than between man and beast. Do you recall the Old Testament history of creation? Adam had for company the beasts of the fields, and yet God said, "It is not good for man to be alone" (Gen. 2:18). The reason God is not to be pitied for loneliness rests, then, not on the fact that He has the angels and saints but rather on an awesome truth. That truth is the Holy Trinity. God is one, but in God there are three persons really distinct yet equal. God is not lonely, for in God there is the infinite companionship of the Blessed Trinity.

STUDY QUESTIONS

The Power of God

1) What is power? Passive power? Active power? Give example.

2) How are an immanent and a transitive operation distinguished? Exemplify.

3) What does the word "omnipotence" signify?

4) What is meant by relative and absolute omnipotence?

5) Is a thing possible because God can do it or can do it or can God do it because it is possible?

6) Are there any limits to possibility?

7) Why is a contradiction impossible?

8) Has the omnipotence of God been revealed? Cite an occasion.

9) Can the existence of power in God be proved by reason?

10) From what other attributes of God does it follow that He is omnipotent?

11) What is there about sin rendering it impossible to God?

12) Does God's inability to sin imply that sinners are more powerful than God?

13) Does God act from a necessity of nature? Why?

14) How does a wise man differ from a foolish one?

15) Does God's goodness restrict His power?

16) Can God do all the He can do?

17) Can God make a stone so heavy that He can't move it?

18) Can God make a sin committed not to have been committed?

19) Can we comprehend the harmony of divine perfections?

20) Is God necessitated to choose one world, the best, by reason of His wisdom?

21) Could God exercise His power independently of His wisdom?

22) Is there a possible better world?

23) Is God's unused power useless?

24) In what sense is this world best?

25) Does evil in the word prevent it from being "best."

26) Could God make a better man? In what way?

27) What is meant by absolute and ordinary power. Give examples.

28) Can God perform miracles?

The Happiness of God

1) What is the object of Happiness?

2) Can we be happy over evil?

3) Is possession of good necessary for happiness?

4) Why is happiness restricted to intellectual beings?

5) What is beatitude?

6) Is God happy?

7) How is God's happiness unique?

8) Is beatitude of the intellect or of the will?

9) Can God be sad?

10) Did God need the world to be happy?

SUMMARY

The Power of God

1) Power may be active: the ability to do, or passive; the capacity to suffer. Active power may extend to an operation perfecting the agent or to the production of an effect extrinsic to the agent. The fullness of power is omnipotence, the power of doing all intrinsically possible things.

2) In God there is no passive power, for such implies imperfection. He is possessed of active power to produce external effects, for He is pure activity and most perfect. Further, He is omnipotent. Hence, His power rests upon the plenitude of His being.

3) In the exercise of His power, God can in no way be necessitated. Whatever He produces outside Himself, He produces freely. Sin on His part, the obliteration of the past, an absolutely best world!—these contain

inherent contradictions and hence are impossible in themselves.

The Happiness of God

1) Happiness is the perfect good of an intellectual nature. It demands the conscious possession of a good.

2) God is supremely happy, for He is the Supreme Intelligence in most perfect union with the Highest Good, Himself.

3) God is the highest happiness of all intellectual creatures Whatever of happiness earth can give is pre-contained in God infinitely.

12

Trinity In Unity
A Consideration of the Three Persons in God

James M. Egan, O.P.

Introduction

This pamphlet concludes the theological tract which is concerned with the consideration of God in Himself or *Deus in Se*. As such this pamphlet with the eleven preceding ones constitutes a series on a portion of dogmatic theology which is most important, for the basis of all religion stems from the fundamental concepts contained in this series. Thus the first dozen pamphlets of the series *Theology for the Layman* provides sufficient material for a year's work for study groups.

Meanwhile these pamphlets comprise but a part of a projected series which shall embrace the whole content of Catholic theology as interpreted by St. Thomas Aquinas in his *Summa Theologiae*. In time then the Catholic laity will be provided with an integrated and systematic survey of all Catholic thought.

TRINITY IN UNITY

Private Lives

Do you remember the time you were asked by your best friend to meet his aunt at the station? You had never met the woman before, hadn't the faintest idea what she might look like. Naturally, you'd asked: "How am I going to tell your aunt from the hundreds coming in on that train?" Let's hope you did not receive the answer that was once given to that question: "Oh, she's very intelligent looking." If she were not wearing a very special sort of dress or carrying a golden rose in her hair, you probably were given a few vague details about her looks, just sufficient to enable you to pick her out from all the rest. Perhaps, after meeting her and depositing her in your friend's room, you heaved a sigh of relief and skipped out. Or perhaps she was not that kind; to your delighted surprise she turned out to be about your own age and it struck you that further acquaintanceship would be most desirable. In fact, your friend had a difficult time seeing much of his aunt during that visit. Who knows, you might now know her much better than your friend ever did; perhaps you married her. Things like that do happen.

The pamphlets that have preceded this one have done the job of introducing you to God so that you'd recognize Him if you ever met Him. They gave a more or less offhand description of the externals of God; as though they said, "Oh, He is broad and stockily built, wears glasses, has a very pleasant smile, and red hair." What they said would be enough to identify Him and distinguish Him from all others; nothing that they said gave you an intimate glimpse into the inner life of God. You have still to get really acquainted with Him.

No matter how long you have lived with a man or how much you have had to do with him, if you have never become his friend, there is a wealth of detail about him still unknown to you. Every man has an inner life, a life known only to himself and to his most intimate friends. This inviolability of a man's private life can scarcely be denied to God Himself. Common sense forces one to admit the fact that God too has an intimate life hidden from the most penetrating glance of the most perfect created intellect. "No one knows the Son except the Father; nor does anyone know the Father except the Son, and him to whom the Son chooses to reveal him" (Matt. 11:27).

Reasonable Faith

Even when a friend reveals to you his most intimate thoughts and feelings, the personal experience that is his own is not entirely communicated to you. He can never completely reveal himself to anybody else. The same is even more true of God. He has chosen to reveal His inner life to us; yet until the moment we see Him face to face in after life we have but the vaguest idea of what that life really is. Whatever we know about God's inner life is contained in the pages of Sacred Scripture and in the tradition and teaching of the Catholic Faith. That is why the Catholic faith has so many mysteries; it is so much concerned with God Himself, with truths about Him so exalted that even when they have been revealed they escape the grasp of human intelligence and must be accepted on the infallible word of God Himself.

That there are mysteries in our faith is no mystery; if the faith really tells us something about the intimate life of God it must be mysterious. But, then, why should we be loth to do more than assent to the truth of these mysterious statements about God? Why should we scrutinize them, take them apart, try to understand, if only in the vaguest way, what they are all about? For two reasons: first, because in a sense, we must; our minds are made to understand. Some day, in the beatific vision, we shall understand perfectly; until then we shall continue to get what light we can from the very statements of God in which His mysterious truth is hidden. Secondly, we investigate the truths of faith to show ourselves and others that they are not irrational; they do not contradict reason, they are simply beyond it; intelligible as they are to God Himself, they can be assented to by us only through faith. Yet this is completely reasonable faith, for we have plenty of assurance that God is really speaking to us through His prophets, and lastly through His Son and His Son's Mystical Body, the Catholic Church.

Before we approach a mystery of our faith with the intention of trying to penetrate somewhat its meaning, we must remember two things: first, that we are trying to understand what can be understood in the mystery; secondly, and more importantly, we are trying to understand just where the mystery lies. In other words, our aim is to see what we can and cannot understand about the mystery. There is always one or more precise points in any doctrine that constitute the mystery as such. When we have recognized them we are in a better position to assent to the doctrine as a whole.

The mystery of the Most Holy Trinity is one of the most profound in our faith. Little of it was known to the peoples before Christ, little even to the chosen people, the Jewish nation. In the light of the New Testament we can see some vague foreshadowings of the Trinity in the Old; not enough, however, to have enabled its readers to grasp the full meaning of it. With the coming of Christ in the fulness of time, the mystery of the Trinity was finally unveiled. It would be useless to start an explanation of this doctrine without first giving its foundation in the words of Sacred Scripture.

Tri-unity

To an unprejudiced reader of the New Testament, three things are clearly expressed: 1) there is a plurality of Persons in God; 2) the Son and the Holy Spirit are in a real sense God; 3) that despite the plurality of Persons, there is only one divine nature, one God.

1) Fittingly enough the first clear indication of the fact that there were several Persons in God was given to a young girl of Nazareth, a virgin, named Mary. An angel came to visit her one day and told her that she was to be the mother of an extraordinary child, who "shall be called the Son of the Most High." Mary, a virgin dedicated to God, simply asked: "How shall this happen, since I do not know man." The angel had his answer ready: "The Holy Spirit shall come upon thee and the power of the Most High shall overshadow thee; and therefore the Holy One to be born shall be called the Son of God." While this is not yet a perfectly clear indication of the Trinity, that is what it can only mean. St. John the Evangelist assures us that the child born of Mary was the Word of God: "In the beginning was the Word, and the Word was with God, and the Word was God." The child of Mary grew up and before beginning His public life went to the Jordan and sought baptism of John

the Baptist, the son of Elizabeth. And as He was being baptized: "Behold the heavens were opened, and he (John) saw the Spirit of God descending as a dove and coming upon Him. And behold, a voice from the heavens said, 'This is My beloved Son, in whom I am well pleased.' " And if we have yet any doubts, there are the words of Christ Himself establishing the rite of His own baptism: "Go, therefore, and make disciples of all nations, baptizing them in the name of the Father, and of the Son, and of the Holy Spirit." As the hour of Christ's death approached and He was to leave His disciples alone, He gave them this precious promise: "I will ask the Father and He will give you *another Advocate* to dwell with you forever, the Spirit of truth whom the world cannot receive, because it neither sees Him nor knows Him." Christ then continually mentions three Persons in connection with God; can it be that the Son and Holy Spirit are not divine?

Son and Spirit

2) There can be no real doubt that Christ claimed He was God and the Son of God. In fact, He died because He "blasphemed"; the last solemn asseveration that He made during His trial before the Sanhedrin was in answer to this question: "Art Thou the Christ, Son of the Blessed One?" "Thou hast said it," was the simple reply that sealed our Lord's doom. During His previous ministry among the people He had time after time asserted His divinity: "I and the Father are one"; "The Father is in Me and I in the Father."

It is also sufficiently clear that Christ considers the Holy Spirit divine, as He Himself is divine. The testimony of the apostles is also forceful. Even at the earliest times, Christians recognized the divinity of the Third Person. You remember the story of Ananias, whose name has become a synonym for liar. To him St. Peter says: "Ananias, why has Satan tempted thy heart, that thou shouldst lie to the Holy Spirit. . . . Thou hast not lied to men, but to God." The consciousness of the divinity of the Holy Spirit was as clear to Peter as it is to us.

3) It is quite certain that Christ, while insisting on the fact that He and the Holy Spirit were divine, had no intention of destroying the belief in one God that had dominated the Jewish people for centuries. The God of the New Testament is the same as the God of the Old; the whole purpose of God's dealings with His Chosen People was to keep alive the belief in monotheism. The unity of Father, Son, and Holy Spirit in one divine nature is a mystery, not a myth. The evidence that Christ revealed the doctrine of the Trinity is adequate; the Church has defined it as a doctrine of faith.

Catholic Formula

It is true that the ultimate formulation of the Trinitarian doctrine is technically more precise than the scattered texts of Sacred Scripture; yet this precision does not involve distortion. It is exactly the same truth expressed in another way. Centuries of thought and prayer, the continual guidance of the Holy Spirit directed the Church in her formulation of the mystery of the Trinity. Here is that formula: "The Catholic Faith is this: that we worship one God in Trinity and Trinity in Unity, neither confounding the Persons nor dividing the Substance. For there is one Person of the Father, another of the Son, and another of the Holy Spirit; but the Godhead of the Father, of the Son and of the Holy Spirit is one—the glory equal, the majesty co-eternal" (*Athanasian Creed*).

This is the mystery of the Most Holy Trinity as revealed in Sacred Scripture and crystalized in the doctrine of the Church. What can any human mind do in the presence of such a profound truth? First of all, it must humbly accept it on the word of God with a complete act of faith. No mind, however keen, can escape that first step; if one does not take it, there is no need to go further. But once the mind has given its assent on faith, it can start seeking greater enlightenment. But where?

We must again return to the words of our Lord! Among the number of passages in the New Testament on the Trinity (we did not give all of them above, of course), there are several that contain a very meaningful word. Of Himself, He says: "For from God I *proceeded* and came." And of the Holy Spirit: "But when the Advocate has come, whom I will send you from the Father, the Spirit of Truth who *proceeded* from the Father, He will bear witness concerning Me." Note the word *proceed*. It is no exaggeration to say that on it, or rather on the divine reality it expresses, lies the whole weight of the Trinitarian mystery. If one could perfectly understand just what it means, one would know what the Trinity is, the darkness would be removed. It is the only key to the mystery we have: it will not unlock it for us, but if we can get a slight glimpse of its meaning we shall somehow know that at least the key fits the lock and we can scarcely expect more.

Procession

We shall be using the noun form "procession" more than the verb. If there were no real processions in God, there would be no plurality, no distinction of Persons. It is, in a sense, because there are processions in God that there is a Trinity of Persons.

When one says "procession," there probably arises in the mind an image of a line of altar boys and priests, headed by a cross bearer and acolytes, ending with the celebrant carrying the monstrance. It is right to call up such an image; in an extremely crude way such a procession can be used as a starting point for our investigation of the Trinity. What is the common note of all processions? They start at a certain point and end up at another point; they have an origin and a termination. The passing from one point to the other is the procession. This, we repeat, is a very crude example, because so external; a group proceeds from one place to another place, but the places remain outside them.

There are other types of processions, although we are not accustomed to call them by that name. When the wife prepared dinner, or a carpenter makes a chair, there is a procession of the dinner from the wife, the chair from the carpenter. Here the origin is within the person, the termination is outside, there is a procession from within outward.

Can we discover now a procession that is wholly within? What happens when we know and love. Say from our experience we know what a good dinner or a good chair is. Is not the idea of a dinner or a chair something that has originated in our mind and ends there (not the dinner itself or the chair itself, but the idea)? The idea of a chair is certainly not the chair, nor is it the mind; it is a product of the mind. Deep within the human mind there are processions, having their origin in the mind and their termination in the mind. Often enough the interior procession is prolonged outside when the wife cooks the good dinner she thought of, or the carpenter makes the chair he *conceived*. But the first product is within the mind itself.

One of the most interesting of these interior processions takes place when a man knows and loves himself. Here he produces an idea of himself, which is distinct from himself; you certainly have no doubt that your idea of yourself is not yourself. It would not be even if you had a perfectly complete knowledge of yourself. The same is true of love though it is not so clear.

Inside God

Now we can say, with the firm support of Sacred Scripture, that the processions, which we know exist in God, are processions of His intellect and His will and are somehow connected with His knowing and loving Himself. There are external processions in God, we know, for all creation has proceeded from Him. We know too that He has created by the decree of His intellect and will, "Let there be light." Faith now tells us that there are processions within the very nature of God and give us a hint as to their explanation.

God certainly knows Himself; in that act of knowledge the Son originates from the Father; together the Father and Son love each other with a mutual love and the Holy Spirit is originated. The Father's knowledge of the divine nature is the Son; the Father's and Son's love of the divine nature is the Holy Spirit. So the procession of the Son is the origin of the Son from the Father; the procession of the Holy Spirit is the origin of the Holy Spirit from the Father and the Son. Note carefully that the Father does not originate from any other person. The Second and Third Persons are the only ones who originate. We have now arrived at the most general notion of "procession"—the origin of one from another.

Here we are really at the heart of the mystery. The First Person is the principle of the whole Deity, the Second and the Third proceed from Him. Now to our way of thinking that which is the principle of a thing is also the cause of a thing; there is a causal connection between the originator and the originated. We cannot apply this idea to God, though, for the reason that the cause is superior to the effect, which depends upon the cause. Now the Son and the Holy Spirit are not effects of the Father, nor are they dependent on Him. How the Son can have His origin from the Father and yet not be dependent on Him, caused by Him, inferior in any way to him is beyond our powers of understanding. What we can know is that the Son is *not caused*, the Holy Spirit is *not caused;* the reason is clear enough. We know by faith that the Son is God, that is, He possesses the perfection of the divine nature, and there is no cause of the divine nature; God is the *uncaused cause*. The same is true of the Holy Spirit. There is, then, an order of origin between the Persons; yet all are equally God.

Our faith has given names to these two processions in God; the procession of the Son is called *generation*, the procession of the Holy Spirit is called *spiration*. These names are actually taken from the names that Sacred Scripture gives to the two Persons who proceed. If the Son is really a Son, His origin from the Father must have been a generation; if the Holy Spirit is really the breath of divine Love, His origin must have been, in a sense, a breathing, or a spiration.

God's Relatives

The processions, we have said, are the foundation of the distinction of Persons in the Trinity; they are not the Persons. This may be clear from another example taken from creatures. A human father is a father because he generates a son; the son is son because he has a father. Yet the act of generation is not the father or the son; rather it is the basis of a real relation between father and son. When you come right down to it that is all a father is—one who is related to another human being who has been generated by him; a son is one who is related to another human being who has generated him. Of course, being individual men, father and son are distinguished by many other qualities; each does have a distinct human nature. We know that the divine nature is one and the same in the Father and the Son, yet they are really distinct, because really related to one another as generator and generated. In other words, the divine nature, which the Father possesses as Principle of the Son, is also possessed by the Son as received from the Father by way of generation.

Something similar is true of the Holy Spirit. We know that the Father and Son as one principle spirate the Holy Spirit; the distinction between the Father and Son and the Holy Spirit is constituted by the real relation of Lover and Beloved. These real relations, arising from the fact that the Persons originate from each other, are the only really distinct things in the oneness of God.

What we have been trying to express here has been said briefly in the Athanasian Creed: "The Father is made of none, neither created nor begotten; the Son is of the Father alone, neither made nor created, but begotten; the Holy Spirit is of the Father and the Son, neither made nor created nor begotten, but proceeding.... And in this Trinity none is before or after another, none is greater or less than another; but the whole three Persons are co-eternal together and co-equal."

Person and Nature

By this time, the reader may be probably very much puzzled by the repetition of the words "three Persons in one nature." He may think that the idea of person and nature is foreign to him; probably he has never thought of person and nature as two different ideas. Yet in fact he knows that there is a distinction.

There have been countless numbers of human beings who have lived before us, countless numbers will live after us; at present there are millions upon millions of other men besides ourselves. Each of these human beings could say with perfect truth: "I am a man." That is a significant statement. The word "man" belongs to each and every human being, to everyone, in fact, that has human nature. The "I" is the expression of something unique; the "I" in each statement by these countless human beings refers to what is individually peculiar to each of them. Another point; only men and angels and God use the pronoun "I". In other words, the "I" always refers to a distinct being that possesses intellectual nature. Intellectual knowledge and free will are necessary to a person.

We can push this a little further. We all say: "I think, I love, I sleep, I eat, I walk." Such a diversity of actions attributed to one thing. We also say: "my will, my arm, my eyes"; here again we are attributing a number of things to one central reality—the "I". The totality, then, to which all else is attributed and by which ultimately one intellectual being is distinguished from another, the reality called "I" is the person. The nature is that through which the person operates. The human "I" does certain things because of human nature; the angelic "I", because of angelic nature; the divine "I", because of divine nature.

Three Distinct Persons

Usually in our experience every individual intellectual nature is at the same time a distinct person. This human being is John Jones; this one is Jim Smith. This individual angelic nature is Raphael, this one is Gabriel. There are two exceptions. We know that the individual human being Christ has no human personality; in Him the human nature is united to a Divine Person, so that Christ the Person has a divine and a human nature. From what we have said above, we know too that in the divine nature there is not just one person, but three. The Father says: "This is My beloved Son in whom I am well pleased." The Son says: "I and the Father are one." There is no place in Scripture where the Holy Spirit speaks in His own Person, but if there were, He too would say, "I". Moreover, Christ speaks of Him as a Person.

If Jim Smith is a person because he is distinct from John Jones within human nature, if Gabriel is a person because he is distinct from Raphael within angelic nature, then the Father, Son and Holy Spirit are also Persons because they are distinct one from the other in the unity of the divine nature. If we keep in mind this difference we shall not go wrong: Jim Smith and John Jones possess each a distinct and separate human nature; Gabriel and Raphael possess each a distinct and separate angelic nature; the Father, Son, and Holy Spirit possess one and the same nature; there is no distinction or separation on the side of the divine nature, it is simply one. This does not deny the fact that they are nevertheless distinct, for, as we have seen, the Father is not the Son, the Father and the Son are not the Holy Spirit; they are distinct by reason of the real relations of origin.

Let us take one more step now to make sure that we do not form an incorrect notion of the Trinity. The Father is identified with the divine nature, the Son is identified with the divine nature, the Holy Spirit is identified with the divine nature. In other words, the divine nature, being completely simple and indivisible, belongs wholly to each of the Persons. The Father has neither more nor less than the Son, the Holy Spirit neither more nor less than the Father and the Son. We always come back to the simple statement: the Father is God, the Son is God, the Holy Spirit is God, three Persons, one God.

Not Mathematics

By this time the mathematically minded readers are probably ready to object strenuously. In fact, all of us have enough mathematical knowledge to know that one cannot be three and three cannot be one. And it is true enough, if we were talking about mathematics; we aren't, we are talking about God. Three units are certainly not one unit, nor is one unit three; but then you can look at a mathematical unit in only one way. We do not say that the one divine essence is three divine essences, or that the one divine Person is three divine Persons; we do say that the three divine Persons are one essence or nature.

There is another famous mathematical axiom that may also come to mind: two or three things equal to the same thing are equal to each other, or better two or three things identical with the same thing are identical with each other. We just said that the three Persons are identical with the divine nature; therefore, are they not identified with each other? The answer is no; for they are not identical in every way. In so far as each Person is identical with the divine nature, He is God; but He is still distinct from the others, not by reason of the divine nature, but by reason of a real relation of origin.

There is much more that could be said in our search for an understanding of the mystery of the Trinity. Let us again reaffirm our faith in the Catholic doctrine that there are three Persons in the one divine nature. We shall now turn to look at each of the Persons separately, trying to know them better. For this purpose we shall find many hints that will make us better acquainted with each Person. These hints will be found especially in the names applied to the Persons as proper to each of them. Unfortunately we have lost the art of naming persons with names that really fit them. Mr. Fisher may never have gone fishing and Mr. Goldsmith may work in a iron foundry. But Scripture has given names of the three Persons that fit them; in fact some names fit only one of the Persons and not the others, some names could be used for any Person, but are reserved for one or the other. Since our knowledge is so limited we must cherish each name of God or of a divine Person as a special token of affection; for it is God Himself who tells us His names.

God the Father

The First Person of the Most Holy Trinity has been given three names by Catholic tradition—Father, Principle, and Unbegotten. The first name is most proper of all, the reason in fact for the other two; for He is Principle and Unbegotten inasmuch as He is Father. He is Father precisely because He has a Son; He simply would not be a Father, and, therefore, not a distinct Person if He did not generate a Son.

Even though the mystery of the Trinity had never been revealed to us, we should still call God our Father. This name would be an adaptation from human parenthood; just as the father is the cause of his child and provides for it, God is the cause of the world and provides for it. In every creature there is at least a trace of God; so Job asks "Who is the father of the rain? or who begot the drops of dew?" In a more perfect way, men, made to the image and likeness of God, are children of the Father. When we say, "Our Father, who art in heaven," we are calling on the three Persons of the Trinity, on God, not just on the first Person.

Now, through revelation, we know that God can be called a Father in the truest sense; He has generated a Son. As St. Paul confesses: "I bend my knees to the Father of Our Lord Jesus Christ, from whom all fatherhood in heaven and on earth receives its name." Human parenthood is but a pale reflection of the perfect parenthood of God the Father.

In generating the Son, the Father gave to Him the perfection of the divine nature, which included the power to spirate the Holy Spirit. Together then Father and Son are one principle of the Third Person. For this reason we can say that the Father is the Principle of the Holy Trinity, or even the Principle of the Divinity; the Son has divinity from the Father, the Holy Spirit from the Father and the Son; the Father simply has divinity. He receives it from no other divine Person; therefore He is also the Unbegotten, or the Unproceeding.

Beginning and End

The central position of the Father in the Trinity is constantly present to the mind of Jesus Christ. Anyone acquainted with the Gospels is struck with the insistence of Christ on His Father's will. In fact, the first words of Christ are these addressed to His Mother: "How is it that you sought Me? Did you not know that I must be about my Father's business?" His last words on the Cross were, "Father, into Thy hands I commend My spirit." His last recorded words before His ascension to the Father are, "And I send forth upon you the promise of my Father. But wait here in me city until you are clothed with power from on high." And this thought of the Father's centrality takes on a vaster meaning when we recall the words of St. Paul: "Therefore let no one take pride in men. For all things are yours, whether Paul, or Apollos, or Cephas; or the world, or life, or death; or things present, or things to come—all are yours, and you are Christ's, and Christ is God's." All things are brought back to Christ by His Mystical Body, the Catholic Church, and Christ returns them to the Father. The Father is therefore the beginning and the end of all things.

Lastly, we must remember that we are the adopted sons of the Father. Adoption takes place in baptism, when original sin is wiped away and sanctifying grace is poured into the soul. This is not the place to discuss the nature of sanctifying grace at length; we should be able to see, though, that the regeneration of the soul through grace is something like the generation of the Son by the Father. Within the Trinity God the Father gives the totality of the divine perfection to His Son; in adoption He gives a share or a participation of the divine nature to men, and this share is sanctifying grace. For the same reason we are children of Mary and brothers of Jesus Christ.

God the Son

The Second Person of the Most Holy Trinity has three names that are proper to Him—Son, Word, and Image. From what we have said about the Fatherhood of the First Person we gather a sufficiently clear idea of the Sonship of the Second Person. He is really generated by the Father, the First-born, the only-begotten. There can be no doubt about this fact for the Catholic; it is clearly expressed in Sacred Scripture and defined by the Church. We can, however, ask, "How is it possible for God, a spiritual being, to have a Son?" Here the other two names given to the Son in Sacred Scripture give us considerable assistance.

What is a "word"? We can imagine a word, we can utter a word. The imagined word and the uttered word are symbols of a concept that we have in our minds. The concept is an inner word, a spiritual word that proceeds from our act of understanding something. This may not be immediately clear to us, but a moment's reflection will help us grasp what it is we do when we understand something. Take for example another man, a new acquaintance. We have been introduced to him by a mutual friend. Immediately our senses bring to us an impression of this individual; further intimacy sharpens the picture we have of him, until we come to possess within our minds a clear idea of "this man." This concept is distinct, for instance, from our concept of our brother or sister. It is the man more or less perfectly existing in our minds; this mental existence is a product of our act of understanding.

Before applying this to the Word of God, let us try to see what happens when we understand ourselves. We can do this only indirectly, by standing aside, as it were, and observing ourselves in action. But gradually we become better acquainted with ourselves; we have an idea of ourselves that has been produced within our minds. The idea proceeds from us, remains within us, and yet is certainly not us. Even were I to form an adequate idea of myself, that idea would be the same thing as myself. "I" and "I as understood" by myself would be distinct, for the "I as understood" would proceed from me, yet remain with me.

God Understood

The Word of God, then, is God understood. The Father understands Himself and the whole divinity; in that act of understanding Himself, He speaks a Word. This Word is a perfect reproduction of the Father, yet is not the Father, for He proceeds from the Father's act of understanding. The Word terminates the Father's act of understanding, somewhat as my concept of myself terminates my act of understanding myself. This seems to be clear enough, for God, being spiritual has two operations, those of His intellect and will; that which terminates the operation of His intellect is the Son, that which terminates the operation of His will is the Holy Spirit.

Because the Son is the Word of God, He is also the image of God. An image is a likeness, not any sort of likeness, but one that is produced just to be a likeness. One egg is like another egg, it is not the image of another egg. A portrait is the image of a man because it was made to be like the man. The son is the image of his father because the whole process of generation tends to produce a likeness, another human being. From what we said about the intellectual conception in a previous paragraph, we can see that the idea is also always an image. My idea of an acquaintance would not be of much use to me if it were not like him. My idea of myself is an intellectual image of myself. The same is true of God. The Word of God, proceeding from the mind of the Father, is a likeness of the Father. The Son is a perfect reproduction of the Father; like to Him is everything but His Fatherhood. Is it any wonder that Christ's words had and still have such a powerful effect in the hearts of men, since His is the Word of God.

God the Holy Spirit

Probably the reader has been struck by the fact that very little has been said about the Holy Spirit so far. What little was said has been rather obscure. There is a very good reason for this obscurity and it lies in ourselves. While the core of any Catholic mystery is divine, the concepts used to express it are always human; therefore, when we have rather clear concepts about ourselves, this very clarity helps us to understand the divine a little better when we apply our concepts to God. It is a simple fact that the human processes of knowing are clearer to us than the processes of loving. We are much better able to give an account of what we know and how we know than of what and how we love.

The Third Person of the Trinity proceeds by way of the divine will, by way of love. This much we are certain of. To get further knowledge of this Person we must have recourse to the names that Sacred Scripture uses when it speaks of Him—Holy Spirit, Love, Gift. In a sense none of these are proper to Him, as, for example, Son is proper to the second Person. They all apply equally well to the Holy Trinity. Yet, if the Third Person is the mutual love of Father and Son there is active spiration (akin to paternity in the first Person); on the side of the Holy Spirit there is passive spiration (akin to filiation in the second Person).

Impulse of Love

Hence, the names that we do use for the third Person have to be, as it were, reserved for Him, even though they also apply to the other Persons as well. Take, for instance, the name that we are most familiar with, "Holy Spirit." Certainly, God is a Spirit, an immaterial substance; certainly, God is holy, the all-pure. Yet there is something in our use of the word "spirit" that makes it appropriate to the third Person. For "spirit" indicates a motion or an impulse; we call the breath and the wind by this name. Now it is also the property of love to move and impel the will of the lover towards the object loved. This aspect of love is undoubtedly well-known to all of us. We know how calm we can be in the pursuit of knowledge; we can sit back and take in knowledge without the slightest impulse to do anything else. When, however, what we know arouses love in our wills, we start to do something about it. We are not satisfied with just knowing; we want with all our strength to possess the thing that has aroused our love. That is why a lack of school "spirit" is interpreted as a lack of love for the school. The excitement and urge of love is therefore the source of spirit. The Person who proceeds from the infinite love of the Father and the Son may well be called the Spirit of God. He can be called (if we are careful to understand aright) the motion or the impulse aroused in the Father and the Son at the sight of the infinite goodness of the divine nature.

There is another point that we must mention here. It will be noticed that we have spoken of the Holy Spirit as proceeding from the Father *and the Son*. One of the differences between the Catholic and the Greek Orthodox Church is precisely this question of the procession of the Holy Spirit from the Son. The Greek Church denies that the third Person proceeds from the second; the Catholic Church has always insisted that He does. The reason for the Catholic view is this; if the Holy Spirit did not proceed from the Son, He would not be distinct from the Son. This may seem difficult to grasp at first, yet we have already given the basic reason for it. In the earlier sections of this pamphlet we saw that there is no real distinction within God except there are opposing relations, of fatherhood and sonship, of active spiration and passive spiration. We also saw that such opposing relationships can be founded only on the procession of the Persons, one from another. Thus, if there were no real generation there would be no real relationship of Father and Son; that seems clear enough. The same thing must be true of the Holy Spirit. If He is really distinct from the Father and the Son, He must originate from them.

Unity of Love

Note here, too, that the Father and Son are one principle in spirating the Holy Spirit; while remaining distinct Persons, they unite in this activity. Which is not at all strange, when we think about it. What unites two human persons more perfectly than love for the same object? In fact, the most perfect unions we are capable of spring from love. Even the union of husband and wife, with each the object of the other's love is deepened when a third person arrives to turn the combined love of the parents to itself. The Father and Son, then, unite in loving the perfection that is theirs, and the love is another divine Person, the Holy Spirit. In a way that is beyond the capacity of creatures, Father and Son can unite in their love, because they are one in nature; no matter how closely two human beings are united in love, there are always two loves.

From what we have said so far about the Holy Spirit it is clear that the other names given to Him, Love and Gift, while also applicable to the whole Trinity are most appropriately applied to Him. Just as to speak is to produce a word, and to flower is to produce flowers, so to love means to spirate love, or produce love, which in God, as it proceeds from the Father and the Son united in one principle, is a substantial and subsisting Person, the Love of the Father and the Son.

Gift of God

Closely connected with the name Love is the name Gift. Again this name can be applied to the whole Trinity, to the Incarnate Son of God, to all the perfections of nature and supernature that God heaps upon His children. Yet it is most appropriately given to the Holy Spirit. What is a gift? It is an object that is capable of being given. What is given bears a relationship both to the giver and to the receiver of the gift. For it can be given only by one whose it is to give and it is given to someone to be his. I don't give my father's cigarette lighter to my friend, for it is not mine to give. I don't give my friend the Brooklyn Bridge, for it could not be his. Does any of this apply to a divine Person the Holy Spirit? He certainly belongs to the Father and the Son, since He originates from them; they can and do give Him. But to whom is He given? To any one in the state of sanctifying grace, who alone is able to receive and enjoy the Gift of God. "Charity is poured forth in our hearts by the Holy Spirit, *who has been given to us.*"

No other gift of God better deserves the name of Gift than the Holy Spirit Himself. For a gift is given without thought of return or recompense; it is a free donation. It is free for it comes from love; we give gifts to those we love. Hence love itself must be the first of all gifts; before anything else we give our hearts. It is fitting then that the Holy Spirit be called the Gift of God, for, as St. Augustine says: "By the Gift, which is the Holy Spirit, many particular gifts are given to the members of Christ." We must never forget that of all the gifts that God has given, none is greater than this; He has given us Himself.

Strictly Personal

We have finished our explanation of the inner life of the Trinity; before turning to the concluding sections on the relation of the Triune God to created reality outside God, let us summarize the important truths we have learned. There is only one God, one divine nature. Faith tells us, though, that there is a distinction within the very unity of the divine nature, a distinction of three real Persons.

Apart from the Persons, there can be no distinction in God. Each Person is something that the other Person is not (even though they are all identical with divine nature); or to accommodate the truth to our ways of understanding, we might say that each Person has something that the other two do not have, a note that is entirely personal. Thus the first Person has Paternity, is the Father; the second has Filiation, is the Son; the third Person has passive spiration, is the Holy Spirit. The first and second Persons have something that the third Person does not have, namely, active spiration. All else is common to the three Persons; in everything else they operate as one.

Here, whenever God operates outside Himself, as it were, that operation is common to all three Persons. The Creation of the world, the guidance of all things to their respective destinies, the redemption of man, the forgiveness of sins and so forth, are all effects of the entire Trinity. We cannot say, for example, that the Father does anything that the Son and Holy Spirit do not do; the same is true of the other Persons in relation to the Father. The creation of a human nature and the uniting of that nature to the second Person of the Trinity in the mystery of the Incarnation is the work of the three Persons, although the human nature is united only to the second Person. Whenever the God-man, Christ, acted as God, He did not act without the Father and the Holy Spirit.

Manner of Speaking

This will probably bring up a difficulty to the mind of the reader; the Catholic Church does speak as though the Father created men, the Son redeemed them and the Holy Spirit sanctified them. There are many other instances where the language used by the Church seems to contradict what we said above. Actually there is no contradiction; moreover it is most important to understand what takes place here, so that we may have a clearer notion of our relation to God. We are dealing here with what is technically known as *appropriation* (making proper what is really common). We have just seen that only Paternity, Filiation and Passive Spiration are really proper to the three Persons; everything else is common. Nevertheless we can take something that is common to the three and attribute it, or appropriate it especially to one. Whenever we do this, it is because, to our way of thinking, that which is common has a special relation to that which is proper to the Person to whom we attribute the common. Take, for example, the fact of creation. Creation is obviously a manifestation of power, the absolute beginning of all the things we know. The entire Trinity created; yet is it not true that from what we have learned about the Father, namely, that He is the source of the other Persons, we feel that the relationship to Creation belongs to Him more than to the other Persons? We already saw that all the names we give to the third Person apply primarily to the entire Trinity; nevertheless, they do express what is peculiar to the third Person and so we appropriate them to Him.

Why do we use this device of appropriation? Simply because it helps us get better acquainted with the three Persons. There is so little we know about them as Persons that it helps us to divide up, so to speak, what we know about the divine nature among the three Persons. Before leaving this question let us explore one of the most common sets of appropriations and see how it helps us realize the personal relationship we have with the Triune God.

Traditional thought has always attributed power to the Father (for He is the Principle of the Godhead), wisdom to the Son (for He proceeds from the understanding of the Father), and goodness to the Holy Spirit (for He proceeds from the love of the Father and the Son). In accordance with these appropriations, we also attribute works of power, such as creation, to the Father, works of enlightenment to the Son, and works of goodness and love, such as the justification of sinners, the infusion of grace, to the Holy Spirit. In a similar manner, we can distinguish sins against the distinct Persons, though, in fact, every sin is against the Trinity. Yet sins of weakness, of passion, are against the Father, sins of ignorance are against the Son, sins of malice, against the Holy Spirit. Weakness and ignorance are, in a way, excuses for the commission of sin and hence are more easily pardoned. But sins of malice, deliberate defiance of love are sins against the Holy Spirit and are remitted with more difficulty. The unforgiveable sin is directly against love, for it is the final refusal of God's love and pardon at the hour of death.

Cradle to Grave

In a former pamphlet *(The Heights and Depths)* we say that God is present to every soul in the state of grace as an intimate Friend. We can now add that the Trinity is present in such a soul. St. Paul calls Christians, "the temples of the Holy Spirit." This does not mean that only the third Person is present; no, the entire Trinity is here. Christ has promised to send the Paraclete, the Spirit of Truth, to every soul that loves Him. Moreover, He has promised that "we (the Father and I) will come and make our abode with him." Within the soul of the just man the Father is generating the Son, and the Father and the Son are spirating the Holy Spirit, for these are eternal processions. Simultaneously the Son and the Holy Spirit are manifesting themselves to the soul through the gifts of grace and leading the soul back to the Father, from whom they have come forth. Within the soul of one in the state of grace, then, the processions that originate from the Father in some way return to the Father, bringing back the fruit of a redeemed soul.

The Christian should be ever conscious of his intimate relations with the Trinity. The Church tries to impress this fact on his mind by putting the Trinity at the beginning and end of Christian life. At the baptismal font the child of Satan is transformed into a child of God "in the name of the Father, and of the Son, and of the Holy Ghost." The last words that strike the ear of a dying man are these uttered by the attending priest: "Go forth, O Christian soul, out of this world, in the name of God the Father Almighty, who created thee; in the name of Jesus Christ, the Son of the living God, who suffered for thee; in the name of the Holy Spirit, who sanctified thee."

STUDY QUESTIONS

1) What is the source of our knowledge of the inner life of God?

2) Why should we be concerned with the mysteries of our Faith?

3) How should a mystery of our Faith be approached?

4) What three aspects of the Holy Trinity are expressed in the New Testament?

5) What is the formula of the Athanasian Creed concerning the Trinity?

6) What is the meaning of *procession* concerning the Trinity?

7) What are some of the more possible kinds of procession?

8) What is meant by *generation* and *aspiration* in the Trinity?

9) What is the distinction between *person* and *nature?*

10) How is *person* and *nature* applied to the Holy Trinity?

11) What is distinctly taught regarding the Father?

12) What is distinctly taught regarding the Son?

13) What is distinctly taught regarding the Holy Spirit?

14) What is the difference in doctrine between the Catholic Church and the Greek Orthodox Church regarding *procession?*

15) What is distinct about the operations of the Trinity?

16) What is meant by *appropriation?*

17) What is distinctly attributed to each of the Persons of the Trinity?

18) What sins can be distinguished against each Person of the Trinity?

19) How do the Persons of the Trinity manifest themselves to the soul?

20) How does the Church impress the doctrine of the Trinity on Christian life?

13

ALL OR NOTHING AT ALL
A Consideration of Divine Creation

REGINALD COFFEY, O.P.

Introduction

This pamphlet begins the consideration of the universe. It is confined to an explanation of creation objectively studied. The subsequent pamphlets will treat of the various aspects of creation and the continuation of the universe. As in the previous pamphlets which were concerned with an objective study of God and His nature, a series of questions are appended for the use of study clubs or discussion groups.

Though each of these pamphlets is complete in itself, the whole series will provide an integrated and systematic survey of the whole of Catholic theology. Previous pamphlets are still available.

PART I

In the Beginning

Long before the advent of that people's university which is the Sunday supplement and popular expositors of science such as Herbert George Wells, who hands out airy, unsubstantial and unsubstantiated theories with more assurance and aplomb than a convention of professors, men were interested in the world, its origin and its composition. This interest goes back to the beginning of recorded history and takes a second place only to those questions most vital to man: Who am I, where did I come from and where am I bound? And since it is natural to man to try to learn something about his surroundings after he has found out something about himself, he speculated in much the same fashion about the earth, the place of his habitation.

Different ages have given different answers to all of these questions according to the mental outlook of the age. In one age—the early Greek period—the principal stress seems to have been put on man, and all things were considered in relation to him. Given the fact that man is naturally interested in himself and his fellows, this was to have been expected. As a matter of fact it is quite remarkable that in the later Greek period especially as it is represented in the persons of those stupendous men, Plato and Aristotle, the chief interest of man seemed to be not the world or himself but the Creator of both.

During the Middle Ages, in a world that had received the fullness of revelation, the thinkers naturally occupied themselves chiefly with God and the relation of all things to him. However, it is necessary to note that the creatures of God must be given a very important place in any consideration of God. Otherwise, one would wonder why in the classics of theology that have come down to us from that period, exhaustive works such as the *Summa,* so much time was spent by the authors on problems that are seemingly of purely mundane consideration. These men, although they realized as the men of other ages did not, that the chief study of mankind was God not man, nevertheless appreciated the fact that a complete study of God entailed a careful study, not only of man, but of the earth on which he lived. And given the fact that they did not have telescopes, microscopes and advanced mathematics to aid them in their inquiry they did a pretty good job.

They did not find out the whole story but the best of them never advanced the fantastic theories with which the modern Sunday supplement so frequently entertains its readers. And since they based their theories upon principles of sound reason they did not have to revise them every few months as many of our modern scientists are forced to do, whose theories are based upon speculation on the facts discovered so far. For today it is not uncommon to see some brash scientist (who in spite of his brashness enjoys an international reputation) put out some wild theory concerning, say, the Martian man, whom he takes for granted, only to have Mars entirely depopulated a few months later by some other scientist. Of course the sad aspect of this situation is not the fact that new theories are formulated but that new theories are taught as new facts.

Backstage

St. Thomas Aquinas like the other Catholic theologians realized that the Bible was never intended to be a text-book in physical science. He knew that the sacred writers in relating the story of the creation were restricted in so doing by the scientific knowledge that they themselves possessed. But he was aware that while the biblical account of creation might not have been entirely satisfying to the mind of the scientific man of the thirteenth century in detail, it was, nevertheless, completely and substantially true. It was because of the teaching of her theologians, through the guidance of the Holy Ghost, that the Catholic Church was not shaken to her foundations with the advent of Darwin as were so many of the Protestant sects. While some of the Protestant sects lost faith in their only norm and guide for faith—the Bible, because modern science had proved it "false," others adopted the fanatical stand of the fundamentalists and insisted that seven days meant seven days of twenty-four hours each and that none of the findings of the evolutionists could possibly be true. But the old and wise Catholic Church read the data uncovered by Darwin, Huxley and the others, stifled a yawn and, passing the paper back to the discoverers remarked without too much enthusiasm, "Evolution is back again, huh? If you'll go to the trouble of pulling down a few books from the top shelf in the dark corner of the library you will find that one of my smartest sons, Augustine of Hippo, did a little work on that subject back in the fifth century. You will also find the subject treated by a lad named Thomas of Aquino in the thirteenth. They both seemed to think that the idea was rather reasonable but they both had enough brains to realize that something doesn't come from nothing and that no monkey can be the father of man. Good day, gentlemen, I've got to say my prayers now."

In his tract on the creation of the world St. Thomas Aquinas, having proved at the very beginning of his *Summa* that God exists, does not here take time out to repeat the proof. His task at this particular juncture is to examine the Deity in the role of Creator and determine just what took place.

We won't even start setting the stage where the drama is to be enacted. About all we will have time for is an interview with the stage-manager. In his eight articles on the subject Saint Thomas discusses eight important points that must be cleared up before the creation of the world can itself be treated. These are: 1) What is creation? 2) Whether God can create anything? 3) Whether creation is anything in the very nature of things? 4) What things are created? 5) Can only God create? 6) Do the three persons or one person of God create? 7) Whether any trace of the Trinity is to be found in created things? 8) Whether the work of creation is mingled with the works of nature and of the will?

In the first article Saint Thomas finds that the verb create is very, often wrongly used. People, in his time as in ours frequently said "create" when they meant "make." To make a thing there is required something existing out of which the thing is made but to create means the production of something out of nothing. And so if we use the word correctly God is the only creative artist.

All Or Nothing at All

This all seems very clear. Nevertheless Saint Thomas finds several subtle objections to offer to the doctrine. One is a captious objection based on the use of words. We say that a statue is made from brass and a table is made from wood but what sort of material is this thing called "nothing" from which something is made. Of course since the objection is founded on a play on words it can be cleared up by changing the words. So if instead of saying a thing is made from nothing, you say a thing is not made from anything the grounds for the objection disappear.

In considering whether God can create we have the reason why He did create and we have a proof for the existence of God. Because the very fact that there is a world in existence points to the fact that there is a Being who put it into existence. This Being did not fashion the world from material already in existence because if such material already existed of which He was not the cause, He would not be the first cause. So the only way by which God could bring the world into existence was by creation—producing it from nothing. The act of creation is unique and belongs only to God. A man may generate another man but he generates him from already existing material. A sculptor can fashion a statue but he can't produce the marble by snapping his fingers. A big oak is a tremendous result— an almost miraculous thing to come from an acorn but if you cut down the oak and submit any portion of it to chemical analysis you will find that it contains nothing not contained in the acorn, the soil and the air, etc. The material from which nature fashioned it was at hand. Only God can create.

Creation is a unique act, so unique and so far beyond our experience that it is all but impossible for us to imagine it. It is not change, really, for nothing does not change into something. Change means that something is different now from what it once was. Sometimes the change is very great and the something existing now bears no resemblance to what it was before. It is hard to see the oak in the acorn. But in creation where the whole substance is produced from nothing there is no comparison to be made, for nothingness is beyond comparison. So while the word "make" is not a good synonym for create it is better than "change" for while "change" signifies a comparison, "make" signifies cause and that at least is clear in the act of creation. But strictly speaking there is no synonym for creation because the act is as unique as God Himself.

How About Causality

One of the first principles of philosophy is the axiom: *Ex nihilo nihil fit*—from nothing nothing is made. It is a very important principle since it is one way of expressing the principle of causality. Throughout the course of this series a great deal has depended upon the principle of causality—even the proof for the existence of God. What do we do in this case? Throw out the principle? In offering the objection Saint Thomas in his role of objector points out that not even the almighty power of God can run contrary to a first principle. He cannot make a part that is greater than its whole. He is not able to produce a square circle and if He creates an irresistible force, it is impossible for Him to create an immovable body. So the query is: Is creation an exception to this principle? St. Thomas answers that this axiom is a statement of the principle of causality as it applies to particular causes. It has no place he says "in the first emanation from the universal principle of things." Far from being an exception to this principle—creation is a proof of it because it shows the need for a first uncaused cause.

The being who does the creating has been, among philosophers, a cause of dissension. Many who admit that the power to create belongs to God alone have held that He communicated this power to some inferior creature, an angel, for instance, who did the creating as an instrument of God. Avicenna, the great Arabian, was one who held that God so delegated His power. According to him the first substance created by God created another after itself: the substance and soul of the world. All inferior bodies according to this fantastic theory are subsequently created by the substance of the world. Even the great authority among the scholastics of Saint Thomas' time, Peter Lombard, the Master of the Sentences, opined that God could communicate to a creature His creative power. These philosophers pointed out that material creatures are able to beget their own likeness. Man, for instance, can beget man and fire generates fire. And following the teaching of Aristotle who taught that what is perfect can produce its own likeness, the philosophers who held the opinion of ministerial creation pointed out that since this ability is found in material things it must surely be found in immaterial things since these are the more perfect. And since an immaterial thing can be produced only by creation then it must follow that all immaterial substances can create.

No Need for Delegation

"But such a thing cannot be," replies Saint Thomas, "because the secondary instrumental cause does not participate in the action of the superior cause, except inasmuch as by something proper to itself it acts dispositively to the effect of the principal agent. If therefore it effects nothing, according to what is proper to itself, it is used to no purpose; nor would there be any need for certain instruments for certain actions." The cutting of wood is the proper action of a saw, Thomas points out, but the fact that the pieces of wood cut form a bench was not the intention of the saw but the sawyer. If the sawyer could have made his bench without the use of the saw he would have been foolish to have made a saw first and then to have gone to all the trouble of sawing. In the case of the sawyer and his saw the instrumentality of the saw is necessary in the building of the bench. But in the work of creation instrumentality is bootless. For says Thomas, "the proper effect of God creating is what is presupposed to all other effects, and that is absolute being. Hence nothing can act dispositively and instrumentally to this effect, since creation is not from anything presupposed, which can be disposed by the action of the instrumental agent." In other words in creation there is no wood to saw or marble to chisel—there is nothing but nothingness.

Less Than Angels?

To bring something out of nothingness requires divine power. And while it is true, as Aristotle says, that a perfect thing participating any nature makes a likeness to itself, it does so not by absolutely producing that nature, but by applying it to something else. An individual man cannot be the cause of human nature because he would then be the cause of himself. But a man in generating his offspring is the cause of human nature being in the son. "But as an individual man participates human nature, so every created being participates, so to speak, the nature of being; for God alone is His own being. Therefore no created being can produce a being absolutely, except forasmuch as it *causes being in this:* and so it is necessary to presuppose that whereby a thing is this thing before the action whereby it makes its own likeness." In other words John Brown can produce a son who is like unto himself and a member of the same species because John Brown is a composite being and he does not produce John Junior out of nothing but disposes the matter into which the form is received. But an angel is nothing but form. It is a simple and not a composite being so therefore there is no matter to be predisposed. Every angel is its own species and every angel, unlike every man, is created and not made. So because of the lack of matter to be predisposed no angel can reproduce even though the angel is a more perfect being than man.

Most Catholics have learned from their catechism at some time or another that to the three persons of the Holy Trinity are assigned roles that are proper to each. Thus it was the Son who became man and suffered and died for the sins of men because the work of redemption is proper to the Son. To the Holy Ghost is given the work of sanctification and government. To the Father belongs the work of creation. But it would be a mistake and heresy to believe that in the works proper to the several persons the whole Holy Trinity is not concerned. The world was redeemed in the person of the Son but it was a work in which the Father and the Holy Ghost were as intimately concerned as He. In the work of creation what might be called the leading role is given to the Father but the work of creation "belongs to God according to His being, that is, His essence which is common to the three Persons. Hence to create is not proper to any one person but common to the whole Trinity. Nevertheless the three divine Persons, according to the nature of their procession, have a causality respecting the creation of things. For God is the cause of things by His intellect and will just as the craftsman is the cause of things made by his craft. Now the craftsman works through the word conceived in his mind, and through the love of his will regarding some object. Hence also God the Father made the creature through His Word, which is His Son; and through His Love, which is the Holy Ghost."

But as divine nature, while common to the three Persons, belongs to them in a kind of order since the Son receives the divine nature from the Father and the Holy Ghost from both, so also the power of creation while common to the three persons belongs to them in a kind of order. The Son receives it from the Father and the Holy Ghost from both. Creation is attributed to the Father as to Him Who does not receive the power of creation from another. And of the Son it is said *Through Him all things were made* inasmuch as He has the same power but from another. And to the Holy Ghost, Who has the same power from both is attributed the government of what was created by the Father through the Son. And so properly speaking creation is the work of God and not of any one Person of God.

Triple Seal

And the Holy Trinity to keep man mindful of this fact has stamped upon every creature its threefold divine seal. Saint Augustine states that the trace of the Trinity appears in creatures and Saint Thomas agrees. But Saint Thomas goes farther than mere agreement with Augustine. Like Saint Patrick plucking a shamrock to preach more clearly upon the mystery to the heathen Irish, Saint Thomas points out where these traces are to be found. But first he finds it necessary to define a few words. What, for instance, is the difference between a trace and an image? Every effect, Saint Thomas says, represents its cause but in different ways. Some effects represent only the causality of the cause. They show that such and such a cause is present. Where there's smoke, says the old saw, there's fire. And such a representation as smoke is a good example of what a trace is. A trace shows, for instance, that someone has passed by but not *who* has passed by.

Other effects represent the cause as regards the similitude of its form. A statue of George Washington, for example, is a much better representation of George than is his foot-print. Such a representation is called an image.

Now in all creatures, Thomas finds, there is at least a trace of the Trinity and in rational creatures there is even an image. For rational creatures possess intellect and will and therefore in them is to be found the word conceived and the love proceeding, as in the Trinity the Son proceeds as the word of the intellect and the Holy Ghost proceeds as the love of the will. In the lesser orders of creation is to be found a trace of the Trinity "inasmuch as in every creature are found some things which are necessarily reduced to the divine Persons as to their cause. For every creature subsists in its own being, and has a form, whereby it is determined to a species and has relation to something else. . . Therefore as it is a created substance, it represents the cause and principle; and so in that manner it shows the Person of the Father, who is *the principle from no principle*. According as it has form and species it represents the Word as the form of the thing made by art is from the conception of the craftsman. According as it has relation of order it represents the Holy Ghost, inasmuch as He is love, because the order of the effect to something else is from the will of the Creator."

PART II

No Starting Point

Saint Thomas Aquinas and his fellow thinkers of the despised Schools had no telescopes it is true. But even without telescopes they realized how small man is. They had no microscopes to aid them in their observation of the infinitesimal. But even without microscopes they realized far better than do the moderns how great man is. And without the aid of either some of their conclusions concerning the world are still more sound than the most modern. For example consider the question of the age of the world about which modern science has concerned itself greatly. The astronomers, the physicists, the geologists, the chemists and other professors of specialized science have pooled their knowledge to determine the age of Mother earth. But with true feminine wile the old orb seems to have duped the investigators prying into so personal a secret. Between the highest estimate, put out by one group, and the lowest advanced by another, there is a difference of several million years. Of one fact they are almost all certain and that is that the earth had a beginning and that this fact can be proved.

Saint Thomas Aquinas was equally certain that the earth had a beginning in time but he did not believe that the fact could be proved from reason. Yet his knowledge was more certain than that of the moderns because he had this knowledge on the word of God Himself. Thomas would have been overjoyed if he could have proved the fact from reason because to him it would have signified a further demonstration of God's condescension in allowing us to discover His secrets for ourselves. But since he respected reason in proportion as he respected the God who created it he would not try to twist the proof to suit his own desires.

That the world began, Saint Thomas knew from the *Book of Proverbs* in which the Holy Ghost says, "The Lord possessed me in the beginning of his ways, before he made anything from the beginning." Because of this and many another text in Sacred Scripture the Church under the guidance of the Holy Ghost had dogmatically decreed that the world was not eternal. But Thomas, after examining the problem and taking into consideration the arguments of the ancients, decided that neither the eternity of the world nor its beginning in time could be proved from reason. And this for the simple fact that there is no starting place for the proof. We can prove the existence of God by starting with His visible effects. We can prove certain things about His nature by starting with what He is not. We can prove the existence of the human soul by starting with the nature of its activity. But how to prove the eternity or non-eternity of the world?

Let us start with the world itself which would seem to be the most likely place to begin such an argument. There is nothing in the nature of the world that is an argument for or against time. The things in the world are subject to continual if not endless corruption and generation and there is nothing about them to indicate that they are continual rather than endless. Substances break down and new ones are produced and we cannot say for certain that this was or was not eternally thus. All the information we can garner from the world itself is that it and the things in it did not just happen. We know that they were caused.

So having failed to discover the age or agelessness of the world from the world itself, we can proceed to examine the problem from the viewpoint of the surest thing about the world, which is the cause—God. From this point nothing on the problem can be determined because since God has existed from all eternity and is unrestricted in His action He obviously could have created from all eternity had He so chosen. There is nothing in the nature of the world that would have forced God to create it in time.

Men Propose

Both before and since the time of Saint Thomas Aquinas there has been much speculation and dreaming on the nature of the world and its inhabitants. Men, not satisfied with the world as it is, have dreamed dreams of the world as they would like it. And they have found God's explanation of what He did as unsatisfying as they have found the deed. So they have fashioned their own worlds, peopling them as they choose and running them as suited their fancies.

One point that has always seemed to trouble the more sentimental of the speculating brethren is the apparent inequality of the creatures that inhabit the world. Pollyannas of the extreme variety who, as Chesterton's Father Brown points out, make the mistake of spelling dog backwards have never been able to swallow the apparent injustice evidenced in the inequality of creatures. Some of the more fanatical have refashioned the world to their own liking by simply denying the existence of any inequality. Others have invented fanciful explanations to explain it away.

Origen, for instance, who happens to hold an honorable and respected position, a position he achieved by splendid writing before *his mind* led him into extravagant error, asserted that in the beginning all things were created equal by God. At first, says Origen, God created only rational creatures which were all equal. Inequality arose among them from free will, for some turned to God more or less and others more or less turned away. Those rational creatures which of their own free will turned to God were promoted to the state of angels according to the diversity of their merits. Those who turned away from God were bound down to bodies according to the diversity of their sins. Saint Thomas who quotes and rejects this opinion, condemns it because it makes the diversity of creatures hinge upon the punishment of sin rather than on the goodness of God. And upon this argument that the diversity of creatures shows forth the goodness of God, Saint Thomas bases his whole explanation of the phenomenon.

For some obscure reason there has always been a tendency among men to identify inequality with injustice. That the tendency is not new, may be seen from Origen's acrobatic ratiocination to explain it away. But possibly never before has this unreasonable theory been so widespread as it has been for the past two centuries, the centuries that have witnessed the penning of the immortal and ambiguous line proclaiming that all men are created equal, the centuries that have seen the slogan: *Liberty, Equality, and Fraternity* take the place of the *Hail Mary*. For reasons best known to himself Satan has seen fit to attack the free will of God and bind Him to conditions to which no just man would consent to be bound. In theology this attack has been centered chiefly upon grace; and God's right to give grace to whom He chooses has been sacrificed to the right of individual men to receive grace.

God Disposes

Excellence in the creature, it would seem, arises not from what God gives it but from the effort employed by the creature. The honor rightly due to our Blessed Mother has been withheld partly because of the reluctance to admit her surpassing excellence which she did not and could not merit. Mary's excellence like all other excellence came from God and was His free gift. And from the pseudo-Catholic denial of God's right to give His grace as He chooses to the communistic assertion of man's brotherhood in Satan a whole plot is pieced and directed by the one master mind, the angelic mind of the god of the damned, who uses the pride of man in a futile effort to defeat God.

The diversity of creatures Saint Thomas saw as the result of and the reflection of the goodness of God. And this is the only rational view. After rejecting the reasons advanced by Democritus and Anaxagoras who attempted to explain the problem according to the principles of their respective unreal philosophies, and after examining the theories advanced by Avicenna and Algazel which were equally unreasonable because they attempted to explain the diversity in some mysterious manner apart from God, Saint Thomas concludes:

> Hence we must say that the distinction and multitude of things come from the intention of the first agent who is God. For He brought things into being in order that His goodness might be communicated to creatures and be represented by them; and because His goodness could not be adequately represented by one creature alone, He produced many and diverse creatures, that what was wanting to one in the representation of the divine goodness, might be supplied by another. For goodness, which in God is simple and uniform, in creatures is manifold and divided. And hence the whole universe participates together the divine goodness more perfectly and represents it better than any single creature whatever.

Thus, each work of creation is called *good*, but the ensemble is called *very good*. "God saw all things that he had made and they were very good." (Gen. 1:31)

Evil, Men Knew

There are few things that have so concerned the mind of man and concerning which more error has been advanced than the problem of evil—its nature and its cause. In this series thus far this problem has been touched upon several times; before the completion of the series it will be treated many more times. In this instance, the teaching of Saint Thomas is concerned with the problem of evil. Men in pondering upon the nature and the cause of evil have, in the main, followed the same course they pursued in settling other problems which they found distasteful. Some have tried to deny the face of evil, protesting that the seeming existence of evil is an illusion and these were very near the truth. Others, of a more pessimistic turn of mind, have declared that everything is evil. And these were far from the truth. Still others have identified evil with matter and good with spirit. And while these had a portion of the truth, their unreasonable identification led them into all sorts of extravagant theological error.

For instance, it was from this school of thought that there arose the error denying the humanity of Christ. This error and modifications of it seem to have their common origin in the East, and this view of matter is still the main motivating force behind many of the religions of India. In the West the best known, perhaps, of all the exponents of this school of thought are the so-called Christian Scientists who are much more Brahmanistic than Christian and far more superstitious than scientific.

There are those that admit only half the problem and deny the rest. At this half-way station are gathered those who admit physical evil and deny moral evil. To some of these, physical evil is the only misfortune that can befall mankind, and it is to be sedulously avoided. Man's highest, in fact man's only happiness, they say, consists in avoiding pain, misfortune and accidents. To this school (if it can be dignified by the name), pleasure is the chief interest of man and should be sought at all times and in spite of all law. To this selfish and purblind doctrine many modern materialists give assent. Up to very recent times it was the major tenet in the moral theology of the neo-pagans. But in our time we have seen a change. The swing today seems to be away from pagan hedonism to pagan stoicism, wherein physical evil is endured as a sacrifice to some materialistic end. For instance the doctrine that the state grows great over the suffering of its members is today a widespread theory with the Nazi and Communistic regimes in Europe as its greatest exponents.

The problem of the cause of evil has also produced various and fantastic errors. Probably the most common is the denial that God the cause of all things, is the cause of the evil in the world. To people who fail to see beneath the surface of things, physical evil and sin cannot be reconciled with the goodness of an all-good God. In the present crisis many pious Christians comfort themselves with the thought that the present war is none of God's doing. Hitler and his satellites, they think, were completely under the domination of the devil and they get all their power from him. God , they say, could not be so unjust as to be the cause of all this suffering.

Some not-so-pious Christians have taken the opposite but equally short-sighted view. If God is all-powerful, they reason, why does He allow such a terrible evil as war to occur? Does it please Him to see men suffer with wounds on the field of battle? Does He derive some sort of obscure sadistic pleasure in witnessing the anguish of parents, wives, and sweethearts who have loved ones away at war? In some sad cases the Faith of the people who reason thus cannot cope with their intellectual deficiency and so they turn their backs upon God.

Either / Or

Then there are some who hold that all physical evil is the result of chance and moral evil the product of man alone and so they remove two great realities from beneath divine domination. They would excuse God from having any share in the sickness and misfortunes of man. He is too good they believe to be the cause of any suffering.

It was something of the same desire to defend the goodness of God at the expense of several other of His attributes that brought into the world the double-principle theology which makes God the cause of all good and the devil the cause of all evil. And it was this theology, in direct contradiction to Christianity, that was followed by the Gnostics, the Manicheans and many other sects that caused so much trouble for the Church in centuries past. And the doctrine still has influence upon the minds of some Catholics.

Saint Thomas Aquinas approached the subject of evil, its nature and its cause with the same open mind that he brought to every other problem. He knew, of course, that since God is good He can do no evil. He also realized that since God governs all things there could be nothing in existence that was exempt from His government. He was convinced that since God is the universal first cause nothing, including evil, could exist without His causation. So Saint Thomas starts off his study of the question faced with a dilemma, namely, either evil does not exist or God is its cause.

So, in his inquiry into the cause of evil in the world which he considers in the forty-eighth and forty-ninth questions of the first part of the *Summa,* Saint Thomas first attempts to establish the nature of evil. Does evil really exist? Quoting the authority of Pseudo-Dionysius on what appears to him to be the correct side of the question to the effect that evil is neither a being nor a good, Saint Thomas seeks to determine the nature of evil by recalling to the mind of the reader the nature of good.

Good, Saint Thomas points out, is anything that is appealing and since every nature desires its own being and its own perfection it must be said that the being and perfection of any nature is good. Now, since evil is the opposite of good, it cannot be that evil is any nature or being. Since this is true it must be that evil is the absence of good, something negative rather than positive, as darkness is the absence of light and blindness the absence of sight. This must be, says Saint Thomas, because everything that is, is good and where there is no good, there can be no positive existence. This does not mean that Saint Thomas denies the reality of evil any more than he would deny the reality of darkness or the reality of blindness. He would no more think of calling evil an illusion than he would consider referring to the absence of John Smith from class as an illusion.

Evil A Necessity

All three are facts. But all three are negative facts. They indicate what is not, rather than what is. They are the results of beings rather than beings in themselves. For example, if there were no such thing as sight, blindness would not and could not be. If light did not exist, we would never have had darkness, and if John Smith were not created, he could never be absent from class. Evil is in things but it is not itself a *thing.*

Of this fact Saint Thomas is certain and he inquiries into the reason for the fact. Evil, Saint Thomas finds, is a necessity. The perfection of the universe requires it. Just as the perfection of the universe requires inequality in things. Both inequality and evil are needed in the cosmic economy so that all grades of goodness may be realized. There is and must be only one grade of goodness that cannot fail, namely, God Himself. All other goods are merely relative and to that extent they are subject to evil. This grade of goodness is found in existence itself, for in existence there are some things which cannot lose existence, incorruptible beings such as the human soul. But there are also beings which can lose existence, corruptible things, such as the human body. And both sorts of being are necessary for the perfection of the universe. This requirement demands also that there be beings which can fail in goodness. As a matter of fact corruption itself is a failure in goodness. And since things can so fail it follows that sometimes they do so fail and evil results, for this failure in goodness is evil.

In the third article Saint Thomas hastens to clear up a difficulty that might lead to possible misunderstanding and confusion. Here he emphasizes the fact that not any absence but only absence understood in a special sense constitutes evil. Absence of good taken negatively, he points out, is not evil. If this were true, the absurd statement could be made that everything that does not exist is bad. A gold mountain does not exist therefore a gold mountain is bad.

Winged steeds do not exist therefore they are bad. Absence taken in this sense as being synonomous with evil would mean also that everything in the universe is bad, for the absence in one being of the good belonging to another would make that being bad. For example, a man who had not the strength of a lion, the sight of an eagle and the fleetness of a deer would be a bad man for these are all good. But such an absence of good does not constitute evil.

Evil comes about when good is absent in the sense of privation. Thus blindness is an evil because a man is deprived of the sight which belongs to him. And since evil is the absence of good from a being, it follows that evil cannot exist except in good because the being from which some particular good is absent, is itself (since it is being) something good.

Ways and Means

A problem very prevalent in any discussion of evil is whether or not evil can corrupt the whole good. Can the evil be so strong that the subject in which it inheres becomes all bad? The reply to this query would seem to be an easy one, for it is against the very nature of being to be bad, and had evil the power of so corrupting good that it became entirely bad, then it would seem that a being could exist which was evil and not good. However, Saint Thomas does not handle the problem so summarily. For a full consideration of it, he says, three aspects of good must be considered. One kind of good, he goes on, is wholly destroyed by evil and this is the good that is directly opposed to the evil. Thus sight is entirely destroyed by blindness, as light is wholly destroyed by darkness.

There is another kind of good that is neither wholly destroyed nor diminished by evil and that is the good that contains the evil. The air, for example, is not injured by darkness. And there is still a kind of good that is diminished by evil but is not destroyed. This good is the aptitude of a subject to some actuality. It is necessary to point out that the dimunition which occurs in this case is not by way of subtraction, as happens when the butcher cuts a slice of meat from a side of beef; it is a dimunition can be carried to infinitude without entirely destroying the good.

The great example of this dimunition of good is had in sin. The more sins we commit the less is the aptitude of the soul to receive grace, for like bodies interposed between the sun and the earth, are sins interposed between God and the soul. Yet the aptitude of the soul to grace is never wholly destroyed since this aptitude belongs to the soul by its very nature.

Saint Thomas next considers the division of evil, but he considers this division only as applied to voluntary agents. Within this limitation he finds that evil can be adequately divided into affliction and fault. In order that this division may be clearly seen it is necessary to remember that evil consists in the privation and not mere negation of good. So every defect, as Saint Thomas points out, is not evil in itself. Thus it is not considered evil because a tree cannot see since a tree is not expected to see. And so evil arises from a defect of good which belongs to a subject. And whereas blindness in a tree is not evil, it is so in a man because sight naturally belongs to man.

Good, then, consists in perfection and act and a thing is better in that it is more perfect and more actuated. Now, as has been seen in previous pamphlets, act is twofold, namely, first and second act. As has also been seen the first act consists in the integral existence of a thing while the second act consists in its operation. Therefore, evil is also twofold. In one way it consists in the subtraction of any part required for the integrity of a thing, for example, the loss of an arm or a leg to a man is an evil because two arms and two legs belong to the integrity of a man's body. Blindness is an evil because sight naturally belongs to a man.

Affliction and Fault

In another way evil exists as it affects an operation. This occurs by the withdrawal of a normal and natural operation either because it does not exist or because it has not its due mode and order. This second sort of evil is found in a special way in rational creatures who have good for the object of their wills. Now the evil which comes from the lack of integrity in a thing has the nature of affliction. Of this kind is the loss of an arm, blindness or any sickness. And such evil is not according to the will of the person so afflicted, for it is the very nature of affliction to be against the rational will. But the second kind of evil which consists in the subtraction of due operation in voluntary things, is in the nature of fault, for it is a fault for anyone to fail in any action over which he has dominion.

So when a person says of another that he or she continually lies but means nothing by this habitual mendacity, then he is excusing the liar either because for some reason the culprit does not have dominion over his acts or because the person defending does not realize that such an act of falsehood is voluntary and therefore must mean something. Perfection in the operation of speaking demands speaking of the truth. Anything that falls short of the truth is a defect in this operation and must be so considered as evil and, in the ordinary course of events, culpable evil.

Having established the adequate division of evil into affliction and fault Saint Thomas proceeds to inquire which of the two is the greater evil. In this contest for the dubious honor of being the more evil the palm is easily won by fault. There can be no question but that fault is a greater evil than affliction, even taking affliction men refer to bodily affliction, such as the loss of an arm or a leg, hardship, an incurable disease or even the loss of a fortune. But Saint Thomas here explicitly states that he is not confining himself to a consideration of affliction from this angle only when he says that fault is the greater evil, but he is considering affliction carried to its utmost to include the privation of grace and glory.

And there are two reasons why fault is more evil than affliction—any affliction. The first reason is that one becomes evil by the malice of fault rather than by the evil of pain, or as Pseudo-Dionysius expresses it: "To be punished is not an evil but it is an evil to be made worthy of punishment." But there is more than the authority of Pseudo-Dionysius to substantiate this assertion. The reasoning of Saint Thomas is much more convincing than the rhetoric of Pseudo-Dionysius. Since good, he says, consists in act and not in the possibility of an act and the ultimate act is operation or the use of something possessed, it follows that the absolute good of man consists in the good operation or the good use of his powers. Now, everything which man possesses he uses by the acts of his will. Hence men who use their wills rightly are called good men and men who use their wills for evil are commonly considered to be bad. An evil man can use even good or an evil end as, for example, a scientist who culpably uses his glibness and authority to convince the unlearned of untruths. Therefore, since fault consists in the disordered act of the will and affliction consists in the privation of something used by the will, fault is more fundamental and has more of evil in it than has affliction.

Evil for Good

The second reason can be seen from the fact that God Who is the author of affliction is not the author of fault. God may strike a man blind, He may afflict him with cancer of the brain, but He will never make him steal. But the evil of fault is directly opposed to the uncreated good because it is opposed to the fulfillment of God's will. It is likewise opposed to divine love whereby the goodness of God is loved for itself. And so it is plain that fault is more evil than affliction. As a matter of fact the proof is around us always all during our lives. We see people sanctified through affliction. Saint Paul was struck blind on the road to Damascus, but only for the purpose of making him see how evil were his ways. It took a cannonball to knock Saint Ignatius off the highroad to Hell on to the straight and narrow path. And even though God can and does use even moral evil to affect a transformation in a soul that is humble, it takes a greater display of the wondrous power of grace and is not so directly ordained to the good as is physical evil.

The cause of evil which has brought so much disturbance to pious souls who have tried to blame it on to everyone and everything but God, has been used with great joy by the impious who have refused to let the blame be put on anyone but Him and have thus employed the evident and undeniable existence of evil as a proof that there is either no God or He is no good. Saint Thomas, refusing to be drawn into any of the sentimental snares that lay in his pathway, lays the blame (if you could call it blame) for evil on the doorstep of the begetter of the evil. But since evil is not one, as we have seen, but two, it was necessary to find two doorsteps on which to put the basket, for these apparently twin children are in reality not twins and each has a different father. There is a great surface similarity between them but the similarity stops with the surface. Saint Thomas, however, does not rob the universal Father of credit for paternity in one case, attributing that credit to chance or the devil, simply because the baby does not, at superficial inspection, resemble the Father.

Saint Thomas Aquinas logically begins his investigation with the effort to determine whether or not good can be the cause of evil. At the very start he quotes, as a very healthy moral backing, the authority of Saint Augustine who asserted that there is no possible source of evil except good. Then he proceeds to find out if Saint Augustine was right and if his dictum can be supported by the internal reasons. At the very beginning he demands recognition of the fact that evil has some cause but he does not demand that the fact be accepted on his say-so. He points out that since evil is the absence of a good which naturally belongs to a thing, the thing can only fail to achieve its proper end because there is some cause operating to draw the good belonging to it away from it.

Action Not Effect

If it is natural, for example, for a flat-iron dropped from the Empire State building to hit the ground and with a tremendous thud, a flat-iron so dropped will surely achieve its end unless somebody catches it either with his hand or his head before it reaches the ground. Some cause must intervene to frustrate the natural tendency of the dropped iron. Now, since we are speaking of impeding causes, it should be pointed out that nothing but good can be a cause—any kind of a cause—because nothing can be a cause only inasmuch as it is a being and evil is not a being. This is true of any of the four causes. Only good can be the material cause of evil because as has been shown, evil cannot exist except in something that is good. And evil has no formal cause because it consists in the privation of form. It has no final cause because it is the privation of order to a proper end. But evil does have an efficient cause although an accidental one, rather than a direct efficient cause. The efficient cause of evil is accidental since evil is caused in the action rather than the effect.

For example defect of motion in an animal can be caused by weakness, as in children, or by ineptitude, as in the lame. But, on the other hand, evil is caused in a thing only by the proper effect of the agent, sometimes by the power of the agent and sometimes by reason of a defect either in the agent or in an instrument. It is caused by the power of the agent when there follows on the form intended by the agent, the privation of another form. For example, a goldsmith in applying heat to a gold bar destroys the symmetry of the bar. The goldsmith's intention is to liquefy the gold and the more heat he applies the more surely will the bar be destroyed. But the destruction of the bar is accidental because the application of heat is intended merely to melt the gold. Hence, it follows that evil has no other than an accidental cause and so not only can good cause evil but only good can cause evil.

This brings us to the question as to whether evil can be caused by the supreme good, namely, God. One thing is clear: that the evil which consists in a defect of the action, and is a result of a defect in the agent, cannot be caused by God because in the action of God there can be no defect. But evil which consists in the corruption of some things can be reduced to God as a cause. And this applies to voluntary things as well as to natural, for as was pointed out above, the agent which produces corruption and defect by its very power can be said to be the cause of the corruption and defect. As we have seen, too, that God chiefly intends in created things the good order of the universe, so that order requires that there should be some things which can and do fail. Thus God in causing the good order of the universe causes also as a consequence, and as you might say, by accident, corruption of certain things. God, in short, may be the author of the evil of affliction but He is not and cannot be the author of the evil of fault.

Not At All

A question that was much discussed in the time of Saint Thomas because of the activity of the Albigensian heresy was whether there could be one supreme evil that is the cause of all evil. Although the answer to this question is patent and, indeed, contained in the other articles on the subject, Saint Thomas makes it a point to refute explicitly the error that there is a supreme principle of evil. The answer to the question is, of course, a very decided nay. The doctrine involved in refuting it is worthy of perusal.

There is no one first principle of evil, says Saint Thomas, because the first principle of good, as has been shown, is essentially good. But nothing can be essentially bad, for every being as such is good, and evil can exist only in so far as good becomes its subject, or as it is located in something good.

The first principle of good is the highest and perfect good which pre-contains in itself all goodness. But there cannot be a supreme evil because although evil can lessen good, it can never entirely consume it. Therefore, as Aristotle says, if evil were an entirety, it would destroy itself.

The very nature of evil militates against the idea of a first principle both because evil is caused by good and because evil itself can be only an accidental cause. Thus it cannot be a first cause because an accidental cause is subsequent to the direct cause. In finishing off the article Saint Thomas indulges in a few remarks that are about the nearest to rhetoric of anything in the *Summa*.

"Those who upheld two first principles," he writes, "the one good and the other evil, fell into this error from the same cause, whence also arose other strange notions of the ancients, namely, they failed to consider the universal cause of all being, and considered only the particular causes in particular effects. For on that account, if they found a thing hurtful to something by the power of its own nature, they thought that the very nature of that thing was evil; as, for instance, if one should say that the nature of fire was evil because it burned the house of the poor man. The judgment, however, of the goodness of anything does not depend upon its order to any particular thing, but rather upon what it is in itself, and on its order to the whole universe, wherein every part has its own perfectly ordered place."

"Likewise, because they found two contrary particular causes of two contrary particular effects, they did not know how to reduce these contrary causes to the universal common cause; and therefore they extended the contrariety of causes even to the first principles. But since all contraries agree in something common, it is necessary to search for one common cause above their own contrary proper causes; as above the contrary qualities of the elements exists the power of a heavenly body; so above all things that exist, no matter how, there exists one first principle of being."

STUDY QUESTIONS

1) What is the proper study for man?

2) Why isn't the Bible a scientific textbook?

3) What two saints and theologians were concerned with the theory of evolution?

4) What does the word *create* mean?

5) Why is creation a unique act?

6) Doesn't creation violate a first principle?

7) What is meant by ministerial creation?

8) Why isn't instrumentality needed in creation?

9) Can an angel reproduce itself?

10) How do the three Persons of the Holy Trinity create?

11) What creatures possess a trace of the Trinity?

12) What creatures possess an image of the Trinity?

13) What was Saint Thomas' thought regarding the origin of the world?

14) Why is there inequality among creatures?

15) What is the nature and cause of the problem of evil?

16) What is double-principle theology?

17) Is evil necessary?

18) What is the difference between affliction and fault?

19) Why is fault more evil than affliction?

20) Why isn't there a first principle of evil?

14

"Spirit World"
A Consideration of the Angels

James M. Egan, O.P.

Introduction

The universe is a finite mirror of God's perfections, wherein each creature represents some facet of the divine beauty and goodness. It is by examination of the creature that one grows to a knowledge of the Creator. First among these creatures is the one which most closely resembles the divine nature, the spiritual creature, the angel. Then one will examine the material creature and finally that creature which is both spiritual and material, man. The following pamphlet considers the angels in their natural and supernatural state and in their contacts with the world.

War in Heaven

"For our wrestling is not against flesh and blood, but against the Principalities and the Powers, against the world-rulers of this darkness, against the spiritual forces of wickedness on high" (Eph. 6:12). Perhaps for the first time, we who live today can appreciate the meaning of St. Paul's words of warning. Unfortunately, "the spiritual forces of wickedness" have, for the most part, been successful in hiding their identity, making us forget their very existence. Now the objects of our fear and trembling are human beings, flesh and blood, with well-known names and faces; we are led to believe that physical weapons, that can thrust themselves through flesh and spill blood, are sufficient for our purposes: Yet, St. Paul's words are a warning lest we forget that men can be instruments of higher powers even when they are not conscious of their subjection. Moreover, these men need not be only those who are our avowed enemies; they may be, and in fact are, within our own household.

In our wrestling, we who are flesh and blood are powerless against the world-rulers of this darknessif we are not instruments of a greater power; we must lose the fight if we trust in ourselves and not in the power of those who have already overcome the enemy—Christ and His Blessed Mother. It is also encouraging to realize that they are King and Queen of the Angels, those other members of the spirit world who are always willing to aid us in our fight against Satan and his cohorts. "And there was a great battle in heaven, Michael and his angels fought with the dragon, and the dragon fought and his angels; and they prevailed not, neither was their place found any more in heaven. And that great dragon was cast out, that old serpent, who is called the devil and Satan, *who seduceth the whole world;* and he was cast upon the earth, and his angels were thrown down with him. . . . And when the dragon saw that he was cast into the earth, he persecuted the woman, who brought forth the man child" (Apoc. 12:7–9, 13). This is a prophecy and a picture; the picture presents us with details of the continual struggle between the good and the bad angels in the midst of which we find ourselves. It behooves us, then, to know more about this spirit world that surrounds us; to understand, as much as possible, the nature of these great beings who are bent on leading us either to heaven or to hell. We are not going to attribute all the evil that befalls us to the devils; nor are we going to ignore the many aids that come to us from the blessed angels who see the face of God. We shall try to give a sober account of the nature and the activity of angelic spirits so that we may beware of the evil some of them can cause and be grateful for the good the others do us.

Are we embarking on a childish task, telling a fairy story that goes back to the days when men saw supernatural powers in everything? Are angels and devils mere remnants of man's primitive imaginings, with no more basis in fact than the sandman or the bogeyman? The modern mind in its superior wisdom dismisses the Catholic belief in the spirit world as superstitious ignorance; it seems that science has explained away the realm of spirits and substituted the reign of the subconscious. Take up any book on psychology, and especially psychiatry, and note that the author dismisses the whole contribution of Christianity to our knowledge of the soul and its ills, because during the Middle Ages some cases of insanity were mistaken for diabolical possession; it is more scientific, apparently, to mistake cases of diabolical possession for insanity, as we do today. Often enough men have held the right conclusion for the wrong reasons. When our primitive ancestors heard the groans of a demon in the roar of a waterfall or felt the lash of an angry God in the wind and the storm, they were wrong. It is equally wrong to fall into the fallacy of denying the existence of good or evil spirits because our forefathers were naive.

Undimensional

Our certitude about the existence of angels and devils is based on the revealed word of God. On almost every page of the Scriptures we come across the divine witness to the existence of a world of spirits. Angels were at hand to witness the introduction of man into the universe; they began at once their tasks—the devils to prevent man from reaching his final goal, the good angels to fulfill the commands of God, act as His messengers, and guard man in his fight against evil.

The Church formulated her belief at the Fourth Lateran Council in these words: "We firmly believe that there is one God, creator of all visible and invisible things, spiritual and corporeal; Who, by His omnipotent power, from the beginning of time made both the spiritual and corporeal creature, the angel namely and the earthly, and then the human creature from both spirit and body."

There is a definite suggestion in these words that the angels were created at the same time as the visible universe, yet before man. They are, therefore, a part of the universe, if we take this term as applying to the whole world of God's creation and not simply to the visible creation. The angels are intimately connected with the development of the visible universe and with human destiny. "Are they (the angels) not all ministering spirits, sent to minister for them who shall receive the inheritance of salvation" (Heb. 1:14).

They do not belong to the visible universe, for they have no bodies. This is the striking difference between the angels and other creatures of God. They have no dimensions—no height, breadth, depth or length. They are not extended in space by quantity—that is why they are invisible to us. We know directly only objects that have an extended surface, for we get all our knowledge from our external senses which are themselves extended in space. It is difficult for us to understand what an angel is like because we are familiar only with objects that are extended and visible to us; even when an object is so small that it escapes our naked eyes or even a microscope, it does leave a visible trace of itself that helps us to know it. And the smallest particle of matter is always extended and can be measured, if we had the instruments.

We get our idea of the angels by denying that they are extended in space, measurable by any unit of quantity whatsoever. They are pure spirits, whose activities are those of knowing and loving; they do possess intellects and wills, but no eyes, ears, hands, or feet. They are, in fact, more like God than we because they are purely spiritual; that is why we have difficulty in knowing what they are like, for of all things we know ourselves best and other things insofar as they are like us.

Could we know about the existence of angels without divine revelation? Perhaps not; although some thinkers maintain that we can. At least, we could make a good guess. Aristotle, who was not influenced by divine revelation, except perhaps remotely, was forced by an examination of the visible universe to explain many of the events that occurred in it by supposing the existence of intellectual

and incorporeal beings, which he called "separated substances."
St. Thomas Aquinas formulated the best argument for their existence in the light of Christian philosophy. He states bluntly that
there must be angels or the work of God would be imperfect. For
if there were no angels man would be God's most perfect creature
and he is a poor one to fill that role. Now God certainly had in
mind the perfection of the universe when He created it, and the
universe is perfect only insofar as it reflects divine perfection; that
creature is most perfect who most closely resembles God in the
very act of creating.

Now, you have seen in a previous pamphlet that God creates by
an act of His infinite intellect and will: "Let there be light." The
divine command was all that was needed to bring about the existence
of light—and of all other created reality. If, then, man is the most
perfect creature in existence, there is no one who approaches this
perfection of God—the ease of operating by a simple command
of the intellect. When man wishes to make something, he must
issue a command also; but that is not the whole story, as experience testifies. Man must depend upon his body to carry out his
command—on nerves, muscles, hands, eyes and so forth. We are
always painfully aware of our dependence upon our bodies. Even
thinking and willing are influenced somewhat by bodily conditions.
If we are the peak of created intelligence, the resemblance of the
universe to God is very distant.

What Difference

Moreover, in us intellect is united to matter; in the animals and
below them matter exists without intellect. Why, then, should there
not be a higher level of created reality in which intellect exists free
from the constraints of matter.

Reason points to and faith assures us of the existence of angels—
pure spirits, who closely resemble God in that they operate by
intellect and will alone and can work even within the visible universe
simply by applying their intellect to the effect desired.

Certainly the angels complete the picture of the universe; with them we have the three possible degrees of being: the purely material—minerals, plants and animals; the purely spiritual— angels; and the mixed, both spiritual and material—men. Of course, God could omit adding the perfection of angels to His universe, but given His wisdom and the order He actually placed in His creation, we may say with St. Thomas that the angels are necessary for the perfection of God's creation.

In the course of Christian speculation about the angels, there have been some who thought that while the angels do not possess bodies as men do, they have some material element in their makeup, a subtle airy kind of matter that is invisible to human instruments. Probably the popular conception of a spirit is similar to this idea of a being with very fine matter—very much like a ghost. There was a good reason for insisting that there must be some matter in the angels: they were creatures and had only limited perfection. It would seem that if they were pure spirits there would be no way of distinguishing them from God.

However, St. Thomas found a better way of limiting the angels and of keeping them distinct from God; therefore, he rejected the notion that the angels have anything material in their nature and his opinion has been generally accepted by Catholic thinkers since his time. The thing that limits an angel is not matter, but his very essence; he is essentially a creature, that is, he does not exist of himself, but by a free decree of God's will. God alone exists essentially, cannot not exist. But every angel receives existence from God and is constituted on a definite level in the graded perfection of creation. Hence each angel is finite and a part of the general scheme of the universe. There is no possibility of his being confused with God, for he *shares* with all other creatures, though in an excellent manner, the perfection of God.

How many angels did God create? It might seem offhand that there should be but a few angels. There must be vast hordes of men, animals and plants, because in their imperfection they can manifest the divine perfection only by the multiplication of their numbers. If, as we have said, the angels are so perfect in themselves, a few of them should suffice to accomplish God's purpose.

However, the testimony of Sacred Scripture is to the contrary. Thus we read: "Thousands of thousands ministered to him, and ten thousand times a hundred thousand stood before him" (Dan. 7:10), where the reference is obviously to angels. And we recall the statement of our lord to St. Peter: "Thinkest thou that I cannot ask my Father and He will give me presently more than twelve legions of angels?" (Matt. 26:53).

When God produces something good, He is not niggardly about it; the very perfection of the angels is the reason why there are so many of them. We have no way of saying just how many there are, but we can be certain that there are more than we can imagine. Countless angels fell from grace and were cast into hell by God; yet even with this defection, the remaining faithful angels are innumerable.

Greater Than Man

There is another idea of St. Thomas, which, when we understand it, leaves us gasping at the magnificence of God's designs and helps us also to appreciate the place we hold in them.

When you have a number of things that are or seem to be alike, you have to find out what makes them distinct. It is important to find out how things differ as well as how they resemble each other. One often sees the same statue of Our Lord in several churches; they are alike because they were cast from the same mold; they differ because the matter (plaster of Paris, perhaps) was different from each statue. Men are essentially alike; they differ because of the material element of their being, which is the basis for their multiplication. If it were not for the fact that there can be an indefinite number of human bodies, there could not be a number of human souls. It is only through matter that things which are essentially alike can be multiplied. When multiplied by the divisions of matter, the things remain more alike than different: thus two men are more alike than different, as can be seen by comparing both of them to an animal or a plant. Their differences are accidental and do not destroy their essential identity.

Now, we have seen that the angels are pure spirits with no material element in their make-up. Hence, we cannot say that angels are multiplied as men are; for there is no common matter that can be the basis of distinction. So, we are forced to the conclusion that each angel is more different from the other angels than he is like them. True they are all spirits; but they differ one from another as plant differs from animal and animal from man. In other words, each angel is a distinct species all by himself.

Perhaps we can get some idea of what this means by turning to the visible universe. We know that the fundamental reality of the world is the inanimate elements and compounds of chemistry. Next we have the plants, then the animals and finally man. Now the plant possesses the perfection of the lowest order of being—inanimate matter—and adds life; the animal possesses both matter and plant life and adds sentience—the capacity to know and feel on the level of sense. Man gathers up within himself all three lower levels and adds a fourth—the capacity to know and love in a spiritual way. Yet on each of these levels there are countless individuals who share, in varying degrees, the perfection of that level. No plant, no animal, no man exhausts the possibilities of its own degree of perfection. In the angelic world we can perceive a likeness to and a difference from this order of the visible universe. The lowest angel possesses the minimum of angelic perfection; each succeeding angel possesses the perfection of the lowest angel and adds something of his own, making him specifically distinct from the others. No two angels have the same degree of perfection; no two share more or less in the same degree; each one exhausts the perfection of his own grade of being.

There is, then, a vast extension of the grades of perfection beyond man. True, men are at the peak of the visible universe; but they are also at the bottom of the spiritual world. We have no immediate experience of angelic perfection and of the grades to be found therein. In the following pamphlet there will be found an explanation of the differences between the angels from the viewpoint of their activity, especially their intellectual activity. From the grades of perfection in the angelic intellect, we get some notion of the essential differences that distinguish them.

The angels, then, are pure spirits, invisible, without bodies. Moreover, they are incorruptible, immortal; once they receive existence from the hand of God, they retain it forever. There is no way for an angel to cease existing, unless God Himself wills it. As Fr. Farrell puts it: "Looking at it in the concrete, we can destroy a fresco by scraping it off the wall or by tearing down the wall it beautifies; that is, either by destroying the thing itself or that on which it depends. There is no chink in the armor of the angel into which we might plunge the lance of destruction. The angel cannot be taken apart or erased; it cannot be destroyed by destroying that on which it depends, for it depends on nothing but God." (*Companion to the Summa,* Vol. I, 199–200. New York: Sheed & Ward, 1941).

Clothing the Spirit

The very name *angel,* used so frequently in Sacred Scripture, tells us an important truth about the splendid beings who bear it. For it means "messenger." They are God's messengers—to whom? To men. The angels, therefore, play a vital role in God's dealings with men. To fulfill this special function of their being, the angels must come into contact with the visible world. When they do, some strange things happen, things that modern science in all its sophistication refuses to consider as possible, but which human experience throughout the centuries insists has happened and does happen. Angels have appeared to men countless times with bodies that seemed human. Many pages of Sacred Scripture testify to this fact. The lives of the saints also bear witness to it. The devil, likewise, has appeared in human form to accomplish his work of seducing men. Not all contact of the spirit world with ours involves this assumption of human form, but some of it does. What explanation can we offer for these phenomena?

Basically, the explanation lies in the power of a spiritual being over matter. We know from our own case that the spiritual human soul can work on material reality, transform it, shape it, move it. We can hardly deny that the angels have even greater power over matter. They are not united to it as the human soul is, to make it live; but they can use it to form for themselves a visible body very much like a human body. Our bodies are manifestations of the spiritual powers of our souls. The angel, when he wishes to converse familiarly with men, assumes a corporeal shape that also manifests his spiritual powers.

Where does the angel get the stuff out of which he forms a body? We do not know for sure, but it is not inconceivable that he can gather enough elements together to form a visible body in the likeness of a man. Perhaps he simply condenses some of the rarefied elements of the air. There is plenty of matter for him to work on; and he has the power to form the body so perfectly that it seems human.

Of course, it is not a human body; it is not even a living body. It is merely matter shaped into the likeness of a body. The angel Raphael, after having been a genial companion to the young Tobias and a blessing to his family, let slip the secret of his presence. "Peace be to you, fear not. For when I was with you, I was there by the will of God: bless ye him and sing praises to him. "I seemed indeed to eat and drink with you: but I use an invisible meat and drink, which cannot be seen by men. It is time therefore that I return to him that sent me" (Tobias 12:17–20). These words recall similar ones of Our Lord: "My meat is to do the will of him who sent me" (John 4:34).

This power of faking human shape, or even animal shape, also belongs to the devils; there is plenty of evidence in the lives of the saints for this statement. Such a power belongs naturally to the angelic beings of the invisible universe and can be used by them whenever God wills of permits them to associate with men.

We must also note that in their relations with men the angels do not always assume bodies. They have power to act in the visible universe without assuming a body. This follows simply from the fact of their spiritual natures, which do have power over matter and the affairs of this universe. What roles do they perform when they are in contact with visible reality? Such functions as guarding individuals, groups, towns, cities, nations, churches, and so forth: directing those whom they are guarding away from evil and toward good. This function is accomplished by the action of the angel on the imagination of men. No angel can directly act on the intellect or will of men; they can act indirectly, in a manner similar to that in which one man influences another, although much more perfectly. Finally the angels can move any bodily object that they wish to. This explains many phenomena that occur, for example, at spiritualistic seances that are not due to fraud on the part of the medium.

God's Assistants

The lives of the saints afford us many examples of the power of evil spirits over matter. Henri Gheon, in his *Secret of the Cure d'Ars,* gives us a list of some of the "tricks" the devil used to disturb the saintly priest: "The devil was there, but unseen; he had at his disposal gusts of wind, crowbars, every sort of musical instrument; he gave the impression of being everywhere and nowhere; of being one and myriad; for his name is Legion. He varied his effects, then repeated one endlessly. . . . The house was infested with him; he swarmed like a rat. At first M. Vianney thought it *was* a rat. . . . Satan tried new amusements. He set the bed curtains tossing, upset chairs, disarranged the furniture. He hammered nails into the floor, plied saw, plane, and axe as though he would smash the house to pieces."

Another interesting point is brought out in the above quotation. Only God can be everywhere; no angel possesses such power. The angels are limited in the area of their influence according to the perfection of their nature. One angel might be able to operate over a whole city at one time, another might have to be satisfied with a house in the city. But within the limits of his power he can operate in what to us seems different places. He can operate on the floor and ceiling of a room without acting in between. This is not so difficult to understand if we remember that a long-limbed person could pick his hat up off the floor and snap on the light at the same time, whereas a smaller person would have to do one thing after the other.

So far we have been considering the natural perfection of the angels as they were created by God. They are His most perfect creatures, more closely resembling Him than man, for they are pure spirits, capable of operating through intellect and will alone. They were created with the rest of the universe, for they are a part of it; they are God's assistants in governing the visible universe.

The angels came from the hand of God in the full perfection of their natural being; here again they differ greatly from ourselves. We start life in a very imperfect state. Only after a long, drawn out, but intensely interesting process do we arrive at the natural perfection of our being; and then, at least physically, we start on the down road again. There is no such process for the angel; he receives the fullness of his natural perfection at the first instant of his existence.

We know from divine revelation, however, that these perfect natural beings have achieved very diverse destinies; some "see the face of the Father in heaven"; others have been plunged into an eternity of hell. How did it happen that such an auspicious start had such divergent endings? Once again we must turn to revelation for the answer; there we find that God did not create angels or men for a purely natural end. His goodness wanted all His intellectual creatures to share in His own happiness. So a higher goal was placed before the angels, which, if they sought rightly, they would infallibly obtain, but which they also ran the risk of losing through their own fault.

On Trial

It is not part of this pamphlet to describe the failure of many angels to attain heaven; we have to consider rather how all the angels could have reached that goal and how some of them actually did. The fall of the angels will be considered in the following pamphlet.

Happiness is a condition that can be had only by intellectual creatures, for it results from the conscious possession of one's proper good. When an intellectual being knows that he possesses the perfection due to his nature he is happy. There is a happiness proper to God, another proper to the angels, a third to men; for the perfection of each differs from that of the other. Clearly, God alone is perfectly and inexhaustibly happy in the possession of His own supreme goodness; no creature can be happy simply in the possession of itself, without reference to God. Men and angels are naturally happy when they possess a knowledge and love of God proportioned to their more or less limited capacities. No creature has the capacity or the right to be happy as God Himself is happy.

Yet God, by an act of infinite mercy, granted to men and angels the undreamed-of promise of being eternally happy with Him. The final goal of all God's intellectual creatures is to be made happy by possessing the same object that God possesses, that is, the divine goodness, and in the same way, by an intimate knowledge and love. True, the knowledge and love of which a creature is capable even through grace is only a participation in the knowledge and love that God has for Himself. Yet it makes us very like to God.

The angels were not created in this state of blessedness. We sometimes say that the rebellious angels were cast out of heaven. This expression leads to confusion. The word "heaven" usually means the place where those who see God face to face are. It is the place where Christ and Mary, together with the angels and saints, now are. But the word "heaven" also signifies the highest reaches of the universe, wherein, according to St. Thomas, the angels were created at the dawn of time. As a matter of fact, these two places are probably the same; but when the angels were created in "heaven," they did not enjoy the vision of God.

God could have created the angels with the beatific vision, perfect, therefore, supernaturally as well as naturally. But since no creature has by nature a right to such a benefit, God willed that by their own actions they acquire a right to it; heaven was to be a reward for their faithful service to God. He wished that they should undergo a trial; he placed them on probation, as it were, and by freely conforming to His will or rebelling against it, they determined their own eternal destiny.

The angels, then, were not created with the beatific vision; but they were created in grace, raised, right from the first instant of their existence to the supernatural order. The reason for this is simple enough: God wanted them to have a supernatural destiny: He wanted them to merit such a destiny by their free activity: yet naturally they were incapable of doing anything to merit a supernatural reward: hence He had to give them grace, which elevated their natural faculties to a supernatural plane and proportioned their activity to the supernatural goal they were destined for.

The angels, therefore, had to merit the vision of God, that is, under the motion of God's grace, which they could have resisted (in fact, many of them did); they had to choose God freely, above all other things, in preference especially to the enjoyment of their own naturally perfect being.

Did it take the angels long to make their choice? Was theirs a long drawn out trial? Was their *way* to heaven as lengthy as ours? Not at all; for the angels take but an instant to make up their minds and once they do they never change them. (This will be more fully explained in the following pamphlet).

Instant Choice

So some of the angels unhesitatingly chose God as the supreme object of their love, as the only One who could make them happy. They all echoed the cry of their leader, Michael: "Who is like unto God?" An instant after they had made their decision, they were admitted to the intimacy of divine life.

We have no reason to be jealous of the angels, feeling cheated because they could obtain the reward in an instant while we must plod along for a lifetime. We must remember that our condition has its recompense. The angels who rejected God never had a chance to repent. If we were angels, many of us might already be in hell. It is only to men that God gives another chance, and another, and another.

We pointed out earlier that the angels differ from one another in natural perfection. They received grace in accordance with the perfection of their nature, used it according to the abundance of its giving, and received a reward in heaven proportionate to the perfection of their nature and their grace. So the order of the angels in glory corresponds to the order of their natural perfection.

We should remember that while men never surpass in natural perfection the angels (this is true even of Christ and Mary), they can surpass the angels in grace. So by grace Christ and Mary are superior to all the angels and saints. Many of the saints are also, we may presume, superior to at least some of the angels. If the devils foresaw that such an arrangement would hold in heaven, we can understand somewhat why they didn't want to go there.

"In the end you shall be judged by love," say the Holy Scriptures. That applies to both men and angels. The essential discretion between good and bad is made on the basis of love of God and love of self. The difference in the degrees of happiness and misery depends on the intensity of each love. Each angel, therefore, received the substantial reward of his love when he entered heaven. There can be no change in that; he can enjoy an increase of accidental joy in the knowledge that he helps men on their road to salvation, and also in the realization that there are countless others who enjoy with him the vision of God, the Common Good of all.

The following stanzas from Fr. Faber's poem *The Holy Angels* will summarize what we have said:

> Angels and Throne and holy Powers
> And Ministers of light—

God's primal sons and mystic bands
In various orders bright,
And hidden Splendors wheeling round
In circles infinite—

Celestial priests and seraph kings
In links of glory twine:
And spirits of departed men
In saintly luster shine,
With Angels dear that fold their wings
Above the awful shrine—

Chariots of living flame that fill
The mountain's hollow side,
Breezes that to the battle-field
Over the forest ride,
Spirits that from the Bridegroom come
To wait upon the Bride—

These are among us and around
In earth and sea and air,
At fast and feast and holy rite
And lonely vigil prayer,
Morning and noon and dead of night
Crowding the heavenly stair. . . .

The Only Missing Link

Even though we may not be able to grasp all the traditional doctrine
about the angels, their nature and their contact with our visible
world, we cannot without great loss to ourselves ignore the fact of
their existence. A modern writer, Mark Van Doren, in his *Liberal
Education* testifies to the plight of modern man in a world wherein
man thinks himself supreme. "The educated person knows his own
species as well as he can. But today he is at a disadvantage because

he lacks a scale whereon to set the object of his examination. Too few other beings are available for comparison. There are the animals, whom we have with us whether or no; and we do use them for the purpose, frequently admiring the mirrors more than our reflection in it. The comparison of men with animals, however, is at best a meager exercise. A richer field existed when there were gods and heroes, as with the Greeks, or God and the angels, as with the Christians. Without the idea of angels we have a poorer knowledge of that creature who once was lower than they, though he was higher than worm or ox. And since angels were still lower than God, and different from Him, the cloud of distinction thickened into something solid which intellectually we have lost. Seeing man in a middle position between animals and angels lights up his dimensions as nothing else does." (p. 20).

There is a concentrated effort on the part of many scientists to reduce man to the level of the animals; looking at only one aspect of man, his body, which is the only view available to them as scientists, they see the continuity between man and the brute. Their error lies in the denial of the other side of man, which is just as clearly presented to the unprejudiced mind. From his spiritual side man manifests his continuity with the angelic world above him. He is truly the link between the two worlds; one might even say that he is the only "missing link."

Study Questions

1) Can men be unconscious instruments of higher powers?

2) What has the modern mind substituted for the realm of the spirits?

3) What is our certitude for belief in the angels?

4) When were the angels created?

5) What did Aristotle think regarding the angels?

6) What is the popular concept of a spirit?

7) How does an angel exist?

8) How do we know that there are many angels?

9) What is meant by distinct species?

10) What distinguishes the angels from plants, animals from men?

11) How can an angel be destroyed?

12) What does the word *angel* mean?

13) How can an angel assume human form?

14) What was Raphael's explanation?

15) What do angels do for visible reality?

16) Are the angels ubiquitous?

17) How do the angels operate?

18) Why did God create the angels?

19) Should we be jealous of the angels?

20) What is the relation of man with the angel?

15

STANDING ROOM ONLY
A Further Consideration of the Angels,
their Intellect and Will

PIERRE H. CONWAY, O.P.

Introduction

The previous pamphlet has explained the angels' physical contacts with the world, their power of moving material things,
their assumption of bodies, and also their supernatural life, their life
of grace. This pamphlet has endeavored to state something of the
essential nature of the angels, which is intelligence and will. We hope
that it has made better known these tremendous spiritual beings,
so near and close to us, who play such a vital part in the universe,
and yet so remote and unknown because of the very perfection of
their being which transcends the realm of sensible and material
things we know so well. May the angels reward those who read
this pamphlet and plod faithfully through its many rather abstract
and intangible sentences with their heavenly aid and protection.

World About Them

In the Middle Ages it is somewhat dubious that the purveyors of
public spectacles ever found themselves obliged, with mixed feelings of pride and distress, to hang out a board inscribed in quaint
Gothic script with the words: "Standing Room Only." When the

portly burgher said to his buxom spouse, after wiping the pearly remnants of a tankard of ale from his moustache with the back of his hand, "let's take in a show," that could only mean a miracle play to be performed on the steps of the cathedral in front of the town square. Here there was room for all, and seats could be had at windows, in the branches of trees, on the tops of carts, on upturned baskets, and on solid wood benches.

However, it is not beyond the realm of possibility that some Connecticut Yankee versed in the ways of Broadway might have found occasion to hang up those classic words at another type of medieval gathering. In those benighted days, before the tabloids, the radio, the movies, and the variegated digests and picture magazines made all further thinking superfluous, men were gnawed by an insatiable curiosity about the world about them, both visible and invisible. Of course, this was more or less inevitable since when they looked up at night they usually saw the stars instead of a neon sign, when they traveled they saw the birds and the beasts, the trees and flowers, instead of the vertiginous blur resulting from speeds of eighty miles per hour and over. They had no telescopes with which to discover new planets, yet in their simple, yet painfully acute way, they reached out beyond the limits of the universe, reasoning that since all material, visible things are limited, the power that limits them must be immaterial and spiritual. Besides the existence of the immaterial and omnipotent First Mover and First Cause, it was quite reasonable to recognize the existence of other immaterial beings who should provide intermediary steps between the first, omnipotent and infinite spiritual being and the limited material world. These would be immaterial, intellectual beings, spiritual yet limited as are all beings other than the Supreme Being. The ancient philosophers such as Aristotle and Plato postulated the existence of such beings to fill in the descending hierarchy of existence from the infinite spiritual being down to the finite material being. The men of the Middle Ages, thanks to their faith, were certain of their existence. They were called "angels" from the Greek word "angellos" meaning "messenger" since men had come to know these spiritual beings as bearers of tidings from God to man.

Packing 'Em In

Because of their importance in the hierarchy of being, because of their greater closeness to God even than that of man and consequently greater reality, because of their vital role in salvation, both as messengers of God and executors of His providence over man, it was not extraordinary that the thinkers of the Middle Ages should have spent a great deal of time pondering over the angels. On the contrary, it is greatly to their credit that they should have spent so many days and nights and filled so many patiently written books pondering over the mysteries of the universe rather than spending their time at the movies or with their ears glued to the pre-digested gems of wisdom sponsored by soap manufacturers that float through the airways and out through the loudspeaker without wear and tear on the brain since as that perspicacious sage Aristotle observed, the perfection of man must consist in the development of that which is most perfect in him, which is, lest we forget, his intelligence.

By this time, the Connecticut Yankee from Broadway is tired of carrying his sign around with no place to pin it up, but he has not long to wait. As previously stated, the men of the Middle Ages gave a great deal of thought to the angels. St. Thomas Aquinas, the Common Doctor of the Catholic Church, is also known as the Angelic Doctor, to some extent because of his masterful treatise on the angels from which this pamphlet is gleaned. It was customary during his time for the professors and students of the University of Paris to gather at certain times to discuss disputed questions. Impish tradition likes to aver that one of the questions discussed was that of how many angels could stand on the point of a needle. If such were the question, the Connecticut Yankee could at last find a place for "Standing Room Only" as a fitting summary of the delicate problem presented by angels alighting in force upon the point of a solitary needle. He might even tack it up with reason on the door of the hall where the discussion was being held since these gatherings were always packed and even at best the students were usually content with a few straw-filled sacks as seating facilities. To be honest, this latter would be the Connecticut Yankee's only excuse to affix the said familiar vestige of Broadway he had been so faithfully trundling about, since, as a careful peruser of the previous pamphlet knows, the problem of angels congregating on the point of a needle really has no point at all, since any number of the angels, being spiritual creatures, could be present at the point of a needle, if they so choose, and several other places also at the same time, without any crowding whatsoever. However, we do thank the Connecticut Yankee for a title with which to titillate the reader's appetite, while begging the latter's forgiveness for such unbecoming ruses with the promise of truly enlightening facts about the majestic angelic hosts.

As Time Goes By

The angels have played a prominent part in the story of man. Angels have been present at all the great turning points of our history. It was a fallen angel, Satan, who tempted our first parents. It was an angel who was posted at the entry of the garden of Eden with a fiery sword, once our first parents had forfeited the garden of pleasure God had made for them. Abraham was given the first intimations that his seed was to become the chosen people when he received three travelers who were angels in the guise of men. An angel slew the first born of the Egyptians when they would not allow the Jews to depart from Egypt. An angel carried the prophet Habakkuk by the hair to the lions' den so that he might bring food to Daniel. The archangel Raphael guided the young Tobias on his way, secured him a wife and cured his father. An angel slew one hundred and eighty thousand of Sennacherib's men when they were about to capture Jerusalem. Angels flogged the Syrian general Heliodorus when he endeavored to rob the Temple.

In the life of Our Lord, which is the story of our salvation, angels were constantly present. The archangel Gabriel announced to Zechariah the birth of John the Baptist, and to the Blessed Virgin

Mary the birth of her Divine Son. Angels announced the birth of Christ to the shepherds. It was probably the same archangel who warned St. Joseph to flee the murderous plotting of Herod. Angels ministered to Our Lord after His temptation. An angel comforted Him in His agony upon Gethsemane. Our Lord told His infamous captors that if He so willed He could have legions of angels to defend Him. Angels greeted Mary Magdalene on the glorious Easter morning she came seeking her risen Master. Our Lord warned all men of scandalizing little children since their angels stood before the face of God. Each of us has an angel to watch over us and guard us, and many of the saints have been privileged to see their guardian angel in human form.

It is plain, therefore, that it is well worth our while to learn more of these powerful though invisible friends whom God employs in the work of our salvation and who possesses a beauty and perfection far surpassing any that the world can boast. The pagan philosophers were vividly aware of these spiritual beings. They attributed to them the motion of the various heavenly bodies of the universe, which was to them the primary motion from which all other motion in the world depended. Socrates at his trial spoke of his guiding spirit. One of the most beautiful pieces of sculpture in the world is the winged Victory of Samothrace of the Louvre Museum, attesting to the Greek custom of representing spiritual beings as human forms with wings, as is our wont to represent the angels.

Wingless Angels

It is possibly due to the Greeks that we are accustomed to represent the angels in the above fashion, which symbolizes so well their heavenly origin. For, just as we look toward heaven as being beyond the realm of the sky, so also it is fitting that the spiritual creatures who come to us from heaven should be represented as born upon majestic wings. Actually, of course, the angels, like God, are pure spirits without bodies. They have no need of wings since they traverse incalculable space with the speed of thought and can be simultaneously active in all parts of an area immeasurably greater than the extent of all our known universe as seen through the most powerful astronomical devices. The angels, as the previous pamphlet has explained, are not limited by any human distances, but have a universal presence which though limited is very similar to the universal omnipresence of God. Because the angels occupy a higher place in the scale of being than man, their powers comprise all the powers proper to man in an immeasurably more sublime way as well as their own particular angelic perfection.

But what is it that makes an angel an angel? As we have said, the angels are pure spirits, spiritual substances. Man is being composed of body and soul, of matter and spirit. It is obviously man's spirit which puts him on an infinitely higher plane than other material creatures. With his spirit he rises above and beyond the bounds of space and time. A man would set a single human being above all the material beauties and grandeur of the universe. Why? Because of the infinitely greater beauty of the soul. Just as man rises above the rest of material creation because of the grandeur of his spiritual soul, so do the angels rise above man because of the perfection of their spiritual being.

It is practically impossible to feel that one would be a superior being if one were without a body. One would feel like a sort of intangible mist: no arms with which to embrace one's friends, no taste with which to enjoy the delights of a succulent steak. To talk to a pure spirit would seem to us like sitting down for a quiet chat with a vaporous bed-sheet floating above the arms of the chair. How could anyone possibly fall in love with the charms of a pure spirit? How could a pure spirit enjoy a walk through the woods at autumn, followed by a good stiff drink beside a warming fire: Could you imagine a spirit as a partner for a round of golf? At this point we begin to feel sorry for the angels at the thought of all they are missing for the lack of a body.

Better Mirror

Actually, however, they are missing none of it. They possess it all and incalculably more besides. Just as man possesses all the perfection of lower nature, the materiality of inanimate things, the nutrition, growth and reproduction of vegetable life, the sensory activity of animal life in a far more perfect and complete way than any of these, as well as his own power of knowledge and free will, so also the angel possesses all the perfections of man as well as the peculiar perfections of angelic nature. He does not possess them as they exist in man, but far from lacking them, he possesses them in a more perfect way. This will be illustrated as the pamphlet rambles on. In the meantime, let us attempt to illustrate how man himself places spiritual values above material ones. Because of his love of his fellow man, a man will give up his life, sacrificing at a stroke all the things he holds dear, his family, his home, his simple pleasures. A missionary will gladly place his life at stake in order to bring to savage tribes the spiritual truths of salvation. A mother will sacrifice her youth and beauty in order to raise her children as perfectly as possible. A man will die sooner than surrender his honor. This world, with all its beauties and pleasures, is the handiwork of a spiritual being, God. If He can produce such things for us, certainly He must possess them Himself. likewise those creatures which more perfectly resemble Him, as do the angels with their pure spirituality, must possess all the goods that man enjoys and still greater ones besides.

But precisely what is it that makes an angel an angel? We have said that they are spiritual substances. What does spirituality consist in in man? It consists in his intelligence and power of free will. All his other powers are subservient to these. An angel, therefore, being a pure spirit, is a being so perfect that its intelligence and free will englobe within themselves all the perfections that man attains with his body and soul, and englobes them in a much more perfect way, just as God englobes all the perfections of created beings in His own infinite perfection which is the source of them all. The world is the mirror of God's perfections. Of all material beings, man is the most perfect image of God. But the angel is the most perfect image of all.

What is characteristic of the spirits is intelligence and will. Since the angels are pure spirits, what is characteristic of them is their intelligence and will, an intelligence and will comprising all the perfections of lower beings including man and the material creation.

Not Bread Alone

In a man, all his sensitive powers such as his sight, his hearing, his sense of touch, are ordained to his spiritual being. So are all his physical activities, his traveling, his working. This may seem to contradict experience, but let us examine a few cases. For example, there are men who would find exceeding delight in sitting down before a board with various delicacies, stuffing a napkin in their collar, firmly grasping a knife and fork and then proceeding to eat themselves silly. This does happen and no doubt we have all indulged in the same in varying degrees, but do we not feel an instinctive repulsion for such an individual for whom the supreme bliss of living would center about the stomach? Undoubtedly we do. Why is this? It is because we realize that eating is not an end in itself, but a means to the higher life in man. Oftentimes we come across intelligent people who are addicted to drink, and we are saddened immeasurably to see the light of their intellect gradually blurred and dimmed by the paralyzing effect of liquor which in exaggerated doses, while giving a mild feeling of elation to the senses, completely ties up the intellect. We have nothing but disgust for a man who, because of his love of money, would deprive his family of possibilities of education and decent living. Thus we recognize instinctively that material things are ordained to man, and that in man, the things of the body are ordained to the soul. Whenever any of these things are made an end in themselves to the point that they impede and prevent the development of the spiritual side of man, we recognize there is something wrong.

In a man, the development of his intellectual and spiritual side comes through his senses from material things. The development of his human personality depends on the gradual sifting of the data received through the senses. Animals never rise above this purely sensory plane, but man coordinates and utilizes all his sensory experiences to attain knowledge of universal significance and utility.

The gradual development of the human side of man, the part that distinguishes him from animals, is seen in the gradual evolution of the child, who in his early stages is, outwardly at least, a very charming little animal. He has a soul and a mind, but his intellect must be progressively perfected by the sifting of sense experience. His mind begins as "a tablet on which nothing has been written," to quote the old philosophers' way of putting it. The gradual experience of life sifted through by the power of the mind writes upon it the data of human knowledge.

With the angels, all this preliminary stage, all this gradual development of the intellect is eliminated. From the very instant of his creation, the angel without any laborious and gradual development possesses a fully developed intellect, stored with a range of knowledge far surpassing the knowledge acquired by a man after a lifetime of careful observation, thought and study. A man gradually acquires universal knowledge, he attains the concept of a first cause from which depend all things that exist. In his knowledge of the first cause from which all things depend he has also a knowledge of all things, but this knowledge is very general and obscure, as we quickly perceive when we endeavor to express ourselves on the plane of universal ideas. With the angel, this knowledge is far more clear, and more closely resembles the universal knowledge of God which embraces all the universe down to its smallest detail, numbering the very hairs of our head.

Free Souls

Thus the angel has no need of senses, no need of going to school, no need of long pondering in order to reason things out. From the beginning he knows all the answers. What is typical of man is rational animality. That is, man is an animal who is able by reason to attain to the knowledge of spiritual being. Its intellectual knowledge is concerned with exactly the same objects as man's, but it is a far clearer and deeper knowledge of these things and one which does not have to be derived through a progressive sifting of sense data.

Therefore, one does not see an angel, because being purely spiritual beings, they do not strike the senses. If an angel came in late, he would not have to tiptoe up the stairs, because he has no feet, and also because he can be at the top of the stairs while he is still at the bottom, and this without even going up them, as the previous pamphlet has explained. Yet of course they do have definite personalities. Each human individual has a personality of his own, which is nothing other than the particular stamp, the particular rounding off of his being which makes him himself and not somebody else. Each angel, too, has a very definite personality, and the differences between the angels, being specific, are more clearly etched even than the differences between human personalities.

What distinguishes one angel from another is obviously nothing other than the differences of their intellects, since there is no material or bodily differences with which to distinguish them. One angel is distinguished from another by the greatness of his intelligence.

But are angels nothing but intelligences, brains, so to speak? Obviously they cannot be intelligence alone, since intelligence is not a thing in itself, but rather a quality of a thing or the act of a thing, just as redness or goodness is not a thing in itself. An angel has intelligence, but an angel is not itself intelligence. An angel has its own substantial nature, just as we have human nature. This nature is characterized by intelligence, just as ours is characterized by rational animality. But there is a difference between the substance of the angel and his intelligence, which is a quality of his substance. God alone, Who is absolutely simple, has no distinction within Himself between His substance, His being, and its properties. God's intelligence, His goodness, His omnipotence, are one with Himself. He is goodness itself, power itself, intelligence itself. All other creatures only participate in these qualities. They have intelligence, they have goodness, but they are not intelligence or goodness itself. Thus the angels have intelligence and are characterized by this quality as against man who has a more inferior type of intelligence which is gradually developed through the use of the senses.

Spellbinder

If an angel were ever asked to appear on "Information Please," he would laugh a politely spiritual laugh. If he did consent to appear and assumed a body for the occasion, you may be sure no Encyclopedia Britannicas would be given away. His hand would be up all the time, and even Oscar Levant would be spellbound. Yet he does not go to school. Like a certain fish, he does not write his name or read a book. He does not learn through his senses as you and I. He is born with a mine of information. It is not a pedantic sort of information, with a textbook knowledge of birds and flowers, of ancient history and literary gems. He knows the score of the latest Giants-Dodgers game even before you read it in the paper or hear it on the radio. How does the angel do this?

An angel, being a purely spiritual creature, is the most perfect image of God. Just as God, being the cause and sustaining power of all things, sees all things in Himself, so also the angel, being the image of God, can perceive the traces of God within himself and through God the various activities of God. But of course this knowledge is general, and because of its generality is necessarily obscure as to detail. The angel, perceiving the traces of God within himself, can understand the power of God, the things He can do, the worlds He can create. But He can not perceive within himself definite facts, He does not know whether God has created these worlds or not. Therefore God, the creator of the angels, in order to render their knowledge truly like His own, must give them a universal knowledge of actual things. Just as a man bears within his memory the picture of things he has seen, such as a trip to Europe, the battlefields of France, baseball games he has played in, happy reunions with friends, so do the angels bear within themselves pictures of all of reality. These pictures, if we may call them such, comprehend, in their sum, a knowledge of all things, both actual and possible.

People gathered around a television set can see things which are transpiring many miles away, boxing matches, operas, news events, in the very room in which they are gathered, without being on the scene at all. So also the angels, thanks to the *species,* or pictures, which God gives them, can perceive within themselves the course of events without actually seeing them with their eyes or hearing them with their ears. These pictures extend to more than mere isolated events, they extend to the whole range of knowledge. For example, the angels know the answers to many problems which will continue to torture humans for years to come. They know the nature of electricity, they know the composition of the sun, the possibilities of stratospheric flight, the cause of cancer, the mysteries of economics. In sum, they know what makes the world go round immeasurably better than we, as befits creatures who so closely resemble God.

The Fewer the Better

But naturally they do not know all things in the same way in which God knows them. God sees all things, past, present and future, in one simple vision within Himself, since he is the sole cause of them all. Men, in knowing God, know all things, but in a very obscure way. Our knowledge is contained in consecutive and restricted concepts rather than in a few all-embracing ones. For instance, it would be difficult for us to comprise in a single thought Beethoven's Fifth Symphony, a hamburger, the Notre Dame football team, and that left rear tire which is going to collapse any minute. But an angel could. We have to think of such things one after another, but an angel can embrace them all in a single thought, although the sum total of his knowledge would require several thoughts. That he can do so is not extraordinary in itself, since all are connected. Because of the weakness of our intellect we cannot get such a sweeping view. The angel, because of the God-given power of his, can. We can see this gradation from many concepts to a few even in man, (just as we see the common sense coordinating the data of the five senses, as for example, in an explosion, the eye only sees it, the ear only hears, the sense of touch only feels the concussion, the nose only smells the fumes, yet the common sense co-ordinates all these as a complete whole). A businessman would have to tell a rather dense secretary just exactly whom he wished to see and whom he did not wish to see. He would have to state specifically that he did not want to see Jones, but that he would see Smith, that as far as Hawkins was concerned he had gone to Mexico, but if Bilgewater called up he would be glad to play golf with him this afternoon. The secretary would have to have a new idea for each occasion or situation. However, if said businessman were blessed with a particularly gifted secretary, she would have a more or less universal idea of whom the boss wished to see and whom he wished not to see, and would act accordingly without any reiterated directives from him. A newly-married bride might take a perfectly good steak and broil it to a cinder while piously following the directions of the cookbook, whereas an experienced house-wife, who has something of an overall notion of cooking could take practically any edible scraps to hand and metamorphose them into something delightful to the taste. For the one, each new dish presents a particular problem, for the other, long experience has resulted in a knowledge of the universal canons of cooking capable of meeting any emergency.

Thus it is evident that the development of one's mind is parallel to the extension and universality of one's ideas. The angels have infinitely larger and more complete ideas and consequently much fewer ones. God, of course has just one idea, which is His own substance, and which comprises with the utmost dearness and completeness all things both possible and actual. One angel differs from another by the fewness of the concepts in which his universal knowledge is contained. Those who are closer to God have fewer concepts but of a more universal extension. The lesser angels have more concepts and consequently cannot take in so much at a glance. However, each of their concepts far surpasses the sum total of any knowledge a human possesses with all his many hard-earned ideas. Among humans, as we have said, the most intellectual are those whose knowledge comprises the greatest number of things in the least multiplied number of ideas. This scale gradually tapers down to those who have to have an entirely disconnected thought for each notion, no matter how related such notions may be as in the case of a little boy who is perfectly willing to buy six rolls but would have to ponder deeply before purchasing half a dozen, or the proverbial parent who is perfectly willing to let the children go in the water once they have learned to swim.

Little Knowledge?

But what do the angels think about all day long? Do they worry about who is going to win the fifth race at Pimlico? Do they take polls among themselves as to who is going to win the presidential election? Do they speculate on the possibilities of a future peace? The angels are informed on all these subjects. However, in the interest of universal ideas, which incidentally, depend upon order, it will not be superfluous to set down the objects of the angels' knowledge in an orderly way.

First of all, an angel knows himself, since his spiritual being is immediately present to his angelic intelligence. Such introspection is not boring to him, since an angel is an exceedingly perfect individual. Likewise an angel knows the other angels in the species which God gives him of all things. By his natural knowledge the angel also has a very profound knowledge of God. Just as we can know God, His wisdom, love and power, by the things of this world and by the traces of God within ourselves, so also the angel, being the most perfect image of God, can gain a profound knowledge of Him by observing the traces of God within himself.

However, we can best compare the ascending simplicity of the angels' knowledge with ours when we put it on the plane of material things known to us. The only thing which an angel knows immediately by his natural powers is his own spiritual being which is present to him. However, since an angel is the most perfect natural image of God, he must also be given by God suitable knowledge of all things so that his knowledge will resemble the divine knowledge. Just as man possesses all the perfections and knowledge of inferior nature in a more perfect way than any inferior being, so the angels possess all those perfections beneath them and their own in a still more perfect way more closely resembling the simplicity of the divine perfection. Thus he possesses a more perfect knowledge of material things in fewer ideas than man possesses with many ideas. Thus he knows all the singular material things far better than we do. He knows our friends, the places we live in, the things we do but with a far greater range than if we traveled the world over, saw everything, read everything and knew everybody. Furthermore, the angel does not have to come down and look at these things or travel from place to place because God has given him the knowledge of all these things within himself. As St. Augustine says, God created the world first within the angelic intellect and then in its actual material form.

How and When

To the perspicacious reader, the quality of the angels' knowledge will give rise to an interesting question. If the angel possesses a complete picture of the world past, present and future within his intellect, he must be able to know beforehand what is going to transpire in the future. For instance he should be able to see what day war will end. He could glance at the stock-market two years ahead and tell whether we are going to have a depression, he could tell how many children a family will have ten years from now. But actually it does not happen this way.

There are two ways of knowing the future. One is by knowing events in their causes, the other is by knowing them in themselves as God knows them. Future events which can be known in their causes occur in three ways, by necessity at all times, most of the time or only occasionally. An example of the first way would be the rising of the sun. It is quite possible to predict in the evening that the sun will rise the following morning, since the laws of nature effect this invariably every day. An example of the second way would be the case of a doctor interpreting his patient's symptoms and prescribing a suitable remedy. In nearly all cases, the predicted cure will follow, but in a certain minority of cases, either the symptoms have misled the doctor or the medicine does not follow. The angels' prediction of the future falls into this category. Since their knowledge is more acute and more piercing, they can predict the chances of the future event from its causes much better than humans, just as a more expert doctor can predict a cure more reliably than a less experienced one. The third type of future events comprises events such as those which happen only occasionally or by chance and are consequently unpredictable since they have no proper cause from which they may be predicted, but rather are the result of a chance complexus of events. Such would be the case of a man who went to the railway station to buy a ticket and there met a long lost friend whom he had been trying vainly to locate for a number of years. The result had nothing to do with the intentions of the men involved. This event could not be predicted in its cause, since the cause involved resulted in buying a railway ticket. The meeting was purely a chance effect. Such would also be the case of a man who while walking down one side of the street decides to cross over to buy a pack of cigarettes only to see a grand piano fall from a ten-story window on the spot where he would normally have been had he continued his course. His escape was quite unpredictable in its cause which was his decision to go and buy a pack of cigarettes. Wonder if he got them? Things which depend upon free will are also unpredictable in their causes. Only God who can control the will is able to definitely predict the decision to be made.

Some Foresight

The other way in which future events can be foreseen is in themselves. That is, God who is the total cause of everything which happens, and which makes it take place, obviously is able to foresee future things in themselves since their whole being comes from him. Unless God reveals future events which cannot be predicted in their causes such as events depending upon chance or free will, no one, including the angels, can foresee them, since this is a divine prerogative, and used by God as a sign of His intervention, as when the prophets inspired by God predicted future events as a sign of God's support of their words. In the ideas of all things which God gives the angels from the moment of their creation, future events which are unpredictable naturally are only unfolded in their knowledge as they occur in the world unless God deigns to reveal them beforehand. Therefore the angels' predictions of the future by their own natural powers are restricted to those events which can be foreseen in their causes, such as events which follow normally from the laws of nature.

However, it is well to remember that the angels, because of their great intelligence and deep knowledge, are able to foresee many events in the natural causes which we because of our lesser intelligences do not see, just as a skillful doctor could discern symptoms of a dangerous disease in a man who to the layman's eye appears perfectly healthy. A clever psychologist is able to discern many of a person's inner desires and thoughts merely in hearing him relate the story of his life. Our best concealed thoughts are inevitably betrayed by certain exterior signs which a shrewd person is able to detect, be it only a drumming of the finger or an occasional shifting of the eyes, an avoidance of a certain subject or slightly false ring to the voice. This is quite natural since man is a creature of body and soul, and all his thoughts, purely intellectual as they may be, are accompanied by certain physical reactions, perspiring, blushing, a quickening of the pulse and the like. The newly introduced lie detector has shown clearly how different questions, try as we will, unleash various physical reaction's dependent upon the impression they make upon the one questioned.

No Mind Readers

Does this mean then that the angels can read the most secret thoughts of our heart? It definitely does not. Man is ordained to God alone, and the thoughts of his heart are closed to all but God. Even the angels are not allowed to penetrate these thoughts unless we expressly wish it. An angel can in no way tell what we are thinking directly, since our mind, which is the faculty by which we reach God, finds its end in Him and no creature is permitted to enter in upon it. However, we do betray our thoughts to a certain extent and the angels can read these external signs. They are by no means infallible. For example, we know people who blush furiously when accused of something of which they are perfectly innocent. That same blushing could accompany the mental reaction of a person who was guilty. Therefore the angels are reduced to shrewd psychology. They know our reactions to former situations, they know the things we like and man is always inclined to pursue the things which attract him. Consequently they can give a pretty good guess as to what we are thinking, what we are planning.

This is all very well for the good angels, who are interested in knowing us only in order to help us know and love God better. But all the angels are not good angels. As our faith teaches us, certain of the angels, for refusing to serve God, were cast into Hell. Since that time their hatred of God has led them to use their natural powers to work for the downfall of the souls whom the Son of God saved by His passion and death.

These fallen angels are allowed by God to try their wiles upon humans, not that men may be lost, but that, with the help of God men may, through overcoming trials and temptations, give proof of their fidelity and draw closer to Him. We have all heard of people who have gone to fortune-tellers or other dispensers of occult mysteries and who say: "Of course, I don't believe in fortune-telling, but you know, that woman told me where I was born and all about my operation. Then she said I was going to take a trip, and would you believe it, the next week the doctor told me that I must go out West because of my lung condition." How did the fortune-teller obtain such precise information, and undoubtedly some of them do? Of course, sometimes it is shrewd guesswork, other times it is thorough research work, but there are honest fortune-tellers who will say that these ideas just come to them from nowhere. The wise men of the Church, and principally St. Augustine, tell us that the source of such information is none other than those fallen angels whom we call devils. From what has been previously said, it is quite clear that an angel could glean all the information within the fortune-teller's imagination, thanks to the angelic power of physical motion whereby angels can act upon the senses and that sensory interior faculty which is the imagination. What is their purpose behind this? The purpose is to win the confidence of the person seeking information, and once this confidence is gained, to gradually win that person away from God. Some fortune-tellers are apparently honest, others are possibly in league with the devil who is the source of their livelihood. At any rate, this is the danger of fortune-tellers, especially good ones, since they are often consciously or unconsciously tools of the devil who never does anything, good as it may seem, that is not eventually calculated to lead a soul to its downfall. Therefore St. Augustine warns: "Beware of fortune-tellers and especially those who tell true things."

Never Reason Why

Besides their natural knowledge the angels have, even as we, supernatural knowledge, a knowledge of divine things revealed by God. Like the knowledge of future events dependent upon the divine will, so also the mysteries of faith are gradually revealed to them. The trial of the angels, in which their faith was put to the test occurred before the trial of our first parents in the garden of Eden. The angels who remained faithful were rewarded with the vision of God, as are the souls of the blessed, and, besides their natural knowledge, see all things in the beatific vision of God! However, the various phases of the redemption of man were not fully revealed to them at once. They, like the people of Israel, gained a gradually clearer notion of the coming of the Son of God as it was more and more clearly revealed by the prophets across the years. However, their knowledge, especially that of the higher angels, was no doubt clearer as befitted their lofty state.

As we have seen, the angels do not play golf, do not go to the movies, don't plant crops or saw wood, don't ride bicycles or go for walks in the woods. Being spiritual creatures, their life is essentially intellectual. Since they do not learn from the senses, but have the objects of their knowledge constantly present to them, their intelligences, unlike ours, are constantly active. Since all their knowledge is not contained in a single idea, they do go from one idea to another, but each of these ideas contains far greater knowledge than a human could amass in a lifetime.

Due to the fact that the angels were created with their full perfection, including that of the intellect, they do not reason. For us, to obtain the answer to a problem in geometry we must go through a number of steps beginning with the given data and gradually step by step working towards the conclusion. To know the composition of the human body we would have to study each part of the anatomy separately and gradually coordinate this knowledge into a complete picture. Before deciding whether it is right to do a little washing on Sunday we must refer this problem to our moral principles, to the laws of the Church, and eventually draw a conclusion. With the angels, not so. In knowing the principles of things, they also know all the conclusions that can be drawn from them. We must work to those conclusions by reasoning.

Because of this quality of the angel's knowledge, it is impossible for the angel to make an error. Error occurs not in the principles of reasoning but in the progressive stages of reasoning. The beginning of reasoning is the knowledge that something exists. Error occurs in the determining of what that something is. For example, a man may see an object in the distance coming over the brow of a hill. The beginning of his thought is the perception of that object. He may then decide it is a horse, only to learn on closer inspection that it is a man. A man may walk across a bridge figuring it is strong enough to hold him, only to have it give beneath his weight. The various factors entering into the construction of the bridge were present before his eyes, but he coordinated them wrongly. The angel, since he takes the whole picture in at a glance cannot possibly make a mistake, except about something concerning which he has not complete knowledge, as would occur if an angel refused to accept a doctrine of faith because he understood it not.

Love Too

But is the angel's life solely one of knowledge? What happens when we know something which is good, when we see the face of a friend, when we hear beautiful music? There is a pleasure following such knowledge and an inclination towards the thing which pleases us. This inclination towards that which pleases is called love. In every creature possessing knowledge, there is also love which is the inclination towards the good which is known. The faculty which loves, in intellectual beings, is called the will. Therefore the angels possess not only intellect but also will. Incidentally, it is not superfluous to note that love in all beings, the tendency in all beings to that which pleases them, is nothing other than the tendency of all beings back to God, the supreme good, as seen through the variegated goodness of created things.

The angels therefore have free will, since the goods which they know are none of them sufficient to fully captivate their will which, like ours, was made to be fully satisfied by God alone. Like a man, an angel loves himself and his neighbor, that is, the other angels, as himself. He also loves men, as being the cherished creatures of God especially since the Son of God has seen fit to redeem them with His divine blood and to unite their human nature with His own divine nature for all eternity. Naturally, too, the angel loves God above all things and for the same reason that we do. The angel recognizes far better than we do that all its goodness comes from God and loves God as the source of all this goodness. The part lives for the whole, finds its perfection in its subordination in the whole, as the cog in the machinery finds its perfection in its contribution to the whole machine, wherein alone lies its utility. Just as a man would gladly sacrifice his hand to save his life, so also all the parts of the universe love God more than themselves. As a matter of fact, the very being of every creature, belonging more to God than it does to any of us, naturally loves God, its maker more than all things, more than its own self which is only the participating possessor of its being.

Love Is Not Enough

So far we have talked only of the perfection of the angels. Yet we know by faith that certain of the angels rebelled against God and were made in the image and likeness of God and could not err.

Obviously the angel could not err, mistaking as good something which was evil, as the man who would commit adultery. He could not make a mistake about the goodness of a thing. But merely to love good things is not enough as we all know. Those good things must be loved with proper regard to the love of God. For example, to sit down to a steak dinner is a good thing, but to do this against the will of God on Friday is not a good thing because all good things must be subordinated to God's will. Therefore the only way an angel could sin is in loving something good but in a way not in keeping with the will of God.

We do not know exactly what the sin of the angels was, but one of the conjectures is that the angels were called upon to adore God of their own free will but some of them remained satisfied with their own very great perfection and saw no need of bowing down to a superior being. In finding contentment in their own being they were perfectly right, but to be satisfied with their own being without also acknowledging the superior goodness of God was wrong. Thus the sin of the fallen angels could be nothing but the sin of pride, the sin whereby we admire our own excellence in an unfitting way, that is without the proper subordination to God. This sin is followed by the sin of envy whereby one is sad at the good of another considered as an impediment to one's own good as would be the divine good in comparison to the good of the fallen angels.

The sin of the fallen angels is thus sometimes said to be in wishing to be like God. Obviously the angels by their knowledge knew they could never possess the omnipotence of God, but to be satisfied with one's own perfection, to be content to exist without recognizing the supremacy of God, is to wish to be like God, since He alone is without superior, without dependence.

None of the angels were created evil, first of all since God is in no way the cause of sin as present in the evil wills of the fallen angels; secondly because the terminus of divine creation is invariably something good, which can become evil only through free will which necessarily follows the moment of creation in which the will is good. Because of the belief of the doctors of the Church that the angels were created in grace, rather than having received it some time after their creation, which is equally possible, and because of their knowledge, which requires no pause for reflection, it is probable that the angels who sinned, sinned in the instant after their creation, just as the good angels merited heaven by their submission to God in the instant after their creation.

As has been said, the sin of the fallen angels was pride, an inordinate contentment in the perfection of their own being. Therefore it is very possible that the chief sinner among the angels was the greatest angel, since he had the most reason for pride in his perfection. That the supreme angel among the fallen angels was also the cause of sin among the others is plain from the text of Scripture, which says, for example: "Depart from me, accursed ones, into the everlasting fire which was prepared for the devil and his angels," which definitely indicates a ruler among the fallen angels and the presence of other angels who followed him. How many angels fell and how many remained? Since evil is rather the exception to the rule than the rule itself we may conclude that it was a minority of the angels who fell.

Knowledge of the Damned

How much of their former knowledge remains in the fallen angels? Since knowledge of all things is proper to the angels by their very nature, this knowledge is not destroyed, since punishment does not destroy the nature of a being. However, their knowledge of supernatural things revealed to them by God is diminished because of the perversity of their will which refuses to accept. Finally that knowledge of God which come from the love of God has completely perished within them. The will of the fallen angels remains confirmed forever in evil since because of their knowledge, which is complete, once they adhere to a decision, there is no revoking it, because it is not possible for them to learn that they are wrong since they know all there is to be known from the start. This is not true of human beings who can rightly change their minds and correct their mistakes because of a lack of vision, as long as they remain in this life. Afterwards, of course, no new natural knowledge can come to them which would make them change. The fallen angels do not have sensible pain, but they do have the greatest of all pains which consists in that which is contrary to the will, which is, for them the sight of the supremacy of God, and the salvation of others while they are damned. Even when they act upon earth, the fallen angels bear their hell with them, which is the recognition that they have forever lost their place in the sight of God.

STUDY QUESTIONS

1) How does an angel differ from man?

2) What has an angel in common with man?

3) Why is an angel the most perfectly created image of God?

4) How does an angel learn things?

5) Does an angel have many ideas or few?

6) Does an angel have both natural and supernatural knowledge of God?

7) Does an angel know what we are doing?

8) Does an angel know what we are thinking? What is meant by distinct species?

9) Do the angels know more of the mysteries of faith than we? Do they have complete knowledge?

10) Can an angel know many things at once?

11) Do angels reason?

12) Can they make mistakes about natural things?

13) Besides their natural knowledge, do the good angels know all things in God, just as the blessed?

14) Do the angels have free will?

15) Do angels have the same love that we do?

16) Can an angel sin?

17) Could an angel be created evil?

18) What must have been the sin of the fallen angels?

19) Can a good angel sin?

20) Can the fallen angels repent?

The First Week

A Consideration of the Biblical Account of Creation

Richard T. Murphy, O.P.

Introduction

Following the consideration of the purely spiritual creatures which are the angels, one comes to the consideration of the purely material creatures, that is, the creation of the material world. The account of creation is contained in the first two chapters of the Book of Genesis. The following pamphlet is an examination and explanation of that account and of the objections that science and reason might appear to find in it.

I

Modern Miracles

The most formidable obstacle to the popularization of St. Thomas is that overwhelming sense of superiority most men of today experience whenever their attention is directed to the past. Everything about the past has been smugly set aside, its science, its knowledge, its outlook on life—everything. All has been made new, to paraphrase the Scriptures, in self-sufficient man.

It is easy to be smug over the accomplishments of the present day. Science sees to it that we are made increasingly more comfortable, and has robbed such personal things as toothaches, childbirth, and operations, of much of their pain. We are grateful; grandpa and grandma had to put up with a lot more than we do.

In the field of chemistry there have been the giant strides which led to synthetic rubber, plastics, and the atomic bomb. The fantastic dreams of the ancient alchemists seem almost to have been realized! They sought vainly the secret of changing one element into another; but many performances of modern chemistry, allied with physics, make these ancient dreams appear a bit on the conservative side.

There are our astronomers, who leap dizzying distances into space with a nonchalance never shown by the lad who wore the first seven-league-boots. Back they come laden with secret information about the sun, moon, and stars and planets, revealing their weights and masses, tracing out their orbits and observing their celestial timetables. Even the carefully kept secrets of their physical makeup have yielded to the probing of the spectroscope. Slide rules move quickly and the secret of their distances from the earth, or from each other, is revealed. How fast are the stars and planets moving? Not only do we now know the answer to that one, but we know that the stars have temperatures, and we can take them!

Modern Muddling

Small wonder, then, that modern scientists show disdain for the science of the ancients. Mention the *Physics* of Aristotle, and it is greeted with an indulgent smile. After all, we're grown up now, we've outgrown that stage, and we know a few things. Aristotle for the ancients, say we. In the same way, mention the Bible story of creation, and it is greeted with another smile, one that is even more derisive, more incredulous, and back of the laughter that follows is a hardness that is hardly human.

This looking-down-the-nose-at-Genesis procedure has led to strange theories. At some time or other, almost everyone has heard the weighty pronouncements of some great scientist or mathematician, blandly dispensing a few crumbs from the tables of the mighty to a properly respectful public. It is done so condescendingly, and with such a polite smile, that John Q. Public is charmed. Little does he realize that beneath the frosting on the cake given him by the Nice Man there is a lethal dose of poison. Poison destroys life; poisonous doctrine destroys it with equal effectiveness, and with much more frightful consequences, no matter how sympathetic the smile accompanying it.

Evolution

The food then, provided for public consumption or served at university tables of learning, has to be inspected. If the story of creation as told in Genesis has to be rejected, we want to know what substitution is going to be made. If creation is to be thrown into the outmoded ashcan, what is going to take its place? The answer is—you've guessed it—evolution.

(1) Evolution may be considered first, *as a scientific hypothesis*. The word "scientific" will distinguish it from the two other species which very appropriately will bring up the rear. As a scientific hypothesis, evolution is merely a working theory, an attempt to discern *the general law* that governs the life and development of all created, material nature. It is a very polite and honest kind of evolution, giving itself no airs, and not even attempting to appear as the last word in explanation of the universe. It is a working theory only, and pursues its way unconcerned with the origin of such immaterial things as souls.

(2) Much more spectacular is the "Sunday Supplement" type of evolution, with which we are all familiar, although we shouldn't be caught reading the stuff. This is the kind of evolution that makes scientists (the real ones) tear their hair, for it is only superficially scientific and casts discredit on honest science and scientists. It is gaily proposed as if it were the last word in any argument, a universal rule measuring everything. As such it is recklessly employed by men who speak neither well nor wisely. Is it not scientific nonsense to apply the theory of evolution to such widely divergent things as religion, morality, and marriage? Not for the Sunday Supplement! Actually there never has been any conclusive evidence advanced

to prove the fact of evolution in these three fields. There is, on the contrary, an ever accumulating pile of sober evidence showing that the more primitive the people, the more pure its ideas and practices in religion, morality and marriage.

(3) The third and last type of evolution masks itself as a serious philosophy, and sets itself up to answer the serious questions concerning the origins of the world. And very interesting, this one. To become a member of the lodge, it is merely required that you deny all causality and all finality. Let's watch this one at work.

In the first place, the account in Genesis is considered as childish, wrong, and therefore dispensable. The universe came into being either by chance or by change. Long, long ago, an area in space was occupied with a mass of gas; gradually by its own gravitation, this was drawn together, until the increased density made the whole thing luminous, and thus a star was born. Only an impertinent lunatic or a sober scholastic would dare question the process, but if he did, doubtless he would be told with annoyed finality, that this all took place millions of years ago, and many times too.

This is a favorite trick of the pseudo-scientists, pushing things back a few million years. The public is prepared for it, having heard much learned talk about light years. New stars float within our vision, whose distance from the earth is so great that not ordinary numbers but light years are used to express it. One light year is the distance light travels in one year at the rate of 186,000 miles per second, approximately six trillion miles. Before long the astronomers were measuring stellar distances by the "parsec" and now by the "mega-parsec," a mere 3,258,000 light years. Imagine the distances involved! It all takes time, so a few million years at a time are invoked without the flicking of an eye. *As if the fact that it happened a few million years ago answers these crucial questions:* How did the gases come into existence? What commanded them to assemble? Why did they become lightsome, why did they explode, and how did the various pieces cool off to become earth, or other various celestial bodies? Then, as now, nothing happened by chance; everything has a reason. How strange that this is only seriously denied when our mental gymnastics have landed us back in never-never-land! Curiouser and curiouser, it is in our own day that the questions just asked are adjudged impertinent and not to the point. If you deny that all this happened by chance, you are anti-modern, ultra-conservative, out of date and behind the times.

Another tidbit? You may have nibbled all unknowing at this between the pages of textbooks, or seen it all in pictures in that ambitious animated cartoon where magnificent symphonic music was invoked to convey the idea across the oceans of time. It goes like this: once, long ago, a mysterious *life force* forced its inexorable way up through matter. It is unimportant where the life force came from, or whence the matter in which it struggled. What is important is that from this beginning, the process evolved and is still evolving, and furthermore it will continue to develop and evolve. Where to? What is its final goal? Why? and What? are suspicious questions released immediately without examination by the very men who profess to police the *facts*.

What Would Thomas Say?

If St. Thomas were alive, he would probably reply to these three theories as follows: (1) I answer that there cannot be a real contradiction between creation, understood as the ultimate explanation of the universe, and physical science, which is uninterested in last causes and ultimate explanations. (2) Most stupid (after the fashion of David of Dinant) is the theory of evolution which lumps together, without proof, all human living and the development of the material universe. For the human soul cannot be the product of material evolution, since it is spiritual and comes only from God. Application of this theory to marriage, morality, and religion is indefensible. Primitive revelation teaches that marriage was originally monogamous (one man with one wife), and only later degenerated into polygamy; morals were of the highest order at the beginning, and became progressively worse as sin obtained a stronger hold on the world. As for religion, it totally exceeds the field in which evolution might possibly be applied. In conclusion, a glance at the fluctuating and unfortunate history of scientific discoveries (and especially the conclusions drawn from those discoveries) within the past generation, shows that this evolutionary theory, which is contrary to the Faith, leads actually by its excesses to the scorn even of unbelievers. (3) The third type of evolution involves a twofold error. The first of these is the denial of causality, which no right reason can justify, for potentiality can never reduce itself to act, but must be reduced to act by something possessing act; otherwise we would be led to the hopeless position of holding that a watch or a ship produced itself, which is simply absurd. The second error lies in the fact that a process of change (whose origin is unexplained) is postulated, and is said to consist wholly in the process of change itself. To put it graphically, it continues after the manner of a child that was never born but nevertheless is constantly growing! It is a process of change without before or after, without beginning or end, without purpose, without meaning; as such it contradicts the order of the entire universe.

Evolution, then, as a theory to answer the problem of origins, cannot be successfully maintained. Above all, it does not apply to the sphere of morality or religion, despite the grave assurance of our university professors, for in these fields the evidence all points the other way. However, it may be used as a scientific hypothesis which limits itself to discover the general laws controlling the material universe.

II

Medieval Reasonableness

Because he was ruthlessly rational and hardheaded, for all that he was a theologian first of all, St. Thomas did not dodge the question of creation. Either this wonderful world, which cannot adequately explain itself, came forth from the hands of an intelligent creator or it does not exist. None but a wild idealist would think of maintaining that the universe does not actually exist. Therefore it must have been created.

Our Faith tells us there is one God, Father almighty, Creator of heaven and earth. This is likewise found in the Scriptures, in the first book of the Bible, in the first chapter of Genesis. Perhaps few things so condemn St. Thomas in modern eyes as the fact that he was so gullible as to accept the biblical story of creation at its face value. Why, everybody and his brother knows that this account is a "myth!" True, it was universally accepted once, but that was before the clear light of science was played upon it, revealing it for what it was! Moderns almost to a man have rejected the Genesis account, and in their haste to do this they have discarded the momentous fact of creation.

For St. Thomas and all Catholics, anything contained in the Scriptures is of the extreme importance, and should not be dismissed, unceremoniously or otherwise. The Bible is not an ordinary book. Even after learning (at what cost!) the intricacies and vagaries of the documentary theories evolved by scholars concerning the composition of Genesis, we can still assert with confidence that Moses did write it, and he was led to write it as he did by the Holy Ghost. The Bible is inspired. This means that it has God as its author in a very special way.

If God is the author of all the books of the Bible—and He is— then since He can neither deceive nor be deceived, everything in the Bible must be true. St. Thomas did not shrink from the important conclusion; he accepted it, and many times in his remarks on the works of the six days, he answers objections with the sample statement: "the authority of the Bible is sufficient."

But the Bible had often been commented upon by the time Thomas came to write on creation and a number of commentaries had by their superiority been singled out from a host of inferior writings. The standard commentaries on creation were those of Augustine, Basil, Chrysostom, Bede and others. Strabo the geographer takes a bow. The great Jewish symbolist, Moses Maimonides (of whom the Jews said: From Moses to Moses, there is none like Moses) was well known, and St. Thomas quotes from him. Add to these the writings of Aristotle and Plato, with which the "Dumb Ox" was well acquainted, and you get a good idea of his library.

Thomas makes no bones about his preferences. Here, where much of the argumentation depends upon the authorities cited, he invariably opens with St. Augustine. But as it was frequently a case of "Augustine against the field" he has occasion to say: "On this point, holy men differ," meaning by that Augustine, Bede, Chrysostom, and especially, Basil. Saints disagree just like the rest of men! What is worth noting is that St. Thomas was acquainted with the very best authors; his bibliography was unimpeachable. He is always guided by reason, not sentiment. "In order to be impartial," he says in one instance, "we must meet the arguments of either side." The arguments of such a man should not be scoffed at, at least before scanning them!

Science

However, few targets have been so pitilessly riddled with shafts of ridicule as the physics of Aristotle. Anyone who associates himself with Aristotle is hopelessly outmoded. Thus St. Thomas Aquinas betrays himself to modern eyes as being very definitely dated by reason of his "scientific" pronouncements, which were largely those of Aristotle. For example: spontaneous generation of living from non-living bodies; all bodies composed of the four elements of earth, air, fire, water; incorruptible heavenly bodies, propelled through the heavens by angels; the firmament a solid, transparent substance.

When the laughter dies down, it will be seen that we excel the ancients in science largely because of the instruments at our disposal, because of the telescopes and microscopes and stroboscopes, etc. Now we know that our razor blades look like saw-teeth; the microscope says so. But we knew before, that though they looked smooth and sharp to the naked eye, they did often feel like can-openers. How much more do we know about the nature and purpose of razor-blades now that we know what their profile really looks like? Can't we say: "So what?" Can't we say "So what?" to many of the modern statements of science? In other words, much of modern knowledge is purely factual and leads to the development of Quiz Kids, but doesn't indicate any appreciable advance in mentality and the use of intelligence over our predecessors. For the instruments at their hand, they made many startlingly accurate observations; for want of instruments, some of their statements are amusing—but never unreasonable.

Rules of the Game

In St. Thomas' time everyone thought the earth was the center of the universe. Over it stretched what looked like an inverted bowl, which in the Scriptures was called the firmament. Since the Scriptures spoke of it, so did St. Thomas. What he says here is of great interest and is instructive: "In discussing questions of this kind, two rules are to be observed, as Augustine teaches. The first is, to hold the truth of the Scriptures without wavering. The second is, that since Holy Scripture can be explained in a multiplicity of senses, one should adhere to a particular explanation only in such measure as to be ready to abandon it, if it be proved with certainty to be false; lest Holy Scripture be exposed to the ridicule of unbelievers, and obstacles be placed to their believing."

He himself followed this rule to the letter. The firmament, he said, was firm, 1` s1`and solid. The stars were fixed in it! Like everybody else he had doubtless seen the stars rise in the east, wend their unhurried way westwards, keeping pace, decorously, with each other. Maybe the vault was solid. But he would have been willing to drop this explanation for another and better one. Everyone considered the universe as comprising seven concentric planetary spheres, the eighth being that of the fixed stars, or firmament; and since there were eight notes in the scale too, Dante and others spoke of the "music of the spheres." Above the firmament began the invisible world. First there was the watery or *crystalline* heaven, where the rains came from. Over this stretched the third heaven, called the *empyrean* or fiery heaven; it was a place of light and the home of the blessed. "It rests only on the authority of Strabo and Bede, and also of Basil, and all agree in holding it to be the place of the blessed." Just the observation you would expect of a cautious man. Easy to see he is not staking everything on this conclusion. Answering an objection he says: *If* by firmament you mean the starry heaven . . . or *if* by it you understand the cloudy region of the air . . . thus indicating his willingness to learn just what really goes on up there. After all, no one but St. Paul had been rapt to the third heaven, and even St. Paul didn't talk about it except to mention the man who was: "caught up into paradise; and heard secret words, which it is not granted to man to utter" (2 Cor. 12:4).

Detail

Spontaneous generation is mentioned at least three times by St. Thomas in this section. Without a knowledge of microbes, who might not say the same? Is he to be laughed at for observing the growth of microbes (only he didn't know them as that) in rotting matter? Something was growing, that was evident. It had to come from somewhere, so he assigned a cause for this appearance. Don't forget, Pasteur was laughed at just as heartily as St. Thomas.

Just so long as a cow is permitted to wear its hide, a steak has the warmth of all living things. How come it is warm? It feels damp as you put it on the grill, and as the fire or heat reaches it, it sweats and steams, and all too easily (as many a bride knows) burns to an unsavory crisp. From this and similar observations, the ancients thought everything was composed of fire, water, earth and air. Modern science has further specified the names, speaks of calcium, iron, phosphorus, proteins and such. Well, so what?

Finally, the planets with their own proper motion (west-east) seemed not to grow or diminish. Thomas thought they were incorruptible, and were subjected to a heavenly pushing around from the angels!

III

Such a lengthy preamble gives some idea of Thomas' interpretation of Genesis. Where did the world come from? From God who made it. Where was it going? Back to God as to a final cause. The eternal ideas in God's mind are the formal or exemplary cause of all things, and both the matter and form of all earthly things were concreated by God.

To his orderly mind, the tale as related in Genesis resolves itself into three headings: (1) the work of creation; (2) the work of distinction; (3) the work of adornment.

Visible things are not made by an evil principle, as certain heretics held, but by God, maker of heaven and earth and all things. Origen thought, wrongly, that corporeal creatures were a sort of divine afterthought, something devised to punish the sin of spiritual creatures! Others held that the first product of omnipotence was the angels, who in turn produced everything else. Thomas insisted that creation was God's exclusive monopoly. All that now exists came from nothingness to being. Only the long arm of God could bridge that gap; no created being can so create.

The work of creation fell into two parts, distinction and adornment. Obviously, before it can be decorated, something must exist. On the first day therefore, God distinguished light from darkness. On the second day the firmament was separated from the waters; and on the third, the waters of the earth were separated into seas, and dry land made its appearance. Followed next the pleasant task of adornment. On the fourth day the stars, sun and moon, were artistically hung in the heavens. The fifth day saw the air decorated with graceful birds, and the sea with glittering fishes; and on the sixth day, the earth was adorned with its great variety of animals, one of which was man. On the seventh day, God rested.

Attack

The Scriptural account of creation presents some obvious difficulties. Men like Darrow and Ingersoll and other "free thinkers" of a past generation found the Bible a wonderful joke book. For a build-up they would extol science which had benefited man so much. It taught that the sun was the source of light. Everybody knew that now, for since Galileo's time such knowledge was every man's property. Then—portentous pause—how can the Scriptures be upheld when they place the production of light on the first day, whereas the source of light made its tardy appearance on the fourth day?

It never failed, or almost never. Yet St. Thomas had asked the same question long ago, and before him many men had pondered over the possibility of having light without the sun. None of them found the difficulty incompatible with their faith. Thomas gives an answer from Pseudo-Dionysius which isn't too satisfactory, and it was probably not meant to be. He says that the light made on the first day was "formless" but later, on the fourth day, it was given specific power to produce determined effects. Well—we talk wisely about the corpuscular or wave theories of light, but we remain much in the dark still! By the way, the stars do not depend on our sun for their light! And we do not know where either the sun, or stars, or light came from, if we do not subscribe to the account of creation.

There were, and are, many more such difficulties. We know them, for our Faith is not the blind, trusting, ignorant, unreasoned, or emotional thing our enemies think it is. The Scriptures talk of the sun's rising and setting; any child in the lower grades knows that to be nonsense. In Joshua, ch. 10, an incredible command is hurled at the sun: Stop moving. As if it ever had. Job describes the heavens as something stretched out overhead as a skin; and they are elsewhere described as a huge brass vault. The Book of Leviticus contains a list of animals considered clean and unclean and there the rabbit or hare is declared to be unclean and not to be eaten because it cheweth its cud. Conclusion: (*to be uttered effectively it must be enthusiastic, triumphant, loud, and with gleaming eye*) Therefore the Scriptures are wrong, and contain error. They contradict science, scientists, facts. They are a lot of nonsense.

Most Provident God . . .

That conclusion is what is known as "'loose talk." Loose talk has been known to cause grievous damage, and this type of loose talk did cause great damage in the Church. Many thought these objections to the truthfulness of the Bible were unanswerable and once this opening wedge was established, it was not long before the Faith itself would be denied. It was imperative that the children of the Church be reassured by their loving spiritual Father, and on November 18, 1893, the supreme Pastor, successor to St. Peter, Pope Leo XIII, issued one of his greatest encyclicals, *Providentissimus Deus*. It sets forth the Church's reply to its critics, and especially to its scientific critics. It could be read with profit right now, along with that latest encyclical of Pope Pius XII, *Divino afflante Spiritu,* which commemorates the fiftieth anniversary of the *Providentissimus.*

Leo in his encyclical first pointed out how vigorously the Church has defended the Holy Scriptures. He urged those who read his letter to read the epistles and gospels and Old Testament too. After all, these speak of Christ, and ignorance of the Scriptures is equivalent to ignorance of Christ, to quote St. Jerome. Not very often do secular magazines help a man's soul; often quite the contrary; but the Scriptures cannot be neglected without the risk of a bad case of spiritual anemia.

The Bible is a holy book containing God's words to man, man's prayers and words to God, and it still outsells all the best-sellers. Even if it were not holy, it should be defended, fought for, protected against the men who wish to destroy it, not realizing that with the destruction of the Bible, much that is beautiful, worthwhile, fruitful in hope and assurance, would disappear from human living.

Inspiration

The principal reason for the Church's care for the Scriptures is that they are *an inspired work.* This means that they are the product of human authors writing under the direct and special influence of the Holy Ghost, who moved them to conceive rightly in their mind, to wish to write faithfully, and express fitly with infallible truth all those things and only those things which He Himself should command. God and man formed an extraordinary writing-team, one was the divine and principal author of the Scriptures; the other was the human and instrumental author. Since God was the prime mover behind the composition of the Bible, it is therefore His book,

His work; He is its author. Consequently there *cannot be anything wrong or erroneous in His book.*

The Answer

But the rabbit! The sunrises and sunsets! The fanciful imaginings concerning the heavens! In *Providentissimus Deus* Leo XIII uttered a phrase from St Thomas which at once calmed the storm raging around the subject of the Bible and Science. "The sacred authors, or to speak more accurately, the Holy Ghost 'who spoke by them, *did not intend to teach men these things* (i.e., the essential nature of visible objects), things in no way profitable to salvation.' Hence they did not seek to penetrate the secrets of nature, but rather described and dealt with things in more or less figurative language, or in terms which were commonly used at the time, and which in many instances are daily used at this day even by eminent men of science. Ordinary speech primarily and properly describes what comes under the senses, and somewhat in the same way the sacred writers (as the Angelic Doctor reminds us) *'went by what sensibly appeared'* or put down what God speaking to man signified, in the way men could understand or were accustomed to."

Simple, isn't it. The Bible makes no pretense of teaching science, any more than you do, or I, or the editors. If then we do not intend to be teaching science or talking scientifically, we cannot be accused of making formal scientific blunders! For all our vaunted education, we still talk of beautiful sunsets, and warble sweet songs about sunrise. Actually the sun does *seem* to rise and set. When I say just that, I make no claim to speak scientifically; I merely state a fact recorded by my sensible eyes.

That is just what Moses, and Joshua, and Job, and the Psalmist did when they wrote. Imagine the goggle-eyed stare that would have greeted Moses if he had proposed the theory of an expanding universe (learned, let us suppose, through a special revelation) to his people! Or if he had declared the immobility of the sun, or that the heavens were not what they seemed! Suppose he mentioned the heliocentric system of Copernicus, and discoursed learnedly of the stars, planets, gases, nebulae, and such. Would he have accomplished his purpose? Not by several light years, he wouldn't! He would probably have been run out of the camp, or perhaps treated with the pity reserved for the poor unfortunates possessed by an evil spirit.

Scientific knowledge would have been as incongruous as a top-hat in Moses or the other sacred writers, whose mission in life it was to tell the people about God, and instruct them what He wanted men to do. They could do this only if they acted as men of their age. So they did. Writing for an ignorant, semi-nomadic people, they wrote very simply, describing things as they appeared to be on the surface, and by this very homely means they were able to inculcate the highest, most refined, religious truths the world had yet known.

There is, therefore, no conflict between the story of creation as related by Moses, and true science. The Bible is no scientific textbook. It is a religious and a holy book, containing no formal error, for God is its author as well as man.

IV

It begins to look as if we will have to accept the account of Genesis! But the theologians who all accept the *fact of creation by God,* are by no means in agreement over the interpretation of Moses' story.

Creation is the complete and whole production of a thing out of nothing. Only God can, in the proper sense, create. How did He go about creating? By a simple, single decree of His eternal Will. This involves absolutely no change in God. The decree to create, made from all eternity, was to be realized in time.

Moses described the first week as a work-day week, with God playing the role of a cosmic piece-worker. At the end of six days, the job of creating was accomplished. "So the heavens and the earth were finished, and all the furniture of them. And on the seventh day God ended his work which he had made. And he rested on the seventh day from all his work which he had done" (Gen. 2:1–2).

The real difficulty comes when we compare that with Sirach (a book in the Bible!) 18:1: "He that liveth forever created all things *together*." Creation in an instant versus creation spread over six days makes quite a problem! There are no less than four solutions advanced by good men.

(1) St. Augustine, realizing that "day" implied a change and a before and after, held rightly for instantaneous creation (as far as God's *Fiat* was concerned), and evolved an ingenious theory, according to which "day" represented a stage in the knowledge of the angels. Each evening and morning represented an advance, a progression in *their* knowledge of things already created, as God infused new species into their intellects.

(2) Most authors, however, brush this explanation aside, and advance in its stead another which is much more improbable. They attempt to reconcile the Bible with science, although the two move in different spheres entirely. The discoveries of geologists and paleontologists raise the question of time, for days of twenty-four hours duration fit only awkwardly into a scheme involving the hundreds, thousands, and even millions of years demanded for the evolution of the universe and the things in it. The resurrected bones of the old dinosaurs won't disappear with the wave of a hand. Much time *must* have elapsed between the formation of the earth's crust and the appearance of man. Came then the dawn, and a rare solution.

The "days" stand for epochs, or long, undetermined periods of time. In Genesis the sun was not made until the fourth day; therefore, it is argued, the days previous to the creation of the sun were not of twenty-fours duration; without the sun they couldn't have been of that length of time. Once grant this, and there is no reason why the same elasticity should not be extended to the days numbered five, six, and seven. So "day" represents a long, long epoch; as long as any geologist or paleontologist desires.

The Biblical Commission in Vatican City, a body of learned men which from time to time reminds Catholic scholars of the limits to which they may push their inquiries, declared (June 30, 1909) that the word "day" may be taken to signify a certain space of time, so you may hold the above opinion if you wish. But it also stated that "day" may be taken in its strict sense as the natural day. Opinion (2) has, you see, its Achilles heel, its weaker points. In the first place, the Hebrew word for day (Yom, as in Yom Kippur [Expiation]) ordinarily signifies a day of twenty-four hours, since it has a morning and an evening. More serious still is the criticism that the day-epochs of Genesis fail to correspond to geological periods, for while in Genesis each day sees the beginning and completion of a work, there were no such carefully demarcated periods in the natural evolution of the globe. The stars were not formed at any special epoch, and the formation of the earth continues even now, this long after the appearance of life; and plants and beasts have developed together, not one after the other. But the real weak spot in this explanation is that it makes a textbook out of the Bible, and a Newton, or Einstein, or Eddington, or James Jeans, out of Moses.

(3) Leave science to its own sphere then, and leave Moses in his. He was interested in only one thing: telling the Israelites that God was the creator of the whole world, and of everything in it. Over and above this he taught that the week, with its Sabbath day of rest, was of divine institution. Everything else in the story is subordinate to the all important doctrine that *God created everything, and sanctified the Sabbath* and ordered men to keep it holy. In other words, Moses didn't care how things came about from a scientific point of view, but he did use the framework of the week with its days so as to inculcate the two great fundamental truths that everything came from God, especially man, who owes God recognition and submission.

(4) St. Augustine, with his very acute mind, appreciated the difficulty of reconciling the Sabbath "rest" of God with the emergence of new things: new plants, species, souls, and so on. Creation was supposed to have been over and done with, according to the Scriptures, and yet it seemed to continue on throughout the centuries. His solution, famous now, agreed that God did not have to bestir Himself anew with each new generation; creation once decreed was final. At the same time, he argued that such a creation implied the existence of *rationes seminales* which means that in the act of creating, God produced everything that was ever to be created, but some of these things were produced at once, while

others were decreed or produced by Him only in germ form, or potentially, and would like Snow White or the sleeping princess in the fairy tale someday awaken to the kiss of life. Sometimes centuries would elapse before this would be realized, but all the while these things existed in the divine mind. And thus both the Scriptures and theology have been safeguarded, and we have all been properly impressed with the infinite sagacity and wisdom of the Divine Workman at whose instant word the complex orderly world we know so well, and so little understand, came forth from nothingness into existence.

In conclusion, then, we have two answers to the question of the world's origin: the answer of creation, and the answer of evolution. Only one of them, the answer of creation, makes sense; the other dispenses with it. Only one of them gives man an explanation, challenges him with truth, and demands his admiration for the marvelous order which he cannot help but observe wherever he turns his eyes. The other answer deprives life of reason, of a goal, of personal value. We cannot afford to adopt that position; it leads too quickly to despair. Our answer makes life worth living for and worth fighting for, for it began with God, and it will go back to Him.

STUDY QUESTIONS

1) Can an inspired book contain any error?

2) What is the notion of biblical inspiration as proposed by Leo XIII in the *Providentissimus Deus*?

3) How is it possible to reconcile the Bible with Science (e.g., the sun "rising")?

4) What is the Biblical Commission? What authority is to be given to its decrees?

5) Mention four specific scientific "mistakes" prevalent in the Middle Ages? Discuss reasonableness or *naivete* of such interpretations of phenomena of nature. Is

the authority of St. Thomas lessened because he held these theories?

6) The scholastic theory of Matter and Form meets with difficulty in the account of Creation. How would you reconcile the two? Can "formless" matter exist? Can light exist without the sun?

7) Give the medieval conception of the heavens. Why does the water said to be stored in the crystalline heaven not run off the concave firmament?

8) How is the term "day" used in the story of Creation? Is it to be understood in a strict sense? Is any other interpretation defensible?

9) What did St. Augustine mean by the "Rationes seminales" or "Seed-essences?"

10) Can Evolution be maintained as a scientific fact? May a Catholic hold for any kind of evolution? Is evolution compatible with the story of creation as narrated in the first chapter of Genesis?

www.ingramcontent.com/pod-product-compliance
Lightning Source LLC
Chambersburg PA
CBHW020917140626
46545CB00015B/75